Decision Making with Computers

The Spreadsheet and Beyond

Decision Making with Computers

The Spreadsheet and Beyond

John S. Edwards

and

Paul N. Finlay

PITMAN PUBLISHING

London · Hong Kong · Johannesburg · Melbourne · Singapore · Washington DC

Dedicated to our wives, Janet and Ann, and to our children, John Michael and Susie, for giving us the time to get on and write this book.

PITMAN PUBLISHING
128 Long Acre, London WC2E 9AN
Tel: +44 (0)171 447 2000
Fax: +44 (0)171 240 5771

A Division of Pearson Professional Limited

First published in Great Britain 1997

ISBN 0 273 62128 9

British Library Cataloguing in Publication Data
A CIP catalogue record for this book can be obtained from the British Library

10 9 8 7 6 5 4 3 2 1

Typeset by Pantek Arts, Maidstone, Kent
Printed and bound in Great Britain by Clays Ltd, St Ives plc

The Publishers' policy is to use paper manufactured from sustainable forests.

CONTENTS

PREFACE

RATIONALE AND FOCUS

The falling cost of hardware and software has brought powerful computer facilities well within managers' budgets – and those of students! A recent review of the software used by degree students from Aston Business School in their industrial training year showed that all had used a computer during their placement and that 90 per cent had used a spreadsheet. The availability of spreadsheets has meant that almost anyone can now do calculations with little in the way of a mathematical background. This has been tremendously liberating both for individuals and for organisations. However, very often this liberation has been accompanied by a lack of organisational control on standards, allowing spreadsheets to be developed in an *ad hoc* manner and as a consequence be very difficult to maintain. While the facilities offered by spreadsheets encourage DIY, this approach can only be successful in the medium to long term if there is self-control on the part of the developer: he/she needs to follow good practice in spreadsheet design. The principal aim of this book is to offer a practical guide to the necessary good practice.

This book is aimed at DIYers. Specifically, it is aimed at the *developer as user*, taking into account that the developer may well wish to show some of the spreadsheet outputs to colleagues. Thus this book is not specifically targeted at the developer who is creating a spreadsheet for use by someone else, although there is a great deal in the book that is likely to be of value where this is the case.

It is assumed that all readers of this book have some knowledge of what a spreadsheet can do and have used one. It is also assumed that the spreadsheet will currently be the major (perhaps the only) software tool that is under their total control – they have grown to know and love it! The book will help readers make the best use of their current spreadsheets and suggest how they might extend their computer support into other, related applications.

TERMINOLOGY AND FORMAT

To be precise, developers develop and users use *spreadsheet application systems*. However, for the sake of brevity we will use the term spreadsheet to mean a spreadsheet application system and use the term spreadsheet package to refer to the software that is purchased (such as Excel and Lotus) and within which specific applications are developed.

There are many spreadsheets in existence and the current ones will develop and change and new ones will be introduced. While there is a convergence of capability and functionality, no two spreadsheets are the same. In general, rather than focus on one particular spreadsheet, a standard 'generic' spreadsheet form has been used in this book. However, the review of spreadsheet usage by Aston students showed that around 45 per cent used Excel and 35 per cent used Lotus 1-2-3 during their business placement year. Thus where specific examples are required, it is these packages that are used.

Terminology can present difficulties. While there is a degree of commonality between the terms used in spreadsheet packages there are also many differences. This is partly due to the idiosyncrasies of the spreadsheet package developers, but also reflects the different backgrounds of the two groups involved in spreadsheet development: the management scientists who have historically concerned themselves almost solely with the relationships between variables, and the computer scientists whose focus is on data. We hope that these problems have been lessened for you in this book through the use of a common set of definitions and by the provision of a full glossary of terms.

To avoid charges of gender bias by using either masculine or feminine terms and to avoid the repeated and annoying use of he/she and him/her, it has been decided to use the terms 'they', 'them' and 'their' even for singular cases. This might offend the purists, but until better terms are generally accepted we feel it is the best we can do.

We use the term 'manager' throughout. It should not be inferred from this that the book is exclusively for people with the term manager in their job title: it is for anyone who has responsibility for resources and wishes to plan and control their use.

A book like this is mainly a 'how to do it' book. It is not a book of reference. So as not to deflect the reader too much we have been sparing with references in the text, preferring to suggest a few additional readings. These serve to acknowledge sources and to guide further reading should readers and/or their mentors require it.

The book is split into two parts. Part One is concerned with the work of managers, the role of spreadsheets and the fundamentals of building spreadsheets. Part Two is concerned much more with specific applications, extending the use of spreadsheets to offer managers significant help in many aspects of their jobs.

Part One

OVERVIEW OF PART ONE

There are a great many situations in business in which some numerical calculations are required in order to get a better view of what's going on. To take a very simple example, if you were about to purchase 20 items at £1.50 each you would need to multiply £1.50 by 20 to know what the total cost would be. This is such a simple task that you could do it your head.

However, suppose that things weren't so easy – that you wanted to buy 23 items at £1.42 each. Some people can do this sort of calculation in their heads, but they are fairly few and far between. You may be able to do the sums using the proverbial 'back of the envelope'. With either method the average person is unlikely to be 100 per cent confident of getting the right answer every time. To be sure it is likely that you would resort to using a calculator.

If you are buying one article costing around £1 it may not be worth your while to 'shop around' for the cheapest price. However, as the unit price rises and the number of articles you want to buy increases, it may become so. Suppose the price per item were around £1000. Then you would want to consider several suppliers' prices. Now you are doing the calculations several times. Programmable calculators are useful here, but what you really want to do is to have the calculated values set out for you in a way that allows you to compare easily the total costs of each option: with a calculator you would need either to write down the results of each calculation as you make it or to hold each result in a different memory location and switch between them – a tiresome way of working. It would be much better if the results could simply be set alongside one another and compared directly. This is exactly what a spreadsheet allows you to do, as is shown in Fig O.1

Fig O.1 A spreadsheet for comparison purposes

	A	B	C	D
1	Cost of article from supplier A (£)	900		
2	Cost of article from supplier B (£)	945		
3	Cost of article from supplier C (£)	995		
4	Cost of article from supplier D (£)	980		
5				
6	Units bought	20	30	40
7	Total cost from supplier A (£)	18000	27000	36000
8	Total cost from supplier B (£)	18900	28350	37800
9	Total cost from supplier C (£)	19900	29850	39800
10	Total cost from supplier D (£)	19600	29400	39200
11				

But there are other reasons for using a spreadsheet. A spreadsheet allows you to record what you have done – the values that you have used and the way in which the calculations have been performed. This provides an audit of what you have done, documenting the important features, so that if you are doing the calculations again in the future you know what you did and thus how to repeat it. This is efficient in that you are not 'reinventing the wheel', it is also valuable because the spreadsheet is holding knowledge – obviously very simple knowledge in the specific example we have used, but not trivial in other cases.

A further reason for using a spreadsheet is to allow exploration of possibilities, particularly to ask 'What if?' questions. This is shown in our example in Fig O.1 where we are in a position to alter any of the suppliers' prices and see what the consequences are for the costs.

It is likely that you will want to show your spreadsheet results to other people: it is rare in organisations that people decide matters completely on their own. This leads on to a further powerful reason for using a spreadsheet – it allows you to show the results (and indeed how the results have been obtained) to other people. Modern spreadsheets are particularly good at displaying results impressively and thus extracting information from data.

Since a spreadsheet user is often not operating in isolation from their organisational surroundings, in order to get the best out of spreadsheets there is a need to appreciate the context in which spreadsheets will be used. This topic is covered in some detail in Chapter 1 where managerial roles and managerial activities are considered. Planning and control are highlighted as two of the tasks most likely to be helped by using a spreadsheet. The emphasis in the chapter is on the brevity and 'scrappiness' of managerial life and the effect this has on spreadsheet design and use.

The information handling that is associated with planning and control is taken up in Chapter 2. The distinction is made between data, information and intelligence. Data is the raw material for producing the information that is recognised as being of value to the manager and intelligence is the result of melding together individual pieces of information. The rationale for much of Chapter 2 is to set spreadsheets and their extensions in the wider context of application systems in general. Management information systems and decision support systems are considered as two types of application program. The emphasis in this book is on decision support systems.

Chapters 3 and 4 provide the links between the managerially oriented first two chapters and the details of spreadsheet development that are covered in Chapters 5 to 8. In Chapter 3 we discuss how a manager might structure their view of the world before developing a spreadsheet. Several approaches are considered: in structural modelling the manager would be identifying those factors that affect their unit's activities; with fishbone diagrams and cognitive mapping the emphasis is on explicitly identifying cause-and-effect links; and in soft systems methodology where the emphasis is on finding the most appropriate way forward by comparing an 'ideal' with the present situation. The end result is a scenario encapsulating a manager's view of their world. It is within this scenario that a manager sees issues arise and focuses on a portion of their scenario – a local scenario – in order to make sense of their situation and define the issue facing them. Having defined that issue the manager might seek help to tackle that issue by developing a spreadsheet.

In moving from a local scenario to a spreadsheet, the manager is taking a portion of the local scenario – a set of vaguely stated relationships between ill-defined variables – and translating it into a coherent and consistent set of relationships between well-defined factors. They are converting an imprecise yet rich view of the issue into a precise yet much more poverty-stricken view, encapsulated in the spreadsheet. They do this because they believe that the insights and information the spreadsheet can generate outweigh the costs of the development effort.

However, it is not necessarily the case that it is appropriate to develop a spreadsheet. In Chapter 4 a set of guidelines is presented that consider how valuable it would be to have a spreadsheet to help tackle the issue at hand, where the major difficulties are likely to arise in spreadsheet development, how detailed the spreadsheet should be and how to ensure that the spreadsheet, especially its output, is acceptable to other people. So, at the end of Chapter 4 we have described approaches which managers can use to structure their issue – forming a scenario and local scenario – and have presented a set of guidelines to help with the development of any subsequent spreadsheet. Only at this stage do we move on to discuss the building of spreadsheets.

Spreadsheets can be considered as consisting of three main components: a logic model that contains all the relationships between factors, a data model that contains the values associated with the factors, and a human–computer interface through which the spreadsheet is developed and information presented. We discuss these three components in Chapters 5 to 7.

Chapter 5 is concerned with the 'building blocks' of logic models and the forms of the relationships between them. The process of logic modelling by which the logic model is created is fully explored. Chapter 6 is concerned with data modelling, the process by which the data model is created containing the specific values associated with the factors that are needed to generate specific results.

Apart from the very smallest spreadsheet, the display of information that a spreadsheet provides will be an extract from the full spreadsheet. These extractions are presented through what we term the results interface. Chapter 7 is concerned with showing data as information through representations such as tables, graphs, charts and pictures designed with a very specific purpose in mind. This specific purpose is to communicate an answer, a pattern or an insight – to oneself and/or to others.

Chapter 8 is concerned with best practice in spreadsheet design. This includes ensuring that the data and logic models can be built easily, being aware of those aspects of design that will make subsequent operation easy, efficient and, as far as possible, error free, and ensuring that the resultant spreadsheet allows for easy maintenance and enhancement.

The flow of the topics and their chapters is indicated in Fig O.2, super-imposed on the process for creating an appropriate spreadsheet within the relevant business context.

Fig O.2 Overview of Part One

1. The nature of managerial work
2. Spreadsheets in business activity

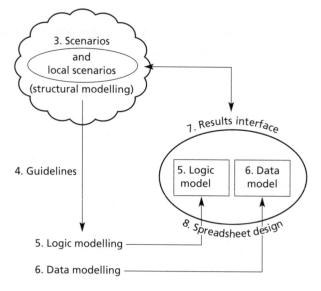

CHAPTER 1

The nature of managerial work

Chapter aims	The aim of this chapter is to introduce the organisational context within which spreadsheets are developed and used. The chapter opens with a consideration of the nature of managerial work – the roles of managers and the pressures under which they are working. Since spreadsheets are primarily used to aid planning and control, it is considered appropriate to focus on this aspect of managerial work, particularly on how issues are handled. The structuring of issues prior to obtaining detailed understanding is described, and the need for managers to have a broad perspective of their operating environment is explained.

- What managers do
- Planning and control
- Problems, decisions and issues: solving, resolving, dissolving, absolving and handling
- The structuring phase
  - Managerial scenarios • Issue detection • Issue definition

It would be inappropriate to use a saw to hammer in a nail, and it would be inappropriate to use a spreadsheet to handle the basic accounting processes of an organisation. Less grossly perhaps, it would also be unwise to use a tenon saw to cut down a tree, or a chain saw when cabinet making – just as it would be unwise to use a spreadsheet to handle complicated mathematical techniques. You can see from these analogies that it would be inappropriate to plunge directly into considerations concerning the development of spreadsheets without first considering the nature of the business activities that the spreadsheets are supporting – within the business context.

WHAT MANAGERS DO

The classical view of a manager as almost totally occupied in directing organising, planning and controlling the operations of an enterprise does not stand up to investigation: a large part of a manager's time is spent performing many other roles. In the 1960s the Canadian management guru Henry Mintzberg tracked the activities of top managers and identified ten managerial roles. First, there are three interpersonal roles, where the manager is acting as a figurehead (for example, greeting touring dignitaries) being the leader and also liaising with people. Next, there are three informational roles: monitoring activities both within and outside the organisation, disseminating information as appropriate and acting as a spokesperson for the group they head. Finally, there are four decisional roles: as entrepreneur, disturbance handler, resource allocator and negotiator.

Mintzberg's research not only shows that a manager has many roles to play, it also highlights the fragmentary nature of management work. In his words, management activities are characterised by 'brevity, variety and discontinuity'. He found that half of the activities engaged in by the chief executives in his study lasted less than nine minutes, and only 10 per cent of activities exceeded one hour.

The theme of Mintzberg's study is the homogeneity of management work: although the specifics will change from manager to manager, the broad patterns of work will remain the same. More recent studies have looked at the activities of middle managers and have found similar patterns concerning the general nature of managerial activity. However, these later studies tend to emphasise the variability of work patterns among managers and indicate that to a large extent this variability is caused by the preferences of the managers themselves.

Management work is thus characterised by many brief segments of action following one another at a hectic pace. These segments may be *ad hoc*, one-off activities, but more often than not they will form part of a continuous thread of interacting activities. Managers are like jugglers, trying to make sure that they keep all the balls in the air at once!

The sources of the information that managers use are significant for the design and use of spreadsheets. While managers will get some of their information from written sources – computer printouts, company statements and trade magazines, for example – much comes to them orally. There is very strong evidence that managers greatly favour oral information, through meetings, one-to-one discussions and telephone calls. One reason for this is that managers like both the richness of informal information and its timeliness, and very often this must come from the web of contacts that any good manager cultivates. Usually this information is fragmented and 'soft' (gossip and rumour), and as such is difficult to handle in a systematic way.

A final point is that management work is highly interactive, not reflective: scheduled meetings are often the single most time-consuming element. Studies show that between 30 and 80 per cent of a manager's time is taken up by meetings. This gives credibility to the reply often given by secretaries when you phone a manager: TIAM – they're in a meeting!

◆ **Key concept**

Although managers have a fair degree of control over their working lives, most spend a hectic, fragmented and highly interactive working day. Soft information tends to be prized and managers have little time for reflection and formal analysis. This has implications for the design of formal support aids such as spreadsheets.

PLANNING AND CONTROL

Although Mintzberg wished to highlight the many roles of managers, he was not implying that planning and control were not important aspects of managerial life: rather that they were not well-defined and self-contained activities. Indeed, it could be argued that in the widest sense all ten managerial activities are linked to planning and control. In particular, both monitoring and liaison are significant in control and the four decisional roles are central to planning.

The classic view of control is that shown in Fig 1.1. This model applies very widely, from such things as central heating systems to many of the control systems used within organisations: for example, the budgetary control systems that are used in (almost) every business. For an organisation, what is termed the system in Fig 1.1 is all or a part of the business. One input might be the raw materials that are converted by the business to a product or service. The output may be the number of units made per day, the wastage of materials or some measure of quality. The output is compared with a corresponding performance standard that has been set previously. Should the comparison be unfavourable (an *adverse variance* in accounting terms) – for example, a higher than wished for wastage of raw materials – then this would signal that action should be taken in order to prevent this deficient performance occurring in future.

As Fig 1.1 stands, the control system is solely reactive: it only indicates that corrective action is required *after* the unwanted deficiency has occurred. Although reactive control is necessary, what is also necessary is proactive control. Proactive control is in fact planning; it is getting the organisation to consider the future and take the necessary action before this future becomes the present. To use a nautical analogy, proactive control for the captain of a ship is to furl the sails and batten down the hatches before the storm strikes. For managers it is to assess possible future opportunities and threats and alter their organisations accordingly.

♦ **Key concept** *Control is reactive when corrective action is taken after an unwanted result has been obtained. Control is proactive either when preventive action is taken before the unfavourable circumstances occur or when action is taken to get the organisation in a position to take advantage of future favourable circumstances.*

Fig 1.1 Management as a control system

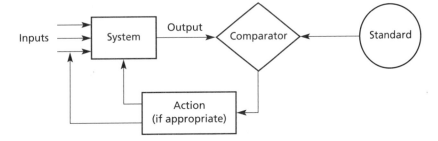

In the model of planning and control set out in Fig 1.1, the monitoring of performance against standard provides alerting information that suggests that some action might be needed. Sometimes the move from being alerted that something needs to be done to carrying out the appropriate action is automatic. This is shown in Fig 1.2a with the existence of the alerting stimulus leading directly to action. A simple example of such automatic action is when you are reading and the daylight fades (the alerting stimulus) – without any thought you switch on the light. Similarly, in the managerial situation where sales fall unexpectedly the sales manager may have met this situation before in the same or a similar context. This experience allows them to act without much thought and they resort to the use of a tried and tested method. For example, they may lower the price of the item – this has worked in similar situations in the past

Fig 1.2 The response to stimuli

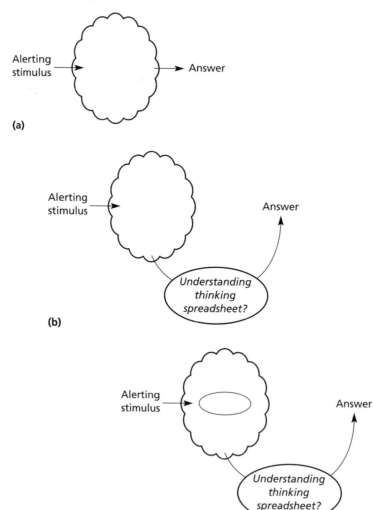

and should work again. However, in other cases, where there is some novelty in the situation there is a need to understand the situation better: the tried and tested recipe is no longer appropriate. Sometimes understanding can be helped by a formal, more reflective and less direct approach, such as that depicted in Fig 1.2b. This approach may involve the use of a spreadsheet.

PROBLEMS, DECISIONS AND ISSUES: SOLVING, RESOLVING, DISSOLVING, ABSOLVING AND HANDLING

Very generally, problem solving can be considered as the process of moving from a unsatisfactory to a more satisfactory state. Decision making is part of problem solving. Sometimes decision making is considered rather narrowly as simply making a selection between various courses of action: sometimes it has been taken to include other aspects of problem solving, such as the need to obtain further information and the associated modelling. Although such distinctions between problem solving and decision making can be made they will not be made in this book – because neither term will be used! There are two reasons for this. First, the opportunity for a manager to increase market share, to increase profits or to reduce costs would not normally be considered a problem and few managers would term it so. Second, the term decision making is too narrow for what we are going to consider in this book. In order to get over these difficulties, it is easier and more appropriate to consider opportunities, problems, decision situations and threats – in fact, any facet of the managerial daily grind that has to be attended to – under the generic term 'issue'. Thus we will be concerned with managerial issues in this book.

There are four general ways of handling an issue: solving it, resolving it, dissolving it and absolving it. Solving is where an optimum or best solution is sought, resolving is where the person with the issue seeks only to obtain an answer that is good enough, while dissolving occurs when conditions are changed to eliminate the issue. Absolving is where the issue is ignored in the hope that it will disappear. The following example will make these distinctions clearer.

Consider someone working in Birmingham and living in Nottingham, a distance of 50 miles. They wish to keep doing this, yet public transport between the two places is difficult and their partner wants the use of the car to ferry their children to school. Another car seems to be called for. The issue then becomes what car to buy.

To solve this issue would require finding the optimum solution.[1] This in turn would require that they completely and precisely specify their requirements and also scour the literature to determine all relevant particulars about all potentially suitable makes of car. Visits to showrooms and test drives would also be called for. This could be an extremely time-consuming business, and even if an optimum match of car and requirements could be found, it is very unlikely that the choice would remain optimum for long: their overall requirements might change, and certainly new cars (for which new claims would surely be made) would come on to the market.

This little example should suggest to you that the search for the best answer is often a search that is not worth the effort. Most managers have realised that optimising part of an issue is not necessarily a greater help in handling the total issue than is an answer that is sensible and understandable and not grossly wrong: resolving or being 'good enough' is the stuff of a great deal of management activity. In the car-buying issue, to resolve the issue they would need to have identified broadly their key requirements – the car must be able to seat five people and be very reliable, for example – and then have selected a car from the half dozen they liked the look of. This process would not be nearly so time consuming as optimising and would get them a reasonable car (although not necessarily the best one).

To dissolve the issue the issue context has to be changed. The car-buying issue would be dissolved if they changed their place of work to Nottingham or if they went to live in Birmingham. The need for a car would now no longer exist, or the need is so transformed that the original issue no longer exists. Finally, the issue could be absolved by ignoring it, hoping that they retain the use of the present car or that public transport will suffice!

◆ *Key concept*

There are four ways of handling issues: solving, resolving, dissolving and absolving. Solving is where an optimum or best solution is sought. Resolving is where the person with the issue seeks only to obtain an answer that is good enough. Dissolving occurs when conditions change so as to eliminate the issue or fundamentally alter it. Absolving is where the issue is ignored in the hope that it will go away.

A model of issue handling consisting of three phases and seven stages is set out in Fig 1.3. The structuring phase is discussed in detail below. The understanding phase includes the design and construction of spreadsheets that are helpful in exposing the important aspects of issues and of the context in which the issues arise. Design and construction will be considered in Chapters 5–8. Exploring courses of action will be considered in Part II. The action phase, in which change is implemented in the 'real world', will not be considered further in this book.

Fig 1.3 Stages and phases in handling an issue

Phases	Stages
Structuring	Detection
	Definition
Understanding	Model construction
	Exploring courses of action
Action	Choice
	Implementation
	Review

Please don't let Fig 1.3 make you think that handling an issue is a totally sequential process, starting with issue detection and moving continuously and without interruption through the seven stages to the implementation of the desired changes and the associated review. Although this is the broad direction that most issue-handling processes take, there is also likely to be much back-tracking and iteration among the stages. Furthermore, the time to move from the initial detection to implementation may be weeks or months; this in itself gives much latitude for second thoughts and redefinition.

THE STRUCTURING PHASE

Managerial scenarios

It is only possible to detect an issue if a manager has an appropriate overall view of the issue situation. For example, a person without any medical knowledge would be quite unable to detect whether someone with a temperature of 38°C was likely to be ill or not: probably they would not even be aware that temperature is often an important symptom! They would be unable to detect the issue because they have no model of the workings of the human body to guide their thoughts. This need for an overall view, termed a scenario, is now considered.

The term scenario has a rather grandiose ring about it and has tended to be reserved for very high-level strategic considerations, such as the economic state of Greenland in the year 2050! A dictionary definition is 'a sketch of a plot of a play' and the word is reputed to have entered the business world in the 1950s via the Hollywood film industry. A film scenario is simply a sketch of how the film may turn out, with the director and screenwriters fleshing out the skeleton that is the scenario as film-making develops. It can be seen how appropriate the word scenario is – meaning a sketch or outline of the world in which managers do and will operate and within which they handle issues. How managers can think about and formalise their scenarios is considered in Chapter 3.

◆ **Key concept**   *A scenario is a managerial view of the world. It is an outline of the world in which they are currently operating and in which they think they will be operating in the future. This sketch provides the context within which an issue will be handled.*

Issue detection

A manager's initial awareness that an issue exists may start simply as a 'gut feeling' that something is wrong or that an opportunity exists to be exploited. In many cases, this awareness develops during an 'incubation period' while further stimuli are sensed that support these initial feelings. There are four sources of such stimuli. First, there are the internal performance measures, such as those generated from an organisation's budgetary control system. Second, there is 'client' reaction, either from the customers outside the organisation or from those within the organisation to whom the manager is supplying a product or service. Third, there are the stakeholders other than customers – shareholders, employees, suppliers and in some cases government. Fourth, there are changes in the political, social, economic and technological environment within which the organisation is operating.

Eventually a point is reached when the general evidence shown by the signals appears so convincing that the issue is deemed to exist, and it is clear that something might have to be done about it. In general terms it is the importance and urgency of an issue that forces managers to consider it: it is the feasibility of being able to do something about the issue that impels further deliberation and action.

As an issue develops it may be at a stage where it is so ill defined that the most appropriate course of action is inaction – it is best to wait until matters become clearer. At other stages the issue might have ceased to be important and thus no longer require attention (until the next time!). The importance and urgency of issues can and do wax and wane. Issues have life cycles and the phase that an issue is in can have an enormous impact on the form of any spreadsheet that is developed.

Assuming that the importance and urgency of an issue means that the manager has no option but to confront it, it is at this point that the issue needs to be defined.

Issue definition

Let's consider Fig 1.2 again. The unspecified 'cloud' in this figure represents a managerial scenario. In Fig 1.2c it is shown open to prompting by an alerting stimulus. In the light of this prompting, the issue area within the scenario will be defined and, if no recipe will suffice, this portion of the scenario is then focused on in a search for an appropriate response.

Remember that managers are not confronted by one issue at a time that can be sorted out and put away for ever. Rather they are confronted by a set of interacting and overlapping issues – what the American academic Russell Ackoff calls 'a mess'. Thus it can be seen that it would be unwise for managers to concentrate solely on a single issue: they need to take account of the inter-action of any particular issue with the other issue areas. Without such knowledge, action may make the issue worse or, as often seems to be the case in medicine, the symptoms of a particular issue may be made to disappear, but the 'cure' causes other issues to surface.

The wider issue area will be called a local scenario and is represented by the ellipse in Fig 1.2c. The local scenario would be wider than an initial considera-tion of the issue would suggest, but narrower than the whole scenario (represented by the cloud). In practice, there would not be a clear distinction between the local scenario and the rest of the scenario; a gradual weakening of the influence of factors in the scenario would be expected to occur as you move away from the centre of the local scenario.

◆ **Key concept**
A local scenario is the portion of the scenario brought into focus under pressure from an alerting stimulus. A local scenario is likely to be wider than an initial consideration of the single in-focus issue might suggest, but narrower than the whole scenario.

How an issue is defined determines how it will be handled. An example from the annals of management science will illustrate what this means. In a tall office block, concern was expressed about the lift service. At peak times – in the morning when people arrived for work and in the evening when people went home – the office workers claimed that too much time was spent waiting for a lift to arrive. The management scientists were asked to look into the issue and to suggest answers. They saw the issue as one involving a reduction in the time people waiting for a lift ('wasted' time). Answers were sought in terms of speeding up the lift, having the lifts stop only at alternate floors, etc. No answer was really satisfactory. All seemed lost until someone came up with the idea of putting mirrors next to the lifts. The reasoning behind this was that the women would look at themselves in the mirrors and the men would look at the women. Sexist stuff from the politically incorrect dark ages! But it worked, in the sense that complaints about delays reduced dramatically. What had happened was that the issue had now been defined in a different way, with an emphasis on the behavioural rather than the mechanical aspects – the objective was seen as one of preventing people *feeling* that they were wasting time rather than *reducing the time* spent waiting for a lift. A different definition, a different way of handling the issue.

SUMMARY

Empirical studies of managerial work patterns indicate the wide range of activities in which managers are involved. Whereas formal planning and control are activities where spreadsheets may be heavily used, most of the other managerial activities do not readily lend themselves to the use of spreadsheets, or indeed to any form of information technology. Consequently, the scope of spreadsheets in the totality of a manager's professional life is limited. However, the high variation between individual managers comes about in part through choices made by the managers themselves, and thus it would appear that scope exists for spreadsheets to be developed by those who wish to do so.

It may seem odd to begin a book on spreadsheets with a chapter that plays down their role in a manager's working life, and it would be unfortunate if the reader were to infer from this that spreadsheets have a negligible role to play in business operations. Spreadsheets do have a role to play, but it is important that this role is seen within the wider context of business life, and that the development of spreadsheets is tailored to fit the realities of managerial activity.

The difficulties with using the term problem in a managerial context and the specific meaning attached to the word 'solving' leads to the phrase 'issue handling' instead of the more cumbersome 'solving, resolving and dissolving issues', unless one specific way is to be explicitly discussed.

END NOTES

1 The term *optimum* means *the best*. It covers both the finding of a maximum value (of a profit, say) where this is best and the finding of a minimum value (the least cost for making a product, for example) where this is best.

FURTHER READING

The classic reading about what managers actually do is work by Henry Mintzberg. The original article was entitled 'The manager's job: folklore and fact' and appeared in the *Harvard Business Review*, July–August, 1975, pp49–61. The paper is reproduced in the book by Henry Mintzberg and James Brian Quinn entitled *The Strategy Process: Concepts, Contexts and Cases*, 2nd edition, Prentice Hall International, 1991.

EXERCISES

1 What implications for spreadsheet design and use lie in the fact that managers' working lives are hectic, fragmented and highly interactive?

2 Managers apparently have little time for reflection and formal analysis. How might this affect spreadsheet design and use?

3 Managers apparently rely heavily on soft information, including gossip and rumour. How might this affect spreadsheet design and use?

4 Reflect on the issues with which you have been confronted recently. Did you solve, resolve, dissolve or absolve them? Was there any pattern in the types of issues that were given similar treatments?

5 It has been stated that issues have life cycles and that their importance and urgency wax and wane. Think of issues that you have experienced over the last few months which have become very important/urgent and then ceased to be so.

6 What differences would you expect between spreadsheets designed to solve, resolve and dissolve an issue?

7 It has been stated that a local scenario will be wider than an initial consideration of the issue would suggest, but narrower than the whole scenario. What does this mean and why should it be so?

8 Consider your own situation. Write down a list of 20 important factors that make up your scenario. Now consider an issue affecting you at the moment. What portion of the scenario would constitute your local scenario when handling this issue?

CHAPTER 2

Spreadsheets in business activity

Chapter aims   The aim of this chapter is to discuss the role of spreadsheets within the context of the managerial activities that have been described in the previous chapter. First, the meanings of the terms data, information and intelligence are defined. Next, the elements of application systems are considered and the characteristics of the two types of managerial system – management information systems and decision support systems – are discussed. Finally, the concepts of models and systems are formally considered together with the place of spreadsheets in a manager's planning and control system.

- **Data, information and intelligence**
- **Components of management application systems**
- **Management information systems and decision support systems**
- **Systems and models**
  - **Systems • Models**

A working definition of an application system is that it is a computer-based system to deliver processing power directly to an employee. Such systems are different from software systems such as operating systems which work 'behind the scenes' and are not themselves used directly. Spreadsheet systems are application systems. The previous chapter closed with a consideration of the place of the manager's scenario in issue handling, culminating in Fig 1.2c which is reproduced in the bottom left-hand corner of Fig 2.1. The question we are addressing in this chapter is where exactly the query *Spreadsheet?* in Fig 1.2c fits within managerial application systems and within the manager's scenario. To answer this question we need first to consider the major elements of application systems – data, information and intelligence and the system components.

DATA, INFORMATION AND INTELLIGENCE

The alerting stimulus shown in the bottom left-hand corner of Fig 2.1 is information. In a business context, information may be defined as data that are perceived by employees to be of use or potential use to them in their job. For application systems, data can be considered to be those stimuli from outside the system that pass the rules embedded in the interface between the system and its surroundings (the term interface is used for 'boundary' in computerspeak). For example, a part of the interface of a computerised order-entry system might be constructed so that only numeric values are accepted: non-numeric values (such as a name) would be rejected.

For data to be treated as information, it is almost always necessary for the data to be combined in some way. For example, an information system for the management in a sales department might be designed to provide the total values of sales over the preceding month. Thus the information system has built into it the rules or formulae by which this total could be derived.

This data/information perspective allows the left-hand side of Fig 1.2c (within the dotted box) to be translated into the left-hand side of Fig 2.1 (again, within the dotted box).

Figure 2.1 shows a myriad of environmental stimuli being vetted by the receiver and filter at the interface between the system and its environment. Those stimuli that pass the tests imposed pass into the database. The base of data that is built up in this way is used to provide two sorts of information to the manager. First, there is the alerting information that the manager compares against what they take as their standard. This information is generally derived according to rules that are embedded in the system (such as the calculations necessary to derive monthly sales figures). Second, there is the information which is extracted depending on the requirements of the particular issue that is being handled: for example, if managers are considering the introduction of an early retirement scheme, they may wish to know the number of employees over 50 years old and who have over 20 years' service with the firm. The rule to derive this information is unlikely to be an embedded rule, as it is one that is needed for only this one purpose. Such a rule is an *ad hoc* rule.

Fig 2.1 A management application system

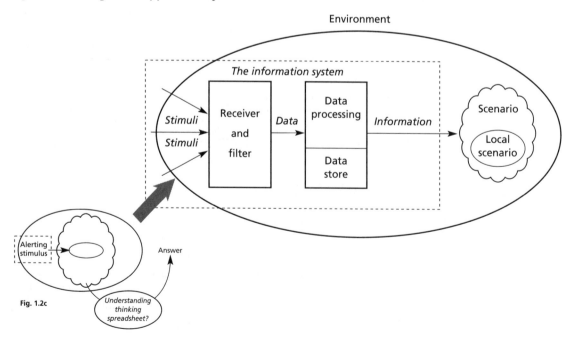

Without an efficient means of filtering and aggregating data, a manager could easily be in the situation of being data rich, yet information poor.

Intelligence is the outcome of the meshing and reconciliation of a set of information. Unlike information, intelligence has the property that the whole is greater than the sum of the parts – the sum of the informational inputs. For example, an issue might require a manager to meld together information on sales forecasts, production costs and salesforce morale: they would develop for themselves an intelligence 'picture' from these three dissimilar pieces of information. Just as data is the raw material for information, so information is the raw material for intelligence

One of the great values in using a spreadsheet is that it can allow managers to experiment and to learn from experience. For example, a spreadsheet might have many relationships that together link *Sales* with *After-tax profits*. Accountants would probably find it fairly easy to pick their way through these relationships and understand the extended linkage, but many managers would not be able to. Through experimentation, however, they can get a feel for how changes in the values for *Sales* link to the corresponding changes in the values of *After-tax profits* – and thus create intelligence for themselves.

This concept of intelligence is important because there is a big difference between application systems that provide information and those that provide intelligence. Information is only a means to enable managers to form a better scenario than they had achieved previously. The scenario is the sum of all the intelligence that they possess, with intelligence about a particular issue equivalent to a local scenario. Managers need help with building and updating this local scenario: simply providing them with information is not providing them with all that they really need. Information may be the raw material for intelligence, but managers often need help to interpret it.

Figure 2.1 can be extended to encompass these terms and concepts and to include the links between decisions and the consequent actions affecting the (task) environment. A view of planning and control from an application system perspective is shown in Fig 2.2.

This figure depicts an application system for management – a system to provide managers with information and intelligence. This model is applicable to any type of cognitive system, not solely to computer-based ones. Naturally, it is valid for application systems involving spreadsheets.

Data are those stimuli from outside the application system that pass the rules embedded in the interface between the system and its environment.
Information is data that are or may be useful to a manager in their job.
Intelligence is the product of the meshing together and reconciliation of information. (Note that as used here intelligence has nothing to do with the possession or otherwise of mental ability!)

Fig 2.2 Planning and control from an application systems perspective

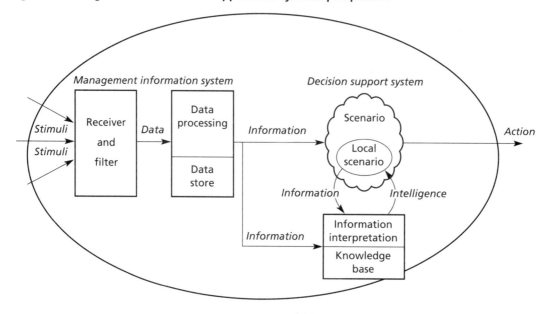

COMPONENTS OF MANAGEMENT APPLICATION SYSTEMS

A simple example from budgeting will make clear the components of a management application system. Budgeting has been chosen because most readers will have had some exposure to the budgetary process.

Virtually every organisation uses budgets in which its activities are represented as a set of cash flows – of incomes and expenditures. Indeed, budgeting is *the* classic business example of the control system shown in Fig 1.1.

Figure 2.3 shows a very simple example of part of a budget. Two things have had to be done to obtain this spreadsheet. First, the rules of calculation have had to be defined. Second, the input data required to 'start the model off' have

Fig 2.3 A simple budget

	A	B	C	D	E	F
1						
2		January	February	March		
3						
4	Sales	10000	11000	10000		
5	Price (£)	11	11	12		
6	Revenue (£)	110000	121000	120000		
7						
8						
9						

had to be selected. The rules of calculation constitute a logic model, while the input data make up a data model. Together, the data and logic models make up the complete model, which is what will be meant when the term 'spreadsheet model' is used from now on.

The result of applying the input data to the rules (or put another way, of linking the data and logic models) is the budget shown in Fig 2.3. Creating the data and logic models is the process of modelling. The modelling lying behind the budget figures is shown in Fig 2.4.[1]

Both the logic and data models used in this budgeting example are extremely simple. In particular, it should be noted that the data model hardly does justice to the data models holding vast amounts of corporate data that are found in many large organisations today.[2]

While the logic and data models will form the core of an application system, they are not the whole of it. In the simple budgeting application, for example, there is a need to consider how the results will be displayed and how the models will be developed and maintained. Here the concern is with the human–computer interface. The display of the results – in tables and graphs, for example – is through a 'results interface'. Although the word 'application system' is much overused, there seems no good alternative to describe this totality of models and interface.

◆ Key concept

*A spreadsheet **model** consists of a logic model and a data model. The data model consists of the data needed to 'start the model off', with the logic model composed of the selected factors and the relationships according to which the data are used to derive results. A spreadsheet **system** consists of the logic and data models and the human–computer interface.*

Fig 2.4 The logic and data models and their relation to the outputs

Logic model			Data model			
Revenue (£) = Sales × Price (£)			Sales	10 000	11 000	10 000
			Price (£)	11	11	12

	A	B	C	D	E	F	G
1							
2		January	February	March			
3							
4	Sales	10000	11000	10000	← Data model		
5	Price (£)	11	11	12	← Data model		
6	Revenue (£)	+B4*B5	+C4*C5	+D4*D5	← Logic model		
7							
8							
9							

Before leaving this section, it is important to stress that all application systems are built on a systems 'infrastructure' and thus are part of bigger computer systems. At its lowest level this infrastructure combines the 'computer' and other associated hardware with the systems software that is needed to make the hardware function (such as an operating system). One level up from this are the application packages that provide the tools to allow application systems to be easily developed. Microsoft Excel and Lotus 1-2-3 are examples of spreadsheet application packages. At the highest level there are the application systems themselves. It is the specific use of an application system that delivers information and/or intelligence to managers. The budgeting example is one such case.

MANAGEMENT INFORMATION AND DECISION SUPPORT SYSTEMS

Roughly 20 years ago, the American Steve Alter put forward perhaps the best-known classifications of managerial application systems. His major categories were defined by the degree to which a system's output directly determines decisions. The major split was between data-oriented and model-oriented systems, following the traditional split between computer science and management science. By data oriented Alter meant that the major development effort lies with the data model: we term these systems 'management information systems' (MIS). By model oriented he meant that the major development effort lies with the logic model: we term these systems 'decision support systems' (DSS).

MIS are one type of management application system used to inform planning and control. They are computer-based systems that provide managers with the information they require to do their jobs. The information may be quantitative (such as that usually provided by spreadsheets) but may also be qualitative – such as that provided by geographical information systems that are being used extensively in such areas as local government and retail store location planning, where much of the information is in the form of maps. The information may be obtained from within the manager's own organisation – from individuals or from corporate databases – or from external sources providing such information as stock-market prices, newsclippings and exchange rates.[3] The data-processing and database portions of Fig 2.2 constitute the main parts of the MIS that provide information. The MIS aspect of spreadsheets is returned to in Chapter 16.

DSS are a second form of management application system. As their name suggests, they are systems to support decision making, or in our terminology issue handling. As with MIS, they may be predominantly concerned with quantitative information (as would normally be the case where spreadsheets are involved) or they could be handling qualitative information in the form of pictures, graphs and diagrams. DSS are used to support the handling of what are termed semistructured issues – issues that have sufficient structure to allow formal structuring methods to be useful, yet at the same time are not so prescribed that there is no need for support. The cases of 'recipes' given in Chapter 1 – switching on the light when darkness falls and reducing prices in the face of falling sales – are examples of very structured situations where the use of DSS would not be necessary. On the other hand, many of the non-financial decisions taken by government, for example, are too ill structured for the use of DSS. Among issues that *are* suitable for DSS are production planning, capital investment appraisal and financial planning. (Many examples are discussed fully in subsequent chapters.) As shown in Fig 2.2, DSS would be helping with information interpretation.

The major distinctions between MIS and DSS are listed in Table 2.1. MIS tend to be developed by information systems specialists and business analysts with a focus on internal control and efficiency: on doing the thing right. Since they are tending to deal with 'facts' (from the past and present) they are providing answers, often in the form of standard reports. In contrast, DSS are often created by users and are concerned with planning and with effectiveness – with doing the right thing rather than simply doing the thing right – and helping to improve intelligence with *ad hoc* outputs providing insights and learning.

Usage of MIS tends to be largely mandatory, generally stretching over an extended period and usually context independent, whereas the opposite is generally the case for DSS. An MIS is context dependent because it will be used in essentially the same way whatever ups and downs the organisation goes through: for example, weekly variance reports will still be needed, managers will still be using personnel statistics and so on whatever the context the

Table 2.1 The emphases associated with MIS and DSS

	Management information systems	Decision support systems
Created by	IT specialists/business analysts	Users/business analysts
Focus	i) Internal control/budgeting ii) Efficiency	i) Planning ii) Effectiveness
Time scale	Past and present	Present andfuture
Output	i) Standard reports ii) An answer, information	i) User created, iterative and interactive reports ii) Insight, learning, intelligence
Usage	Largely mandatory	Discretionary
Duration of use	Long	Short
Context	Context independent	Context dependent
Development	On structured information flows and data structures	On flexibility, adaptability and quick response
Objectives	Prespecified	*Ad hoc*, contingent
Design perspective	Organisational	Individual/small group
Type of situation	Within fixed policies	Within given scenarios
Design methodology	Classical systems approach and prototyping of inputs and outputs	'Breadboarding' , i.e., flexible trial and error
Form of models	i) Fixed logic ii) Definitional relationships iii) Deterministic data iv) Ratio and interval scales	i) Evolutionary logic ii) Judgemental relationships iii) Probabilistic data iv) All scales
Exactness	Precision and lack of bias	Lack of bias
Validation	Verification	Appropriateness

organisation finds itself in. This is certainly not the case with DSS: for example, the importance of the factors to be taken into account in considering whether to go ahead with a capital investment is likely to change over time – perhaps even day to day. The decision is almost certain to depend on the cost of money, the alternative uses for the funds, perhaps on exchange rates and perhaps on forthcoming but as yet unfinalised government legislation.

The development of the two forms of application system is quite different. MIS are concerned primarily with structure – of the information flows and of the data – with prespecified objectives framed within fixed, organisational policies. A classic systems development cycle approach or some variant of it, applied by systems analysts, is the predominant design methodology. However, prototyping is the approach whereby some of the needs of individuals can be met. The term prototyping is borrowed from engineering: a prototype is an early version of a system that exhibits the main features of the later, operational system. Prototyping is employed because theory and experience are not powerful or detailed enough to define every element of the final system.

The prototyping approach is for the user to provide a general specification and for the systems developers quickly to develop an initial version. The user would then try this version and, in the light of the experience gained, modifications would be suggested. The cycle of modification–trial–modification is continued until an acceptable system is developed. However, it is just not feasible to prototype significant portions of an MIS of any substantial size. Prototyping of the input and output screens is possible, however, and is a valid approach to involve the manager and their staff in development, and to show them that progress is being achieved.

DSS are developed within a much looser framework: the system objectives are dependent on circumstances and reflect the scenarios of individual managers or of small groups. DSS are developed in situations where users do not really know where they are going, and thus with objectives not clearly definable at the outset. In such situations it is unlikely that the systems development cycle – where objectives must be clearly agreed from the outset – would be suitable.

A more appropriate approach for DSS is 'breadboarding', a term borrowed from electronics. A breadboard is a board with a matrix of holes in it, arranged so that electronic components can be changed around very easily. This flexibility is needed because of the trial-and-error process sometimes used in assembling 'breadboards'. This same flexibility is needed in DSS, where constant feedback and refinement are part of the evolving system and where managers do not always know at the outset the final system which will be appropriate.

The logic models required for MIS and DSS are also very different. The logic models in MIS are very often simple, with a fixed and easily defined logic consisting of relationships between factors that have been defined to be as they are (as is the case with the financial and accounting relationships used in budgeting models). In contrast, DSS employ relationships which are not predefined but in which the developer has to use judgement in deciding what form of a relationship is most appropriate. The emphases in the data models are also different, with MIS needing to be concerned with the precision of the data (as MIS purport to deal with 'facts'), whereas precision, which is a measure of the random error in a piece of data or information, is of much less significance in DSS, where the focus is on the future with all the uncertainty that this implies. The question of precision is dealt with in more detail in Chapter 6.

Finally, the approach to validating an MIS tends to simply be one of checking that the system carries out its computations as intended, i.e. that there are no bugs in the system. Although a lack of bugs is to be welcomed in DSS, a further, very important consideration here is the appropriateness of the system – whether the system is available on time, whether it covers the area of interest, whether it addresses the issue in a suitable way etc.

Spreadsheet packages *are* used to build MIS, since the simple grid framework within which data is processed and the capability of spreadsheets to present information are useful. In particular, spreadsheets might be used to provide two of Alter's types of data-oriented systems, especially within a spreadsheet DSS. The first of these are *file-drawer systems* providing rapid, *ad hoc* access to a set of prestructured data in support of a regular operational task. A system consisting of personnel records would be a good and common example of such a system. The second are *data-analysis systems* providing straightforward analyses, reports and graphical output of predefined situations. Predefined variance reporting is a good example of such a system.

Such uses of spreadsheet packages to build MIS are rare, however: the predominant uses of spreadsheets are as DSS. The relatively small use of spreadsheets as MIS arises out of several of the distinctions between MIS and DSS given in Fig 2.5. In particular, because MIS tend to be used widely within an organisation and for a much longer period, they need to be designed in a very formal way and with formal tools. Also, since the requirements of MIS are much more standard than are those of DSS, ready-made packages can more easily provide what is required. This has meant that there is a great deal of applications software available to help create MIS, and much of it is far more appropriate to use to build MIS than are spreadsheet packages.

♦ **Key concept** *Managers make use of two forms of application system. Management information systems (MIS) are systems to provide information to managers. Decision support systems (DSS) are systems to provide support to managers faced with semistructured issues. This support is through providing help in information interpretation to produce intelligence. In general, spreadsheet packages are used to develop DSS rather than to develop MIS, although the database facilities in spreadsheets allow for limited MIS applications.*

In the last two sections, the discussion has been about generic forms of management application systems, of MIS and DSS. It is appropriate now to become more specific and talk in terms of spreadsheet systems. From now on we will only be considering spreadsheets that are DSS or, as described in Chapter 16, where the MIS is part of a DSS. The place of DSS spreadsheet systems in the application systems representation in Fig 2.1 is shown in Fig 2.5. Also shown here are the four main components of a spreadsheet.

Fig 2.5 The place of spreadsheets in management application systems

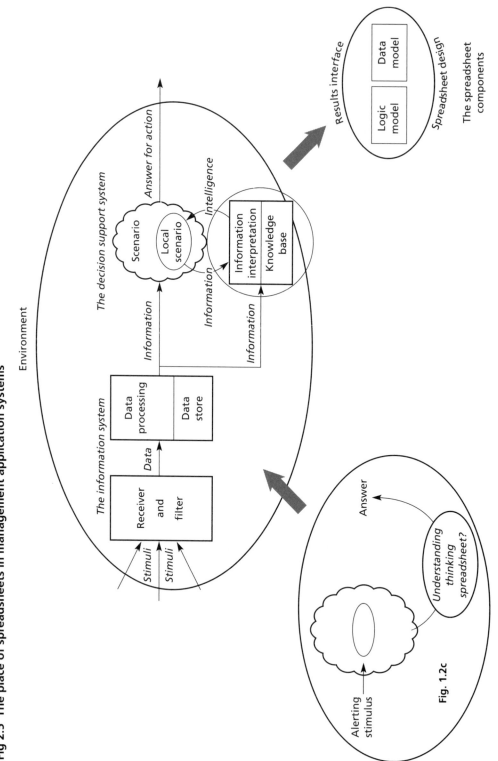

SYSTEMS AND MODELS

So far, the terms system and model have been used without their meaning being formally defined, and with no explanation of the interaction between the two. Since these two terms will be used extensively throughout this book, it is important that you have a solid grasp of what is meant by them.

Systems

A system may be defined as a set of interdependent things connected so as to form a complex unity. One crucial feature of a system is that the whole is greater than the sum of its constituent parts – the system has properties that the elements do not. For example, molecules have properties that atoms do not (for example, colour and smell), and in turn organisms have properties that the molecules do not (for example, the ability to reproduce). These properties that exist at the higher level are called emergent properties.

Hard systems are those for which objectives can be clearly defined and in which causal relationships between factors are well understood. In such systems little time needs to be spent discussing what has to be done (since the objectives can be defined quickly and unambiguously) and the systems thinking reduces to designing and implementing a system that meets these objectives in the best way: the problem can be solved. Systems of this class may be civil engineering projects; for example, given that a bridge is needed over the river Thames, the requirement is how to achieve this under constraints of time, money etc. If the scope of the system were widened to include considerations of why the bridge should be built at all, including, for example, the operations of the whole of the Ministry of Transport, then the system would be considered a soft system. *Soft systems* are those whose objectives are difficult to define and impossible to state with any precision, and where cause and effect are only hazily understood. What, for example, are the goals of the Ministry of Transport? What is the link between the level of motorway provision in a country and the quality of life of its inhabitants? Indeed, what do we mean by quality of life? The example suggests a nice play on words – that hard systems are soft (easy to handle) while soft systems are hard (difficult to handle).

◆ **Key concept**

A system may be defined as a set of interdependent things connected so as to form a complex unity. One crucial feature of a system is that the whole is greater than the sum of its constituent parts – the system has what are termed emergent properties. Hard systems are those for which objectives can be clearly defined and in which causal relationships between factors are well understood. Conversely, soft systems are systems whose objectives are difficult to define and impossible to state with any precision, and where cause and effect are only hazily understood.

Hard systems are soft (easy): soft systems are hard (difficult).

Models

A succinct definition of the term model is 'a representation of reality'. However, this definition is rather limited if reality is taken to mean only that which presently exists. Many exploratory tools have been constructed to explore situations that do not yet exist – for example, models for new cars, or financial plans for an organisation covering the next five years. To encompass such tools under the term model, reality must be taken to include that which could come about in the future as well as that which presently exists.[4]

It is valuable to consider the assumptions underlying modelling. These are that modelling assumes that the world is systematic (or at the very least that a systematic approach to understanding the world is likely to be better than an unsystematic one) and that we have some idea of the nature of the relationships between important variables in this world. It also assumes that things in the world are measurable.

◆ *Key concept*

If you intend to develop spreadsheet models then you are assuming that understanding the world is best approached in a systematic manner and that you have some idea of the nature of the relationships between important variables in this world. It also assumes that things in the world are measurable – i.e. that a data model can be constructed.

It is worth building models to aid decision making for the following reasons:

- models make the structure of an issue explicit
- models can usually be analysed more readily than the original issue
- it is possible to experiment with models and thus answer 'What if?' type questions (as is explained fully in Chapter 9)
- the process of model building leads to a deeper understanding of the issue
- the process of model building and experimenting with the model leads to a better-formed and richer view of the scenario when handling subsequent issues.

◆ *Key concept*

A model is a representation of reality – either of something that already exists or of something that might exist in the future. The models in a spreadsheet are part of the spreadsheet system. The spreadsheet system is used to help managers plan and control the (real world) system for which they have responsibility.

SUMMARY

This chapter has been concerned with some fundamentals of application systems. The terms data, information and intelligence have been defined, with information seen as the raw material for the creation of intelligence. A model has been developed out of the planning and control model of Chapter 1. The terms model and system have been discussed, with data and logic models providing the heart of application systems.

The two types of managerial application system – MIS and DSS – were introduced. MIS are formal means whereby information is provided to alert managers to the presence of problems and to provide information to DSS. DSS are systems for helping managers to interpret information to support issue handling and helping them develop a scenario of their system and its environment.

The major distinctions between MIS and DSS have been described. Although spreadsheet packages may be used to develop either MIS or DSS, they are predominantly used for DSS. This is because there are many more appropriate software packages available to create MIS, which are systems for widespread and continual use. The tools that will be introduced in this book include selection from external databases, which comes under MIS, but also simulation, risk analysis, project management and many others that are DSS.

END NOTES

1 Note that the budget (i.e. the output from the spreadsheet model shown in Fig 2.3) is itself a model, since it is a (financial) representation of the expected operations of the organisation.

2 Budgeting is only one area where financial modelling is used: similar modelling is involved in capital investment decisions and in long-range planning. However, it must be stressed that modelling goes far beyond financial modelling, into such areas as scheduling, resource allocation, preference determination and ideas management.

3 Executive information systems are one form of MIS that obtain much of their power from providing managers with external information.

4 There is more to this point than might be immediately apparent. The question of whether 'the world' is a meaningful concept is not just one for philosophers, but for professional modellers too. Fortunately for us here, this does not usually raise problems in issues where a spreadsheet model is likely to be helpful.

FURTHER READING For a good all-round view of information systems, including how to implement prototyping and the life cycle approach, the book by Carol Cashmore with Richard Lyall, *Business Information Systems and Strategies*, Prentice Hall International, 1991, is to be recommended. Ralph H. Sprague Jr and Barbara C. McNurlin provide good, readable coverage of DSS and group support systems and multimedia in *Information Systems Management in Practice*, 3rd edition, Prentice Hall International, 1993. A fairly advanced book on DSS is that by Ralph H. Sprague Jr and Hugh J. Watson, *Decision Support for Management*, Prentice Hall, New Jersey, USA, 1996.

EXERCISES

1 What is the distinction between efficiency and effectiveness?

2 In this chapter, three levels of hardware/software have been introduced. What are they?

3 What are the differences between prototyping and breadboarding? Where would each be used?

4   What is the difference between embedded and *ad hoc* rules?

5   Where using a spreadsheet, where does information interpretation take place?

6   According to some information theorists, information is used to shift the probabilities associated with the options facing a decision maker. What do you think of this?

7   Consider the application systems that you know about. Look at Table 2.1 and assess how many of the attributes you can place in either the MIS or DSS categories. Are there many cases where the characteristics are partly MIS and DSS, or is it the case that the systems fit all MIS or all DSS characteristics?

8   A scenario is the sum of a manager's intelligence. Why is it not the sum of both intelligence and information?

9   The 'breadboarding' approach suggests that you should not plan much about the DSS you are building – just get on with it and allow the system to evolve. What do you think of this?

10   A model is a representation of reality. A system is a set of interdependent things connected so as to form a complex unity. Can you have a model of a system? Can you have a system of a model?

11   What is the interaction between the local scenario and information interpretation?

CHAPTER 3

Constructing local scenarios: structural modelling

Chapter aims

It is not much good managers going ahead and starting to build spreadsheets unless they have some idea of the support they want from them – in other words, unless they have first got a local scenario which describes their situation and requirements. Constructing a local scenario is an important stage in spreadsheet design and is achieved through a process called structural modelling, which is the focus of this chapter.

- System and environments
- Managerial variables
  - Fishbone diagrams
- Constraints
- Expressing a local scenario
- Complementary approaches
  - Rich pictures • Cognitive maps
- Tips on constructing local scenarios

It could be argued that if managers are building the spreadsheets themselves there is no need for them to articulate their requirements for it: it is all in their heads! However, except for very simple cases, without some sort of formal specification a great deal of effort could be spent continually modifying the spreadsheet to take account of requirements that suddenly become apparent. The aim of this chapter is to prevent such large-scale modification through the use of a formal structuring process, whereby managers can quite easily articulate a view of their local scenario in a way that allows for the fairly simple translation of appropriate portions of it into spreadsheet form.

A scenario is a managerial view of the world within which issues are detected. An existing local scenario is the portion of the scenario used to define the issue once it has been detected. However, once the issue has been defined it will often be necessary to refine and develop the local scenario further to provide the necessary understanding to handle the issue. The process by which this refinement and development are undertaken is called structural modelling, since it allows the broad structure of the situation to be modelled. Structural modelling does not aim to model at the level of detail required to build a spreadsheet. Rather, the aim is to provide a solid base from which subsequently to build one if one is required: thus it is a preliminary to spreadsheet design. While few managers will have carried out structural modelling with any great formality,[1] all will have done it implicitly or they would not be able to manage.[2]

There are three main steps to structural modelling:

1 Identification of the managerial variables in the local scenario.
2 Identification of the constraints on the values that variables can take.
3 Formalisation of the local scenario by expressing the broad relationships between managerial variables, including the associated constraints.

These steps will be discussed following an introductory discussion of systems and environments.

◆ *Key concept*   *Structural modelling is a systematic way of capturing managers' perceptions of their world. It does not attempt to determine goals, nor to optimise performance: rather it attempts to identify all the factors that are important to the manager, to specify the broad relationships between them and to recognise the ranges of values associated with these factors.*

SYSTEM AND ENVIRONMENTS

Managers need to understand their system and its interactions with its environment in order to plan and control it. To achieve this understanding they need to distil from their world the fundamental elements and relationships – discarding any unnecessary detail or 'mental clutter'. In other words they must model: take a snapshot or a 'mental video' of their system and its environment.

The world in which managers operate can usefully be divided into two main parts – their system and its environment – with the system boundary separating them. These boundaries need not be physical boundaries (such as the factory gates) but can be conceptual, social, political or psychological. The distinction between the system and environment is clear – the system consists of those things over which the manager has control, the environment being all else of relevance. In many cases it is helpful further to subdivide the environment into local and remote environments. The local environment is where, although managers have no direct control in the sense that 'their word is law', they can nevertheless exert a significant influence, and where their performance is significant. Generally the local environment can be taken to be the rest of the organisation in which the manager works. A person's boss is perhaps the most obvious example of an element within a manager's local environment – they can't tell the boss what to do but they can influence what they do. An example of a part of the local environment which lies outside the organisation would be where an organisation is very dependent on a retailer and thus the retailer can exert a powerful, indirect influence on the organisation. Both organisation and retailer would most certainly see the other as part of their local environment.

Fig 3.1 System and environments

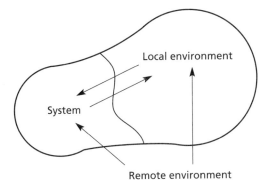

The second part of the environment is the remote environment over which managers have no significant influence but which has a significant impact on them and their system. Almost always, the remote environment models the world outside the organisation. Examples of factors in the remote environment would be monetary exchange rates and government legislation.

In Fig 3.1 the three divisions of system, local environment and remote environment of the manager's world are shown together with the interactions between them. The interactions from the remote environment affect the system either directly or indirectly via the local environment. An example of the latter would be the effects of changes in consumer demand on a system for buying raw materials: the production and marketing departments are likely to have stockholding and scheduling procedures to damp down the effect of sudden changes in consumer demand on this system.

♦ **Key concept**

A manager's system may be defined as consisting of those things over which they have control. Their environment is all else of relevance to them when doing their job. It may be appropriate to subdivide the environment into two parts: a local environment where, although managers have no direct control, they can nevertheless exert a significant influence, and where their performance has a significant impact; and a remote environment over which they have no significant influence, but which has a significant impact on them.

MANAGERIAL VARIABLES

Managers are measured by how well they meet objectives set for them by their bosses. These objectives are generally the more obvious output variables of the manager's system. One example of an objective for senior management would be the level of annual profits: for a middle manager examples of objectives would be the costs incurred, sales made and the level of customer complaints. Further output variables would be the other factors that the manager wishes to know about since they contribute to the organisational objectives – and to their own personal objectives! Examples would be the morale of the workforce and the amount of stress the managers themselves feel. Output variables may be quantitative and reasonably precisely defined variables such as turnover and profit, or more nebulous ones such as morale and flexibility.

The system for which managers are responsible will be subject to many factors in the environment. To plan and control managers must make decisions – to take advantage of environmental opportunities or to mitigate the effects of environmental threats – so as to meet the outputs required of them. The ability of managers to take decisions implies that there are things in their system that they can vary (such as advertising expenditure for a marketing manager and manning levels for a production manager). These 'levers' are called decision variables.[3] Decision, output and environmental variables are depicted in Fig 3.2.

To clarify the concepts outlined above, consider the operation of a restaurant. Suppose the restaurant is owned by a group of gourmets and run by a manager. The first thing needed for structural modelling is to be sure whose scenario we are concerned with and the issue that has arisen.[4] This is most important: for instance, the gourmets may be concerned only with the social aspects of the restaurant's operation and hardly concerned with financial matters at all as long as they don't lose money, while the manager's focus is likely to include financial considerations – especially if their salary is performance related!

Let's take the role of the manager and see how we might go about structurally modelling their system and environment. The manager is going to be held responsible by the owners for the overall financial performance of the restaurant as this affects them (and thus their profit). The manager will also have their own additional output measures, such as customer comfort, staff morale and type of clientele – and the performance-related salary! They will have at their disposal several decision variables, the values of which they can change, and they are exposed to the effects of several environmental variables. Some of these variables are listed in Table 3.1. Note that several of the variables (for example, staff morale and restaurant ambiance) are likely to be

Fig 3.2 Decision, output and environmental variables

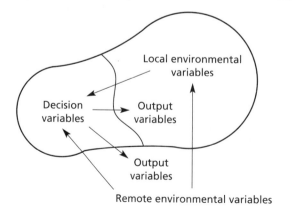

ill-defined. This is of little consequence as long as there is some broad basic understanding of their meaning. What must be avoided at this stage is any over-emphasis on definitions that might inhibit the capturing of the richness of the real-world situation in the local scenario. Precise definitions come in any subsequent detailed modelling.

Sometimes it is not obvious whether a variable is a decision or output variable: for example, type of clientele is listed as an output variable in Table 3.1 but it could well be considered as a decision variable. Sometimes variables are both decision and output variables: as are salaries and wages in Table 3.1. Don't worry if you have difficulty categorising the variables: in practice the key thing is to have identified them.

Table 3.1 Typical variables in the restaurant system

Decision variables	Local environmental variables
Number of staff Number of customers/sitting Stock policy Staffing policies Salaries and wages	Suppliers' delivery schedules Other restaurants – especially the new one Warehousing Hours of work for the manager's partner Space in the bar area Size of the restaurant car park
Output variables	**Remote environmental variables**
Profit Salaries and wages Stock held Wine revenue Customer comfort Restaurant ambiance Staff morale Type of clientele Manager's (performance-related) salary	Legal opening hours Unfair dismissal laws Health regulations Violence Duty on alcohol Value-added tax Bank lending rules

Fishbone diagrams

The list of variables in Table 3.1 was obtained by focusing on the decision, output and environmental variables in the manager's local scenario. A complementary approach to identify the variables of significance is to focus on resources and forces, and this is what is done when using fishbone diagrams (also known as Ishikawa diagrams after their Japanese developer). Fishbone diagrams have been extensively used in improvement programmes where they map out the possible sources of problems. However, they are also useful in identifying the important factors in any sort of issue.

A fishbone diagram for part of the restaurant example is given in Fig 3.3. It is easy to see why it is given this name! Drawing a fishbone diagram is simple. First, select the main dimensions of significance to the issue under consideration. The chosen dimensions nearly always include the people and systems dimensions; it is the other dimensions – such as government in the case of the

Fig 3.3 Fishbone diagram for the restaurant

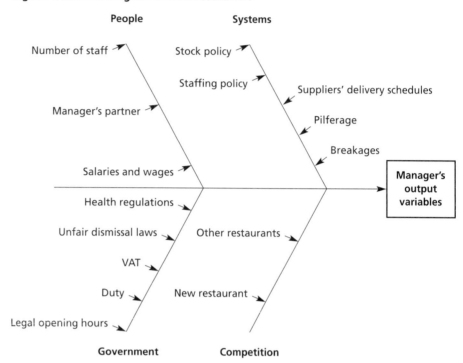

restaurant – that are peculiar to the particular situation. Then, taking each dimension in turn, the variables thought significantly to affect the issue are drawn in – adding flesh to the bones.

◆ **Key concept**
A variable is any factor whose value is not fixed. One approach to scenario development is to consider scenarios as composed of three types of managerial variable. The output variables are the dimensions along which managers would measure themselves and be measured by others. Factors whose values the manager can alter are their decision variables. Important variables in the environment are termed environmental variables.

A second approach to scenario development is to consider scenarios as covering the resources under the manager's control and the forces acting on their system.

CONSTRAINTS

So far in this discussion of systems, and of the restaurant example in particular, a list of the managerial variables of concern has been developed (as in

Table 3.1 and Fig 3.3). Two more steps are needed before the structural modelling is complete. The next step is to identify broadly the range of values which a variable can take, and this requires consideration of the constraints that exist in the system and its environment. They limit the range of a decision variable, either directly (such as the effect of suppliers' delivery schedules on the stock policy) or indirectly through limits imposed on output variables (such as the effect of a strict minimum imposed on the stock held). An environmental constraint is an imposition on the system from outside. It might be physical and very tangible – for example, a local government restriction on the size of the restaurant's car park – or it might be more behavioural – for example, the social view of what constitutes fair play in the handling of employees. A constraint arising from within the system is a self-imposed constraint. Often such constraints are intangible – for example, a feeling of inadequacy limiting a person's perception of what they are capable of achieving; an example of this would be if the restaurant manager did not think that the restaurant would be able to provide the standard of food that the gourmets sought, although there was no real reason for this to be the case. But constraints can also be more tangible. For example, the restaurant manager may believe that the available storage is limited to that on the restaurant premises, while in fact there may be warehousing available for rent nearby and nothing to prevent its use. Some of the constraints in the case of the restaurant might be as listed in Table 3.2.

♦ **Key concept**

Constraints are limitations on the values that variables can take. An environmental constraint is an imposition on the system from outside. A constraint arising from within the system is a self-imposed constraint.

Although Fig 3.3 only contains variables, a fishbone diagram can be augmented with constraints if this is considered useful.

Table 3.2 Constraints in the restaurant example

1	The manager's partner won't work in the restaurant during lunch times.
2	The banks have a policy of only giving money for restaurant modernisation up to half of annual turnover.
3	The owners require that the restaurant doesn't lose money.
4	The space in the bar area restricts the number of customers taking a drink before their meal to 20.
5	The maximum number of customers which the restaurant can comfortably accommodate is 50.

EXPRESSING A LOCAL SCENARIO

The third and final step in structural modelling to produce the local scenario is the expression of the relationships between variables, constraints and constants in a language understandable to all relevant people. One approach is to express these relationships verbally. In the UK this verbal expression would naturally be English, but perhaps using 'organisational English', i.e. incorporating jargon where appropriate and using such well-known symbols as $+$, $-$, $\times$, $/$ and %. Some of the statements relevant to the restaurant example might be along the lines shown in Table 3.3.

Table 3.3 Statements for the restaurant local scenario

1	Customers like a relaxed atmosphere in the evening.
2	The new health regulations will mean costly changes in the kitchen.
3	When it opens, the new restaurant down the road will affect trade quite a lot.
4	Staff morale depends on two main items – staff wages and the restaurant's social atmosphere.
5	Wine revenue = Bottle sales $\times$ Price
6	Present stocks = Previous stocks + Receipts – (Sales + Breakages + Pilferage) up to maximum stock governed by the size of the cellars.
7	At peak times one waiter can, on average, attend to 10 customers.

COMPLEMENTARY APPROACHES

The structural modelling approach described above results in a local scenario expressed in words. The attraction of this verbal approach is that it allows for the fairly simple translation of appropriate portions of it into a spreadsheet. However, there is no reason to limit the scenarios to a set of sentences and it may well be that it is appropriate to consider using some other form of representation to act as an intermediary step between issue definition and the formalised, 'verbal' local scenario. Two other approaches that are complementary to this 'verbal' approach will now be discussed, using rich pictures and cognitive maps.

Rich pictures

Rich pictures have been used to handle issues in soft systems for many years. For the more semistructured issues – those that might be aided by the use of spreadsheets – it is less usual to draw such pictures, but there are times when pictures might prove valuable. Pictures have the properties that:

- they provide a feel for the overall shape of a local scenario
- they can show far more information in the same space than can a verbal description
- they show multiple relationships far more easily than a (linear) verbal description
- they summarise the local scenario in a way that can be readily appreciated by others.

This latter point is important if the results from the spreadsheet are to be shown to others who might have contributed in preliminary discussions.

One such rich picture for part of the restaurant example is shown in Fig 3.4. Any forms of icons, words, symbols etc. may be used in a rich picture: the only limitation is your imagination – and appropriateness, of course!

Cognitive maps

A further form of representation of the local scenario is through a cognitive map – so called because it reflects (maps) graphically a person's or a group's thought processes, particularly cause-and-effect thinking. A cognitive map for a portion of the restaurant example is given in Fig 3.5.

In a cognitive map arrows are drawn pointing from a cause to its effect. For example, in Fig 3.5, car parking is shown leading to staff morale and type of

Fig 3.4 Part of a rich picture of the restaurant

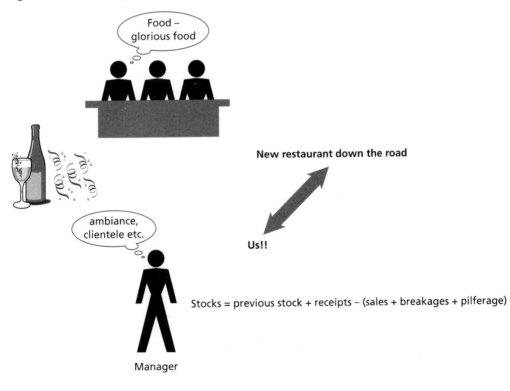

Food – glorious food

New restaurant down the road

ambiance, clientele etc.

Us!!

Stocks = previous stock + receipts – (sales + breakages + pilferage)

Manager

Fig 3.5 A cognitive map for a part of the restaurant situation

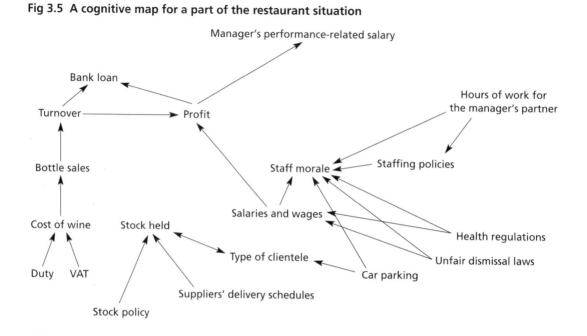

clientele: i.e. the quality of the car-parking provision affects both staff morale and the type of clientele. Note that arrows can be double-headed, reflecting a two-way interaction: for example, the stock held both affects the type of clientele and is in turn affected by the type of clientele.

TIPS ON CONSTRUCTING LOCAL SCENARIOS

There is no best way to produce a description of a local scenario that is suitable for all people in all circumstances. Use the method or combination of methods that suit you – verbal, fishbone, rich picture, cognitive mapping or anything else that you like. However, you are likely to find that a final representation that consists of verbal statements will be easier to convert into any subsequent spreadsheets that you build.

Tips for constructing local scenarios are as follows:

- Think of an appropriate time scale. Remember that you are planning for the future.
- Try to consider the issue from several different perspectives – perhaps through discussion with colleagues.
- Pick out the important factors. Here a good starting point is to consider that you are a new manager just arriving to take over your system. Ask yourself what information you need to handle the issue and what resources and forces you have to contend with.
- Include both hard and soft information.
- Look for slowly changing things – the structure.

- Look for continuously changing things – the process.
- Look at the political, economic, social and technological facets (the PEST factors) in the remote environment.

SUMMARY

A scenario is a managerial view of the world within which issues are detected. An existing local scenario is the portion of the scenario brought into focus to define the issue. Once the issue has been defined, it will often be necessary to probe more deeply in order to handle the specifics raised by the issue, and this will require that the local scenario is refined and developed. The local scenario contains a description of the issue situation as seen by the manager.

The process by which the local scenario is refined and developed is called structural modelling. This is a systematic way of capturing a manager's perceptions of their world. It does not attempt to determine company or departmental goals, nor to optimise performance: rather it attempts to identify all the important factors in an organisation and its environment, to specify the broad relationships between these factors and to recognise the broad ranges of values associated with them. Structural modelling may involve the drawing of rich pictures and the use of cognitive maps as well as verbal statements. You should use whichever approach best fits your way of working.

There are three main steps to structural modelling:

1 Define the local scenario – the variables in the manager's system and its environment.
2 Identify the constraints on the values that variables can take.
3 Formalise the local scenario by expressing the broad relationships between managerial variables, including the associated constraints.

END NOTES

1 The need for any formal approach might be questioned, however, since many managers seem to perform very well without one. But if you agree with the reasons for model building put forward towards the end of Chapter 2, you will accept that a formalised approach is likely to help in communication with other people and between a manager's unarticulated local scenario and any subsequent spreadsheet design.

2 The discussion that follows throughout the chapter implies a *single* local scenario. But we know from experience that sometimes the future will be very different depending on the outcome of one of two events. For example, the construction industry in many countries is the driver of much other economic activity and for this reason governments use it as a control for the rest of the economy. Thus planners in construction firms develop scenarios to sketch out a set of futures, often developing a scenario relevant to each political party that stands a chance of getting into power in the time period of concern.

3 Important features of the environment may be constant or variable (over the planning time frame of the typical manager, accounting conventions will normally be constant while monetary exchange rates would be expected to be highly variable). Although managers must be knowledgeable or at least aware of important environmental

constants, it is the environmental variables that are of paramount importance, since containing or taking advantage of environmental change is largely the stuff of true management. It is for this reason that the emphasis is placed on variables.

4 It may seem odd to discuss here who the scenario is for, since the whole book is aimed at managers who are building spreadsheets for themselves. However, in many cases spreadsheets are built for use with other people whose cooperation is needed. Incorporating some of these people's local scenarios into the structural modelling (to provide a 'composite scenario') may be necessary.

FURTHER READING A book that contains descriptions and discussions of the soft systems methodology that uses rich pictures, cognative mapping and other methods useful in scenario development is that edited by Jonathan Rosenhead, *Rational Analysis for a Problematic World: Problem Structuring Methods for Complexity, Uncertainty and Conflict* published by John Wiley, Chichester, 1989. A second book that provides a wide and discursive look at issue handling is that by Michael J. Hicks, *Problem Solving in Business and Management: Hard, Soft and Creative Approaches*, Chapman and Hall, London, 1991. More information on rich picture development is given in Peter Checkland and Jim Scholes' book, *Soft Systems Methodology in Action*, John Wiley, 1990.

A book by five people at Warwick University – Nigel Slack, Stuart Chambers, Christine Harland, Alan Harrison and Robert Johnson – *Operations Management*, Pitman, 1995, presents some more detail on fishbone diagrams.

EXERCISES

1 What is the difference between an environmental and a self-imposed constraint?

2 What is the difference between an organisational objective and an output variable?

3 In Fig 3.1 there are no arrows going from the system or local environment to the remote environment. What does this mean and is it correct?

4 How does Fig 3.1 link in with Fig 2.2?

5 Add further decision, output and environmental variables to the list given in Table 3.1.

6 Complete the fishbone diagram in Fig 3.3. [You may feel that you would like to add further dimensions.]

7 Complete the rich picture in Fig 3.4.

8 Complete the cognitive map in Fig 3.5.

9 Fishbone diagrams represent a means of identifying variables of importance in producing a local scenario that is complementary to the approach which relies on identifying the decision, output and environmental variables. What is it that each approach offers that the other does not?

10 Consider an organisation which you know something about. It may be the company you work for, a part of that company, your university department, a club or church to which you belong. Think of some issue that is important to

that organisation. With this issue as a focus, identify the managerial variables and constraints.

11   Following on from exercise 10, move forward and develop a scenario for the 'owner' of the issue you identified. In building the scenario, try out all three ways of representation that have been described in this chapter: verbal statements, a rich picture and a cognitive map. Discuss the pros and cons of each representation.

12   The emphasis in this chapter is on refining a local scenario in the light of a detected issue. How does this enhancement of the local scenario affect the (full) scenario?

13   What are the consequences for spreadsheet development when there are two or more scenarios?

14   In Chapter 2 the prototyping and breadboarding approaches were discussed. In this chapter, it was suggested that structural modelling is a means of preventing the necessity for redoing/reformatting a spreadsheet. How do you reconcile these two approaches?

15   Construct a local scenario for yourself for an important issue in your personal life.

16   Consider the Readyread case. Derive what you think might be a suitable local scenario for the managers most affected.

17   Consider the Strongarm case. Derive what you think might be a suitable local scenario for the managers most affected.

18   Make a list of likely decision, environmental and output variables for
(a) the production manager in the Proteus case
(b) a university lecturer.

CHAPTER 4

Spreadsheets and managerial support: guidelines

Chapter aims

In the previous chapter structural modelling was introduced as a means of producing a formalised description of the manager's local scenario. Before moving on to Chapters 5 through 8 where spreadsheet development is considered in detail, it is valuable first to consider the situations for which spreadsheets are appropriate and where spreadsheet builders should best put their efforts. The aim of this chapter is to help answer these questions through the use of a set of guidelines.

- How valuable would it be to have a spreadsheet?
- Where will the major difficulties arise in spreadsheet development?
- How detailed should the spreadsheet be?
- How do I ensure that the spreadsheet, especially the form of its output, is acceptable to other people?

A manager's view of the world is a set of perceptions encapsulated in a scenario. It is within this set of perceptions that a manager sees issues arise. Having defined the issue through the development of a local scenario, the manager will move on to handle the issue. Will a spreadsheet help? If so, what should be its scope?

What is happening when a spreadsheet is created is shown in Fig 4.1. Here the modeller is taking a portion of the local scenario – a set of vaguely stated relationships between ill-defined variables – and translating it into a coherent and consistent set of relationships between well-defined factors in a spreadsheet. The modeller is converting an imprecise yet rich view of the issue situation into a precise yet much more poverty-stricken view – they will often be moving from a soft to a hard model. They do this because they believe that it is worth the effort to create the spreadsheet since the insights and information its use generates are helpful in handling the issue.

Very few practical issues do not involve some number crunching, even if all that is needed is a quick, back-of-the-envelope calculation. So the question to ask is not whether to carry out number crunching or not but rather what amount of it is appropriate. Sometimes, of course, this is very obvious, especially when

Fig 4.1 The translation from local scenario to spreadsheet

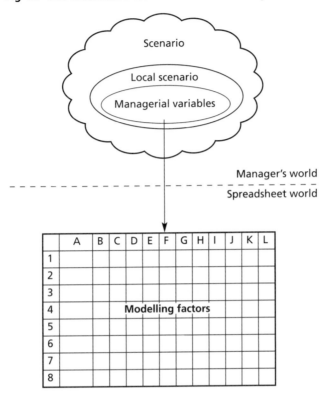

applying a well-known technique in a straightforward manner: a simple example would be the calculation of the average of a set of data. On the other hand, the circumstances may be such that considerable resources may be committed to building a spreadsheet that may provide little or no benefit.

Conceptually the process of deciding what constitutes the appropriate level of modelling is a cost–benefit exercise. In such an exercise you consider the opportunity costs of the resources: i.e. seeing if there is any better use that can be made of the time and money spent creating the spreadsheet and comparing the costs with the benefits you think you will gain from having the spreadsheet. This comparison is very difficult to do in practice, however.

The difficulty in determining costs and benefits can be bypassed to some extent by considering an issue situation in the light of a set of broad guidelines about the use of spreadsheets in organisations. Such guidelines can be grouped conveniently into four areas. These address the questions:

- How valuable would it be to have a spreadsheet?
- Where will the major difficulties arise in spreadsheet development?
- How detailed should the spreadsheet be?
- How do I ensure that the spreadsheet, especially its outputs, is acceptable to other people?

Note that the guidelines are generally expressed as simple relationships between two factors – in the form of *the more is A the more is B*; *the greater is X the smaller is Y* and so on. Given the complexity of the contexts in which spreadsheets may be used, it would be inappropriate to go further – for example, to try to combine the guidelines in some way to cover more complex situations. When faced with a situation that might call for the development of a spreadsheet, it is for you to use your common sense and any experience you may have to make the necessary trade-offs between these rather bald statements.

HOW VALUABLE WOULD IT BE TO HAVE A SPREADSHEET?

The seven guidelines given in this section are intended to help managers judge the potential value of having a spreadsheet to help handle an issue.

Guideline 1 The more important an issue, the greater the potential value of a spreadsheet

Guideline 1 may appear to contradict what was said in Chapter 1, that the impact of spreadsheets on strategic issue handling has been and is likely to remain small. But this is to confuse potential value with ability to contribute. Guideline 1 is simply saying that as the importance of a issue rises – as the size of the irreversible allocation of resources increases – management should use all relevant tools and techniques to generate and explore options. Spreadsheets provide one such tool.

Guideline 2 The greater the number of people who are involved with an issue, the greater the potential value of a spreadsheet

One of the most important uses for a spreadsheet is to focus the discussion surrounding the opinion-forming process that precedes the adoption of a course of action. The greater the number of people who are engaged in such a debate, the more need there is for the discussion to be structured, for a common terminology to be used and for a generally accepted picture of the world to be available. Spreadsheets and their outputs can usefully act as the basic core around which some of the discussion flourishes.

Guideline 3 The greater the number of factors involved in an issue, the greater the potential value of a spreadsheet

The number of factors that need to be taken into account is a measure of the complexity of the issue. Some researchers write of 'the magic number 7 ± 2', believing that people can only deal with around seven things at a time. It is impossible for a manager to deal effectively with many variables unaided and spreadsheets are able to help by effectively reducing this number. For example, the financial appraisal technique of discounted cash flow, with which most readers will be familiar, enables many variables (the cash inflows and outflows over many years) to be represented by a single figure – a very great simplification.

Guideline 4 The more often the same or similar issues are met, the greater the potential value of a spreadsheet

This guideline is quite straightforward, since any help that a spreadsheet (or any other support, for that matter) can give is multiplied by the number of times it is used, and this is obviously linked to the number of times similar issues are met. Discounted cash flow calculations present a good example of where similar calculations are performed many times – and thus are an obvious candidate for spreadsheet support. Another area which obtains a great deal of spreadsheet support is financial planning.

Guideline 5 The more an organisation values intelligence in issue handling, the greater the potential value of a spreadsheet

Some organisations are concerned that the quantitative parts of issues are rigorously handled, and seek out all relevant information and intelligence before coming to a conclusion. It is in such organisations that spreadsheets are likely to be valued. Other organisations are less concerned with intelligence, prefering to rely more on hunch and unarticulated views.[1]

Guideline 6 The greater the importance of 'soft' variables in an issue, the less the potential value of a spreadsheet

A soft variable is a variable that cannot be fully or easily quantified. Examples of soft variables would be 'restaurant ambiance' and 'staff morale'. When the importance of these soft variables is high, it makes little sense to do much in the way of spreadsheet modelling – which is concerned with quantitative modelling. A personal experience will demonstrate this. Some years ago a company with which one of us was associated decided to move its offices out of central London. The determination of the new location seemed an obvious case for a spreadsheet, with a model encompassing such things as the present location of staff, staff reallocation expenses, the number of business trips north and south (and thus the need to be near a railway station), the number of overseas business trips (and thus the need to have good access to a main airport) and so on. A perfect case for a cost–benefit study. However the boss, being very much versed in the ways of the world, instructed us to keep out of the debate. He thought that the preferences of the directors (and of their spouses!) would be the determining factor. And he was right.

Guideline 7 The more the overall decision is determined by political and organisational considerations, the less the potential value of a spreadsheet

This guideline could be seen as an extension of the previous guideline as the concern is again with soft variables. However, these soft variables are of a hidden and complex kind. Issues are seldom concerned only with information interpretation; almost all major decisions have political overtones and have organisational implications.

◆ **Key concept** *The potential value of a spreadsheet is directly related to the importance of the issue; the number of people involved; the number of factors influencing the issue; the number of times the same or similar issues will be met; and the value that the organisation places on intelligence. Conversely, as the importance of soft variables rises and the political and organisational influences become more significant, the potential value of a spreadsheet diminishes.*

WHERE WILL THE MAJOR DIFFICULTIES ARISE IN SPREADSHEET DEVELOPMENT?

If it has been decided that the potential value of a spreadsheet is such that spreadsheet development is a definite possibility, the next question concerns the main difficulties that may prevent a suitable spreadsheet being developed – or strongly curtail its scope. These conditions lead to four guidelines.

Guideline 8 The less well recognised the relationships between managerial variables, the more difficult it will be to create a satisfactory model

A logic model is a set of precisely defined relationships between factors. If the model is reflecting a set of precisely defined, well-recognised relationships in the real world, then it should be easy to construct since the translation from one set to another is easy. Many accounting models are of this form, since the accountants have been clever enough to construct their own 'real world' as a set of relationships that are as they are by definition.[2] However, it is a very timid manager who restricts their spreadsheets to accounting relations: they can use spreadsheets to explore less precisely defined areas as well. Just because the relationships in these areas do not have the strong claims to validity that attach to accounting relationships should not prevent their use.[3]

Guideline 9 The wider the range of values a relationship is expected to handle, the more difficult and time consuming it will be to construct an adequate spreadsheet

A relationship between variables that take a wide range of values often poses problems. This is because it is likely that the form of the relationship will be different over different ranges of values of the variables. For example, when an organisation is making profits the corporation tax paid will vary directly with the profit made, i.e. if the profit rises by 10 per cent then so will the tax. However, this relationship will not hold if the company is making a loss!! If foreign investments began to play a part in the profit then a further form of relationship between profit and tax would be appropriate.

There is also the problem of coping with discontinuities. For example, as demand increases it is often the case that at some stage the production department of an organisation will need to change how it works – perhaps working a second shift, perhaps bringing in more workers to operate an additional machine. In such cases the costs of production will not be smoothly related to the quantity produced: as the new working practices are introduced it is likely that costs will be discontinuous, often being stepped.

Guideline 10 The more difficult it is to obtain data, the less likely it is that a suitable spreadsheet can be produced

It is all very well thinking of developing a spreadsheet that is going to astound your boss, but it will remain stillborn if the data needed cannot be obtained. Two examples from our own experiences will perhaps drive home the point. The first involved producing a spreadsheet for a production department that worked on a four-week 'month', whereas the financial data was only available for calendar months. The second case concerned the construction of a spreadsheet to predict production staffing costs in a factory over a wide range of demand. Although elaborate and very elegant relationships were derived to create the logic model, the managers, feeling threatened by a spreadsheet that would generate 'their' staffing costs, refused to release the precise data that would have allowed the spreadsheet to be considered credible.

Guideline 11 The more indirect the empirical measure of a variable, the less the model should depend on the variable

An empirical measure is one that will provide data. This is in contrast to a theoretical measure which will not. For example, height and weight are empirical measures, since a tape measure and a weighing machine will produce data. Goodness and evil are theoretical rather than empirical measures, since data cannot be obtained about them – certainly not directly.

For some managerial variables the empirical measure is extremely straightforward. For example, if a value were required for the average number of people using a railway station during an evening, one way of getting this information would be to have someone at each entrance to record all the comings and goings over the period of concern; from the resultant data, calculation of the average would be very easy. The empirical measure is straightforward in this case. What now of an empirical measure for 'employee morale'? Does one exist? A survey might be used to obtain this information, but this costs money and takes time to administer. It might be possible to use an indirect measure – say, absenteeism. Absenteeism itself is a simple empirical measure reflecting unplanned absence from employment and values for it can usually be obtained from attendance records. So it might at first glance seem a good indirect measure for morale. However, you are always on potentially dangerous ground with indirect measures, since agreement to their use will have to be obtained from all interested parties. Also, agreement will be needed on when their use would be appropriate: if an epidemic were to occur in the area, would absenteeism still be regarded as a reasonable measure for morale? The study into the siting of London's third airport should be a lesson to us all. One infamous part of the study concerned the assessment of the value of the mediaeval churches that would have to be demolished at one of the possible airport sites. The best valuation that the researchers came up with was the insurance valuation placed on the buildings – a very low figure! This was seen by almost everyone involved in the study to be a very poor indirect measure and the credibility of the study suffered accordingly.

◆ *Key concept*

The difficulty in developing an appropriate spreadsheet will be directly related to how well recognised are the relationships between the managerial variables, the range of values the relationships need to accommodate, and the difficulty in obtaining suitable data and the indirectness of the empirical measures.

HOW DETAILED SHOULD THE SPREADSHEET BE?

Detail generally costs money, and detail in spreadsheet development is no exception. Thus there is a need for guidelines to help the modeller decide the level of detail that is appropriate. Two guidelines follow.

Guideline 12 The less the abstraction of the logic model underpinning the spreadsheet, the more detail there will need to be in the spreadsheet

Abstraction is almost the essence of modelling: it involves stripping away the inessentials to lay bare the essentials. Seeking greater 'reality' through more detail will almost certainly involve greater effort on the part of the modeller and for this reason alone should probably be resisted. But very often it should be resisted for better reasons as well. The more detailed the model the more 'realistic' it may become, but clarity is likely to be lost and the data-input requirements are likely to rise. For example, an organisation may have ten product groups, each consisting of 100 products on average. It may be more 'realistic' to include all 1000 products in a spreadsheet, but it would certainly be more cost-effective – and clearer – simply to model the characteristics of the ten groups.

Guideline 13 The more uncertain the environment, the less detailed the spreadsheet needs to be

This guideline can be nicely summed up in the aphorism: 'What's the point of landscape gardening with an earthquake about?' The practical effect of this can be seen by contrasting the top and lower levels in a business organisation. The top level has to deal with a uncertain, remote environment, while the lower levels have a much more stable environment within which to act (the upper level acting as an intermediary, stabilising force – essentially converting an external environment into a local one). Thus it would be expected that spreadsheets would be more detailed at lower levels, and this is borne out by their use in such areas as stock control and production planning; at the highest levels (for example, when considering strategy) modelling is not likely to be so detailed or so much in evidence. For example, when estimating contribution (revenue – variable costs), what is the point of calculating the variable costs to the nearest 0.01 per cent if the revenue cannot be estimated to be better than 5 per cent?

◆ **Key concept** *The appropriate level of detail in a spreadsheet is inversely related to the level of abstraction permitted and to the level of uncertainty in the environment.*

HOW DO I ENSURE THAT THE SPREADSHEET, ESPECIALLY THE FORM OF ITS OUTPUT, IS ACCEPTABLE TO OTHER PEOPLE?

Although there can be situations where a manager works on an issue totally independently of other people, it is generally the case that issues are handled by a group of people. It is easy to see why this should be so. Many issues do not simply affect one manager's system: other areas in the organisation have to be considered and the people responsible for them must be consulted. A group should be able to supply many more perspectives than can an individual, unless this individual is exceptionally gifted. Thus to be of maximum use in the issue-handling process, a spreadsheet must appeal to more than the rather mythical lone user. It is this aspect of spreadsheets – the use of its outputs to influence people in the organisation other than the spreadsheet developer and direct user – that will now be addressed. Seven guidelines follow.

Guideline 14 The better the communication between the spreadsheet developer and the intended audience during the building of the spreadsheet, the greater the chance of the spreadsheet being accepted

The assumption underlying this guideline is that the managers who comprise the intended audience for the spreadsheet, especially for its outputs, will better understand the models underpinning the spreadsheet through actively contributing to its development. This will prevent them being placed in the position of either having to believe the results derived from the spreadsheet without understanding them, or rejecting them out of hand.

Guideline 15 The better the professional reputation of the spreadsheet developer, the more likely it is that the spreadsheet will be accepted

This is the reverse of the old adage: 'give a dog a bad name and hang him'. A good reputation will mean that users and potential users will tend to take for granted that the spreadsheet is OK. Thus people are validating a spreadsheet simply by validating the person who has developed the spreadsheet in the first place.

Guideline 16 The greater the intended audience's ability to validate or make credible the models underpinning the spreadsheet, the more acceptable will be the spreadsheet

To use a spreadsheet or the results from one, managers need confidence in the models used. As well as having confidence in the spreadsheet developer, they can apply two other checks. First, they can check the credibility of the model by understanding and agreeing its internal workings. Second, they can treat the model as a 'black box' and validate the box by looking at the transformations it carries out between inputs and outputs.

Guideline 17 The more familiar the intended audience is with any technique used in the spreadsheet and the more numerate they are, the more complex the logic model can be without sacrificing acceptability

A technique that is familiar carries with it its own seal of approval: if it has been used many times before it must be good! The discounted cash flow technique is a good example of this; it is widely used in investment appraisal and this widespread use generates even greater use. If managers are familiar with a technique then the use of that technique is unlikely to faze them.

Two personal examples will help make this point clear. When working in a marketing-dominated organisation, we realised that we were limited in the modelling techniques we could use. The background of the managers was such that simple spreadsheet modelling would be generally acceptable, but more complex types of modelling – such as linear programming – could only be used with one or two managers, and even then only after we had discussed the technique with them very fully. In a different organisation employing many highly numerate engineers, we could discuss printouts obtained directly from a computerised linear-programming system. The background of these engineers was such that they understood the fundamentals of the technique and were happy dealing with numbers and with computers.

Guideline 18 The more familiar the terminology used, the more acceptable the model will be to its intended audience

What you have to do is to prevent the user having to carry out 'mental gymnastics' on the spreadsheet in order to find it useful: i.e. to prevent the user having to work to convert data to information. For example, in developing a logic model of the operations of a café/bar, a modeller may choose to work in terms of litres of beer sold per day. This would be suitable to people in most of Europe, but working in litres would surely be less acceptable to a British manager who would feel much more comfortable with pints. A model framed in terms of litres of beer would be less easy for them to use; they would have to perform mental gymnastics to convert from the quantities the model produced to those with which they could easily deal. And if pints were used care would need to be taken when Americans are involved: they have a different-sized pint to the British!

Guideline 19 The greater the number of people involved in an issue, the simpler and more extensive the underlying models must be for the spreadsheet to be organisationally acceptable

One of the uses of spreadsheets is in the debate concerning the most appropriate course of action to be taken. For a spreadsheet to be useful there must be a general consensus that the underlying models are reasonable representations of reality. Since this consensus may be required from managers in areas outside their own direct experience and competence, the models representing these areas must be straightforward: such a requirement generally demands simplicity. Because the spreadsheet must appeal to a group of managers, the modelling is likely to be more extensive than that covering the concerns of just one manager. This more extensive modelling means that a set of models (or one model in modular form) may be more appropriate than a single, large model.

Guideline 20 The greater the effort required to maintain a spreadsheet, the less likely the model is to be accepted

Maintenance is the process of keeping a spreadsheet up to date, involving keeping both the logic and the data models current. Often a split of responsibility is made with the spreadsheet developer responsible for maintaining the logic model and the information systems department responsible for keeping the data up to date (see Chapters 16 and 17). Experience with building spreadsheets tells us that the logic model is often altered considerably over the first period of intensive use as experience with the spreadsheet is gained, but not much thereafter. The picture is very different for the maintenance of the data model, where making available valid and up-to-date data can be very tedious and time consuming and require efficient data management. Maintenance can be especially demanding if the data needed for the model do not fit the way the data naturally occur within the organisation: to repeat a previously used example, a production spreadsheet geared to months of either four or five weeks' duration would have difficulty where the necessary financial data were only readily available on a calendar month basis.

♦ **Key concept**   *The acceptability of a spreadsheet is directly related to the quality of the communication between developer and the people they wish to influence and the professional reputation of the developer. It is also directly related to the audience's ability to validate the underlying models and their familiarity with the technique and terminology used. The acceptability is inversely related to the number of people to be influenced and to the effort required to maintain the spreadsheet.*

SUMMARY

While scenarios give the necessary general picture, spreadsheets give a more specific one that is both precise and well structured. The models that underpin spreadsheets are a set of precisely defined abstractions, while business systems abound with loosely defined, often ill-articulated perceptions. No well-defined steps exist that allow unequivocal specification of the degree of effort that should be undertaken to produce the spreadsheet. The best help that can be given to channel the modelling in fruitful directions is a set of guidelines that pull together accumulated experience. The full set of guidelines is set out in Table 4.1.

Table 4.1 Guidelines for spreadsheet development

1	The more important an issue, the greater the potential value of a spreadsheet
2	The greater the number of people who are involved with an issue, the greater the potential value of a spreadsheet
3	The greater the number of factors involved in an issue, the greater the potential value of a spreadsheet
4	The more often the same or similar issues are met, the greater the potential value of a spreadsheet
5	The more an organisation values intelligence in issue handling, the greater the potential value of a spreadsheet
6	The greater the importance of 'soft' variables in a issue, the less the potential value of a spreadsheet
7	The more the overall decision is determined by political and organisational considerations, the less the potential value of a spreadsheet
8	The less well recognised the relationships between managerial variables, the more difficult it will be to create a satisfactory model
9	The wider the range of values a relationship is expected to handle, the more difficult and time consuming it will be to construct an adequate spreadsheet
10	The more difficult it is to obtain data, the less likely it is that a suitable spreadsheet can be produced
11	The more indirect the empirical measure of a variable, the less the model should depend on the variable
12	The less the abstraction of the logic model underpinning the spreadsheet, the more detail there will need to be in the spreadsheet
13	The more uncertain the environment, the less detailed the spreadsheet needs to be
14	The better the communication between the spreadsheet developer and the intended audience during the building of the spreadsheet, the greater the chance of the spreadsheet being accepted
15	The better the professional reputation of the spreadsheet developer, the more likely is it that the spreadsheet will be accepted
16	The greater the intended audience's ability to validate or make credible the models underpinning the spreadsheet, the more acceptable will be the spreadsheet
17	The more familiar the intended audience is with any technique used in the spreadsheet and the more numerate they are, the more complex the logic model can be without sacrificing acceptability
18	The more familiar the terminology used, the more acceptable the model will be to its intended audience.
19	The greater the number of people involved in an issue, the simpler and more extensive the underlying models must be for the spreadsheet to be organisationally acceptable
20	The greater the effort required to maintain a spreadsheet, the less likely the model is to be accepted

END NOTES

1 It would appear that small businesses do not place such an emphasis on intelligence as do large companies, and so there might almost be a guideline relating use of spreadsheets to the size of the organisation!

2 Types of relationships, including the definitional relationships beloved of accountants, are fully discussed in Chapter 5.

3 The spreadsheet developer should be cautious when using less well-recognised relationships and the results from spreadsheets that contain them. Care should be taken to check out all such relationships before their inclusion in the spreadsheet. The checking of relationships is fully considered in Chapter 8.

EXERCISES

1 The assumption underlying the use of a spreadsheet is that a manager's world – or at least a part of it – is amenable to a systematic and quantitative approach. What do you think of this view?

2 What is meant by an empirical measure?

3 How do Fig 2.2 and Fig 4.1 relate to each other?

4 What is the role of the manager's scenario (as opposed to their local scenario) in using the guidelines?

5 Where do you think that the main difficulties would lie in carrying out a cost–benefit analysis before deciding to build a spreadsheet?

6 Consider the Readyread case. Use the set of guidelines to answer the following questions:
   a) How valuable would it be to have a spreadsheet?
   b) Where will the major difficulties arise in development?
   c) How detailed should the spreadsheet be?
   d) How would you ensure that the spreadsheet, especially the form of its outputs, is acceptable to other people?

7 If you have any experience of using a spreadsheet in handling real issues, think through the set of guidelines in the light of this experience. Discuss with fellow students those which you have found to be important. Add any further guidelines that you think are particularly important.

CHAPTER 5

The logic model and logic modelling

Chapter aims

Logic models form one of the main components of spreadsheets and it is their construction that we will be discussing in this chapter. First, the building blocks of logic models are explained and their links to the managerial variables are discussed. Then, the types of relationships between the building blocks are considered. After these two preliminary sections the stages in the construction of a logic model are described. While the manager and modeller are the same person, the type of thinking needed in the modelling (or spreadsheet) world will be very different from that in the manager's world – richness will be suppressed and precision will be emphasised.

- The building blocks of logic models
  - Input factors and calculated variables • Parameters • Constants and coefficients • Managerial variables and modelling factors
- Types of relationships between the building blocks
  - Definitional relationships • Prescriptions • Judgemental relationships • Linearity
- Stages in logic modelling
  - Stage 1: Conceptualisation • Stage 2: Verbalisation • Stage 3: Formalisation

The tangible end product of the structural modelling discussed in Chapter 3 is a local scenario made up of a set of broad-based statements in English about a system and its environment.[1] While this set of statements is likely to be reasonably comprehensive, the statements are unlikely to be in a form that will allow managers to see the full consequences of their actions if they were to alter the value of a decision variable. For example, it would be quite difficult for the manager in the restaurant example (Chapter 3) to determine the effect on profits of different stocking policies. What is required to explore such consequences is a detailed and explicit decision support system, building on the framework provided by the local scenario and appropriate to the issue at hand.

THE BUILDING BLOCKS OF LOGIC MODELS

Input factors and calculated variables

If a spreadsheet is to be useful, some or all of the managerial variables must be transformed into 'spreadsheet factors'. You would expect that many of the managerial variables would be included directly and unchanged in the spreadsheet model: if this was not the case it is likely that the substance of the managerial issue would be lost. However, it may be necessary to convert the softer variables that a manager may use (for example, morale) into precisely defined factors (such as *Absenteeism*). It may also be convenient to introduce new factors which ease the model building. More fundamentally, however, model factors may be used in a way that is different from the way in which managers would use and think about their variables. To see this, let's follow through a simple spreadsheet for marketing managers.

Marketing managers generally have control over the *Price* at which their organisation's goods are sold, and through pricing and advertising they also have some influence over the level of *Sales*. Their decision variables are *Price* and *Advertising spend*, while their output variables are *Revenue* and *Sales*. The environmental variable is the price of the (single) competitor's product. Suppose that initially they develop a logic model consisting of just one equation (they have not included *Advertising spend* and *Competitor's price* in their model at this stage):

$$Revenue = Sales \times Price \tag{5.1}$$

With this simple model they would insert a pair of values for *Sales* and *Price* and allow the spreadsheet to calculate the corresponding value for *Revenue*. It is apparent from this that some factors are being treated differently from others in the model: values for *Sales* and *Price* are being obtained *outside* the logic model, while the value for *Revenue* is being calculated *within* the logic model.

◆ **Key concept**   *Consider a logic model that consists simply of the single equation:* Revenue = Sales × Price. Sales *and* Price *are termed* **input factors**, *since their values would be input to the logic model – their values would be derived <u>outside</u> the model.* Revenue *is termed a* **calculated variable**, *since its value would be calculated <u>within</u> the model.*[2]

Factors may change from being input factors to being calculated variables, usually as the model is extended. Suppose now that the model is expanded to incorporate the view that *Sales* are dependent on *Price*, *Competitor's price* and *Advertising spend*, with the model now containing two equations:

$$Revenue = Sales \times Price$$

$$Sales = 50 \times \left\{ \frac{(Competitors' \ price)^2}{Price} \right\} \times Advertising \ spend \tag{5.2}$$

where *Price* is the price of the company's product. There is now no longer a need to input a value for *Sales* – putting in values for each of *Price*, *Competitors' price* and *Advertising spend* allows the value of *Sales* to be calculated. So *Sales* changes from being an input factor to being a calculated variable.

> ◆ **Key concept**   *The values of the input factors in a logic model constitute the data model.*

Parameters

Very often a manager wants to use a spreadsheet to explore how variables are interrelated. For example, it may not be obvious how *Revenue* is related to *Advertising spend* in the two-equation model as the link through *Sales* is a complex one. So managers may like to try inputting various values of *Advertising spend* and see what happens to the value of *Revenue*. What they might very well do is to fix the value of all other input factors (*Price* and *Competitors' price* in the example being considered) while the value of the remaining input factor, *Advertising spend*, is changed – possibly many times. In this way, managers can explore the influence of these changes on the calculated variable of concern (in this case *Revenue*) for one set of fixed values of *Price* and *Competitors' price*. Then they might change the value of one of the input factors (say, *Price*) to a second fixed value and again explore the effect of alterations of *Advertising spend* on *Revenue*. When this sort of change is made to a factor (in this case *Price*) – keeping its value fixed over a period of use of the model, changing its value and then again freezing its value over a second period and so on – the factor is called a parameter.

> ◆ **Key concept**   *In logic modelling a parameter is a factor whose value is held constant over a given period of time or during the exploration of given relationships. (Note that in everyday speech the term parameter is very often used much more loosely to cover anything of significance to a topic under consideration.)*

Constants and coefficients

So far the only factors or 'building blocks' of the logic model that have been introduced have been variables: even a parameter is a fixed variable! The term variables has been used (rather than variables and constants) since it is both convenient and illuminating to start by considering all factors to be variable: i.e. capable of taking on a range of values. This is not so daft as might appear, since it fits in with the old saying that everything is variable in the long run; many things only appear not to vary if the time frame of concern is restricted or if their impact on the system is judged to be trivial. Many obvious examples may appear to run counter to this proposition. For example, there are seven days in a week, but this division of time is only humanly contrived and could be changed – perhaps to a more 'rational' ten-day week. The laws of physics may be fixed, but their expression rests on humanly contrived definitions and these could be recast if it were thought useful to do so. So you cannot say that something in the real world is constant in an absolute sense, only that it appears not to change significantly within the time scale of interest.

However, some factors are more fixed than others. There are factors whose values are fixed by definition. Examples of this sort include the specific heat of pure water which, under stated conditions of pressure and temperature, is defined to be 1 calorie/gram/degree centigrade; the number of days in the week is seven; and latitude is measured from the equator. All these examples have been fixed by agencies outside an individual business organisation, by government or international bodies. A business organisation can make its own definitions, however: for example, defining the accounting month to coincide with the calendar month, or defining a production month to be of either four or five weeks' duration. Such definitions that are used might be inappropriate, but their values will be exact and contain no errors.

Factors fixed by definition are one example of constants, but they are not the only sort. It may be that there's no point in altering the value of a variable – but on the other hand you shouldn't ignore it. As an example, consider a product made up of two components. Suppose that the cost of one component is very variable and around 20 times as large as the cost of the second component whose value is known fairly accurately. Within a spreadsheet to explore the financial contribution made by the product it would be rather a waste of time and perhaps cloud the issue to treat the second component as a variable. (On the other hand, not to include it at all would introduce a systematic error of 5 per cent into the product cost.) In this case the second component would be *treated as a constant*: as a variable one chooses to hold constant because of the trivial impact its variability has. The constant values given to these sorts of variables are not error free, although any error is likely to be inconsequential.

Coefficients are factors that relate two or more other factors: very often their values are determined by 'rules of thumb'. Their values may have been defined externally; an example is a government decree on the minimum floor space per employee in commercial buildings. Other coefficients are accepted 'norms' that are rarely challenged. For example, the rules of thumb that have been established for the making and setting times of concrete. Sometimes the values of coefficients have been statistically derived from past data: one example is the coefficient used in universities to relate one part-time student to one-third of a full-time student. A second example is an academic society in the UK that can establish a very good idea of the number of paying participants at upcoming annual conferences using the rule of thumb that the ratio of attendances to the number of people presenting papers is 1.6:1. Sometimes the values of constants are decided subjectively, possibly simply by hunch. An example of this might be a marketing manager's view that a 1 per cent increase in sales will follow a 2 per cent increase in advertising expenditure.

The value of 50 in equation 5.2 would probably have been derived from empirical data as giving the 'best' or at least a reasonable fit of the equations to data obtained from past operations. The value could have been obtained from another mathematical model, one of whose calculated variables would be this coefficient. No claim would be made that the value so obtained was error free, just that it was a reasonable estimate. If more or 'better' data became available the new value produced using them would generally differ from the one in use and would replace it.

Coefficients are often treated as constants, not changing as the values of other variables change. But this is not always so: the coefficient in equation 5.2 might vary with the overall level of *Price*.

♦ Key concept

Constants are of two types. There are those whose values are defined to be what they are: for example, 7 days in a week, 24 hours in a day. There are also those whose values are known to vary, but where this variability is relatively trivial to the issue of concern and thus where it is appropriate to treat their values as unchanging.

Coefficients represent a relationship between two or more factors and are thus ratios. Often they are rules of thumb.

Table 5.1 summarises the four types of building blocks used in logic models.

Table 5.1 Types of building blocks in logic models

Variable	a factor whose value varies freely.
Constant	a) a factor whose value is unchanging and has been defined to be what it is b) a factor where the variability in its value is inconsequential and it is thus appropriate to treat its value as unchanging.
Parameter	a factor whose value is held constant over a period of spreadsheet exploration.
Coefficient	a factor representing a relationship between two or more factors.

Managerial variables and modelling factors

It may appear that there is a direct link between managerial variables and the modelling factors. For example, it may appear that the decision variables of the manager always correspond to the input factors of the modeller and that output and calculated variables always relate to one another. In the simple example of *Revenue = Sales × Price*, the decision variable (*Price*) was indeed the input factor, while the output variable (*Revenue*) was a calculated variable. However, when this model was extended to link *Sales* to *Price* (in equation 5.2), *Sales* changed to become a calculated variable. Nothing in the managerial world changed, just the views taken of the factors for modelling purposes.

That there is no fixed correspondence between types of managerial variable and types of modelling factor can be seen in another way. In using the model of *Revenue = Sales × Price* the question being asked was of the form: 'What value will an output variable (*Revenue*) take if a specific value is given to a decision variable (*Price*)?' Here output variable = calculated variable; decision variable = input factor. On the other hand, a different question could be asked: 'What value should *Price* (the decision variable) take, in order that *Revenue* (the output variable) has a specific value?' In this case output variable = input factor; decision variable = calculated variable and the model would effectively be written as *Price = Revenue/Sales*. (However, see goal seeking in Chapter 12.) This second model is different from the first, reflecting the changes in input factors and calculated variables: the managerial variables remain unchanged. This illustrates that modelling may require the factors to be viewed in a way that is different from that in scenarios and this may affect the way in which a model is constructed.

Often it is convenient to define intermediate variables in order to simplify the development and maintenance of the model. For example, the equations in 5.2 may be altered to those in 5.3 with the intermediate variable *Price Ratio* introduced.

$$Revenue = Sales \times Price$$

$$Price\ ratio = \left\{ \frac{Competitors'\ price}{Price} \right\}$$

$$Sales = 50 \times Price\ ratio^2 \times Advertising\ spend \tag{5.3}$$

Before moving on to discuss the forms of relationships between the building blocks, it is important to consider the naming of variables. Above we have specified variables such as *Revenue* and *Sales*. Very often, of course, spreadsheet models will involve several time periods and you will naturally want to distinguish between values of such items as *Revenue* and *Sales* in these different time periods. The spreadsheet form of the simple budgeting example discussed in Chapter 2 is reproduced as Fig 5.1. It is important to recognise that the variable whose value is shown in cell D4, for example, is the variable *Sales-for-March*, and not simply either *Sales* or *March*.[3]

Fig 5.1 A simple budgeting example

	A	B	C	D	E	F
1						
2		January	February	March		
3						
4	Sales	10000	11000	10000		
5	Price (£)	11	11	12		
6	Revenue (£)	110000	121000	120000		
7						
8						
9						

Management variables *and* model factors *are often the same, but sometimes there may not be a direct link between them. The managerial variables are the decision, environmental and output variables. The model factors are the input factors and the calculated and intermediate variables.*

TYPES OF RELATIONSHIPS BETWEEN THE BUILDING BLOCKS

So far, we have discussed the smallest building blocks in a logic model – the variables, parameters, coefficients and constants. These factors are combined to create the relationships that together make up the complete logic model. These relationships are of three broad types: definitional relationships, prescriptions and judgemental relationships. Each of these types can be equations (otherwise known as equalities), which are by far the most common form of relationships in spreadsheet models, or inequalities. Inequalities are relationships such as:

*Number of employees required > Crew members * Number of machines*

(where the > sign should be read as 'is greater than').

Conditional relationships may also be used. Examples are:

If *Profit* > 0 then *Tax* = 40% of *Profit*

If *Output* > 2000 then *Crew numbers* > 25

A relationship is a link between variables, parameters, coefficients and constants. Equations are by far the most common form of relationship in spreadsheet models and are of the form Revenue = Sales × Price. *Another form of relationship is the inequality, where the value that a variable may take is constrained to lie above, below or between set values.*

Definitional relationships

Definitional relationships are relationships that are as they are because they have been defined to be so.[4] Many accounting models are composed entirely of definitional relationships: examples are the balance sheet and the profit and loss account. Accountants have been clever enough to define a set of variables, such as *Revenue*, *Variable cost* and *Contribution*, and from these definitions precise relationships follow. For example:

Contribution = Revenue − Variable cost

Prescriptions

All relationships that are not definitional contain an element of judgement. However, some contain so little judgement after formulation that the term prescriptions will be used for them. An example of a prescription would be the combination of ingredients to make a product – the flavourings in a soft drink, the ingredients in pet foods. The significant feature of prescriptions is that data exist that can be used in objective tests of the 'goodness' or appropriateness of the relationship. Although there is, paradoxically, some element of judgement in the application of these objective techniques, nevertheless the prescriptions so derived are seldom seriously a contentious issue.

Judgemental relationships

The third category of relationships are judgemental relationships. In contrast to prescriptions, data cannot be obtained that would allow one relationship to be universally accepted as an adequate representation of the real world. For example, one person may hold strongly to the view that when launching a new consumer product almost all promotional expenditure should be addressed to the retail trade and very little directly to the ultimate consumer. A second person may hold completely the opposite view. Probably neither is totally correct, but it will be hard to decide where the balance lies. In theory a test seems easy: perhaps launch the product one way in one part of the country and the other way in a second part of the country and see which leads to the greater success. But this raises many questions. Does success mean sales in the first week only, or over the lifetime of the product, or what? Does success mean units sold or total revenue? With definitional issues out of the way, things may then seem clear. However, carrying out experiments in a social context is very different from carrying out experiments in a laboratory where the conditions can be closely controlled. For example, a competitor may launch a new product at the same time as your own launch – and in only one part of the country!

One case where political factors intervened to affect us personally occurred some years ago. We were involved in trying to determine the effects of promotional expenditure on sales during the launch of a consumer product. A statistically designed experiment was planned lasting a few weeks during the test launch. Everything went well until the returns came in from the first week of sales activity. Sales were, fairly reasonably, lower in the area where promotional expenditure was lower. These lower sales naturally depressed the total sales from the test launch and were seen to jeopardise a go-ahead being given for the hoped-for national campaign. The experiment was set aside overnight and more expenditure authorised in the areas where performance was low. The political and organisational context of experimentation and data collection prevented unequivocal relationships being developed.

Sometimes no data are explicitly available. Then precedent is cited or hunch is used. Sometimes even cause and effect are not agreed on – does inflation cause wage demands or do wage demands cause inflation? The use of judgemental relationships in a model will be more contentious than the use of other forms of relationship and much debate will focus on them. However, just because they do not have the strong claims to validity that attach to definitional relationships and to prescriptions, this should not prevent their use, since incorporating judgemental relationships within a logic model can greatly enhance the power of a spreadsheet.

◆ **Key concept**
> *Three types of relationships between factors may be found in logic models.* **Definitional relationships** *are relationships that are as they are because they have been defined to be so.* **Judgemental relationships** *are relationships that include in their formulation the judgements of the modeller and other interested parties. The appropriateness of such relationships is open to argument and the relationships themselves is open to change.* **Prescriptions** *lie between definitional and judgemental relationships in that they have not been defined to be as they are, yet their form is not contentious.*

Linearity

One special form of relationship that needs to be considered in detail is the linear relationship. Such relationships occur very widely indeed and, among other things, underpin the linear programming technique that is described in detail in Chapter 12. Thus it is very important to be sure what is meant by the term 'linear'.

For a relationship to be linear, it must satisfy two requirements: the effects must be in *constant proportion* to the causes and the effects of more than one factor acting at the same time must be *additive*. These requirements are best shown by the use of examples. Consider equations 5.4 to 5.6:

$$Sales = 6 \times Price \tag{5.4}$$

$$Sales = Price^2 \tag{5.5}$$

$$Sales = 30 \div Price + 5 \tag{5.6}$$

Equation 5.4 satisfies the proportionality requirement, since if the value of the variable *Price* changes by a given amount, then the value of the variable *Sales* alters by the same proportion whatever the initial values of *Price* and *Sales*. For example, if the value of *Price* was increased from 1 to 2, the value of *Sales* would increase from 6 to 12, a change of 6; if the value of *Price* was increased by a further 1 (from 2 to 3) the increase in the value of *Sales* would be from 12 to 18 – by the same amount as before (a further 6). Thus equation 5.4 is a linear relationship: in shorthand, equation 5.4 is linear.

Equation 5.5 is not a linear relationship, since a change in the value of *Price* produces a change in the value of *Sales* that depends on its initial value. For example, if the value of *Price* was increased from 1 to 2, the value of Sales would increase from 1 to 4 – an increase of 3. However, if the value of *Price* was now increased by a further unit (from 2 to 3) the value of *Sales* would change by a different amount – from 4 to 9, an increase of 5. Equal increments in the value of one variable do not lead to equal increments in the value of the other.

Equation 5.6 is not linear since equal increments in the value of *Price* do not lead to exactly the same-sized incremental changes in the value of *Sales*.

Fig 5.2 Linear and non-linear relationships

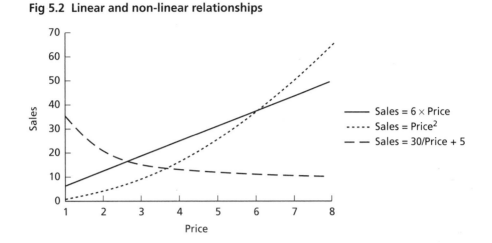

These equations are sketched in Fig 5.2 Using equally spaced scales on the x-axes, a linear relationship is shown as a straight line, a non-linear relationship as a curve.

The second requirement for a relationship to be linear is that the effects of different variables are additive. Consider the relationships 5.7 through 5.9:

$$Variable\ cost = Packaging\ cost + 5 \times Contents\ cost \qquad (5.7)$$

$$Variable\ cost = 6 \times Contents\ cost \times Tax \qquad (5.8)$$

$$Variable\ cost = 6 \times Tax + 5 \times Contents\ cost \times Tax \qquad (5.9)$$

Equation 5.7 satisfies the additivity requirement, since the effect of changes in the value of *Packaging cost* and the effect of changes in the value of *Contents cost* on the value of *Variable cost* are independent. In other words, whatever the value of *Contents cost*, a given change in the value of *Packaging cost* will produce an equally sized change in the value of *Variable cost*. Similarly, whatever the value of *Packaging cost*, a change of a given size in *Contents cost* will always produce a change five times as great in the value of *Variable cost*.

Equation 5.8 is not linear, since the additivity rule does not hold. If the value of *Contents cost* was to change by 3, say, then the resultant change in the value of *Variable cost* would be 18 if the value of *Tax* was 1, but would be 36 if *Tax* had the value 2.

Equation 5.9 is also non-linear, since the second term on the right-hand side (viz. $5 \times Contents\ cost \times Tax$) does not satisfy the additivity rule.

◆ Key concept

One special form of relationship in logic models is the linear relationship. Such relationships are used very widely and, among other things, underpin the linear-programming technique. For a relationship to be linear, it must satisfy two requirements: the effects must be in **constant proportion** *to the causes and the effects of more than one factor acting at the same time must be* **additive**.

STAGES IN LOGIC MODELLING

The construction of a logic model has been split into three stages and these are shown in bold in Fig 5.3. This is an extended version of the bottom right-hand side of Fig 2.5.

As the modelling moves from stage 1 to stage 2 and then on to stage 3, there is unlikely to be much change in model content. What does change, however, is the model form – from the softer, fuzzier managerial view to the precise spreadsheet requirement.

Stage 1: Conceptualisation

Suppose that managers have developed a local scenario of their system such that a issue has been detected and to some extent defined. The issue seems to be a candidate for spreadsheet modelling and thus the move is to be made from the local scenario to an appropriate spreadsheet – to one that will aid the manager to understand better the issue they are facing. Conceptualisation is the first step in this move, and a critical one. It is the vital link between the managerial issue placed in the context of the local scenario and the spreadsheet formulation of it. While the manager and modeller are the same person, the type of thinking needed in the modelling world will be very different from that in the managerial

Fig 5.3 The logic modelling stages

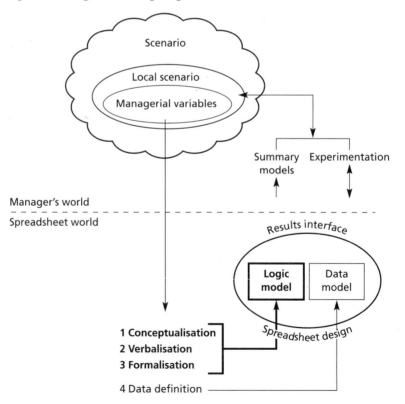

world – richness will be suppressed, precision will be emphasised and rigor will become more important. Thus it is valid to talk of two manifestations of the same issue: a managerial one and a spreadsheet one. The form of the two will be different, but the substance should remain substantially the same.

Conceptualisation is an awesome task, since backwards, sideways and forwards considerations must be made while at the same time keeping the scenario and issue firmly in mind!

The backwards look

First there is a need to reappraise the issue area. Very often the redefinition involves opening up the issue area to prevent suboptimisation, i.e. where one issue is 'corrected' to the detriment of the overall operations of the organisation. Two examples should make this clear. One involved managers who wanted to reduce costs in a production process; they concerned themselves only with material costs, and not at all with the interaction of the materials and the machines using them. This was a narrow view to take, since the variable consistency of the cheaper materials caused machines to jam more frequently than if more costly materials had been purchased, and machine downtime was expensive. The second example concerned managers who made great efforts to obtain data on whether it was beneficial for the company to deal with certain wholesalers, when they ought to have been looking more widely at the issue and considering the best overall way in which to service the market.

Following an acceptable issue definition, the modeller needs to consider further the variables of concern and the relationships between them. While doing this, the goal of the model, the time scales associated with its development and use, the associated costs and the intended range of application of the model should all be considered. The range of application of the model is a statement of the scope of the model. At the conceptualisation stage the specification of the *intended* range of application of the model will only be a preliminary statement on the way to a specification of the *actual* range of application, since it is very common for further limitations to the model's range to be introduced as the modelling progresses. Ideally the model used by the manager should have associated with it a full listing of the assumptions built into it; in the hurly-burly of business life this may be asking too much, but the main assumptions should not be kept hidden.

♦ Key concept

*The **range of application of the model** is a statement of the scope of the model. For example, if a spreadsheet had been devised to calculate a company's profits but not its losses, the range of application would be restricted only to profitable situations. (It may well be that the model would give wrong answers if used for unprofitable situations.)*

The sidewards look

The modeller must look sideways to see if their issue, as derived from the scenario and the managerial issue, fits into one of a class of issues that have been handled before and for which models/techniques already exist. Examples of such techniques are given in Part II. These techniques are in the modeller's toolkit – ready to be used where appropriate. While there are great dangers in applying a favourite technique without considering carefully the context in which it will be used, there are also great benefits in time and cost in using something 'off the shelf'. Why reinvent the wheel?

As with many things, the answer lies in making a judicious choice as to which, if any, technique to use; the making of this choice is very much part of the art of modelling. The modeller certainly needs to know the assumptions underlying the techniques. Just as importantly, they should have a good appreciation of the consequences of offending these assumptions, since it is very seldom that real-life issues fit a technique or previously derived solutions exactly – even in the host of special cases written up so diligently in the management science journals! However, if a modeller felt that they could not use a technique because it did not fit the issue exactly, their tools of the trade would be severely limited. Thus in practice they use the techniques – and introduce new limitations into the model. What they must guard against is if these new limitations are such as to make the substance of the modeller's issue different from the substance of the manager's issue. Examples of approximations that might invalidate the use of a technique would be using a linear model where some of the relationships are non-linear, taking variables to be independent of one another where there is some link between them, and grouping many items into one category. Many modellers have produced very elegant models that have 'solved' the issue their model reflected, but did not help very much with the manager's issue.

The forwards look

The forwards look that the modeller must make is concerned with how the final spreadsheet might be used and maintained: for example, whether a set of models might be more appropriate than one large model, how information from the model might be presented and how the interaction with the model might be handled. Such matters will be considered in later chapters.

MINICASE

An Electricity Board offers electricity to its commercial customers under three tariffs; an ordinary tariff, a 'small-user' tariff and a special 'night-saver' tariff. Whatever the tariff the electricity bill is made up of two parts. Customers opting for the ordinary tariff must pay a quarterly connection charge of £100 and pay at the rate of 3 pence per unit consumed. Customers choosing the small-user tariff are required to pay a lower quarterly connection charge of £50 but with the enhanced rate of 5 pence per unit consumed.

The ABC Company only works during the day and so has little interest in the night-saver tariff. The company is consuming around 3000 units/quarter under the small-user tariff. Since output is rising – and with it the use of electricity – the manager responsible for electricity purchase is wondering whether to change to the ordinary tariff.

The conceptualisation of the electricity tariff issue is straightforward. The managerial decision variable is the tariff to choose based on the quarterly costs for each case, the output variable is the total electricity cost (and possibly the cost of units used). The environmental factors are the connection charges and the charging rate. The model to be created has as the calculated variable the *Quarterly cost*, with input factors the *Units used*, the *Cost/unit* and the *Connection charge*. Sometimes the need to introduce intermediate variables only becomes apparent as modelling develops: however, in this electricity tariff case the variable *Cost of units used* would be an appropriate intermediate variable.

Having decided on the factors that will be in the spreadsheet, it is useful to structure them through the use of an information flow diagram, as shown in Fig 5.4. The arrows in information flow diagrams identify where relationships exist between the factors: for example, Fig 5.4 shows that the factors *Units used* and *Cost/unit* are linked in some way to determine the *Cost of units used*. Note that the input factors are those factors that only have an arrow coming out of them. Calculated and intermediate variables must have at least two arrows leading into them. Intermediate variables always have arrows entering and leaving them.

In Fig 5.4 the left-hand boxes contain the output variables and the right-hand boxes the input factors. (Note that some modellers reverse this convention.) Thus to draw an information flow diagram, it is convenient to establish the output variables and then consider what needs to be known to allow values for these variables to be derived. In deriving an information flow diagram you work from left to right.

Stage 2: Verbalisation

The conceptualisation produces a logic model of part of the manager's local scenario. It is to be hoped that this stage will ensure that the appropriate portions of the local scenario are in focus. The next stage in moving towards the final logical model is the verbalisation stage – the verbal specification of relationships between the model factors.

Fig 5.4 The information flow diagram for the electricity tariff issue

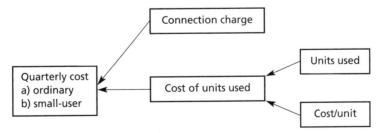

Verbal specification of relationships means an accurate and precise statement of the link between the model factors in a form that can readily be converted into spreadsheet form. 'Verbal' here does not really mean 'spoken', but is shorthand for 'non-symbolic'. For example, the equation *Revenue = Sales × Price* would be considered a verbal relationship, while the equation *Revenue = +C5 * C8* would not. The common arithmetic signs + , − , × , / and =, although symbols, are in such general use that they are acceptable in a verbal relationship.[5] Although not so well known, the following set of symbols are very useful and can conveniently be incorporated in verbal relationships:

> is greater than
< is less than
≥ is greater than or equal to
≤ is less than or equal to

The value of carrying out the verbalisation stage is that not only does it act as a springboard for the spreadsheet formulation of the logic model, but also it is the first time that the logic of the model will have been made explicit: and perhaps the last time that an explicit statement of the logic is in a form that can be discussed between the modeller and their colleagues.

The verbalisation of the electricity tariff issue is the set of relationships set out in equation 5.10.

$$Quarterly\ cost = Connection\ charge + Cost\ of\ units\ used$$

$$Cost\ of\ units\ used = Units\ used \times Cost/unit \tag{5.10}$$

Note that each set of arrows in Fig 5.4 is represented by one relationship in the verbalisation. This is shown in Fig 5.5.

Fig 5.5 The information flow diagram for the electricity tariff issue, including verbalisation

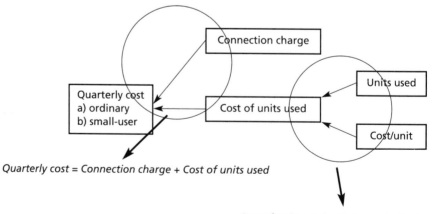

Quarterly cost = Connection charge + Cost of units used

Cost of units used = Units used × Cost/unit

Fig 5.6 A spreadsheet of the electricity tariff issue (poor practice)

	A	B	C	D
1	**Ordinary tariff**		*Verbalisation relationships*	*Spreadsheet relationships*
2				
3	Cost/unit	3		
4	Units used	3000		
5	Cost of units used	9000	= Units used × Cost/unit	+B3 * B4
6	Connection charge	100		
7	Quarterly cost	9100	= Connection charge + Cost of units used	+B5 + B6
8				
9				
10	**'Small-user tariff'**			
11				
12	Cost/unit	5		
13	Units used	3000		
14	Cost of units used	15000	= Units used × Cost/unit	+B12 * B13
15	Connection charge	50		
16	Quarterly cost	15000	= Connection charge + Cost of units used	+B14 + B15

Stage 3: Formalisation

In the formalisation stage, the modeller is moving from the set of verbal relationships developed in the verbalisation stage to the final spreadsheet form. In a spreadsheet the factor is designated by the cell reference and relationships are made up of a set of cell references. A possible spreadsheet model for the electricity tariff minicase is shown in Fig 5.6.

Note that the logic model is the complete set of input factors and calculated variables together with the relationships between the factors and variables. (The data model is the set of the *values* of the input factors.) Note that each line in the verbalisation translates into one spreadsheet cell (and very often into one spreadsheet row).

While Fig 5.6 is a very tiny example, it demonstrates several features of a *poor* formalisation. These features and how to create better formalisations will be considered in Chapter 8.

SUMMARY

Four building blocks for logic models have been discussed: constants, variables, coefficients and parameters. These blocks are combined to form equations and inequalities which represent definitional relations, judgemental relations and prescriptions.

Table 5.2 Summary of the main stages of logic modelling

Conceptualisation	• issue redefinition • redefinition of managerial variables • modelling goals defined, including the intended range of • application of the model • preliminary views of the modelling technique(s) that might be appropriate • consideration of the assumptions underlying these techniques
Verbalisation	• definition of modelling factors • precise statement in English of the relationships between factors
Formalisation	• symbols assigned to the model factors • statement of units used • statement of any conventions used

The main features of the five stages that make up logic modelling are summarised in Table 5.2.

In order to simplify the introduction of the logic modelling, it was convenient to treat each stage as a self-contained activity that followed on from the previous self-contained activity. In practice, however, there will be quite a lot of movement between stages, as the consequences of each stage become apparent and as validation proceeds. Again, the treatment given in this chapter suggests that each stage must always be rigorously worked through. In practice, the stages may be scrambled together in a 'thought process mess' rather than completely separated. However, such cavalier and unstructured behaviour is for those very well versed in spreadsheet development; less experienced modellers abbreviate and scramble the stages at their peril.

END NOTES

1 Of course, you would use your own language (rather than English) if this was more appropriate.

2 Modelling specialists sometimes use special terms. They may use the term *exogenous factor* for *input factor* and *endogenous variable* for *calculated variable*.

3 If Fig 5.1 were extended to include two departments, then the variable would need to be labelled *Sales-for-March-Dept 1* or in some other way to distinguish the different variables.

4 One special form of definitional relationship are definitional equations, which are sometimes termed identities.

5 Note that the / sign is used for divide rather than the ÷ sign as it is the same as the sign used in spreadsheets and also corresponds to the very common usage in everyday life, such as cost/unit for cost per unit.

EXERCISES

1 Which of the following equations are linear?
   a) *Price = Cost + 10% of Cost*
   b) *Total sales = Sales in Europe + Sales in USA*
   c) *Sales = 30 × Advertising spend^2*

2 Consider the equation:

   Number of employees required = 6 × Number of machines

   Draw this relationship. How many employees would be required to run eight machines?

3 Consider the inequality:

Number of employees required $> 6 \times$ Number of machines

How does the drawing of this relationship differ from that drawn for the equation in Exercise 2? What values of the number of employees would correspond to the running of six machines?

4 What are the links between managerial variables and modelling factors?

For the following exercises (5–8), do not bother to attempt any structural modelling: the situations described have effectively already been 'structurally modelled'.

5 Demand for the products of the ABC Company is growing so rapidly that the factory is thinking of moving to a two-shift system spanning the hours 6am to 12 midnight. This might make it advantageous for the company to move to the night-saver tariff, where night-time covers the period 10pm to 5 am. Under this arrangement customers must pay the slightly higher connection charge of £120/quarter with a cost of 3 pence per unit during daytime and 2 pence per unit during night-time.
   a) Augment the information flow diagram of Fig 5.4 to take into account the new tariff.
   b) Augment the verbalisation of relationship 5.10.
   c) Create a spreadsheet model based on this augmented verbalisation and determine at what level of electricity consumption the company might switch to the 'night-time' tariff. (To do this, you will need to make an estimate of the electricity consumption during the day and when the night-saver tariff is in operation.)

6 The Readyread Printing and Publishing Company produces one type of book for the children's market. It manufactures and sells this book (and no others) in the UK.

It is the beginning of 1997 and the managing director has asked you to build a model to produce a simple trading account for the next three years. (Inflation is not to be included.) The data available are as in Fig 5.7.

The spreadsheet should calculate the *Sales revenue, Total variable costs, Profit, Profit per month* and the *Percentage change in profit from year to year.*

Even though this is a simple case you should rigorously apply the three stages of logic modelling before beginning to approach your spreadsheet.

Fig 5.7 Readyread trading account

A	B	C	D
1		Year	
2	1997	1998	1999
3			
4 Sales estimates (million)	2.7	3.0	3.0
5 Sales price (£)	5	5	5
6 Raw materials costs (pence/book)	40	40	40
7 Royalty (pence/book)	75	80	80
8 Labour costs (pence/book)	170	180	180
9 Fixed costs (£'000)	5000	5200	5600

7 An undergraduate is entering the revision period before exams in the final year of their degree and is wondering what type of degree they might attain and how much effort they need to make on each subject.

The final year mark is the mean of the marks in eight modules. The situation that the student finds themselves in is set out in Table 5.3.

The marks are derived as follows:

A module mark is obtained by combining coursework and examination marks. For each module, the module mark is calculated by adding together 25 per cent of the coursework mark with 75 per cent of the exam mark.

The final year mark is simply the mean of the eight module marks.

The final year mark counts for 75 per cent of the overall degree mark. The second year mark counts for 15 per cent of the overall degree mark and the first year counts for 10 per cent.

So far, all marks are known except for the four examinations that have yet to be sat. Carry through the three stages of logic modelling and derive a spreadsheet model to determine:

a) what the overall mark would be if the score in all the remaining exams was 50 per cent

b) what average mark would the student need to get in in these last exams in order to achieve an overall score of at least 60 per cent – and thus be awarded an upper second class degree.

Table 5.3 Students marks

	Coursework %	Examination %	Module %
Final year module			
1	68	65	66
2	69	65	66
3	55	60	59
4	58	50	52
5	65		
6	48		
7	58		
8	64		
Second year mark	55%		
First year mark	50%		

8 A maker of computers buys in components. One component is particularly fault prone and so the company subjects each component to two, sequential tests: a surge test and a vibration test. Over the next month the company requires 100 such components. From the past it knows that on average 20 per cent of components fail the surge test and, of those that pass, only 90 per cent pass the vibration test. Because it can get a better price for ordering in bulk, it wants to get its total monthly requirement in one order. The question is, how many components should the company order? Develop a spreadsheet model to answer this question by working through the three logic modelling stages.

CHAPTER 6

Data models and data modelling

Chapter aims The second main component of a spreadsheet is the data model. The aim of this chapter is to describe the characteristics of data and the sources of data for spreadsheets. First, the subtle interaction between the logic and data models is considered. This leads on to discussing two characteristics of data – the type of variable with which they are associated and the exactness of their values. Sources of data are then considered and this is followed by consideration of the facilities offered by specialist database packages – which might be appropriate when large quantities of data are to be employed.

- Links to the logic model
- Types of quantitative data
- Precision and bias
- Sources of data
- Large data models

LINKS TO THE LOGIC MODEL

It is at the data-definition stage that data values for the input factors are obtained. It may seem strange to leave considerations of the data to such a late stage in the model-building process, but what is meant here is *detailed data* – specific values needed to generate specific quantitative outcomes from the spreadsheet. This is a totally different use to that to which any data collected in the structural modelling or conceptualisation stages would be put. There, the data would be used to give a *feel* to the *scope* and *shape* of the logic model – the bounds over which a model could be said to be an appropriate representation of the manager's world and what might be the important factors. For example, a back-of-the-envelope calculation using simply the magnitudes of certain factors may tell you that a certain part of the organisation is in trouble and that this is the area on which to concentrate: if the size of the labour costs in a factory dwarfs the material costs, this informs us of how much effort to put into a labour cost logic model and how much to put into a materials cost logic model. In these cases the data help to define the logic model.

The situation we are now looking at is where the logic model defines the data required – and thus the content of the data model (see Fig 6.1). That this is likely to be so can be seen from the fact that each input factor in the logic model requires a value (from the data model) or the spreadsheet will not operate. More subtly, the place and role of a factor in the logic model determine the

Fig 6.1 The data-modelling process

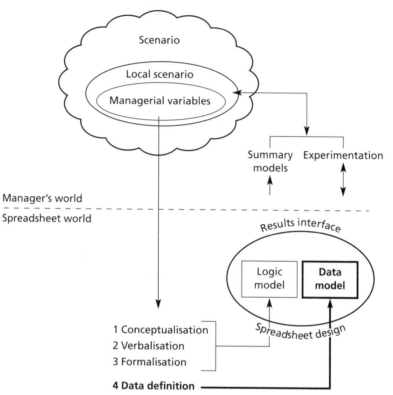

exactness required of its value; this is examined in the later section on precision and bias. Data definition should be left until the latter stages of model building, since the logic of the situation identifies the data that are needed and defines their appropriate exactness. Obtaining data, especially exact data, generally costs time and money and thus it is important to be sure that the effort to obtain the exactness is really necessary.

The end result of the data-definition stage is a data model. It may seem strange that such a thing exists at all; surely data are data are data and that is the end of the story? However, on reflection it will be realised that a choice does exist about which data to use and how the data will be represented. A choice exists about both the form and content of the data model. This choice also exists within corporate databases on which the spreadsheet may call for data, but as will be discussed in the section on sources of data, the choice is someone else's!

◆ Key concept

In structural modelling, the rough magnitude of the data will give a guide to the factors that should be included in the logic model. In data modelling the inclusion of an input factor in the logic model means that a value must be obtained for this factor. The role and context of the input factor in the logic model will determine the appropriate exactness of the data value.

TYPES OF QUANTITATIVE DATA

A quantitative measurement is defined as the systematic assignment of numbers to individuals in a group in order to represent one of their attributes. Under this definition measurement can be any of four levels – nominal, ordinal, interval and ratio. Each level has a characteristic not present at a lower level, as shown in Fig 6.2.

Nominal measurement has only the characteristic of distinctiveness. On this level of measurement the different numbers given to individuals in the group only indicate a difference between the individuals. If in a collection of vegetables it is decided to assign the number 0 to cabbages, 1 to beetroots, 2 to peas and so on, the numbers distinguish between the various kinds of vegetable, but in no sense is it implied that peas are any more of a vegetable than are beetroots. Typical uses of nominal measures by management would be the coding of personal information (e.g. 0 = single, 1 = married, 2 = widowed, 3 = divorced; or S = single, M = married, W = widowed, D = divorced). The use of letters for coding illustrates that there is no implication of 'goodness' in the codes assigned.

Ordinal measurements order individuals according to the magnitude of an attribute they possess: the higher the number assigned, the more of the attribute the individual possesses. If the height order of individuals in a group is to be indicated, then a low number (say, 1) would be assigned to the smallest individual, a higher number (say, 2) to the next smallest and so on. The greater the height the greater the number: but note, that there is no implication that an individual with rank 3, say, is 2 units of any meaningful measure higher than the individual with a rank of 1. Thus ordinal measures do not say anything about *how much more* of an attribute one individual has than another; only that it has *more or less*, or the same. Typical uses by management would be in the ordering of information: e.g. the ranking of sales regions by sales revenue, the ranking of products by their manufacturing costs and the scoring of judgemental responses/opinions (e.g. 1 = poor, 2 = adequate, 3 = good, 4 = very good, 5 = excellent). However, see below on the use of the resulting scores.

An interval level of measurement is needed in order to signify the amount of an attribute. What is required is that equal differences between measurements are represented by the same amount of difference of the attribute being measured. Temperature measurements using the common home thermometer are examples of using an interval scale of measurement. For a given individual, a 3 degree rise in temperature when the individual is cold represents the same

Fig 6.2 Characteristics of scales of measurement

Characteristic	Scale of measurement			
	Nominal	Ordinal	Interval	Ratio
Distinctiveness	*	*	*	*
Ordering in magnitude		*	*	*
Equal intervals			*	*
Absolute zero				*

amount of change in the amount of 'hotness' as a 3 degree rise in temperature when the individual is warmer. The Celsius and Fahrenheit scales of temperature measurement are examples of interval scales, even though there is a zero measurement. This is because the zero does not indicate no 'hotness': the zeros are simply convenient points on the scale.[1] Calendar dates are examples of the use of an interval scale in management: there is no day or year zero.

Having said this about interval scales, such measures are rare and any discussion about them can be included under the ratio level of measurement, which occurs when a measurement of zero represents the absence of a property being measured. The ordinary ruler has this property for measuring length: zero length is represented by zero on this scale. Typical managerial variables that are measured on a ratio scale are the multitude of accounting measures: profit, costs, contribution etc.

While arithmetic manipulation *can* be performed at any level of measurement, the simple operations of addition, subtraction etc. have little meaning when a nominal or ordinal scale is used. It is only with interval or ratio levels of measurement that the real power of spreadsheets can be deployed, and this is only possible when the characteristic of equal intervals is present. It is very common on questionnaires to ask respondents to choose from a 1–5 scale, for example a scale with 1 = very dissatisfied, 2 = dissatisfied, 3 = indifferent etc. This is an ordinal scale. However, it is almost a certainty that the survey organisers will produce means and other summary information from the raw data. They are incorrectly treating this ordinal data as interval data. So think before you manipulate data in a spreadsheet: is the data being measured on an interval or ratio scale? If not, be very wary of any sort of arithmetic manipulation other than simply adding up the number of occurrences of each value.

Quantitative information has the same range of characteristics as do quantitative data. As discussed in the next chapter, the appropriate representations differ for different forms of information.

PRECISION AND BIAS

We mentioned in the introduction to this chapter that you have a choice over the content of the data model. Two people with the same logical model would not necessarily obtain and use the same data; their data models may differ, reflecting their views as to the exactness required. For example, if the forecast annual sales of some simple consumer product like bread is to be used in a spreadsheet, one person may input the value to the nearest million loaves while another may work to the nearest thousand. One person may use last year's data on a competitor if this was very easy to obtain, arguing perhaps that the changes in this year would be likely to be small, while the second person may be willing to pay to obtain this year's data.

'Exactness' itself has two dimensions, precision and bias. Precision is a measure of the random uncertainty in a set of data; bias a measure of the systematic error.[2] The difference between precision and bias is shown very neatly in Fig 6.3, which illustrates the results of rifle shooting at a fairground where the marksman is trying to hit the centre of the target. If they got the grouping shown in Fig 6.3a, where the average location of the shots is far from the centre, they might justifiably complain that the rifle had a systematic bias in it although there is little spread of the shots around each other. If they got the grouping as shown in Fig 6.3b, any systematic bias looks small as the average location of the shots is very close to the centre – although the low precision does somewhat mask the size of any systematic bias. A grouping where the precision is high and the bias is low is shown in Fig 6.3c, while Fig 6.3d is shows the opposite – low precision and high bias.

If a systematic error exists and something is known of its likely size, an attempt can be made to compensate for it. For example, there are two well-known deceits in business planning: overestimating the sales and underestimating the costs. If data is available on previous forecasts of costs and sales and on how these forecasts turned out in practice, then appropriate corrections can be applied to any new forecasts. In general, however, over- or undercompensation will occur since the magnitude of the bias is unlikely to be known exactly.

On the other hand, you should try to determine how any data supplied to you has been obtained and what sort of bias it might have in it. An aid agency

Fig 6.3 Precision and bias

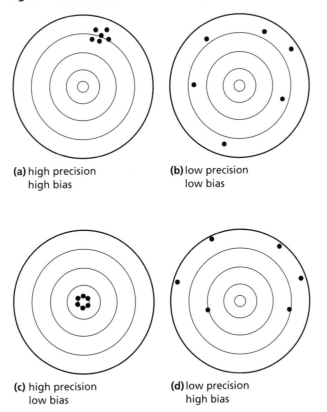

(a) high precision
high bias

(b) low precision
low bias

(c) high precision
low bias

(d) low precision
high bias

wanted to know whether the special food it was giving to babies was having the desired effect and getting the babies to put on weight. Babies in two villages were weighed. The babies in one village had had the special food, the others had not. Weighings were recorded to the nearest 10 grams. In one village the recorders truncated the measurement to the nearest 10 grams (downwards), and in the other they rounded up to the next 10 grams. The procedures had introduced a 'built-in' systematic error in the measurement of difference of 10 grams on average.

Imprecision cannot be compensated for, since it occurs randomly, with any error equally likely to be positive or negative. It may be that the imprecision can be reduced through a more controlled measuring procedure: for example, a more detailed analysis of buying habits may unearth hitherto unforeseen patterns in the data and this enhanced understanding may, in turn, lead to increased precision in forecasting. Sometimes, however, there is nothing that can be done about the imprecision – for example, where sales depend on the weather (e.g. for ice cream and lager) any retailer of these commodities will just have to accept the vagaries of the climate.

However, the presence of imprecision can, paradoxically, ease the effort in determining the values in the data model. Essentially this comes about because if the size of one quantity is known only vaguely, it may not make sense to spend a great deal of time and effort obtaining an exact value for other variables. Consider the relationships 6.1 and 6.2:

$$Expected\ revenue = Forecast\ sales \times Price \qquad (6.1)$$

$$Expected\ contribution = Expected\ revenue - Expected\ variable\ costs \quad (6.2)$$

Say a sales manager considers that the most likely situation is that 10 000 units will be sold, but they know that the sales could quite easily be as high as 11 000 or as low as 9000: i.e. an imprecision of around 10 per cent. If the value of *Price* was precisely known, the values of *Expected revenue* would have the same relative imprecision as *Forecast sales*. (If there was an imprecision in the value of *Price* this would increase the relative imprecision in *Expected revenue* over that of *Forecast sales*.) With this amount of imprecision in *Expected revenue* it does not make sense to attempt to obtain a very precise value for *Expected variable costs* in order to calculate the value of *Expected contribution*: if *Forecast sales* can only be estimated to within ±10 per cent, what is the point of trying to calculate *Expected variable costs* to much better than ±10 per cent?[3]

SOURCES OF DATA

There are several different types of sources for values for the data model and these will be looked at as we consider the simple spreadsheet set out in Fig 6.4. This spreadsheet is used by management accountants and sales personnel to predict the likely performance of a product made in the UK and sold in the USA.

Fig 6.4 A simple spreadsheet with various sources of data

1	Data model (all costs in £ unless otherwise stated)	
2		⎤ value obtained from
3	Unit labour costs	⎦ a database
4		
5		⎤ value obtained from
6	Sales estimate	⎦ another decision aid
7		
8	Unit material cost	⎤ values obtained from
9	Material cost inflation %	⎦ a look-up table
10		
11	Sales price ($)	⎤ values directly input
12	£–$ exchange rate	⎦ by the user
13		
14	Logic model	
15		
16	Total unit costs = Unit labour cost + Unit material cost * (1+Material cost inflation %/100)	
17	Sales price = Sales price ($) / £–$ exchange rate	
18	Unit contribution = Sales price – Total unit costs	
19	Total contribution = Unit contribution * Sales estimate	
20	Total revenue = Sales price * Sales estimate	
21	Total revenue ($) = Sales price ($) * Sales estimate	

The first type of data source we will consider is the database. This is a sources of data held and maintained by someone other than the spreadsheet user: the spreadsheet user has no responsibility for the data values and no control over them.[4] When needed, the data values would be available to be 'downloaded' into the spreadsheet. The databases of concern to spreadsheet users generally contain numeric data, since the strength of a spreadsheet is its ability to manipulate numbers. However, it may be that non-numeric data may be combined in the spreadsheet. Most often the databases associated with spreadsheets will be internal databases originating and maintained by other people in the same organisation as the spreadsheet user. However, external databases are increasingly being made available and being used: for example, there are databases such as Reuters, which provides financial information – share prices and other information regarding company accounts. In the example given in Fig 6.4, data on unit labour costs are held outside the spreadsheet: typically these data would be held in a manufacturing or accounting database and be maintained by personnel in these departments.

The second type of data source is other decision aids. Here data from outside the spreadsheet (and often outside the user's control) are obtained by manipulating base data using a decision aid other than the user's spreadsheet. This is

Fig 6.5 A look-up table

	A	B	C	
1			Unit material	Material cost
2	Product ID	Product Name	cost(£)	inflation %
3				
4	25	Cassette recorder A	51.68	10
5	6	Radio C	34.60	15
6	37	Console	76.22	5
7	27	Radio B	26.98	15
8	7	RC TV	105.57	3
9	9	Cassette recorder B	26.72	4
10	15	TV	60.67	8

the case with the sales estimate in the example. Here, the values of past sales data would have been input to a second decision aid – possibly another spreadsheet, but in this case probably a specialised forecasting package – and an appropriate value for the sales estimate would have been calculated. The value for the sales estimate would then either be input by the user or downloaded from the second decision aid.

A third type of data source is the look-up table.[5] Here the data is part of the spreadsheet but not a central part: it is an adjunct to it. Look-up tables are often held in the same spreadsheet adjacent to the logic model, but they could be in different spreadsheets. The look-up table would generally be established by the user prior to use of the main spreadsheet and it would tend to remain under their control. An example of such a look-up table is given in Fig 6.5. In the example, the costs of materials and the associated likely inflation rates for different products have been listed. In use, values would be selected from the table and used in the relationships in the logic model. Examples of this are given in Chapters 9 and 10.

The fourth and last type of data source is where the data are input directly by the user as they use the spreadsheet to experiment and get results. In the example of Fig 6.4 these values are the sales price and the £–$ exchange rate. The user will be changing these values to see what effect different values of the sales price have on revenue and contribution and the consequences of different assumptions about the £–$ exchange rate.

♦ **Key concept**

Four sources of data can be recognised. First there are data held in databases either inside or outside the organisation. Second, there are data obtained from decision aids other than the spreadsheet itself. Third, there are data obtained from look-up tables. Finally, there are the very dynamic data that are changed by the user as they experiment with the spreadsheet. This sequence broadly reflects the increasing control that the user has over the sources of data.

LARGE DATA MODELS

If you are contemplating handling an issue which involves large amounts of data, it may be that a spreadsheet is not the appropriate software to use. Perhaps it would be more appropriate to use a specialist database package instead. (This will be discussed further in Chapter 16.)

Except for the very simplest, databases always have what is termed a database management system (DBMS) associated with them. A DBMS allows the base of data to be established and maintained and also makes access to the data fairly painless. This easy access is fortunate, since it is unlikely that you will know how the data is structured – and with a DBMS there is no need for you to know. There *is* a need for you to know the field names, however.

There are three basic operations that you can carry out using a DBMS. First there is *sorting*. Here you might wish to sort items into alphabetical order, perhaps reverse alphabetical order, perhaps by rank order depending on the sales made in a given period. As with the selection operation, a good DBMS will allow you to sort on many attributes; for example to sort so that sales areas are listed alphabetically within regions and the regions are ranked in order of the total sales. Spreadsheet packages generally fall short of offering such comprehensive selection facilities, although the gap is closing.

The second basic operation is *selection,* whereby you decide on a selection criterion and ask that all items satisfying this criterion are selected. For example, you might wish to use a sales database to select all sales regions with sales of more than £1 million. Or, more ambitiously perhaps, to select all regions with sales of more than £1 million in Asia which also have sales of less than £100 000 of a particular range of products. This second example illustrates that a good DBMS will allow you to select items using a great many criteria in combination. Again, spreadsheets are unlikely to offer such comprehensive facilities, generally offering only two or three sort fields.

The third important feature of a good DBMS is that it can *merge* data from two or more tables in the same or different databases. For example, the sales to each overseas agent that a company uses may be held in an accounting database, while data about the sales area in which the agents are working may be stored in a table in a sales database. Data from both tables will be needed to produce a report that tells management what the sales in each sales region have been: in other words, data from the two tables will need to be merged.[6] A second example is nearer home. A telephone directory cannot let you know what the telephone numbers of your neighbours are: in general there is no link within a telephone area between phone number and address. The problem is that a telephone directory is structured to give information in one way only. However, if you merge the data on the electoral roll (which links names to addresses) with the data in the corresponding telephone directory, then you can obtain the telephone numbers that you want.

There are further features of a good DBMS that are significant. It will allow you to produce many reports from the same set of data. If you have only been concerned with small data models where the range of possible outputs is limited, this may seem unnecessary. However, once you are dealing with large amounts of data it is important to have an easy means of producing the many reports. Spreadsheets do not offer such an easy means, especially for printed reports. A further advantage of a DBMS is that instead of employing the user-unfriendly macro languages offered by spreadsheets to automate some standard sets of key-strokes, DBMS are specifically designed to provide a user-friendly approach. Most significantly, this approach allows control to be maintained over what you are doing, which you would be hard-pressed to maintain in a spreadsheet if you are using it in an equivalently sophisticated way. A DBMS also controls access by several users at once – not something that spreadsheet packages are intended to do at present. Further considerations of the database aspects of spreadsheets are given in Chapter 16.

SUMMARY

The form of the logic model defines the data required – and thus the content of the data model – and the place of a factor in the logic model determines the precision required of its value. The imprecision inherent in the value of one variable can ease the precision required of the values of other variables.

The characteristics of the four scales of measurement – nominal, ordinal, interval and ratio – were introduced with a warning attached to the use in spreadsheets of the two lower levels. Effectively, the interval and ratio scales can be treated as one, where arithmetic can be done. Four sources of data were discussed: databases, other decision aids, look-up tables and direct insertion into the spreadsheet. This sequence broadly reflects the increasing control that the user has over the source. The appropriateness of spreadsheets when very large data modelling is contemplated was discussed and some of the characteristics of specialised database packages were presented.

END NOTES

1. Since these scales were devised scientists have found that there really *is* a true state of 'no hotness', corresponding to just below –273°C. A measurement scale starting from this *absolute zero* is a ratio scale, but only certain scientists use it.

2. The term precision is identical to what statisticians call random error. The term bias is identical to what statisticians call systematic error.

3. Of course, for *control purposes* it may be that a precise value for the *Expected variable costs* is needed. However, there is no need for this in order to calculate *Expected contribution* for *planning purposes*.

4. Within the spreadsheet the values of data downloaded from a database can be altered, but the originating data cannot be.

5. A look-up table is also a database, but an extremely simple one. It is really only a list with a facility to select a specified matching piece of data. A major difference between a look-up table and a corporate or external database is that the user will know the structure of the look-up table, i.e., will know which data is located where and its relationship to other data, while with a corporate or external database they are unlikely to know the structure.

6. Database terminology for the merging of data from two or more databases is *joining*.

EXERCISES

1 What are the differences between bias and precision?

2 What is meant by saying that in structural modelling the data values help define the logic?

3 What is meant when it says in the text that the logic model defines the data?

4 In Fig 6.4, what choice does the user have over the form and content of the data model?

5 What scales of measurement are used in the following
   a) the goals scored in a football match?
   b) the heights of people?
   c) the nationalities in the European Union?
   d) i) a set of sales regions listed alphabetically?
      ii) a set of sales regions listed by sales revenue?
   e) the scores given in the following opinion scales:
      i) Please select the term that best sums up your view:
         poor   acceptable   good   excellent
      ii) Please indicate on the scale your view of the acceptability of the service you have received:

      _____
      totally   totally
      unacceptable   acceptable

      iii) Please indicate on the scale your view of the percentage of beef in the lamb sausages you have just eaten:

      _____
      0%   100%

6 Suppose that a logic model to forecast future costs has within it the relationship:

   Total costs = Fixed costs + Variable costs

   The *Fixed costs* are forecast to be around £1000 to within ± 10 per cent. The *Variable costs* are forecast to be around £2000. Estimate what precision should be sought for a value for the *Variable costs* if you want to get a value for the *Total costs* that is within ± 15 per cent of the most likely value.

7 Recall the types of factor introduced in Chapter 5 – coefficient, constant, parameter and variable. Relate these different types of factor to the sources of data discussed in this chapter.

8 Draw the information flow diagram corresponding to Fig 6.4.

CHAPTER 7

The results interface: presenting information

Chapter aims The logic and data models have been considered in the two previous chapters. In this chapter we look at the third major component of a spreadsheet – at the human-computer interface and the presentation of information. The value of tabular, pictorial and other representations is discussed.

- ● The concept of summary models
- ● Tables
- ● Continuous and discrete variables
- ● Pictures
  - • The pictorial representation of nominal and ordinal information • The pictorial representation of ratio and interval information • Miscellaneous pictorial representations • Multimedia

THE CONCEPT OF SUMMARY MODELS

Apart from the very smallest spreadsheet, the display of information that a spreadsheet provides will be an extract from the principal (or full) model. These extractions are themselves models – they are representations of 'reality' and they are termed *summary models*. The budgetary example given in Chapter 2 (Fig 2.3) is a good example of a summary model. This chapter is concerned with summary models: with representations which are subsets of the principal model chosen and which are designed with a very specific purpose in mind (see Fig 7.1). This specific purpose is to communicate an answer, a pattern or an insight – to oneself and/or to others

◆ *Key concept*   *Except for trivial cases, the outputs from spreadsheets are summaries of the principal model that is at the centre of the spreadsheet. They are summary models. The outputs may be a single number or word, but usually would be in the form of tables, charts and diagrams. All these forms of output are models themselves since they are representations of 'reality'.*

Fig 7.1 The results interface

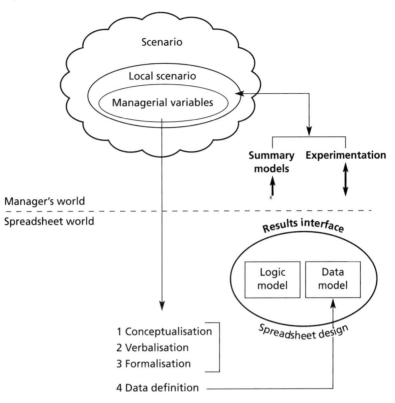

TABLES

Figure 7.2 is a simple table setting out the costs of three components of a product for four consecutive years. It may appear to be a clear table, but can the relevant information in it be clearly seen? For example, the disk drive costs about two-thirds of the subassembly, but this feature is masked somewhat by the number of insignificant digits displayed. To understand the figures in a table requires that the different numbers be related to one another. This tends to

Fig 7.2 Component costs for a product (in £)

	A	B	C	D	E
1					
2	Type of cost		Year		
3		1994	1995	1996	1997
4					
5	Electronics	37.82	34.17	34.36	31.72
6	Subassembly	117.41	123.59	122.36	121.61
7	Disk drive	81.36	86.21	89.27	94.92

mean, even in the age of the electronic calculator, that mental arithmetic will be performed on them. Most people can only manage mental arithmetic on the numbers in Fig 7.2 if they concentrate on two significant digits: for example, rounding the cost of the subassembly in 1997 to £122 and that of the disk drive to £95. Rounding all the numbers of in Fig 7.2 in this fashion produces Fig 7.3

Fig 7.3 Component costs for a product (in £), rounded

	A	B	C	D	E
1					
2	Type of cost		Year		
3		1994	1995	1996	1997
4					
5	Electronics	38	34	34	32
6	Subassembly	117	124	122	122
7	Disk drive	81	86	89	95

Using Fig 7.3 now makes mental arithmetic much easier, and allows patterns to be seen more readily. For example, it can be seen that, while the cost of the electronics was roughly half the cost of the disk drive in 1994, by 1997 its relative cost had fallen to about a third. A rule of thumb for rounding is to round to two significant digits. Note that rounding to two *significant digits* is *not* the same as rounding to two *decimal places*. Under the two-significant-digit rule, a number like 37.82 would be rounded to 38, while a number like 117.41 would be rounded to 117 – three digits shown but with the hundreds digit not considered significant in this case, since it does not change from year to year. By rounding, trends can be seen more easily, but this advantage is accompanied by the disadvantage that the table may not now 'add up'– the totals shown may not be equal to the sum of the individual items. To some people this is such an overwhelming disadvantage that rounding in tables is precluded. But anyone who cannot learn to cope with such rounding errors will probably not get much out of statistical information in any case. The arguments against rounding are that information is lost, and that the compiler of the table is manipulating the figures to highlight things they think should be highlighted, and not allowing the user to carry out the manipulations they want to do themselves. (Obviously this does not apply where the spreadsheet developer and user are always the same person, but the outputs from spreadsheets are often shown to other people.) The counter to this argument is that information is rarely lost through rounding; what are lost from the table are insignificant pieces of data. These bits of data are not lost from the principal model from which the table was derived, however, and if a similar but more precise table were required this could be produced from the principal model. Note that every summary model must show some bias, in the sense that there must be some criterion by which to decide what to include and what to exclude. What is sought is constructive bias.

Where appropriate, a useful adjunct to a table is to give column and row totals and/or means. For greater readability of the table, the means and totals have conventionally been placed at the right-hand edge and bottom of the table. However, with spreadsheets that extend over more than one screen, the means and totals can be shown more easily if they are positioned to the left and at the top: in this way, the means and totals can be fixed (as titles can be in most spreadsheets) and thus kept in view as the spreadsheet is scrolled. Fig 7.4 is Fig 7.3 with the means and totals added.

Fig 7.4 Component costs for a product (in £) – rounded with totals and means added

	A	B	C	D	E	F
1						
2	Type of cost			Year		
3		Mean	1994	1995	1996	1997
4						
5	Total cost	244	237	244	246	248
6						
7	Electronics	35	38	34	34	32
8	Subassembly	121	117	124	122	122
9	Disk drive	88	81	86	89	95

The appearance and impact of the figures in a table can be enhanced if the rows and columns are ordered by size. This is not always appropriate, however: it would not be, for example, where recipients have become used to receiving tables in one constant format, and consequently have learnt to use them in a way that suits them. In such cases, to chop and change the format according to the set of numbers that happen to come up at any one time would not be helpful. An example of this is the sequence of years in the tables discussed: to alter this sequence would generally be inappropriate. However, to give the component costs in order of size could be illuminating, and Fig 7.5 has been derived from Fig 7.4 taking this into account. From Fig 7.5 it can be seen that the subassembly, the disk drive and the electronics make up roughly a third, a half and a seventh (33 per cent, 50 per cent and 15 per cent) of the total cost.

In Fig 7.5 the components have been ordered with the largest cost component first and the smallest last. Also the table gives the latest year at the

Fig 7.5 Component costs for a product (in £) – rounded with totals and means added and values ranked

	A	B	C	D	E	F
1						
2	Type of cost			Year		
3		Mean	1994	1995	1996	1997
4						
5	Total cost	244	237	244	246	248
6						
7	Subassembly	121	117	124	122	122
8	Disk drive	88	81	86	89	95
9	Electronics	35	38	34	34	32

right-hand side. Neither of these two orderings is necessarily better than the other possibilities, since it is very much a question of personal taste. However, it is very likely that some ordering is better than none at all.

Finally, a further decision to make when providing tables concerns which variables should be the rows and which the columns. The significance is that the eye can usually scan more easily down a column of figures than across a row, although the opposite is true for text. In the tables given so far, it has been easier to compare values within years than to compare the values for one disk drive across years. If the more significant comparisons are across years, then the columns and rows should be interchanged. Figure 7.6 shows this – and we hope you agree that comparisons across years is now easier.

Fig 7.6 Component costs for a product (£) – rounded rounded with totals and means added and rows and columns transposed

	A	B	C	D	E
1					
2	Year		Type of cost		
3		Subassembly	Disk drive	Electronics	Total cost
4					
5	1994	117	81	38	237
6	1995	124	86	34	244
7	1996	122	89	34	246
8	1997	122	95	32	248
9	Mean	121	88	35	244

Note throughout the development from Fig 7.2 to Fig 7.6 the value of having a title to a table that tells you what it is about and any special features of its make-up.

In all the above the use of colour to highlight items is to be recommended – if used sparingly! The most obvious is to use red to highlight 'bad' financial items. Also, of course, you can embolden, italicise and otherwise smarten up and highlight the important items.

◆ *Key concept*

It may be that spreadsheet outputs may only be seen by the person creating them. Often, however, other people in an organisation may need to see them. When this is the case there is a need to think of the intended audience and, most importantly, of what you are trying to highlight: is it detail that you want to show, a comparison, a breakpoint, a trend. . . ?

CONTINUOUS AND DISCRETE VARIABLES

Before moving on to discuss non-tabular displays of information, we need to consider a further characteristic of input factors and calculated variables: whether they are continuous or discrete.

Fig 7.7 Weekly sales revenues

175123	155297	156234	132998	152345	179126	169234
153459	143183	142429	157675	166666	147975	136376
158123	162601	144851	142766	155622	165854	138124
132766	141024	165640	159891	154632	145487	173742
144784	140591	125238	157447	173458	171333	141763
164731	159769	154496	135582	142347	133699	156871
128386	137369	158349	155871	141789	163421	149871
151338	143511	131621				

Consider the set of data given in Fig 7.7, which are the weekly sales figures for a retail outlet over the period of a year.

The revenue in any one week may be considered a continuous variable – that is to say, the variable can take any value within a range of values. For example, the height of an adult is a continuous variable – the value 1.725618 meters is a perfectly possible height for someone to be. This is in contrast to a discrete variable where the values the variable can take are limited – 1.725618 is not a feasible value for the number of peas in a pod. The number of peas in a pod is a discrete variable for which the possible values are limited to the positive integers 0, 1, 2, 3 etc.

Note that it was stated above that the weekly revenue *may be considered a continuous variable*. This wording was used because, in the ultimate, revenue is a discrete variable: revenue must be a whole number of £ and pence: a revenue of £121 362.5672 is not a feasible value. However, the pence subdivision (and indeed the units of pounds or even hundreds of pounds) is so small compared to the size of the revenue that on any meaningful pictorial representation the variable can be treated as a continuous one. Thus, although the theoretical distinction between continuous and discrete variables is clear cut, there is some measure of arbitrariness as to how they are treated in practice.

The data in Fig 7.7 are for 52 weeks of the year. Time certainly is a continuous variable, but here, as in many cases in business, it is convenient to take portions of a continuous variable and treat it as a 'chunk' – of a week. But see later!

It should not be thought that continuous variables can take on any value. There may be constraints on possible values: for example, a person's height cannot be greater than 3 metres and there is a lower limit. And discrete variables may also be limited: for example, the number of students in the classroom cannot be negative and there must be an upper boundary – even in these cost conscious-days! Scoring in games is another example of limits on the values which discrete variables can take.

◆ **Key concept**

A variable was defined in Chapter 5 as a factor that could take various values. Some variables can only take a limited set of values: for example, the number of students in a classroom cannot be other than 1, 2, 3 etc. Such variables are called discrete variables (note the spelling – discreet means careful and discerning!). They are to be contrasted with continuous variables whose values are not restricted in this way.

PICTURES

The saying 'a picture's worth a thousand words' has a lot of truth in it, and quite naturally many of the representations of summary models are more graphic than are tables. Microsoft Excel uses the general term *chart* to describe all visual non-tabular forms of representation, while Lotus uses the general term *graph*. We will use the general term *picture*: this is not a perfect term but it does have the advantage that it doesn't favour the usage in either of these popular packages.

While a picture's worth a thousand words, it is also probably true that a picture's worth a thousand numbers, as the cases given by Anscombe so graphically illustrate. In Fig 7.8 four sets of data are set out.

Fig 7.8 Anscombe's four sets of data

I		II		III		IV		
X	Y	X	Y	X	Y	X	Y	
10.0	8.04	10.0	9.14	10.0	7.46	8.0	6.58	N = 11
8.0	6.95	8.0	8.14	8.0	6.77	8.0	5.76	mean of Xs = 9.0
13.0	7.58	13.0	8.74	13.0	12.74	8.0	7.71	mean of Ys = 7.5
9.0	8.81	9.0	8.77	9.0	7.11	8.0	8.84	equation of regression line: Y = 3 + 0.5X
11.0	8.33	11.0	9.26	11.0	7.81	8.0	8.47	standard error if estimate of slope = 0.118
14.0	9.96	14.0	8.10	14.0	8.84	8.0	7.04	t = 4.24
6.0	7.24	6.0	6.13	6.0	6.08	8.0	5.25	sum of squares X – X = 110.0
4.0	4.26	4.0	3.10	4.0	5.39	19.0	12.50	regression sum of squares = 27.50
12.0	10.84	12.0	9.13	12.0	8.15	8.0	5.56	residual sum of squares of Y = 13.75
7.0	4.82	7.0	7.26	7.0	6.42	8.0	7.91	correlation coefficient = 0.82
5.0	5.68	5.0	4.74	5.0	5.73	8.0	6.89	$r^2 = 0.67$

Source: from F.J.Anscombe, 'Graphs in statistical analysis', *American Statistician*, **27**, February 1973, pages 17–21

As can be seen from the values given on the right of the table, all of the summary statistics given are identical for all four sets of data: the means of the Xs and Ys are the same and so on (don't worry if you don't know what these signify – the important features will be explained in Chapters 14 and 15). However, plotting them as in Fig 7.9 shows just how different these underlying patterns are. So, although pictures can lie, so can summary statistics! Both are required.

◆ *Key concept*

*With a picture you lose some of the underlying data. This might seem a disadvantage, but in fact it is the main reason for drawing pictures. The value of a picture is that it **suppresses data** in order to **provide information**. (With the underlying data available if necessary, the data is not, of course, lost.)*

The pictures most often used in business and/or available on most spread-sheets have been selected for consideration below. Most spreadsheets offer variants on the type and class of picture to be described and it will be for you to judge which variant is most suitable for your application. First, the pictorial

Fig 7.9 Data sets

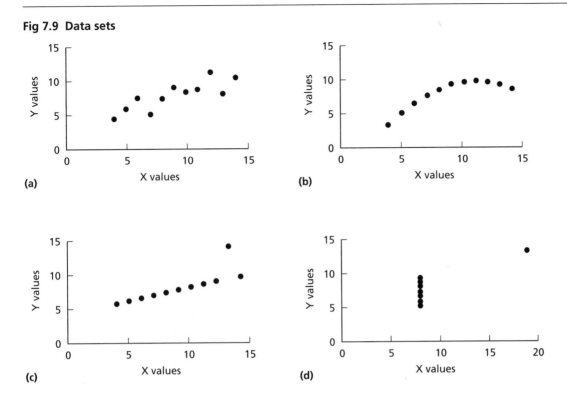

(a)

(b)

(c)

(d)

representation of nominal and ordinal information will be considered: then, the representation of interval and ratio information.

The pictorial representation of nominal and ordinal information

Nominal information is associated with things that can be classified as distinct from each other, but where no other categorisation is useful: examples are sales regions, factories and products.

One way to represent a variable of nominal information is by using a bar chart (column chart in Excel or bar graph in Lotus). Bar charts provide suitable diagrammatic representations where contrasts between sets of information are to be highlighted. An example of a simple bar chart is given in Fig 7.10 where the components of product cost for 1997 are displayed (using the data in Fig 7.2).

The variables may be either continuous or discrete. The height of the bar represents the amount of the characteristic: neither the width of the bar nor its position along the axis is significant.

The changes in the three component costs for, say, four years can be shown either by using a multiple bar chart (stacked column chart in Excel; stacked bar graph in Lotus) as in Fig 7.11 or a stacked bar chart (stacked column chart in Excel; stacked bar graph in Lotus) as in Fig 7.12. Stacked bar charts have the additional advantage that they show the relative contributions of the parts to the whole.

Fig 7.10 Bar chart showing component costs

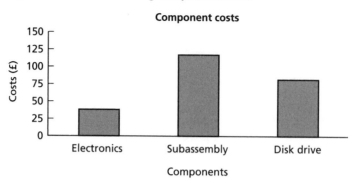

Fig 7.11 Multiple bar chart

Fig 7.12 Stacked bar chart

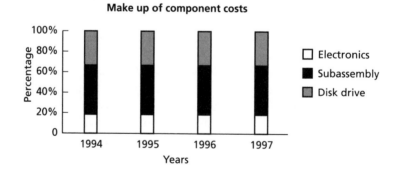

Theoretically there is no limit to the number of characteristics that may be shown on a multiple or stacked bar chart, but as the number rises the increased clutter in the layout is soon likely to reduce the impact of the major informational features. Further forms of bar chart and stacked bar chart are horizontal charts. These are not really different, but they may appeal to some people. Such horizontal charts are shown in Fig 7.13 (termed bar chart and stacked bar chart in Excel).

Two further special forms of bar chart are the pictogram (stretched and stacked picture markers in Excel) and box plots, sometimes termed range bars (hi-lo chart in Excel; hi-lo-close-open in Lotus). In a pictogram, instead of simply using plain bars to show size, little pictures are shown instead, increasing the impact of the information. A pictogram showing the sales of cars over a five-month period is shown in Fig 7.14.

An example of how to draw a box plot is shown in Fig 7.15. This diagram shows one area where such plots are often used – to show share-price movements. The ends of the vertical lines indicate the maximum and minimum prices recorded, with the horizontal lines that make up the top and bottom of the boxes showing the opening and closing prices. (The white rectangle indicates that the closing price is larger than the opening price: the black rectangles indicate the opposite.)

Fig 7.13 Horizontal chart

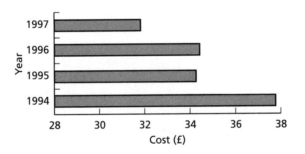

Electronics costs by year

Fig 7.14 Car sales for the first five months of 1997

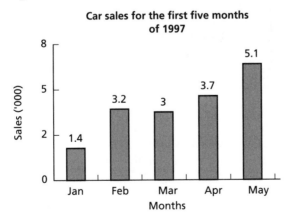

Fig 7.15 A hi-lo plot

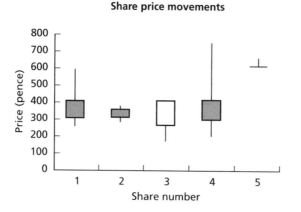

The pictorial representation of ratio and interval information

Before discussing the various pictorial ways in which ratio and interval information can be presented, we need to consider another way of looking at variables. There are some variables that 'cause' other variables. This means that the value of one variable follows from the value of a second variable. For example, all things being equal, the more cigarettes that you smoke the lower your life expectancy. Here, the value of one variable (the number of cigarettes smoked per day) leads to the value of another (years' life expectancy). More subtle is a non-causation case: for example, children (and often adults too!) will get heavier as they get older. When you think about it, the increase in weight follows getting older: getting older doesn't follow from getting heavier. One doesn't *cause* the other, although one is *associated with* the other. The variable whose value is determined by the value of the second variable is termed the dependent variable. The lead variable is known as the independent variable since its value doesn't depend on the value of other variables.

◆ *Key concept*

*Often it is found that the value of one variable depends on the value of another. The variable whose value 'follows' that of the other variable is termed the **dependent variable**. The variable whose value 'leads' the value of the dependent variable is termed the **independent variable**.*

In the following discussion of pictures we will use the terms *x-axis* for the horizontal axis and *y-axis* for the vertical axis where appropriate, since these terms seem to be almost universally used in spreadsheets. These terms arose because it is the values of the independent variable, traditionally labelled *x* in algebra, that have generally been plotted along the horizontal axis. Similarly, it is values of the dependent variable, traditionally labelled *y* in algebra, that have generally been plotted along the vertical axis. Just in case you meet them, mathematical buffs sometimes use the more high-faluting term *abscissa* for *x-axis* and *ordinate* for the *y-axis*. Where a third axis is needed, as in three-dimensional pictures, the term *z-axis* is used.

Fig 7.16 Plot of weekly revenues

It is hard to extract information from the revenue data given in Fig 7.7. You might be able to spot that the maximum and minimum values are £179 126 and £125 238 respectively and that most values lie between £140 000 and £160 000. Ranking the values would be helpful, but a picture may be more so. The frequency of occurrence of the values of sales is plotted in Fig 7.16, with the conventional arrangement of the independent variable plotted on the horizontal axis and the dependent variable plotted on the vertical axis. Such a figure is not very informative, although the maximum and minimum sales revenues are now easily picked out and the density of points gives an indication of where most of the values lie. There is one rare occurrence – one value of revenue occurs twice.

Figure 7.16 has been drawn purely to show the drawbacks of such a representation: representations like this are rarely used since a much more informative picture can be drawn instead – a histogram. Histograms differ from bar charts because only the height of the bar has significance in a bar chart, not the area as in the case of histograms. Figure 7.17 is a histogram (a special form of column chart in Excel and bar graph in Lotus) of the revenue values.[1] It has been produced by grouping data values into classes – values lying between £120 000 and £130 000 are grouped into one class, those values greater than or equal to £130 000 and less than £140 000 are grouped into a second and so on. Unless

Fig 7.17 Histogram of sales revenue

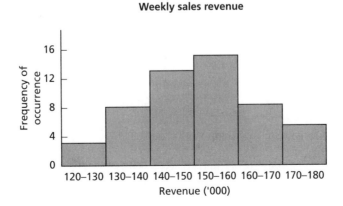

groupings like this are made, the best one can do are diagrams like Fig 7.16 which are not very helpful. By contrast, Fig 7.17 shows how the frequency of occurrence is greatest in the band £150–160 000 and how the frequency falls off on either side of this peak.[2]

The choice of groupings in a histogram is important. Figure 7.18 may also be drawn from the data in Fig 7.7. Unlike Fig 7.17, this does not show a single peak but two peaks, one for the range £135–145 000 and one for the range £155–165 000. The choice of class boundary is all that has been changed, yet a very different-looking histogram has been produced. Although there is no way to prevent this happening, the procedure to prevent unwanted bias creeping in is for the class boundaries to be decided *prior* to the analysis of the data – or, better still, prior to the data being obtained. From Figs 7.19 and 7.20 it can be seen that a person drawing a histogram has to settle for some middle ground, between making the groupings so small that there are very few values in each group or so large that only a few groupings are possible. In the first representation all of the data is present, yet patterns in the data remain hidden; in the second case the broad patterns are exposed at the expense of fine detail. Exactly how to draw the histogram depends on the circumstances and requires judgement. This subjectivity provides the flexibility to lie with statistics!

A feature of histograms is that it is the area associated with a range of values (the class width) that indicates the number of occurrences in the range. In Figs 7.17 to 7.20 the class widths in each individual histogram are the same throughout and thus equal areas (and equal numbers) are reflected in equal heights in each (although not across the histograms). While histograms are often drawn in this way this is not always so: any class widths can be used, but if they are then caution must be exercised in their use. In Fig 7.21 the data of Fig 7.7 are redrawn with an 'open-ended' final class. This type of histogram is very useful when there is a long tail of results: to keep to only one class size means either a huge set of numbers in one or two classes or a set of classes in the tail which contain none or only a very few cases. Since the *x*-axis is continuous, it would be inappropriate to have a gap between the histogram classes.

Fig 7.18 Histogram of sales revenue

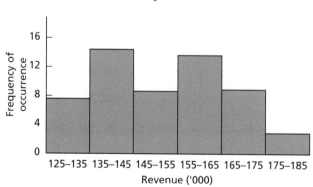

Fig 7.19 Histogram of sales revenue

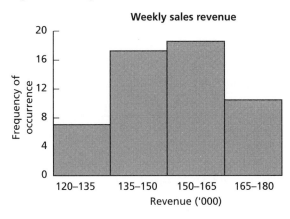

Weekly sales revenue

Fig 7.20 Histogram of sales revenue

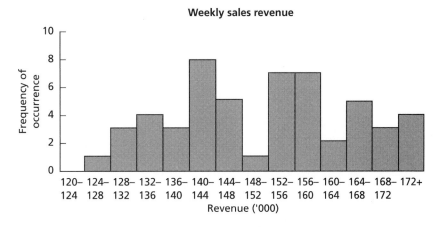

Weekly sales revenue

Fig 7.21 Histogram of sales revenue with open-ended final class

Weekly sales revenue

Fig 7.22 Number of people at work – wrongly drawn as a histogram

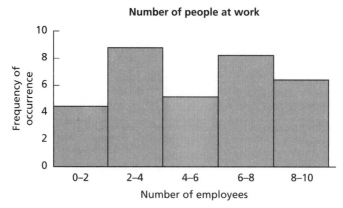

Number of people at work

Fig 7.23 Number of people at work – correctly drawn as a frequency diagram

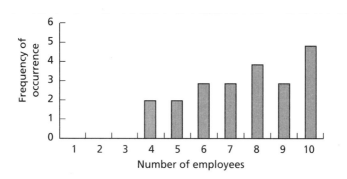

Number of employees at work

For discrete variables it is not appropriate to draw a histogram, since values other than the discrete ones have no significance. The appropriate picture is a frequency diagram. For example, consider an organisation employing ten people which has data available for the number of employees who were at work on any one day over the period of one month (22 working days). Plotting a histogram like Fig 7.22 would suggest that values such as 3.265 are feasible, which is not the case. Here, the frequency diagram of Fig 7.23 is the appropriate picture to draw. This diagram is the same as a bar chart, but the *x*-axis is ordered. (Other illustrations of groupings of data and presenting continuous and discrete data are given in Chapter 10.)

◆ *Key concept*

A histogram is the appropriate picture to show the frequency of occurrence of the values of continuous variables. A frequency diagram is the appropriate picture to show the frequency of occurrence of the values of discrete variables.

If data are available and a continuous relationship between two variables is thought to exist, then the data could be plotted on a graph (X-Y scatter chart and line chart in Excel; X-Y graph in Lotus) to show this relationship. For example, the UK Treasury has a model that includes a relationship relating the amount of duty that will be obtained from tobacco sales in any year to the rate of tobacco duty – because this rate has such an effect on the price of tobacco products or cigarettes. A plot of the rate of tobacco duty and the associated Treasury income looks like that in Fig 7.24.

As was seen with histograms and frequency diagrams, it is not appropriate to draw pictures such as Fig 7.24 for discrete variables. The values may be plotted in the same way, but a curve drawn through the points suggests that values other than the discrete values are feasible and this is not the case.

It is vital when drawing any sort of diagram that it is correctly labelled. Politicians have been known to use unscaled graphs to attempt to prove a point! For example, the two graphs drawn in Fig 7.25 both show the rate of inflation as a function of time. In Fig 7.25a inflation seems almost to be static; in Fig 7.25b the fall in the rate looks remarkable. The difference is caused by the different scales used on the two y-axes. You should always think twice before using a y-axis scale that does not start with a zero. Unfortunately, most

Fig 7.24 Total tobacco duty

Fig 7.25 Yearly inflation rates

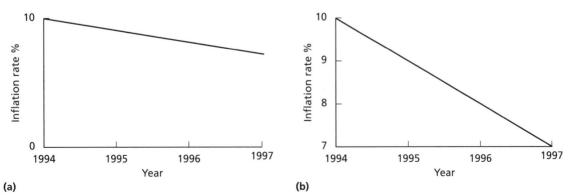

(a)   (b)

Fig 7.26 Breakeven chart

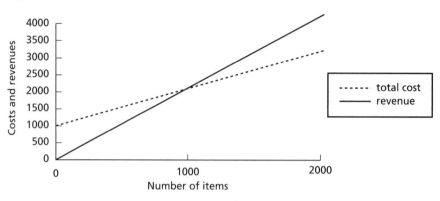

spreadsheet packages default to automatic scaling, which produces results more like Fig 7.25b.

The use of graphs need not be restricted to the plotting of data linking two variables, but can illuminate the relationships between several variables. One example of this is the case of breakeven analysis. In breakeven analysis a calculation is made of the number of items that need to be sold in order to cover costs – to 'break even'. Generally the costs are made up of a fixed component – one that is incurred however many items are made – and a variable component that varies directly with the number of items made. For the simplest of cases, where all the items made are sold, the total cost associated with sales may be written:

$$Total\ cost = Fixed\ cost + Variable\ cost \qquad (7.1)$$

with:

$$Variable\ cost = Variable\ cost/item \times Number\ of\ items \qquad (7.2)$$

Revenue may be written as:

$$Revenue = Sales\ price \times Number\ of\ items \qquad (7.3)$$

With a fixed cost of £1000, a variable cost/item of £1 and a sales price of £2, equations 7.1 and 7.3 can be plotted to produce Fig 7.26. It can be seen immediately from this graph that the breakeven *Total cost* and *Revenue* are £2000 when 1000 units are made and sold; below this values of sales the contribution is negative, above it the contribution is positive.

Miscellaneous pictorial representations

Pie charts, so called because a quantity is represented rather like a pie and the sectors are akin to portions of the pie, are another useful and much used representation – especially, it seems, in company accounts. Pie charts are often the best way in which to show the relative contribution of the parts to the whole. An example of a pie chart is given in Fig 7.27.

Fig 7.27 Percentage split of sales

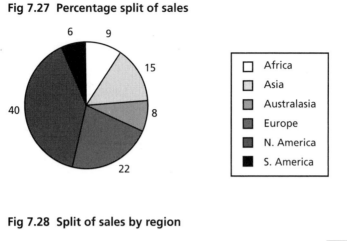

Fig 7.28 Split of sales by region

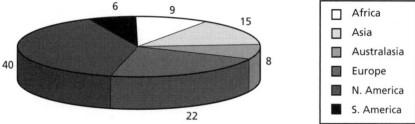

The major 'face' of the 3-D pie chart shown in Fig 7.28 is an ellipse. It does, however, faithfully reflect the percentages of sales with correspondingly sized 'portions'. But beware of 3-D pie charts where the cross-section is an ellipse and the point from which the portions radiate is off-centre. In such cases the size of the 'portions' may well not faithfully reflect the percentage split to the human eye.

Star diagrams are a clear pictorial way of illustrating the strength of the relationship between one variable and each of several other variables. Figure 7.29 is an example of this where the changes in *Raw material costs*, *Labour costs*, *Fixed costs* and *Sales* are plotted against the consequent *Profit* changes. The form of the star is used to highlight the sensitivity of an important variable (*Profit* in this case) to changes in other variables. For example, the diagram shows that *Profit* is more sensitive to changes in *Sales* than it is to changes in *Raw material costs*: a 1.5 per cent change in *Sales* changes *Profit* by 30 per cent while a 1.5 per cent change in *Raw materials costs* changes *Profit* by less than 15 per cent.

Multimedia

Mention has already been made of the use of colour, both to highlight areas of the spreadsheet and to 'jazz up' the overall appearance of a summary model. Other features are sound tags, such as bleeps to indicate an inadmissible entry and the recording of voice annotations. Other possibilities are to link the spreadsheet to video facilities to provide a level of animation.

Fig 7.29 A star diagram

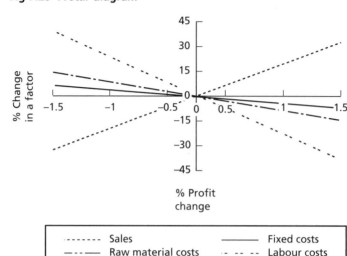

% Change in a factor

% Profit change

| ······· Sales | ——— Fixed costs |
| —·—· Raw material costs | ·- ·· ·· Labour costs |

SUMMARY

Summary models are portions of the spreadsheet whereby significant features of a larger, more complex principal model are highlighted and communicated to convey 'results'. To do this effectively means they have to be visually appealing. In the case of tables, rounding, providing column and row totals and averages, transposing rows and columns and ranking rows and/or columns are ways of improving the presentation of information. With both tables and pictorial representations a clear and meaningful title is very important.

Spreadsheets now offer many ways of presenting summary information. Graphs, pie and bar charts and histograms are now almost instantly available at the touch of a button, in colour and integrated with the principal model. With the computer's sound capability, the 'all singing, all dancing' spreadsheet is close to realisation!

END NOTES

1 Most spreadsheet packages cannot draw true histograms. They draw bar charts with equal class intervals and no gaps between the bars

2 There is always a potential problem with histograms – into which class do you put values that fall at the exact boundary between the classes. For example, in Fig 7.17, where should the value £130 000 be placed – in the first or second class? The problem is easily resolved by simply determining from the outset what the classes should contain. In this example, we have decided that the class limits will be equal to or greater than the lower boundary value and less than the lower boundary value. You could obviously reverse this rule: it doesn't matter as long as you are consistent – and do not choose the boundaries simply to prove a point.

FURTHER READING A beautiful and very interesting book is that by Edward Tufte, *The Visual Display of Quantitative Information*, Graphics Press, Cheshire, Conn, USA, 1983. This gives many examples of good graphical design – and also of how to lie with pictures! The book by Mike Carter and David Williamson, *Quantitative Modelling for Management and Business*, Pitman, 1996, gives some more examples in the chapter on data reduction and its presentation.

EXERCISES

1 What is the information that is almost totally suppressed in Fig 7.16?

2 Under what conditions would you use a histogram and a frequency diagram to represent patterns in data?

3 It is said in the text that a rule of thumb is to round to two significant digits. How sensible do you think this is? It is easy on a spreadsheet to try out any type of rounding. Try rounding to 2, 3 and 4 significant figures. Which summary model is most meaningful and useful?

4 Consider the full Readyread case. How would you show the following:
   a) the relationship between book production and total costs?
   b) the relationship between staff required and book production?
   c) costs and revenues as a function of book production?

CHAPTER 8

Spreadsheet design: model creation maintenance and enhancement

Chapter aims

In the previous three chapters the three major components of a spreadsheet have been considered. This chapter is concerned with two interrelated matters. First, that the spreadsheet is valid so that you can have confidence in its outputs; and second, that best practice is followed to ensure that the data and logic models can be built easily and the resultant spreadsheet allows for easy maintenance and enhancement. In short, it is concerned with spreadsheet design.

- Introduction
- Validation, validity and verification
- Overall systems considerations
- Logic management
  • Checking the 'shape' of a relationship • Checking the dimensions • Checking the units • Checking the range of application of a relationship • Further considerations
- Data management
- Menus and short-cut keys

INTRODUCTION

This book is mainly intended for the DIY spreadsheet user – a person who is both the developer of the spreadsheet and an operator of it. Development and operation are two fairly distinct tasks. The concern in this chapter is with the activities of the developer, in particular with how best to design a spreadsheet so that a valid spreadsheet is built in the first place and then that it is easy to maintain and enhance it. It is also concerned with those aspects of design that will make subsequent operation easy, efficient and, as far as possible, error free.

As developer, the user must design the spreadsheet so that it is easy to maintain and enhance. *Maintenance* is the process of keeping a spreadsheet in a state where it remains valid. This means keeping both the logic and the data of the model up to date. For example, if working practices change, the relationship between costs and output is likely to need amendment in the logic model; when a VAT (value-added tax) rate is changed, its value in the data model needs to be altered. *Enhancements* are changes to a spreadsheet that provide additional fea-

Fig 8.1 Considerations in spreadsheet design

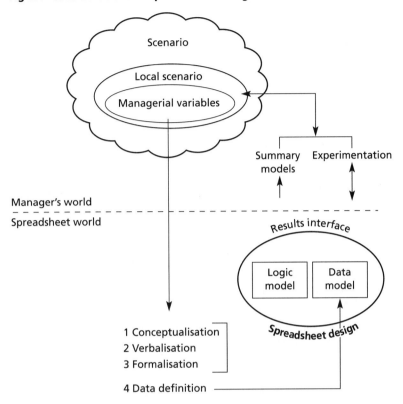

tures: for example, calculating monthly totals where previously only weekly totals were available. A spreadsheet that is easy to maintain and enhance will be *future proof* to a considerable extent – it will be able to accommodate future changes.

The user as developer must also recognise the needs they will have as the subsequent operator of the spreadsheet – the need to be able easily to change the data values (and sometimes the logic) without making silly mistakes. However, there is a balance between ease of use and the increasing effort that is required as a design is improved to incorporate more and more user-friendly features.

Creation, maintenance and enhancement all involve ensuring that the spreadsheet is a valid one. For this reason, the chapter begins by discussing the concepts of validation, validity and the related term verification. There are then two further sections: one concerned with the validity of the logic model and one with the validity of the data model (*see* Fig 8.1).

VALIDATION, VALIDITY AND VERIFICATION

At its simplest, validation can be looked on as the process of testing the fit between the spreadsheet and a portion of the manager's scenario, and thus a valid spreadsheet would be one that has stood up to these tests. There may appear to be a problem with this view, since in many cases where spreadsheets have been created there is no managerial world yet in existence: for example, where a new company is being created to manufacture and sell a new product. This problem is a minor one since the concepts underlying the proposed system must be an extension of current thinking. There *is* a major philosophical problem with the validation process, however, since validation can never be fully carried out. This problem arises because it is not possible to prove that a relationship is valid, only that it is invalid. The fact that the sun has been observed to rise in the east for many thousands of years has led to the 'law', 'the sun always rises in the east'. The observations and the resulting law only make it very probable that the sun will rise in the east tomorrow – it does not and cannot guarantee that it will. On the other hand, if on only one day the sun failed to show this behaviour, then the rule that the sun always rises in the east would have been disproved. Thus, although you cannot prove a law, one genuine, contradictory finding can make a law invalid.

Fortunately, the validation of spreadsheets is not concerned with proving the absolute truth of the underlying relationships that make up the spreadsheet – since this is impossible – but with demonstrating that one can have reasonable confidence that the relationships are appropriate. We use the term 'appropriate' rather than 'right' or 'the truth' since with spreadsheets for managerial decision making the search is for usability, and usability depends on the user's viewpoint and the context in which they find themself – on their scenario. It must be recognised that each individual will have their own scenario. Since it is these mental models that are discussed, argued about and used (and supported by the spreadsheet) it is not reasonable to view the real-world system as definable in absolute terms. It follows from this that validity is not, and cannot, be an absolute: like beauty, validity is in the eye of the beholder. It is for this reason that validity is best considered as an expression of appropriateness – of the spreadsheet in the context in which it is to be used. The process of validation will be taken therefore to be the checking of the appropriateness of a spreadsheet to help handle issues as seen from the viewpoint of those involved in the spreadsheet's creation and use.

Although validation is a process that should take place throughout the development of the spreadsheet, often someone who has had no involvement in this development has to validate the spreadsheet for themselves. So much of the validation might be concentrated on an existing spreadsheet – or on extensions and changes to a spreadsheet that already exists.[1]

◆ **Key concept**

The validity of a spreadsheet is an expression of the confidence we have in its appropriateness to help understand managerial issues. No spreadsheet can be considered completely valid – appropriateness is a relative concept. There are simply levels of validity.

Validation is the process by which a given level of validity is achieved. It is the process of checking the appropriateness of a spreadsheet to help handle managerial issues as seen from the viewpoint of those involved in the spreadsheet's creation and use.

One special and well-developed part of validation is verification, which is the process of testing something to see that it performs as expected:[2] for example, that totals are calculated correctly, and that exceptions are reported appropriately. Verification, therefore, is the testing and debugging of the spreadsheet. Within logic model development it is not concerned with the appropriateness of the relationships that make up the model, only with whether the translation of the relationships into a computer representation in the formalisation stage has been done correctly. In data modelling verification is concerned with whether the data values 'match' the requirements of the logic model, for example, that daily sales figures have been used in the spreadsheet and not weekly data.

In contradistinction to other forms of validation, it is theoretically possible to verify a spreadsheet – that it has completely passed all the tests during the process of verification. However, it may be impracticable to verify the model over all possible cases.

> ◆ **Key concept**
>
> *Verification is the testing and debugging of a spreadsheet. Within logic model validation, verification is concerned only with whether the translation of the verbal relationships into a computer representation has been done correctly. Within data model validation, verification is concerned with whether the data values 'match' the requirements of the logic model.*

OVERALL SYSTEMS CONSIDERATIONS

With a small spreadsheet – one that perhaps only covers a computer screen or two – any problems with creating, maintaining or enhancing the spreadsheet are likely to be trivial. However, once the spreadsheet becomes larger the situation changes radically and it is only by being extremely diligent that changes can be made easily and the chance of errors can be minimised.

It is good design practice to keep all the elements of the major components of the manager's scenario together and to make each component a different module in the spreadsheet. Consider the case of a factory that first takes stored raw materials from a warehouse to the manufacturing area. After manufacture, the finished goods are placed in a finished goods store prior to dispatch to wholesalers. Suppose that a spreadsheet is to be built to determine the costs incurred in each of these four functions (raw materials handling, manufacture, finished goods handling and dispatch). There are two reasons that it would make sense to keep the four major components of the logic model separate. First, the relationships between variables are likely to be more intimate within a function than between functions, reflecting the original reason for grouping the physical activities together into these functions. Second, it may well be that the developer will have to go to the manager responsible for each function and discuss the spreadsheet with them. It then makes sense to have a fairly independent module as the focus for discussion. A diagrammatic representation of this is shown as modularisation 1 in Fig 8.2.

Fig 8.2 Modularisation of a spreadsheet

Modularisation 1		Modularisation 2	
Raw materials handling	Data model	Raw materials handling	Data model
	Logic model	Manufacture	Data model
Manufacture	Data model	Finished goods handling	Data model
	Logic model	Dispatch	Data model
Finished goods handling	Data model	Raw materials handling	Logic model
	Logic model	Manufacture	Logic model
Dispatch	Data model	Finished goods handling	Logic model
	Logic model	Dispatch	Logic model

Within each module it is valuable to segregate (the values in) the data model from (the formulae of) the logic model. One reason for this is that the values of the data are likely to be what is termed volatile – changing quite often – while the logic model is likely to change only slowly after an initial 'bedding-in' period. A second reason for such segregation is that one logic model may be associated with several data models: for instance, when several companies report to head office, they are likely to be providing their own data to the same logic model.

Modularisation 2 in Fig 8.2 is a second way of grouping the portions of the data and logic models that is possibly more suitable for small spreadsheets.

Figure 8.3 is a version of Fig 5.5 – the electricity tariff problem – augmented to include a calculation of the VAT payable. This calculation has been included

Fig 8.3 The information flow diagram for the electricity tariff issue (augmented version of Fig 5.5)

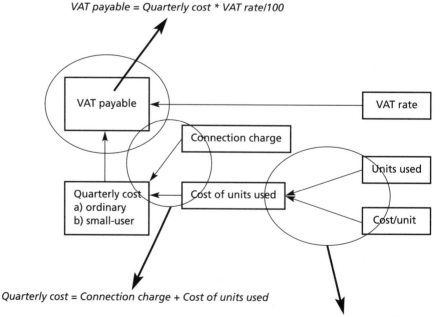

*VAT payable = Quarterly cost * VAT rate/100*

Quarterly cost = Connection charge + Cost of units used

Cost of units = Units used × Cost/unit

Fig 8.4 A spreadsheet of the electricity tariff issue (poor practice)

	A	B	C	D
1	**Ordinary tariff**		*Verbalisation relationships*	*Spreadsheet relationships*
2				
3	Cost/unit	3		
4	Units used	3000		
5	Cost of units used	9000	= Units used × Cost/unit	+B3*B4
6	Connection charge	100		
7	Quarterly cost	9100	= Connection charge + Cost of units used	+B5+B6
8	VAT payable	1365	= Quarterly cost × (VAT rate%/100)	+B7*0.15
9				
10	'Small-user' tariff			
11				
12	Cost/unit	5		
13	Units used	3000		
14	Cost of units used	15000	= Units used × Cost/unit	+B12*B13
15	Connection charge	50		
16	Quarterly cost	15050	= Connection charge + Cost of units used	+B14+B15
17	VAT payable	2257	= Quarterly cost × (Vat rate%/100)	+B16*0.15

in rows 8 and 17 of Fig 8.4. Note that the *value* of the VAT rate (15 per cent) has been included within the equations themselves, i.e. in the logic model. This is bad practice, since if the VAT rate changes it is difficult to ensure that all the formulae using this value will be correctly updated. Figure 8.4 is also a poor formulation because the data and logic models have not been kept separate. A much better version is that of in Fig 8.5, where the data and logic models are separated and the value of the VAT rate is now part of the data model.

A further form of modularisation results from the availability of '3-dimensional' sheets in many spreadsheets. With 3-D sheets (often called 'multiple sheets') you can use one sheet for each department or for each product that you are dealing with. Working in 3-D is made simple because you can copy data and logic from one sheet to another and can do such things as add the values of the same cell 'through' the spreadsheet: for example, if each sheet held data on the sales of each product sold, then a cover sheet could hold the sum of the individual product values – the total sales.

If you are not careful it is easy for the assumptions made during the building of a spreadsheet to be lost. It is therefore good practice to incorporate information about the major assumptions and modelling conventions underpinning the whole of the spreadsheet explicitly *in* the spreadsheet – generally at the top. An assumption for the factory example could be that there was no restriction on the amount of overtime that could be worked (this may turn out to be an inappropriate assumption – for this very reason it should be stated!). Examples of conventions would be that all monetary values were in millions of pounds sterling and that all quantities were in tonnes unless otherwise stated. Where

Fig 8.5 A spreadsheet of the electricity tariff issue (better practice)

	A	B	C
1	Ordinary tariff – quarterly costs		*Spreadsheet relationships*
2			
3	Cost/unit (pence)	3	
4	Units used	3000	
5	Connection charge (£)	100	
6	VAT rate (%)	15	
7	Cost of units used (£)	90	+B4*B3/100
8	Quarterly cost (£)	190	+B5+B7
9	VAT payable (£)	14	+B8*(B6/100)
10			
11	'Small-user' tariff – quarterly costs		
12			
13	Cost/unit (pence)	5	
14	Units used	3000	
15	Connection charge (£)	50	
16	VAT rate (%)	15	
17	Cost of units used (£)	150	+B14*B13/100
18	Quarterly cost (£)	200	+B15+B17
19	VAT payable (£)	14	+B18*(B16/100)

appropriate, assumptions and conventions should also be placed at the beginning of each module. Examples of such assumptions and conventions are shown in the first spreadsheet rows in Fig 8.6. Another way of capturing these assumptions and conventions in Excel is by inserting the name *Assumptions* in, say, cell A1 and conventions, in say, cell A2 and then linking each cell to an *attach note or show information window* made available through the auditing function from the tools menu.

A more subtle piece of documentation is to specify the range of application of the spreadsheet – either of the whole model or of parts of it. For example, it may be that a financial model is only valid for (positive) profits: if a loss were to be made, then the spreadsheet would not provide valid results, because the relationships that would be needed if a loss occurs have not been entered into the spreadsheet. Another example is where the relationship between costs and output may be linear over a certain range of output, but as output rises, over-

Fig 8.6 The inclusion of assumptions and conventions in a spreadsheet

	A	B	C	D
1	*The ABC Company Inc*			
2	**Assumptions and conventions**			
3	Note: all monies in £mn unless otherwise stated			
4	There is no restriction on the amount of overtime that can be worked			

time or subcontracting must be used to produce the extra output and this causes a discontinuous jump in cost levels. If only the linear relationship is in the spreadsheet, then the spreadsheet would not cover overtime or subcontracting and thus the range of application of the spreadsheet would be restricted to outputs that could be covered in normal working. A further important aspect is to state any symbolic conventions that may be used. For example, in investment appraisal it is conventional for cash inflows to be taken to be positive, cash outflows to be negative.

◆ **Key concept**   *It is good practice to document within the spreadsheet itself the **range of application** of the spreadsheet, **other limitations**, any **assumptions** and any **symbolic conventions** underlying the spreadsheet.*

You will probably find it valuable to have the name of the file that holds the spreadsheet entered permanently into the summary model section of the spreadsheet. This means that you will not become confused between the paper outputs that you might produce from different spreadsheets. In addition, it is useful to reduce the chance of confusion even further by arranging for the time and date when the results were produced to be automatically printed with the results.

LOGIC MANAGEMENT

Logic management is perhaps a rather grandiose name for being in control of the logic in the spreadsheet – knowing how relationships have been developed, over what range they are applicable and whether the relationships are appropriate or not. It is about good practice in developing the logic model.

The first element of good practice is further to subdivide the logic model modules into logically integrated subunits – for the same reasons that modularisation of the full spreadsheet was recommended. Assigning titles, such as *Logic model for the manufacturing function*, to the top left-hand corner of each of the spreadsheet modules can be a useful aid.

Recalling the methodology of Chapter 5, verbalisation is the translation of the information flow diagram of the conceptual model into precise verbal relationships. Important aspects of the validation of this translation are to check for each relationship: its 'shape', its dimensions, the units used, and its range of application. These checks will now be discussed in turn.

Checking the 'shape' of a relationship

Consider the case where a relationship links the price of a product and its sales. A relationship with the shape shown in Fig 8.7a might be sketched. There are simple tests that should be applied to check on its feasibility.

Fig 8.7 Checking the 'shape'

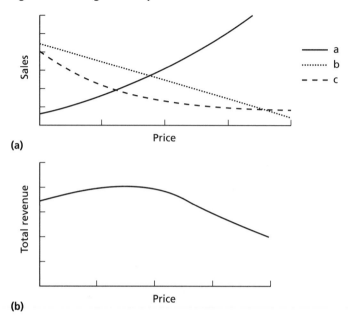

(a)

(b)

The first check is to look at the behaviour of the relationship at the 'extremes', i.e., when the values of the factors are very high and very low within the range of application of the model. With the graphs in Fig 8.7 the test would be at high values of price and close to zero price. Consider curve a. Is it reasonable that low price is associated with low sales and a high price with high sales? This is most unlikely apart from the most exceptional of goods. Thus relationship a would not seem to be appropriate.

What now of the relationship sketched in curve b, which has the attraction that the 'extreme' values look feasible – high price is associated with low sales and vice versa. A further check is on the shape between the extremes. Is it likely that the relationship is a straight line – meaning that the same-sized change in price results in the same-sized change in sales whatever the price might be – at high prices as at low prices? This is unlikely: it would seem much more likely that as prices are raised equal increments in price would have a smaller and smaller effect on sales – and thus curve c would seem to be the more likely 'shape'.

Having checked at the extremes and the general shape in between, another check is of the 'bumps' in the curve. Looking now at Fig 8.7b, which shows the relationship between total revenue and price, a 'bump' in the revenue is expected when the price is 'middling'. Is this reasonable, or would a consistent increase or decrease in the contribution as price is increased be more reasonable?

Checking the dimensions

The second check on the individual relationships is to ensure that the factors used within a relationship have *consistent dimensions*. The factor *Number of peas in a pod* is a simple number, unlike the factor *Cost* or *Distance between Paris and London* which are not, since they have associated dimensions – *Cost* has the dimension of a monetary unit ($US, DM, Fr or some other currency) and *Distance* the dimension of length (km, mile etc). To simply state the numerical value of either the *Cost* or *Distance* would be meaningless. A dimension must be specified and in relationships the dimensions used must be consistent.

Consider equation 8.1, which represents an attempt to relate the fuel used on a journey to other journey characteristics:

$$Fuel\ used = Distance\ travelled \times Speed \tag{8.1}$$

By considering the dimensions of the three factors, it can easily be seen that equation 8.1 cannot be a valid relationship. The dimension of *Fuel used* is a volume, that of *Distance travelled* is a length, and *Speed* has the dimension of length/time. In dimensional terms equation 8.1 becomes:

$$volume = length \times length\ /\ time \tag{8.2}$$

Since volume itself has the dimensions length × length × length (or length^3), equation 8.2 can be written:

$$length^3 = length^2\ /time \tag{8.3}$$

or, dividing by length^2:

$$length = 1\ /time \tag{8.4}$$

which cannot be correct.

A second equation:

$$Fuel\ used = \frac{[Distance\ travelled]}{Distance/Unit\ of\ fuel\ consumption} \tag{8.5}$$

is dimensionally consistent. *Unit of fuel consumption* has the dimension of volume (or length^3), and so in terms of dimensions, equation 8.5 becomes equation 8.6 in which the dimensions on both sides of the relationship are the same:

$$length^3 = \frac{length}{length/length^3} = length^3 \tag{8.6}$$

Checking the units

A further check is needed to ensure that *consistent units* are being used. For example, in equation 8.5 it would be inconsistent to use kilometres for *Distance travelled* and miles for *Distance*. Note that units are not always consistent in the original sources of data. One of us has a car handbook that gives the fuel tank sizes in litres but discusses fuel consumption in miles per gallon!

The specification of units has not been done in Fig 8.4 and this has contributed to a gross error: there is the incorrect addition of *Cost of units used* in pence and the *Connection charge* in £ to calculate the *Quarterly charge*. Such errors are usually picked up and corrected eventually, but sometimes not until a great deal of extra effort has been expended and credibility in the model (and modeller) has been lost. The spreadsheet in Fig 8.5 reduces the likelihood of such errors.

Checks on the consistency of the dimensions and units are a form of verification, in that the tests applied are rigorous and standard: a relationship failing the tests would be deemed 'incorrect'.

Checking the range of application of a relationship

Earlier we noted that it was important to specify the range of application of a spreadsheet: the range over which relationships in the spreadsheet remain appropriate. Here we look at this area in a little more detail.

Consider the minicase of a manufacturing department.

MINICASE Range of application of a relationship

A department in a manufacturing organisation is trying to establish what its variable costs might be over the next year. One large element of cost is the personnel cost. The sales demand and thus the manufacturing requirement are not known with any great accuracy and are bound to be revised several times. It has been decided to formulate a spreadsheet that will allow the number of people and thus the variable personnel costs, to be calculated, instead of repeatedly asking the manager of the department for estimates of the number of people that would be required. To this end the manager has been asked for their estimates and has replied as follows: for an output of 20 million packs per year they estimate that they require 75 people; for 25 million packs per year, 90 people; for 27 million packs per year, 100 people; for 30 million packs per year, 110 people, and to produce 35 million packs they require 130 people. Plotting the values estimated by the manager produces Fig 8.8.

The points suggest that a straight-line relationship between output and number of people required may adequately represent the manager's situation. A fit of the straight line to the points could have been derived using the statistical tech-

Fig 8.8 Relationship of output and people required

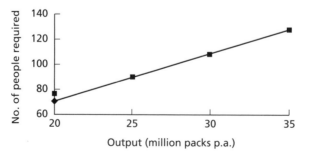

Table 8.1 Comparison of the number of people required

Output	Number of people required		
(Millions p.a.)	Specified	From graph	Difference
20	75	70	–5
25	90	90	0
27	100	98	–2
30	110	110	0
35	130	130	0

nique of regression (see Chapter 15), but very often a fit by eye is perfectly acceptable. The line in Fig 8.8, was drawn in this way. As shown in Table 8.1, the fit of the straight line to the points is very close for all output volumes between 25 and 35 million packs per year. A difference of five people is shown for an output of 20 million packs per year and this may be too large a discrepancy for the relationship represented by the line to be acceptable in the spreadsheet. If it is too large, then the straight-line relationship would not be valid for outputs below 25 million packs. Around outputs of 35 million packs the fit of the line to the points is perfect and thus the relationship is apparently valid in this range. So good is the fit that there must be a temptation to extrapolate the line to cover cases where the output is greater than 35 million packs per year.

Sometimes the situation in which the model is being used forces such extrapolation, but it is always a risky procedure since the relationship is being used in unfamiliar territory, where the comfort of firm data does not exist. Perhaps there are physical constraints that prevent an output of more than 35 million packs per year being possible, or perhaps a double shift would be needed and this would require a great many more people. Because the line drawn in Fig 8.8 is a straight line, i.e. it is linear, the algebraic representation of the relationship between the number of people required and the output volume must be of the form:

$$\text{Number of people required} = A + B \times Output \qquad (8.9)$$

where A and B are constants. Any two sets of values may be used to obtain values for A and B: here the values for 90 people and 130 people will be used. Substituting into equation 8.9 and working in millions of packs gives:

$$90 = A + B \times 25 \qquad (8.10)$$

and:

$$130 = A + B \times 35$$

Manipulating equations 8.10 gives A = –10 and B = 4 thus:

$$\text{Number of people required} = -10 + 4 \times Output \qquad (8.11)$$

where *Output* is measured in million packs per year. Equation 8.11 is not sufficient to fully define the relationship; the range over which it is valid needs to be expressed as well. This appears to be for outputs between 25 and 35 million packs per year. Thus, the relationship can be expressed as equation 8.11 with the caveats: $25 < Output$ and $Output < 35$, where $25 < Output$ means that the *Output* must be greater than or equal to 25 (million) and $Output < 35$ means that the *Output* must be less than or equal to 35 (million). These caveats can be succinctly expressed in the constraint:

$$25 < Output < 35 \qquad\qquad (8.12)$$

It is worth noting that in arriving at equation 8.11 it has been assumed that it was possible to interpolate between the values specified by the manager, by joining up the points with a straight line. In fact, this may not have been valid. It would not have been valid had the relationship been a 'stepped' one, i.e. if at one or more production volumes it had been necessary to make a sharp change in the number of people employed.

♦ **Key concept**

Extrapolation is the extension of the application of a relationship outside the range over which the relationship has been validated. In general, the greater the extent of the extrapolation the less valid the application of the relationship becomes.

Interpolation is the use of a relationship in a region between the points at which the relationship has been tested. The greater the distance between the tested points and the point where the application is to be used, the less confidence one can have that the relationship applies.

Further considerations

Spreadsheet formulae are generally derived from the verbalisation by substituting cell references in place of the factors in each relationship. However, it makes checking and maintenance of the spreadsheet much easier if the factor names, where possible exactly those used in the verbalisation, are used in the spreadsheet. It's a lot easier to interpret *Revenue = Sales × Price* than +D45*F67! However, this is a painstaking job to do thoroughly and in most spreadsheet packages there are limits on the number of names (as low as 100) and the length of names that make it even more difficult.

It is often the case, even for the DIY user, that it is wise to protect or lock some of the entries in a spreadsheet. For example, you may not want to run the risk of corrupting some of the formulae. A particularly common problem – well vouched for by the authors! – is inadvertently to overwrite formulae with data values. Some data values also need protection. For example, VAT rates are changed infrequently and very formally and thus should be protected from the chance of inappropriate change. However, values of variables that are part of an exploratory analysis 'What if? the cost/unit in the electricity tariff case were to change?' need to be quickly and easily accessible. Most spreadsheets offer various levels of protection and the most appropriate form of protection should be considered.

Excel allows you to add notes to cells and indicates that there is a note attached through a small red dot in the top right-hand corner of the cell. This allows the good practice of adding notes to a formula, such as *In this formula, it is assumed that costs are linearly related to output* or *Note that this formula is only valid for positive values of profit.*

Care should be taken when inserting and deleting rows and columns, especially the effect on parts of the spreadsheet that are not visible on the screen at the time of the change. Formulae update OK, but it is very easy to 'ruin' a look-up table by inserting or deleting a row or column in the middle. Graphs and charts can be messed up in the same way, but usually this is easy to identify.

DATA MANAGEMENT

Data management is the efficient and effective disposition of data. A database management system does this for you in specialised database packages. The concern for the spreadsheet user is to ensure that the access paths to the databases are secure and that you know what you are getting from the database.

Databases have been defined here to be those bases of data over which the user has no control. A first significant matter is for the spreadsheet user to understand just what the data values refer to. This is not a trivial point. For example, when sales are considered in a forecast, are these determined when an agreement has been reached that somebody will buy them, when the goods are shipped or when the cash for them is received?

The data in the database is almost certain to be dynamic, being updated continuously or at fixed intervals – once a day or once a week. For decision support, which is geared to the future, it is unlikely that the precise values of the data are important cognitively but they can be psychologically. In one case known to the authors, a decision support system for long-term forecasting was not used because the managers who were to use its outputs were unhappy with the data on the current stock positions that were in the data model. That almost any stock positions would have no appreciable effect on (the cognitive aspects of) decision making cut no ice – the managers were uneasy, and the imprecision in the data gave them an excuse to defer use of the decision aid! Thus it is important to know how often the data are updated in the database and which version of the database is being downloaded to the spreadsheet. It is good practice to ensure that the date on which the downloading took place is recorded in the data model.

Three sources of spreadsheet data other than database were identified in Chapter 6: data obtained from other decision aids, data held in look-up tables and data that is input by the user as operator. Further aspects of specific data sources will be discussed in Chapter 17. We are now going to consider the management of the data downloaded from a database and the other data used in a spreadsheet.

A major consideration is never to input the same piece of data more than once. Doing this is time consuming but it also allows inconsistencies to creep into the spreadsheet. This is one reason, of course, to download data already in a database for use in the spreadsheet, rather than inputting it a second time. Returning to Fig 8.5, note that the VAT rate is input twice: this is bad practice as it could happen that one of the values is changed and the other is not. Thus where the same value is used more than once in different sections it is good practice to open a section to hold such values. This is shown in Fig 8.9.

Fig 8.9 A spreadsheet of the electricity tariff issue (even better practice!)

	A	B	C
1	**Electricity tariff problem**		
2	**General data**		
3	VAT rate (%)	15	
4	**Ordinary tariff – quarterly costs**		*Spreadsheet relationships*
5			
6	Cost/unit (pence)	3	
7	Units used	3000	
8	Connection charge (£)	100	
9	Cost of units used (£)	90	+B7*B6/100
10	Quarterly cost (£)	190	+B8+B9
11	VAT payable (£)	14	+B10*(B3/100)
12			
13	**'Small-user' tariff – quarterly costs**		
14			
15	Cost/unit (pence)	5	
16	Units used	3000	
17	Connection charge (£)	50	
18	Cost of units used (£)	150	+B16*B15/100
19	Quarterly cost (£)	200	+B17+B18
20	VAT payable (%)	14	+B19*(B3/100)

◆ **Key concept**   *Never include the values of any coefficients and parameters within formulae: make these factors part of the data model and refer to the relevant cell in the formulae that use them.*

As mentioned in the previous section, Excel allows you to add notes to cells and indicates that there is a note attached through a small red dot in the top right-hand corner of the cell. This allows the good practice of adding notes to data values, such as *This data value was obtained from the finance director on 6 March* or *Note that this data value is only an initial estimate: a more accurate value is promised by the sales department in July.*

Cell widths and appropriate formats can be used to give visual clues as to anomalies in the data. This can be seen to some extent in Fig 8.10, where the value of 22.2 is visually 'out of line' with the other values. However, this visual clue could be made much more powerful if the width of the cells is made so that data values larger than the cell widths are indicated by a string of asterisks. The

Fig 8.10 Limit checking

	A	B	C
1	Year and Quarter	£–$ rate	
2			
3	1996 Q1	2.3	= IF(AND(+B3>=1,+B3<=2.5),"OK","Rate outside limit")
4	1996 Q2	22.2	= IF(AND(+B4>=1,+B4<=2.5),"OK","Rate outside limit")
5	1996 Q3	1.8	= IF(AND(+B5>=1,+B5<=2.5),"OK","Rate outside limit")
6	1996 Q4	1.5	= IF(AND(+B6>=1,+B6<=2.5),"OK","Rate outside limit")
7	1997 Q1	2.4	= IF(AND(+B7>=1,+B7<=2.5),"OK","Rate outside limit")
8	1997 Q2	1.4	= IF(AND(+B8>=1,+B8<=2.5),"OK","Rate outside limit")
9	1997 Q3	1.4	= IF(AND(+B9>=1,+B9<=2.5),"OK","Rate outside limit")
10	1997 Q4	1.0	= IF(AND(+B10>=1,+B10<=2.5),"OK","Rate outside limit")

value of 22.2 in quarter 2 of 1996 has a width of 4, whereas the required values all have widths of 3. Thus setting the column width at 3 and the format to one decimal place will result in 22.2 being considered too large and being flagged as such through the asterisks.

Limit-checking formulae can also be used to ensure that the data values are sensible. Suppose a set of values of the £–$ exchange rate are input. These inputs (at present!) cannot reasonably lie outside the range of 1 and 2.5. However, you can guard against simple input errors associated with a misplaced decimal point by incorporating the relations shown in column C of Fig 8.10.

The formulae in column C would place the warning message 'Rate outside limit' in cell C4 but not into the other cells in column C.

While range checking has indicated the 'grossly' incorrect exchange rate entry of 22.2 in cell C4, graphs can be used to bring attention to less obvious errors. With the value of C4 corrected to the required value of 2.2, a graph of the set of exchange rates and shown in Fig 8.11 highlights the apparent anomaly in the first quarter of 1997.

You may wish to put into the spreadsheet a reminder that you need to consider (or must change) a particular value. One solution, perhaps, is to use colour to highlight each volatile piece of data. Some values might change systematically (date, for example). Most spreadsheet packages allow for the

Fig 8.11 £–$ exchange rate movements

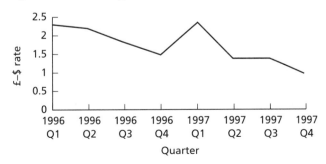

121

automatic entry of today's date. This can be a problem if the user wants to know exactly when something was done in the past.

MENUS AND SHORT-CUT KEYS

Anyone who has used a spreadsheet has navigated around a system by selecting from a 'menu' of items presented on a screen. The selection of an item in one menu often leads to the presentation of a second menu and so on. With such a hierarchy of menus the user can easily and safely select the support that is required.

What generally happens when you operate a spreadsheet is that you wish to alter or simply check certain input values, follow this up with a look at some interim results on the screen and then obtain hard copy. If you have segmented your spreadsheet along the lines suggested earlier in this chapter, you will want to go to certain input areas many times. You can do this through setting up your own system of menus by constructing macros in the programming language provided with the spreadsheet, or you can use facilities that the spreadsheet provides.[3] And you can incorporate these macro instructions within a short-cut key.

In menu design there is the question of 'breadth versus depth'. As a rule of thumb, research suggests that menus should not generally contain more than seven or eight items, although having more does not seem to have any great disadvantages. However, having an extended hierarchy of menus can be most infuriating. Taken to its extreme, one could envisage a set of menus in which the user is simply offered a yes–no choice at each level, requiring many levels to be employed for the user to make a single selection.

SUMMARY

In this chapter the developer's role and specifically the design of the spreadsheet have been considered. The search has been for good practice that produces a valid spreadsheet in the first place, yet also makes the spreadsheet easy to maintain and enhance: i.e. to make the spreadsheet as 'future proof' as is reasonably possible.

The first main feature of good spreadsheet design is to use a modular construction: keeping the logic and data models separate and further modularising these models to reflect the functional structure within the organisation. It is important to document the assumptions and conventions underlying the spreadsheet and, in some cases, to document how relationships were developed and the source of data. Logic management consists of checking the shape of individual relationships and the consistency of the dimensions and units used. Determining the range of application of the spreadsheet is an important issue. Data management is concerned with the efficient and effective disposition of data, especially that from corporate or external databases. Tips to prevent incorrect data being used in the spreadsheet have been given.

END NOTES

1 For the manager who has had a spreadsheet built for them or who acquires a spreadsheet on taking up a new job, a third method of validation exists: they can simply have so much faith in the spreadsheet builders that they leave all the validation to them. The association of particular people with the spreadsheet is sufficient to give the spreadsheet a good name.

2 A note of caution here. The terms validation and verification have been used as they are in the USA. British spreadsheet builders tend to switch the definitions and use validation for verification and vice versa. Our view is that standardisation of terms is helpful: we have chosen to standardise on the US nomenclature purely on the grounds that there are more US spreadsheet builders than British ones.

3 For example, within Excel you could set up a cell called, say, Inputs, and have a note attached to it. This note would specify which cell to go to so that you get to the required input section. Or easier still, use the goto facility within the edit menu to go to a referenced name. For instance, with the four-function manufacturing model earlier, if you have a title to each input section then you need only reference with *Data Input for Manufacturing* or simply *Manufacturing* to have the appropriate module displayed to you. In Excel you can add to Excel's own menu scheme (in the Tools menu) to have your own macros 'on tap'. Lotus 1-2-3 allows you to write your own menus.

FURTHER READING

The book by T. Rubin, *User Interface Design for Computer Systems,* Ellis Horwood, Chichester, 1988, goes into some detail about the design considerations for human–computer interfaces, mainly from an information systems perspective. More directly relevant to decision support systems is Chapter 7, 'Dialog Management,' in Ralph H. Sprague Jr and Eric D. Carlson, *Building Effective Decision Support Systems,* Prentice Hall, New Jersey, USA, 1982.

EXERCISES

1 What are the differences between the user as developer and as operator?

2 What do you understand by the term *volatile* when applied to data?

3 Does the data model include simply *data values* or does it also include the variables themselves?

4 What are the good design practices for a spreadsheet overall?

5 What are the good design practices for the logic model?

6 What are the good design practices for the data model?

7 What are the advantages of putting in data once only? Are there any disadvantages?

8 Define the term *maintenance.*

9 Define the term *enhancement.*

10 Figure 8.12 reproduces Fig 5.7 from Exercise 6 in Chapter 5.
The model should calculate *Sales revenue, Total variable costs, Profit, Profit per month* and *Percentage change in profit from year to year.*
   a) If you haven't already done so, redo your spreadsheet to separate the logic and data models.

Fig 8.12 Readyread trading account

A		B	C	D
1			Year	
2		1997	1998	1999
3				
4	Sales estimates (million)	2.7	3.0	3.0
5	Sales price (£)	5	5	5
6	Raw materials costs (pence/book)	40	40	40
7	Royalty (pence/book)	75	80	80
8	Labour costs (pence/book)	170	180	180
9	Fixed costs (£'000)	5000	5200	5600

b) Add headings to the sections.

c) Add in checking (as described) to check that no silly input values for the sales estimates remain undetected.

d) Consider what assumptions and conventions may apply to the spreadsheet. Investigate the facilities offered by your spreadsheet for adding notes to spreadsheets and spreadsheet cells. Insert the assumptions and conventions into your spreadsheet.

e) Investigate your spreadsheet to see if you can alter its menus to go directly to a specific area of the spreadsheet.

f) Investigate the facilities that your spreadsheet has for protecting cells. Decide which cells you think should be protected and implement this with your spreadsheet.

11 Table 8.2 gives the sales that have been made over the last 12 months. These were to be input from the computer keyboard. Devise one or more checking procedures to ensure that the correct inputs would have been accepted and the incorrect inputs would have been flagged or rejected.

Table 8.2 Sales

Month	Sales	Keyboard Input
January	31015	31015
February	27406	274060
March	24874	24874
April	23657	23657
May	20769	30769
June	20247	20247
July	19657	19657
August	18007	18007
September	18192	18192
October	19400	1940
November	21365	21365
December	28976	28976

Part Two

OVERVIEW OF PART TWO

The intention of this book is to explore ways in which the spreadsheet can be used to help managers to handle the issues they face in their organisations, by building and exploring appropriate models of parts of the local scenario. Although the spreadsheet is not the only tool that can be used for this purpose, it is the certainly the most commonly available and most familiar, perhaps the cheapest and for many people the easiest to use. Part Two of this book starts from the reader's own experiences with using a spreadsheet and the theoretical knowledge of Part One in order to develop practical spreadsheets. This overview discusses how this development has been treated and explains the rationale for the choice of topics.

The assumption we have made about you, the reader, is that you will have used a spreadsheet and thus have some familiarity with its basic features. Part One will have extended your 'theoretical' knowledge. Part Two assumes this level of knowledge and moves on to explore in practical detail the use of specific tools and applications.

Chapter 9 provides a structured explanation of the spreadsheet facilities that managers are most likely to find generally useful, centering on the built-in functions that are available in modern spreadsheets. There are two structurally different types of built-in functions: those that are used instead of a complex or long formula, and those performing calculations that would be difficult or impossible to carry out with a formula using only arithmetic operations. However, we have split them by *usefulness* into three groups. The first group are those we consider essential: these include some of the mathematical and statistical functions, such as sum, count, mean and standard deviation, plus look-up and logical functions. The second group are those that are likely to find a use in several application areas: these include the database and financial functions. Finally, there are the functions that might be useful in a few limited areas: these include the calendar, engineering, information and text functions. Chapter 9 ends with a short discussion on *What if?* analyses, in which we explore the consequences of asking questions such as: *What if the sales were 20 per cent less than expected?* or *What if the VAT rate is reduced to 10 per cent?*

Up to the end of Chapter 9, uncertainty about the values of the input variables is dealt with either by the manager simply changing the contents of the appropriate cells, or by considering all the possibilities. Although such methods have their uses, they represent a rather simple approach to handling uncertainty. In Chapter 10 a more sophisticated view is taken under the heading of risk analysis. Probability distributions and sampling are introduced and the intricacies of dealing with both discrete and continuous variables are discussed. The steps required to build and use a risk-analysis spreadsheet are listed and described.

A simulation also involves a model that includes uncertainty in the form of sampling from probability distributions. Thus, in a technical sense, Chapter 11 which deals with simulation is a continuation of Chapter 10, since the spreadsheets being produced rely for their usefulness on the inclusion of uncertainty. However, there is a significant difference in emphasis concerning what is actually being modelled. Risk analysis is mainly concerned with the sort of variables that would typically appear in financial reports, while within simulation a wider view is taken to include all aspects of a company's operations. Simulations concentrate on issues related to the dynamic behaviour of parts of the local scenario.

To this point, we have examined the spreadsheet facilities that allow *What if?* analysis to be used to explore many of the features of the manager's world incorporated in a spreadsheet model. However, *What if?* or *trial-and-error* approaches – even if they are as systematic as we have described in Chapters 10 and 11 – are not always what is needed. Sometimes the manager will want the spreadsheet to work out answers directly: *What should be?* or *What's best?* rather than *What if?* That's where the two related but different techniques of goal seeking and solving come in. These techniques are fully explained in Chapter 12. Goal seeking and solving are providing what we have termed *solutions* in Chapter 1 – but through interpretation of the output that they provide, they offer much more than a single best answer; they also allow exploration of many of the consequences of possible managerial action.

Managers are often involved in running projects, which we define as a set of integrated activities that need to be completed by a specified date. Although planning complex projects provides managers with some of their biggest problems, even smaller projects, such as producing an advertising leaflet or organising the departmental social trip, can be helped through a systematic approach and computer assistance. Chapter 13 describes some of these approaches, often known as critical path analysis or project evaluation and review technique (PERT). The techniques have been available for many years, but it is only recently that tools have been readily available within or closely associated with spreadsheets. These techniques concentrate on the interaction between time and cost, and enable the manager to work out the answers to key questions such as: *How long will the project take?* or *What effect will a delay in one of the activities have?*

In some of the earlier chapters in Part Two ways of dealing with uncertainty are discussed. What these chapters do not do is treat statistics in any substantive way. Statistics may be thought of as the science of summarising and drawing conclusions from data. It is mainly concerned with quantitative data, but this does not exclude qualitative data entirely. As its practitioners will tell you, there is a certain amount of 'art' in it, too. In Chapter 14 we look at the use of statistics in understanding and exploring the local scenario, and at the facilities that spreadsheets provide to help with this. We concentrate on two aspects of statistics. The first is descriptive *statistics* where the aim is to summarise the most important information that can be gleaned from a set of data, in particular to describe data through such summary measures as the mean, median and mode (for central tendency), and the range, interquartile range, standard deviation and variance (for spread).

The second is inferential statistics, which allows a manager to go further than simply describing a set of data, by drawing inferences about the wider world from the data that is available. This includes confidence intervals (making estimates based on a sample, allowing for the possible effect of sampling error), hypothesis testing (looking at whether apparent differences are really significant or the result of chance fluctuations) and correlation (a technique to measure the association between variables).

Forecasting what is going to happen, both within an organisation and outside it, is one of the core activities of management. All organisations must forecast to some extent if they are to plan for the future. Chapter 15 is concerned with the types of forecasts that meet two requirements. First, they are concerned with quantitative rather than qualitative matters; how many pairs of shoes we will sell next month for example, rather than what next year's fashionable styles and colours will be. Second, it must be assumed that the future will resemble the past in some sense and that relevant past data are available on which to base the forecasts. Two types of forecast are discussed. The first is time series analysis, where past data is directly extended to forecast future values under the assumption that all that you can ever know about the future is contained in the data values for that variable that have actually occurred in the past. The second is causal forecasting, where forecasts are derived from a knowledge of the cause-and-effect relations between different variables – for example, using knowledge of the link between disposable income and spending patterns. Thus causal forecasting can be stronger than time series analysis because it relies on the patterns of the past not simply the data values that happened to occur.

Although there is no doubt that the spreadsheet package is the leading PC software modelling tool for the individual manager, and (along with the word-processor) the package that any individual business user is most likely to use personally, in terms of routine applications the database package is the most important software package for most organisations. Although databases and spreadsheets grew up separately, as with many computing developments the functionality that they offer has converged in recent years. This convergence has been encouraged by the growth of so-called relational database packages, one of the principles of which is that the data are stored in two-dimensional *tables* set out in rows and columns. The similarity of this to a spreadsheet is immediately apparent, and it was a short step to treating parts of a spreadsheet (or indeed all of it) as if it were a relational database table. Relational databases are now the most common form of database, especially on PCs. In Chapter 16 we consider in more detail the relationship between spreadsheet packages and databases, picking up from Chapter 6 in Part One. We look at data in spreadsheets in terms of database concepts and terminology, and examine how to carry out basic database activities in spreadsheets.

In Chapter 17 the various sources of data that might be useful to managers using spreadsheets are described. Six categories of data are considered: personal data, corporate data, commercial databases, on-line databases, databases on CD-ROM, and the Internet and the World Wide Web. We look at these in terms of seven characteristics: data security and privacy, data volume, data formats, data cost, data integrity, data accuracy and data timeliness. These are then related to four longer-term activities involved when using a spreadsheet model, namely maintaining data, accessing data, understanding data and relying on data.

Finally, in Chapter 18 we go beyond the spreadsheet – at least as it has been in the previous 17 chapters! First, because there will be times when it is necessary for the manager to use software other than that available in a spreadsheet in order to build and use an appropriate information or decision aid, we look at some of the spreadsheet add-ins that are available for the manager who needs extended modelling capabilities. Then we review some of the likely spreadsheet tools that the manager may find available over the next five years or so. This 'crystal ball gazing' is helped considerably by the realisation that the chronology of spreadsheet functionality has been quite consistent. Initially, something is only available in a specialised package. Then it becomes available as an add-in for the major spreadsheet packages. Third, it becomes part of the functionality of an up-dated version of the spreadsheet package. The only thing that we can be sure of is that in five years' time the modelling capabilities of spreadsheets will be even greater, and easier to use, than they already are today.

CHAPTER 9

Beyond spreadsheet basics

Various spreadsheet features and facilities have already been used in the examples in Part I. The aim of this chapter is to give a more structured explanation of the spreadsheet facilities that managers building models are most likely to find generally useful. The subsequent chapters in Part II will then explore specific features and applications in more detail.

- Introduction
- Built-in functions
  - Main categories of function • Mathematical and statistical • Look-up
  - Logical • Database • Financial • Calendar/date and time • Engineering
  - information • Text
- 'What if' analysis

INTRODUCTION

Like the ancient Roman god Janus, in this chapter we look simultaneously in two directions. Facing one way, the 'technical' direction, we look at the capabilities of current spreadsheet packages. The illustrative examples of spreadsheets given in Part I have barely even scratched the surface of what a spreadsheet can do as a modelling tool. Much of this chapter will therefore be spent looking at the range of built-in functions available to managers in spreadsheet packages.

Facing the other way, the 'managerial' direction, we consider what support spreadsheets can provide to managers in issue handling. Here we will concentrate on 'What if?' analysis – the home territory of the spreadsheet as a modelling tool. The phrase 'What if?' analysis came from the use of spreadsheets to consider 'What will happen if we do this?' or 'What will happen if this situation occurs?' For example, what will happen to the contribution to profit if we increase all our prices by 5 per cent? Or, in the electricity tariff example in Chapter 5, what will happen to our costs if the connection charges remain unchanged, but the costs per unit rise by 15 per cent? Or by 1.2p per unit?

Naturally, the concepts of built-in functions and 'What if' analysis are even more powerful when used together, but we shall begin by considering them separately.

BUILT-IN FUNCTIONS

Ever since their invention by Bricklin and Frankston, in the form of the VisiCalc package, it has been realised that spreadsheets need to go beyond the basic arithmetic operations of addition, subtraction, multiplication and division. These operations can, of course, be combined; part of the power of the spreadsheet originally came from the ability to do this by putting formulae which refer to other cells, rather than just numbers, into each cell. However, the power of the spreadsheet has also been considerably increased by the inclusion of *built-in functions* to perform more advanced operations.

Some built-in functions are shorthand for arithmetic operations that could be done with a formula, such as the SUM function,[1] which adds up the values in several cells; SUM(A1..A10) is quicker and easier than having to type A1+A2+A3+A4+A5+A6+A7+A8+A9+A10 into a cell! In these days of graphical user interfaces, the range of cells used in the function can usually also be selected by 'pointing and clicking', a further benefit.

Other built-in functions, like MAX and MIN, which find the largest and smallest values in a range of cells respectively, or SQRT, which finds the (positive) square root of a number, perform calculations that would be difficult or tedious to carry out with a formula using only arithmetic operations. In VisiCalc, these typically came from functions or routines that had been found useful in earlier computer programming languages like BASIC or FORTRAN.[2] Since then, the list of functions has grown considerably, thanks to a combination of technological 'push' and demand 'pull', so that whereas an early 1980s spreadsheet might have had 40 or 50 built-in functions, a present-day one might have 250 or more. We shall concentrate here on those functions that make the task of building models easier, whether they happen to be newer additions or 'old faithfuls'. Other functions serve rather different purposes; we will mention some of them, but only in passing.[3]

◆ **Key concept**   *Built-in functions fall into two types: those that are used instead of a complex or long formula involving arithmetic operations, and those performing calculations that would be difficult or impossible to carry out with a formula using only arithmetic operations.*

Note that nearly all built-in functions require extra information in brackets after the function name, for example to tell the SQRT function the number or cell value whose square root is needed. Thus SQRT(16) would return the value 4, while SQRT(C5) would return the square root of the value in cell C5. The entries in brackets are known as the *arguments* of the function. The SQRT function always has just one argument. On the other hand, the SUM function can have a variable number of arguments, to indicate which cell values to add together. These could be either a list of cell references, or a range of cells, as in our example (A1..A10). We shall see later that some built-in functions have more complex sets of arguments, including arguments that serve different purposes.

Main categories of function

For once, there appears to be considerable agreement between the authors of the different spreadsheet packages about what are the main categories of built-in function. For example, Lotus 1-2-3 lists 10 categories in version 4.01, and Microsoft Excel lists 11 in version 5.0. As shown in Table 9.1, these map directly on to each other, with the exception of Microsoft's additional 'DDE & External' category, which comprises only three functions and is associated with linking software within the Windows environment. Other packages have similar category lists.

However, there is not always such close agreement as to which functions come under which categories! For example, we chose SUM as the first built-in function to mention, not only because it is one of the most basic, but because its name is the same in every spreadsheet package we have ever seen. However, while Microsoft Excel categorises SUM under 'Math & Trigonometry', Lotus 1-2-3's @SUM is listed under 'Statistical'. Conversely, the function LARGE, which finds the nth largest value in a range, is 'Statistical' in Excel but 'Mathematical' in 1-2-3! Our advice is to regard the headings as indicative, rather than definitive. In any event, it is essential that you learn the details of any specific built-in functions that you intend to use in your particular spreadsheet package and version.

In the rest of this chapter, we shall use the Lotus 1-2-3 category names, merely because they are shorter. We discuss the categories in what we consider to be descending order of usefulness to the modeller; as we see it, this runs as follows:

Essential
- Mathematical and statistical (wherever the line between them is drawn!)
- Look-up
- Logical

Highly recommended
- Database
- Financial

Table 9.1 List of categories of built-in functions

Microsoft Excel	Lotus 1-2-3
Database & List Management	Database
Date & Time	Calendar
DDE & External	
Engineering	Engineering
Financial	Financial
Information	Information
Logical	Logical
Lookup & Reference	Lookup
Math & Trigonometry	Mathematical
Statistical	Statistical
Text	Text

Not very useful
- Calendar
- Engineering
- Information
- Text

However, any manager may find any function useful in the appropriate circumstances. We would therefore again encourage you to find out, and explore, the complete range of built-in functions for your favourite spreadsheet package.

◆ Key concept   *From the validation point of view you really must know exactly what the functions you are using in your spreadsheet actually do!*

Mathematical and statistical

These contain many of the essential built-in functions for the managerial spreadsheet user, and several more which we shall discuss later in Chapters 10 (Risk analysis), 11 (Simulation), 14 (Statistics) and 15 (Forecasting). They do also contain some which will be of rather less use to managers, such as the trigonometric and hyperbolic functions.

We shall subdivide the essential functions under five headings. The headings are:

- quick arithmetic
- rounding
- counting
- mathematical operations
- 'think of a number'.

Quick arithmetic (SUM, SUMPRODUCT, PRODUCT, MEAN)   We have already said that SUM is one of the most important built-in functions for the modeller. SUMPRODUCT, which adds up the products of the cell values in two ranges of cells, runs it pretty close. Figure 9.1 shows a simplified stock file.

SUM(B2..B9) is used to produce the total number of items in stock, shown in cell B11, and the total value of stock on hand is shown by SUMPRODUCT

Fig 9.1 Use of SUM and SUMPRODUCT

	A	B	C
1	Stock item code	Number in stock	Unit price (£)
2	G1234	85	3.56
3	G1235	65	2.99
4	G1237	92	3.12
5	G1238	12	2.99
6	G1250	1	7.35
7	G1251	63	7.49
8	G1252	86	7.59
9	G1253	44	7.49
10			
11	Total no. of items	448	
12	Total stock value (£)	2281.39	

(B2..B9, C2..C9) in cell B12. As may be seen, SUMPRODUCT has two arguments, corresponding to the two ranges of cells.

On the same lines, there is also PRODUCT, which multiplies the values in a range together, but this is less commonly used in business applications. Often it is easier simply to use * instead.

MEAN (AVERAGE in Microsoft Excel, @AVG in Lotus 1-2-3) calculates the mean of the values in a particular range. It is perhaps the simplest way of summarising a set of values in a single measure; we shall look at this and other ways to summarise data, and the functions used for them, in more detail in Chapter 14.

Rounding etc. (ABS, INT, QUOTIENT, ROUND)

The ABS function returns the absolute value of a number, i.e. removes the minus sign from negative numbers. This is useful in measuring the size of errors or variances from budget, for example, as we shall see in Chapter 15.

The INT function truncates a value to a whole number (integer). For example, INT(3.75) is 3; note that INT always truncates the value 'towards' zero, so that INT(–3.75) is –3. QUOTIENT is closely related; it divides one value by another and truncates the result to an integer, thus avoiding the need to divide first and use INT afterwards.

The ROUND function is similar to INT, but more flexible; it rounds a value to a chosen number of digits and/or decimal places. For example, to round the value in cell C1 to two decimal places, you would enter the formula ROUND(C1,2). The second argument, in this case 2, is the number of decimal places to which the value should be rounded. If this value is negative, the rounding will be to the left of the decimal point, so that ROUND(362,–1) will return a value of 360. Note the difference between rounding, in which digits 5 to 9 go 'up' and digits 0 to 4 go 'down' and the truncation used by the INT function. ROUND(3.75,0) gives a value of 4, not 3. **N.B.** It is vital that you do not confuse the ROUND function with the operation of changing the display format. ROUND actually changes the value, not just the way it is displayed.

As an example of how these might be used, consider an affinity credit card scheme whereby purchases made with the card earn points which translate into money off a new car of a certain make. Typically this comes out as a number with two decimal places, but only whole points earn money off the cost of the car, so although the actual points value for a particular customer might appear in, say, cell D2 of a spreadsheet, the value to be used in calculations of how much money that customer could receive off the cost would be INT(D2).

On the other hand, suppose we are changing money between different currencies in a *bureau de change*. Exchange rates nowadays are usually quoted to four decimal places, e.g. £1 = 7.6612 French francs, but the actual money changing hands must be to two decimal places, i.e. the nearest cent, franc, penny, pfennig, etc. Thus the result of the calculation would need to be rounded to two decimal places. (A good *bureau de change* will not systematically truncate in its own favour!) It is necessary to round, rather than merely change the number of decimal places displayed, in case several converted sums are added together. Figure 9.2 shows a simple example of this; the formula in cell B3 is ROUND(B2*D1,2). Note that ROUND is the first function we have discussed that has two arguments of different kinds; the first is the number or value to be rounded, the second the number of decimal places.

Fig 9.2 Currency conversion example

A	B	C	D	E
1		Exchange rate:	£1=	7.6612	French francs
2	Amount to be changed (£)	25			
3	Amount due to customer (francs)	191.53			

A third possibility is that it is always necessary to round up, for example to determine how much needs to be ordered of a raw material that comes in 1kg packages; so that, if 3.4kg of material are needed, the number of packages to be ordered is 4. If the actual amount needed is in cell E1, say, then the only way to give the correct amount to be ordered that will work in all spreadsheets is to use a formula such as INT(E1)+1. Many spreadsheet packages do have more sophisticated rounding functions, but the precise operation of these functions, and their names, vary between packages. For example, Microsoft Excel's ROUNDDOWN and Lotus 1-2-3's @ROUNDDOWN are not quite the same; @ROUNDDOWN is more like the Excel function called FLOOR! We shall not discuss this any further here.

Sizes and positions (LARGE, MAX, MIN, PERCENTILE, PERCENTILERANK, RANK, SMALL)

MAX and MIN, as already mentioned, find the largest and smallest values of a range of values. These are ideal for operations such as selecting the best performing products or sales staff – or indeed the worst ones! LARGE and SMALL find the nth largest and nth smallest values, respectively, one of the arguments for these functions being the value of n. These are most likely to be useful in circumstances such as when the manager wants to 'find the top three products in terms of sales revenue'; MAX will give the top one, and LARGE can be used to give the next two.

RANK does exactly the reverse of this. Instead of searching for, say, the third largest value, it returns the position of a given value in a list of values. Thus if last month's orders taken by each salesperson are stored in cells B2 to B31 of a spreadsheet, and cell B17 corresponds to Kim Wilson, RANK(B17,B2..B31) will give the position of Kim Wilson in terms of orders taken – say eighth, as shown in cell B32 of Fig 9.3. PERCENTILERANK does this as a percentile; note that the name for this function varies between spreadsheet packages, including PERCENTRANK and PRANK. Note also that the value it returns is usually a *proportion* between 0 and 1 rather than the percentile that its name would imply, and that, whereas the best rank is the smallest, i.e. 1, the best percentile rank is the largest, i.e. 1 again! So PERCENTILERANK(B17,B2..B31) for Kim Wilson might return the value 0.758, say, as shown in cell B33 of Fig 9.3.

Last in this category, but not least, PERCENTILE gives the value corresponding to a particular percentile in a range of values. Again, be careful about the way in which the 'percentile' is entered; as with PERCENTILERANK, it is more likely to be in the form of a proportion, e.g. PERCENTILE(B2..B31,0.8). This gives the 80th percentile for the range of values in B2..B31, say 27560.38, as shown in cell B34 of Fig 9.3.

**Fig 9.3 Use of RANK, PERCENTILERANK
and PERCENTILE**

	A	B
1	Salesperson	Last month's orders (£)
2	Ahmed, Imtiaz	20193.83
17	Wilson, Kim	26850.37
32	Rank	8
33	Percentile rank	0.758
34	80th percentile	27560.38

Counting

There is clearly a need for some kind of COUNT function, to count cells of a particular kind. However, there is no general agreement about what the next most basic counting operation is, beyond simply counting how many cells there are. Possibilities include:

- counting cells with non-zero entries
- counting cells with non-blank entries
- counting cells with values, i.e. not text.

Figure 9.4 shows part of an organisation's personnel file. Column A gives the names of some of the employees. The organisation runs an incentive scheme offering employees the opportunity to buy shares in the organisation at a reduced price. The scheme is only open to permanent staff who have worked for the organisation for at least three years. Column B of the spreadsheet shows the number of share options each employee has purchased. Some of the values

Fig 9.4 Share scheme example (Microsoft Excel)

	A	B
1	Employee name	Number of shares purchased
2	Schmidt	100
3	McGrath	200
4	Lewis	100
5	Moody	0
6	Patel	100
7	Simmonds	N/A
8	Chang	100
9	Robinson	0
10	Dion	N/A
11	Jones	200
12		
13	Number holding shares:	
14	=COUNT(B2:B11)	8
15	=COUNTA(B2:B11)	10
16	=COUNTIF(B2:B11,>0)	6

Fig 9.5 Share scheme example (Lotus 1-2-3)

	A	B
1	Employee name	Number of shares purchased
2	Schmidt	100
3	McGrath	200
4	Lewis	100
5	Moody	0
6	Patel	100
7	Simmonds	N/A
8	Chang	100
9	Robinson	0
10	Dion	N/A
11	Jones	200
12		
13	Number holding shares:	
14	@COUNT(B2:B11)	10
15	@PURECOUNT(B2:B11)	8
16	@DCOUNT(B1:B11,B1, Number of shares purchased>0)	6

are 0, where the employee has decided not to buy the shares offered. Others show as 'N/A' (for 'not applicable'), where the employee is not eligible to buy shares. The manager needs to know how many employees have actually bought shares in the organisation. As Fig 9.4 shows, neither COUNT (which counts the number of cells with numerical values) nor COUNTA (which counts the number of cells with non-blank entries) will do this in Microsoft Excel. Only the more flexible COUNTIF gives the desired information; we discuss IF conditions later, in the subsection on logical.

Lotus 1-2-3's built-in functions share the same features, as shown in Fig 9.5, where the database @DCOUNT function is needed to answer the manager's question. A further complication is that 1-2-3's @COUNT function actually matches Excel's COUNTA; it is @PURECOUNT that is equivalent to Excel's COUNT.

Mathematical operations

Certain models will require relationships that use more sophisticated mathematical operations than can be obtained straightforwardly by the ordinary arithmetic ones. Those you are most likely to encounter are:

- EXP (the exponential function)
- FACT (the factorial of a number)
- LN (the logarithmic function)
- SQRT (the square root of a number)

We will meet some of these in the context of forecasting in Chapter 15.

Think of a number

The built-in function RAND randomly generates a number that is greater than or equal to 0 and less than (but in most spreadsheet packages not equal to) 1, all numbers in that interval being equally likely. The usefulness of this to the modeller may not be immediately apparent, but we will see its relevance in Chapters 10 and 11, when we explore risk analysis and simulation.

Look-up

Arithmetic operations or mathematical functions are not the only ones of interest to model builders. A crucial element of modelling is to be able to present, and work with, information in tables, so that information can be looked up appropriately. This is particularly relevant for a spreadsheet, because the idea of referencing entries by row and column led to spreadsheets being developed in the first place. An example of a look-up table has already been given in Chapter 6. Often tables are the only way to present and store certain information, such as the rates of income tax shown in Fig 9.6. There is no reason that the value in cell C3 should be 24 per cent, except that (presumably) the government has decided that it should be. If the value were not given, it would be impossible to guess it, although one might reasonably expect it to be somewhere in the range 20–40 per cent. This is an example of a definitional relationship, as mentioned in Chapter 5.

Tables can be used for text information as well as for numeric values. The example that is most familiar is a telephone directory. Although the telephone numbers may look like numbers, they are not numerical values in spreadsheet terms; telephone numbers are on a nominal scale, not a higher one (see Chapter 6). To prove this point, some of us are old enough to remember when UK telephone 'numbers' also had letters in them, such as the legendary WHI 1212 for Scotland Yard!

There are two types of built-in function for accessing information in tables: LOOKUP and INDEX. LOOKUP is the more common, and usually comes in two varieties: HLOOKUP and VLOOKUP. The H and V stand for horizontal and vertical respectively. The telephone directory structure, where we know someone's name and want their number, would use VLOOKUP, as shown in Fig 9.7. We go vertically down the first column ('Name') until we find the right person, say Dalton, then look along that row to their number, 0123 456 7890. By contrast, HLOOKUP goes horizontally along the top row of a table first, then down a column to the desired value.

VLOOKUP functions typically have three arguments: the value to look for (Dalton), the range containing the table (A2..C8 – the whole of the range is one argument) and a number indicating the relative position of the column giving

Fig 9.6 Example of a look-up table

	A	B	C
1	Income level (£)		Tax rate (%)
2	0	19999	20
3	20000	29999	24
4	30000	and above	40

Fig 9.7 VLOOKUP for a telephone directory

	A	B	C
	Name	Address	Number
1			
2	Adams		
3	Bi		
4	Chin		
5	Dalton		0123 456 7890
6	Eccles		
7	Featherstonehaugh		
8	Graudyn		

the value to be returned. The order of the arguments, and the definition of the relative position, vary between packages: some packages use the position of that column in the table, starting from 1 for the first column, other packages use the 'offset' – how many columns it is to the right of the one where we looked for the name Dalton. These two different versions would be expressed as VLOOKUP('Dalton',A2..C8,3) and VLOOKUP('Dalton',A2..C8,2) respectively. HLOOKUP functions are similar.

Another advantage of LOOKUP functions is that as long as the entries in the 'look up' column or row are arranged in ascending order, it is possible to look up a value that does not explicitly appear in the table at all. This is often what is required with quantitative data. For example, in Fig 9.6, suppose the manager wants to find the tax rate corresponding to an income of £25 000 per year. The formula VLOOKUP(25000,A2..C4,3) will do this and return the correct value of 24 per cent, even though 25 000 does not appear explicitly in the table. In such a case, the LOOKUP function stops at the last entry which is less than or equal to the one it is looking for.

LOOKUP functions are likely to be frequently used in modelling, because their use makes maintenance of the spreadsheet easier, as it is not necessary to know exactly where the values in the table are, only that they are in the correct order. If the lookup table in Fig 9.6 is defined to be larger than the three tax rates currently shown, say as cells A2 to C10, then it would allow for up to six extra tax bands to be included, and the function VLOOKUP(A2..C10,F5,3) would still always return the correct tax rate corresponding to an income shown in cell F5, say.

INDEX is not as commonly used as LOOKUP. With LOOKUP and INDEX, the relationships and the data in the table may be the same, but the way in which they are accessed by the two functions is different. Unlike LOOKUP, which accesses by value, INDEX accesses by position, for example finding the value in the third row and the second column, or indeed all the values in the third row.

In most cases, it is possible to use LOOKUP rather than INDEX, but there are times when INDEX is essential. The most common is when the manager needs to look up by row and by column simultaneously. Figure 9.8 shows a table giving the cost of a package holiday for a party consisting of varying

Fig 9.8 Holiday cost table, illustrating use of INDEX

	A	B		AA	AB	AC	AD	AE	AF
1	Numbers in party:				Children				
2	Adults	2		Adults	0	1	2	3	4
3	Children	1		1	550	675	900	1050	1180
4				2	650	700	900	1050	1180
5	Total cost(£)	700		3	975	1065	1185	1300	1400
6				4	1100	1150	1275	1375	1450

numbers of adults (shown in the rows of the table) and children (shown in the columns). The table itself is placed well away to the right, starting in column AA; it could equally well be on another sheet of a three-dimensional spreadsheet, or in another spreadsheet altogether. The location of the table may be chosen for convenience, since the rows and columns are identified in the arguments of the INDEX function by a number starting from 1 for the first row/column, rather than by cell references.

Looking at the detail of Fig 9.8, the actual numbers of adults and children for whom the price is needed are shown in cells B2 and B3 respectively. The formula in cell B5 is INDEX(AB3..AF6,B2,B3+1), which returns the correct cost; £700 for this example. Note the need for the column number to be expressed as B3+1, since the first column of the table corresponds to 0 children rather than 1. Note also that these prices are intended for illustrative purposes only! We shall give another example of the use of INDEX in Chapter 11. In some spreadsheet packages, INDEX can also be used to return a whole row or column of the table at a time, which is a further advantage.

Logical

Most of the built-in functions in this category are intended for those writing spreadsheet programs or macros for spreadsheets to be used by other, less able users. However, the IF function, as a simple yet flexible way of including a condition in a spreadsheet formula, is one that everyone should know.

The IF function typically has three arguments, consisting of a condition and two possible values, arranged in the form IF(condition,value1,value2), where 'condition' is any valid formula that gives the result TRUE or FALSE. If the result is TRUE, the cell takes the value value1, if FALSE, value2. The values value1 and value2 can be formulae instead of numbers, giving great flexibility.

This would be useful, for example, in calculating tax due, where the tax is levied at a rate of 30 per cent on profits but not on losses. If the profit/loss figure is in cell D1, then the formula IF(D1>0,0.3*D1,0) would give the correct amount of tax due. The condition is D1>0. If this is TRUE, the tax due is 0.3*D1, if FALSE, the tax due is 0.

The most common conditions that will be useful in building a spreadsheet model are formed using the <, > and = relationships, but more advanced users can incorporate any other expression that evaluates to TRUE or FALSE.

Database

Typically these built-in functions perform the same calculations as essential built-in functions such as SUM, MEAN, MAX and MIN, but for entries in a database table rather than cells in the spreadsheet. They have names like DSUM, DMEAN, DMAX and DMIN. As such, they could be essential if you are working with data that are stored for another purpose; in other words, you wish to build a new spreadsheet using existing data.

As well as linking to external databases, these functions have made it possible to use spreadsheet packages as databases themselves, which we shall discuss in Chapter 16.

Financial

The presence of this category of built-in function is partly the result of the spreadsheet's origin in the needs of accountants and financial managers. These functions are in fact not as essential as might be anticipated for the average manager, even for financial modelling. For most financial applications, such as using a spreadsheet to help devise and monitor budgets, arithmetic operations and the functions under our 'essential' heading will be sufficient.

The majority of the built-in financial functions are concerned with the evaluation of actual or potential investments. Managers for whom this forms the core of their normal work will therefore find the financial functions essential.

Anyone who is intending to use one of these functions should be even more careful than usual about the precise definition of how the function does its calculations. Current spreadsheet packages may have over 50 financial functions, several of them very similar to each other; differences in the assumptions built in to the way that calculations are carried out are often based on different accounting conventions in particular countries or types of organisation. It is vital to be aware that different countries do have different assumptions about how some calculations involved in finance are carried out. For example, 1-2-3's @PMTC function calculates loan repayments based on Canadian conventions, producing results very different from the similar @PMT function, which is presumably based on US conventions. Those who have a mortgage from a UK building society will find that neither of these functions calculates their mortgage repayments correctly; as far as we are aware, no spreadsheet package contains a built-in function incorporating the necessary conventions to do this correctly.

Calendar/date and time

Many of these functions are only needed because the way in which most spreadsheets store dates is not the same as the way in which people write them down. Date formats have been a bone of contention with computer software designers for years, because of the many different ways in which people write them down, for example 27-09-96, 09-27-96, 27-09-1996, to name but three (DD-MM-YY, MM-DD-YY, DD-MM-YYYY in spreadsheet format terms). The solution chosen by the designers of spreadsheet packages was to base the whole

Fig 9.9 Example of date calculation

	A	B	C
1	Date invoice issued	Date payment received	Time taken to pay (days)
2	16/08/97	13/09/97	28

calendar on counting the days from a fixed starting day, so that day 1 was, for example, 1 January 1900 (not all packages start from the same date).[4] The built-in date and time functions were thus originally intended for conversion between 'normal' dates and these 'day numbers'. As a result, they are of little relevance for modelling purposes, although they can be useful for ensuring that the correct date appears on printed reports.

However, one very useful application of these functions is where it is necessary to do calculations on values which are stored as dates, such as working out how many days have elapsed between the date of issuing an invoice and the date of receiving payment. At one time it was essential to use the built-in functions for this, to access the 'day numbers', but more recent versions of spreadsheet packages cope with this automatically. For example, in Fig 9.9, the formula in cell C2 is simply +B2–A2.

Non-Gregorian calendars, for example the Chinese, Hebrew, Indian and Islamic calendars, are not catered for at all in the UK and US versions of spreadsheets, as far as we are aware.

Engineering

There are many built-in functions in this category, but we shall not cover these in any detail here since, as the category name implies, they are intended for use by engineers rather than managers. Bessel functions and the like may well be essential for a few production managers, but we shall assume that they are for a different class of user from the one at which this book is aimed. It is just conceivable that very advanced models could make use of the built-in complex number functions, but this too is beyond the scope of this book.

Information

These are not very useful, despite the encouraging name. Most of these built-in functions are for macro programmers who want to write error-handling routines.

Text

These functions perform such tasks as finding the nth character in a string of text, changing upper-case text to lower case, and converting between text and numeric formats. This is excellent for improving presentation, but not among our main concerns here. The one circumstance in which these functions may be relevant in connection with building a decision support system is when data imported from an external database are in the wrong format, for example numbers stored as text. In this case, the 'conversion' functions may well be essential.

'WHAT IF' ANALYSIS

The point of 'What if?' analysis is for the manager to be able to explore the issues and outcomes in the local scenario of interest. The spreadsheet model helps in exploring the consequences of various possibilities and assumptions, for example by trying different parameter values. Typically, this means leaving the logic model unchanged, but altering the values in the data model, or trying several different data models at once. Spreadsheets normally use the term scenario for one set of data model values, so that the term scenario as we have used it in this book is slightly more general than the term as it is used in spreadsheets, but essentially both are talking about the same thing.

The simplest form of 'What if?' analysis is for the manager to change the numbers themselves. This works, but is time consuming and error prone. If you want to do it that way, it's up to you!

Rather more systematic, and also more efficient, is the use of menu commands such as Fill and Copy to produce tables showing how output variable values change as an input factor value changes. Suppose a company is introducing a new product next week. Figure 9.10 shows a spreadsheet containing a 'What if?' analysis for the weekly sales of this product in one year's time. The verbalisation is:

$$\{Weekly\ sales\ in\ one\ year's\ time\} = \{Initial\ weekly\ sales\} \times \{1 + \{Growth\ rate/100\}\}$$

Values of *Initial weekly sales* between 500 and 1500 have been entered in cells A4..A14 using the Fill command, and values of *Growth rate* from 0 to 30 per cent in cells B3..H3 similarly. The formula $A4*(1+B$3)$ for *Weekly sales in one year's time* was entered in cell B4, and copied to the rest of the range B4..H14 using the Copy command. Note that the $ signs were necessary to 'anchor' the formula correctly by using mixed rather than relative cell references.

Fig 9.10 Use of Fill and Copy commands

	A	B	C	D	E	F	G	H
1	Weekly sales in one year's time							
2		Growth rate						
3	Initial weekly sales	0%	5%	10%	15%	20%	25%	30%
4	500	500	525	550	575	600	625	650
5	600	600	630	660	690	720	750	780
6	700	700	735	770	805	840	875	910
7	800	800	840	880	920	960	1000	1040
8	900	900	945	990	1035	1080	1125	1170
9	1000	1000	1050	1100	1150	1200	1250	1300
10	1100	1100	1155	1210	1265	1320	1375	1430
11	1200	1200	1260	1320	1380	1440	1500	1560
12	1300	1300	1365	1430	1495	1560	1625	1690
13	1400	1400	1470	1540	1610	1680	1750	1820
14	1500	1500	1575	1650	1725	1800	1875	1950

Better still, many spreadsheets now include facilities to guide the manager through this process, avoiding such problems as incorrectly anchoring formulae before Copying them (leave out one of the $ signs in the Fig 9.10 example and the value in H14 will be *huge* – and completely wrong!). For example, we have the 'What if?' tables and the version manager in Lotus 1-2-3 and the data tables and scenario manager in Microsoft Excel, which help to build up 'What if?' analyses with rather less effort.

These two sets of facilities in each of the major packages correspond to two slightly different approaches to 'What if?' analysis. The 'What if?'/data tables systematically investigate what happens if a small number of input factors (either two or three, according to the spreadsheet package used) take a series of values that change in steps. The effect of all possible combinations of these input factors on a single calculated variable is shown in the tables. The rows of the spreadsheet represent the different values of the first input factor, the columns the second input factor and (where this is possible) different sheets represent the third. Figure 9.11 gives an example of this, showing how the calculated variable *amount to be repaid* on a loan varies according to the three input factors of *interest rate*, *principal* (in £) and *term* (in years). Note that the enforced format of 'What if?'/data tables does not make the results quite as easy to read as they should be. There is no ideal place to put the label *amount to be repaid*. More seriously, the values of the third input factor, here *term*, have to be in the top left cell of the table (here C1) on each sheet. This leaves no place for the label showing *interest rate* as 0 in the top row! The format also requires dummy values for the input factors outside the main table (here shown in column B) to be used in a defining formula for the calculated variable, here shown in cell A4 of the first sheet. The single formula B2*(1+B1)^B3 in that cell is used to calculate all the values in the table. The symbol ^ means 'to the power of'; in this compound interest calculation, the *principal* must be multiplied by {1+ *interest rate*} once for each year. Normally it would make sense to 'hide' the result in cell A4, but we have left it in here, in order to show how the table is constructed.

◆ **Key concept**   *'What if?'/data tables systematically investigate what happens if a small number of input factors (no more than three) take a series of values that change in steps.*

Version or scenario manager facilities are intended for more specific and less systematic 'what if?' analysis. They can cope with far more variable input factors (typically up to 32) and with unequal differences between the values, although they are not quite as simple to use as in the 'equal step' case. What happens is that part of the data model is given a name, so that it can be changed easily. This part consists of a set of values for some of the input factors, which corresponds to a particular set of assumptions. This is given a name, enabling values for different input factors to be linked together. All these values can then easily be changed at once, by recalling the named set, which all spreadsheet packages offering this facility (as far as we are aware) call a *scenario*.

Fig 9.11 Three-variable 'What if' table

	A	B	C	D	E	F	G	H
1	Interest rate	0	1	10000	10500	11000	12000	15000
2	Principal (£)	10000	0.02	10200	10710	11220	12240	15300
3	Term (years)	1	0.04	10400	10920	11440	12480	15600
4	10000		0.06	10600	11130	11660	12720	15900
5			0.08	10800	11340	11880	12960	16200
6			0.10	11000	11550	12100	13200	16500
7			0.12	11200	11760	12320	13440	16800
8			0.15	11500	12075	12650	13800	17250
9			0.20	12000	12600	13200	14400	18000

	A	B	C	D	E	F	G	H
1	Interest rate		2	10000	10500	11000	12000	15000
2	Principal (£)		0.02	10404	10924	11444	12485	15606
3	Term (years)		0.04	10816	11357	11898	12979	16224
4			0.06	11236	11798	12360	13483	16854
5			0.08	11664	12247	12830	13997	17496
6			0.10	12100	12705	13310	14520	18150
7			0.12	12544	13171	13798	15053	18816
8			0.15	13225	13886	14548	15870	19838
9			0.20	14400	15120	15840	17280	21600

	A	B	C	D	E	F	G	H
1	Interest rate		3	10000	10500	11000	12000	15000
2	Principal (£)		0.02	10612	11143	11673	12734	15918
3	Term (years)		0.04	11249	11811	12374	13498	16873
4			0.06	11910	12506	13101	14292	17865
5			0.08	12597	13227	13857	15117	18896
6			0.10	13310	13976	14641	15972	19965
7			0.12	14049	14752	15454	16859	21074
8			0.15	15209	15969	16730	18251	22813
9			0.20	17280	18144	19008	20736	25920

A manager might, for example, define optimistic, baseline and pessimistic scenarios when considering next year's profitability. Figure 9.12 shows such a spreadsheet based on the component cost example in Chapter 7. There are four input factors corresponding to various costs (shown shaded); the component costs in cells E4..E6, and the fixed costs in cell B9. These input factors can be defined as making up a scenario; this is done using menu commands. Each set of values is then given a name; the manager might devise three sets called optimistic costs, baseline costs and pessimistic costs. Figure 9.12 uses the baseline costs values, whereas Fig 9.13 uses the optimistic costs values.

Note that some spreadsheet packages only allow a range of cells to be named, not as shown here. However, as all the packages offer the facility to combine scenarios for different parts of the same spreadsheet, this is not a drawback. Thus, for example, the manager could also define high sales, base sales and low sales

Fig 9.12 Spreadsheet for profitability analysis: baseline costs

	A	B	C	D	E
1	Sales and profitability analysis (all figures in £ unless stated otherwise)				
2					
3	Total unit cost	248		Component costs:	
4	Selling price	385		Electronics	32
5	Sales (units)	9500		Subassembly	122
6	Revenue	3657500		Disk drive	95
7					
8	Contribution	1299125			
9	Fixed costs	658000			
10					
11	Net profit	641125			

Fig 9.13 Spreadsheet for profitability analysis: optimistic costs

	A	B	C	D	E
1	Sales and profitability analysis (all figures in £ unless stated otherwise)				
2					
3	Total unit cost	240		Component costs:	
4	Selling price	385		Electronics	32
5	Sales (units)	9500		Subassembly	120
6	Revenue	3657500		Disk drive	88
7					
8	Contribution	1380160			
9	Fixed costs	610000			
10					
11	Net profit	770160			

scenarios, for the values in cells B4 and B5 (shown lightly shaded in Fig 9.14). They can then carry out 'What if?' analysis using any combination of scenarios for the fixed and component cost values and the sales values. All the scenario names need to be different, because the sets of values are selected by name using a menu command. If only ranges of cells may be named, this has the virtue of encouraging the separation of data and logic models, as we advocated in Chapter 8; we deliberately avoided doing this here, to make the point.

Figure 9.14 shows the pessimistic costs/high sales case. As may be seen, revenue (in cell B6) is higher than in Fig 9.12 (baseline costs/base sales), but net profit (in cell B11) is lower.

♦ **Key concept**

Version or scenario managers allow the storage of a set of values for some of the input factors (typically up to 32 factors), which corresponds to a particular set of assumptions. This is given a name, enabling values for different input factors to be linked together. All these values can then easily be changed at once, by recalling this named set or scenario.

Fig 9.14 Spreadsheet for profitability analysis: pessimistic costs/high sales

	A	B	C	D	E
1	Sales and profitability analysis (all figures in £ unless stated otherwise)				
2					
3	Total unit cost	254		Component costs:	
4	Selling price	375		Electronics	35
5	Sales (units)	11000		Subassembly	124
6	Revenue	4125000		Disk drive	95
7					
8	Contribution	1331000			
9	Fixed costs	750000			
10					
11	Net profit	581000			

SUMMARY

In this chapter we have looked at the range of built-in functions available to managers in spreadsheet packages; a range that is increasing almost by the month. Our aim here was to introduce the functions that are most generally useful in modelling. Specific uses of these and other built-in functions will be discussed in later chapters in Part Two. Every manager using a spreadsheet package should have a good understanding of the functions available in that package and their precise names and definitions.

We have also looked at the most fundamental support the spreadsheet can provide to managers in issue handling: 'What if?' analysis – the home territory of the spreadsheet as a modelling tool. This included the use of 'What if?'/data tables, for carrying out 'What if?' analysis on many different values for relatively few factors (up to 2), and version/scenario managers, looking at a relatively small number of different values for a larger number of factors (up to 32).

END NOTES

1 Different spreadsheet packages give different names to their built-in functions, and also use different conventions to indicate that the name is to be interpreted as the name of a built-in function rather than as text. For example, in Lotus 1-2-3 all function names must be preceded by the @ sign, such as @SUM, @MAX. On the other hand, Microsoft Excel tries to interpret any text it encounters in a formula, whether upper or lower case, as a function name, but the formula itself is indicated by a preceding = sign. Our convention here will be to show function names in upper case, for example SUM, MIN, without any special preceding sign or symbol, unless we are referring to a specific spreadsheet package.

2 A similar process has occurred with pocket calculators, which originally began with just +, −, ×, ÷ and = keys, but have since added first a square root key and then a multiplicity of other keys, the number depending on the level of sophistication of the calculator. Each key effectively corresponds to a built-in function in a spreadsheet.

3 No doubt someone, for example, really needs the built-in function ROMAN, which converts a value to roman numerals so that ROMAN(1997) appears as MCMXCVII, but it is of little use in the type of modelling we discuss in this book.

4 This business of dates is still a real can of worms. The 'day counting' approach is inelegant, but at least it works, as long as the list of leap years is correct; in at least one current spreadsheet the list is wrong, but as the error is in thinking that 1900 was a leap year the consequences are minimal. At the time of writing, many non-spreadsheet computer systems which do not use the 'day counting' approach store only the last two digits of the year, and assume that the first two digits are 19, which will cause many a problem on 1 January 2000, if not before. Older versions of spreadsheets are also likely to assume that the first two digits of the year are 19, but at least they do offer the scope to input all four digits.

FURTHER READING Despite the rise in popularity of the spreadsheet, there are virtually no books about 'What if?' analysis. The most important piece of further reading is for you to consult the manual and/or the on-line help for your spreadsheet package. You really must become familiar with the range of built-in functions available to you, precisely what each one does, and also with exactly how the 'What if?' facilities work. This will save you a great deal of effort.

EXERCISES

1 Find out what the functions in your favourite spreadsheet package are that correspond to the ones we have used in this chapter.

2 In the electricity tariff example in Chapter 5, calculate (a) what would happen to the costs if the connection charges remain unchanged, but the costs per unit rise by 15 per cent; and (b) if the costs rise instead by 1.2p per unit.

3 Reconstruct one of your electricity tariff spreadsheets using the 'What if?'/data table facilities.

4 Reconstruct one of your electricity tariff spreadsheets using the version/ scenario manager facilities.

5 Most UK building societies calculate the monthly payments on a 'repayment mortgage' (money borrowed to buy a house or flat) as follows. Interest on the outstanding balance is worked out, and added to the balance, at the end of each six months, so that a typical 25-year-term mortgage effectively consists of 50 periods. The repayments are made monthly, but are not subtracted from the outstanding balance until the end of the six-month period, after the interest has been added on. Develop a spreadsheet to calculate the monthly payment for suitable values of the initial loan and annual interest rate. Note that it is possible to do all of this as a formula in a single cell, but some use of tables is likely to be more helpful, for example to illustrate how little of the initial loan is paid off during the first five years.

6 Carry out a 'What if?' analysis for the Readyread example from the exercises in Chapter 8:
   a) by using 'What if?'/data table facilities to vary two input factors at a time
   b) by using version/scenario manager facilities to link values of all the input factors.

7 Draw up a personal/family budget for a suitable period such as a month, six months or a year, using the 'What if?'/data table facilities and/or version/scenario manager facilities as appropriate.

8 Which of the analyses in Exercises 6 and 7 did you find most useful for which purposes?

CHAPTER 10

Risk analysis

Chapter aims   Until this point in the book, uncertainty about the values of the input
variables has been dealt with either by the manager simply changing the
contents of the appropriate cells, or by listing all the possibilities, as in
Chapter 9. The aim of this chapter is to explain how to perform risk analysis
using a spreadsheet, and how probability distributions and sampling may
be used in a spreadsheet in order to model more complex instances of
uncertainty.

- Introduction
- Why not use 'What if' analysis to handle uncertainty?
- The sampling process in a spreadsheet model
- Data and logic models in handling uncertainty
- The steps in building and using a risk-analysis model
- Generating uncertain values
  - Dealing with discrete probability distributions • Dealing with continuous
  probability distributions
- What if I need more?
- Appendix 10A: Basic probability and probability distributions

INTRODUCTION

As we have been saying since the start of this book, managers face an uncertain
environment. Nobody knows exactly what will happen tomorrow, let alone
next year. Despite this, or more likely because of it, handling risk is one of the
main responsibilities of management. Risk management is a whole area of study
in itself, covering activities such as:

- identifying sources of risk
- identifying proactive and reactive responses to these risks
- identifying what might go wrong with the responses
- allocating ownership and management of risks and responses
- identifying areas of significant uncertainty
- producing base plans and contingency plans

and many more.

Throughout this chapter we shall use the terms risk and uncertainty interchangeably, as this is typical of the way in which the terms are used in the wider

management literature. Both terms denote a situation where one action may lead to any one of several possible outcomes or consequences, as opposed to conditions of certainty, where an action always leads to a single known outcome. However, it is worth mentioning at this point that some people who build quantitative models to help with decision making do distinguish between risk and uncertainty.[1]

◆ **Key concept**

*A decision made under conditions of **certainty** means that there is only one outcome or consequence for a given action. Most decisions are made under conditions of **uncertainty** or **risk**, meaning that a particular action will lead to any one of a number of possible outcomes.*

One distinction that does need to be made here is that between risk analysis and risk management. *Risk analysis* refers to the development and use of quantitative models to help understand the risks and uncertainties involved in a particular local scenario by considering a range of possible outcomes. The term *risk management* is normally used for the more general and qualitative activity, as outlined above, of which risk analysis is only one part. It is on risk analysis that we shall concentrate in this chapter.

◆ **Key concept**

***Risk analysis** means the development and use of quantitative models to help understand the risks and uncertainties involved in a particular local scenario. **Risk management** is a wider activity, considering more general and qualitative aspects of risk, and how to deal with it, so that risk analysis is only one part of risk management.*

To clarify these terms, consider the following simple example. The manager of a bakery is considering the financial implications of making chocolate muffins for general sale (not made to order). The only way in which the future will be known with certainty is if the manager decides not to make chocolate muffins at all; then none will be sold, with no implications for cost or revenues.[2] However, if they do decide to start making chocolate muffins, then the weekly sales figure becomes uncertain. It may still be zero (perhaps no one wants chocolate muffins), but it may also be any value up to the maximum weekly production; see Fig 10.1, where this figure is assumed to be 99.

The many arrows in the 'uncertainty' part of Fig 10.1, as opposed to the single arrow in the 'certainty' part, show the additional complexity when uncertainty is involved. Given that the manager will also want to consider changing the value of *number of muffins made in first week* from 99, the need for a model to help in risk analysis becomes apparent.

To help decide how many muffins to produce in a week, risk analysis may be performed to examine the financial out-turn of a range of production levels and sales figures, which is likely to include looking at the effect of different pricing strategies. This will only be part of the risk-management process, which would

Fig 10.1 Certainty and uncertainty in decision making

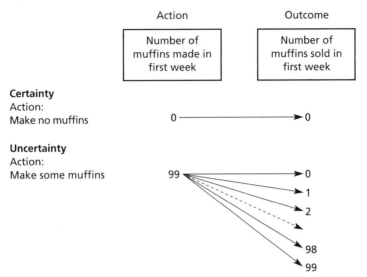

also consider qualitative sources of risk such as interruption to the supply of ingredients for the muffins, what to do to make sure that the muffins taste good enough, whether retailers will be willing to stock the muffins and so on. We shall return to this example later.

Risk analysis is typically used in planning investments such as those in new plant and equipment or in new product development. Examples of several spreadsheet risk-analysis models have appeared in the literature recently, including:

- Comparing different subsidy schemes to give businesses the incentive to locate in a particular local authority's area.
- Deciding which pricing tariff a power-generation company should adopt.

WHY NOT USE 'WHAT IF' ANALYSIS TO HANDLE UNCERTAINTY?

We have already seen in Chapter 9 that one way to handle uncertainty in a scenario is to build a spreadsheet to examine what will happen if the input factors take a particular set of values, and for the manager to vary the values of the input factors to cover all of the possibilities foreseen in the local scenario. This works well enough in simple cases, but it has two major limitations:

1 It does not take any account of how likely each of the different input factor values is. For example, expected sales of televisions next quarter may be between 10 000 and 30 000 units, but the manager may feel that the result is much more likely to be close to 20 000 than at either end of this range. Most charting commands in spreadsheets are designed to work on data series rather than data tables; 'What if' analyses typically produce tables of results, which are thus difficult to chart easily. It can therefore be hard to concentrate on the values of most interest, and get information from the data.

2 If the values of several input factors are uncertain, constructing the 'What if' analyses rapidly becomes unwieldy. The practical limit for a systematic exploration of varying different input factor values independently is three factors, corresponding to the rows, columns and different sheets of a three-dimensional spreadsheet, as we saw in Chapter 9. Linking the values of different factors together as spreadsheet scenarios allows more factors to be varied, but not independently. In addition, in both cases it can soon become difficult to appreciate how the significant features of the output variable values are related to changes in the input factor values.

To deal with these limitations, the manager needs to be able to specify an input factor as taking a range of values from a *probability distribution*, rather than a single fixed value or a set of fixed values. Unless you are absolutely sure that you know all about probability distributions, please read Appendix 10A and come back to the chapter at this point.

The difficulty when working with an input factor that takes on a range of values is that in order for the spreadsheet to calculate the values of variables that depend on this input factor, it must be given *some* particular value. Typically, a spreadsheet model cannot complete its calculations unless all the input factors have specific values. What is needed is to be able to produce specific values in a way that is somehow 'typical' of a range of values; for each uncertain input factor, a process is needed that generates a value that is in keeping with the pattern of uncertainty appropriate for that particular input factor. The pattern of uncertainty can be represented by a probability distribution. The process of generating a value in keeping with this pattern is called *sampling*, and an individual value thus generated from the probability distribution that represents the range of values is called a *sample*. Let's see a simple example of how to do this without using a spreadsheet.

◆ **Key concept**

*Sampling is the process of generating values that are in keeping with the pattern of uncertainty appropriate for a particular variable. The pattern of uncertainty is represented by a probability distribution. An individual value generated by this process is called a **sample**.*

MINICASE 'Top hat' sampling

A bus company runs trips to London every weekday under the slogan: 'no need to book: just turn up!' Suppose that one of the managers is trying to decide how large a bus is needed for tomorrow's trip. Too large a bus, and money is wasted; too small, and there will be some very dissatisfied customers. Data are available on how many passengers travelled on this trip on each of the past 20 weekdays, as shown in Table 10.1. For simplicity, we shall assume that the demand is not showing any increase or decrease, and is not affected by the day of the week. Whatever the manager's decision on the size of bus, the outcome is uncertain. However, the manager can model the uncertain demand by using the past data, without using a spreadsheet, as follows.

**Table 10.1 Number of passengers travelling
on each of the past 20 weekdays**

14	40	51	16
24	17	49	21
41	49	46	56
47	40	31	47
56	24	24	39

1 Take 20 pieces of paper and write each of the demand figures for the last 20 days on one of them. Thus there will be one piece of paper marked 14, but three marked 24, and so on. Put them in a suitable container, such as a hat.
2 Pick out one piece of paper to model tomorrow's demand; the figure on the piece of paper is the value the manager will use in deciding which bus to use tomorrow.
3 Put the piece of paper back again before taking another sample.

If the manager uses this process, the values they generate for passenger demand will follow the same pattern as the past data. The values of the past data form the probability distribution; this is also represented, but in a different format, by the numbers on the pieces of paper. The piece of paper drawn from the hat is one sample. The manager can now generate as many possible 'tomorrows' as they like, in accordance with this pattern. Each new 'tomorrow', where one sample value has been generated for each uncertain variable in a model (there is only one in this example), is called a *trial*, in the terminology of risk analysis and simulation (see Chapter 11).

This method is known as 'top hat' sampling, for obvious reasons.

♦ **Key concept**   *A **trial** is the name given to the results of a spreadsheet model with one set of values for the uncertain variables in the model.*

You may be wondering why the manager would want to go through this process, when for any given size of bus they could simply work out how many days in the last 20 it would have been too small, and take the decision accordingly. We agree that for this simple case the benefits of using the spreadsheet appear marginal. However, suppose that the manager is actually responsible for trips to 15 different places tomorrow, all with uncertain numbers of passengers. Now the calculations certainly need a spreadsheet, and the risks now interact. The manager cannot, for example, assign the bus with the largest seating capacity to all 15 different trips at once. The same procedure described above could, however, still be used to generate samples for this risk analysis. Fifteen sets of past data, fifteen sets of pieces of paper, and fifteen hats would now be required. Each trial would involve taking one piece of paper from each hat (one sample from each probability distribution) to give the values of the 15 input factors. This would indeed work, but it would be somewhat cumbersome. It can be done rather more efficiently using a spreadsheet.

Precisely how do we carry out risk analysis using a spreadsheet? We need to reproduce the probability distribution and the sampling process; these are the pieces of paper and the act of pulling one piece of paper out of the hat from the 'top hat' method. There are many subtleties to the probability distribution part of this, so to begin with we shall concentrate on the sampling process. Once this is clear, it is then more straightforward to discuss the further details of using probability distributions to represent risk/quantify uncertainty.

We can now give a more precise statement of what risk analysis involves; it is the process of letting input factor values vary by sampling from appropriate probability distributions, and then seeing the effect this has on the calculated variable values. Risk analysis is a type of simulation, which we shall consider more generally in the next chapter.

◆ **Key concept** *Risk analysis is the process of letting input factor values vary by sampling from appropriate probability distributions, and seeing the effect this has on the calculated variable values.*

THE SAMPLING PROCESS IN A SPREADSHEET MODEL

Let us return to the manager wondering whether or not to start making chocolate muffins. Suppose the initial production level (*number of muffins made in first week*) is to be 99 muffins per week, as in Fig 10.1. We shall assume for simplicity that the uncertain sales outcome (*number of muffins sold in first week*) can take all the values from 0 to 99 with equal probability. This would be equivalent to putting 100 pieces of paper in our top hat, each with one of the numbers from 0 to 99 on it.

For a computer to reproduce the process of picking the piece of paper out of the hat, or rather to do something equivalent to it, we need to introduce the concept of a random number. A random number is one chosen so that all possible values are equally likely. A series of random numbers has the additional property that there is no connection between one number in the series and the following one, or indeed any of the others. As we mentioned in Chapter 9, spreadsheets have a built-in function RAND that returns random number values. This will be at the heart of our sampling process.[3] Note that the RAND function returns a different value every time the spreadsheet is recalculated. It is therefore essential to change the recalculation mode from automatic to manual when using the RAND function, otherwise the values change whenever any change is made to the spreadsheet, which is confusing.

The RAND function typically returns a value between 0 and 1 (see later for more detail); it does not normally need an argument, but optionally one may be provided, called a *random number seed*. This means that a particular series of random numbers may be reproduced. We shall discuss this point further in Chapter 11. So, to represent muffin sales between 0 and 99, the manager needs to multiply the value returned by RAND by 100 (the value of *number of muffins made in first week* + 1) in the spreadsheet, and round down to the whole number below. The formula INT(100*RAND) will accomplish this, as shown in Fig 10.2, where it appears in cell B2, having been changed to INT((B1+1)*RAND) for generality. This uncertain input factor, *number of muffins sold in first week*, is used as part of a model whose verbalisation is:

$$\text{Profit contribution in first week} = \text{Sales revenue} - \text{Fixed cost} \\ - \text{Total variable cost}$$

$$\text{Sales revenue} = \text{Number of muffins sold in first week} \times \text{Selling price}$$

$$\text{Total variable cost} = \text{Number of muffins made in first week} \\ \times \text{Variable cost per muffin}$$

The other formulae for cells in column B are shown in the end column in the figure. We shall see shortly why some formulae have been 'anchored' by the use of the $ sign. Note that we have repeated the fixed cost row in order to make the calculation clear and yet separate the data and logic models.

One formula using the RAND function is enough to give the result of a single trial in this example, as there is only one uncertain input factor. To carry out more trials, the manager could simply force the spreadsheet to recalculate, but this would not make it easy to analyse the results of several trials simultaneously. A better option is to use the spreadsheet's Copy command to repeat the formula in many cells, each corresponding to one trial, as shown in Fig 10.3. Here the formulae for the cells in column B have been copied into columns C to K, to give ten trials in all. (We choose ten only because it is a round number and the spreadsheet still fits on the page!) For clarity, only those items that vary are shown in each column after the first, except for fixed cost, as it is visibly part of a 'totalling' process. Observe that the set of values in each column is different. Each of these trials is a 'possible' future.

In this case, the manager can see without the need for detailed analysis or a summary model that the chances of making a positive contribution to profit do not appear to be good! This assumes that this probability distribution for sales is a reasonable estimate, of course. We shall discuss the analysis of results later in the chapter.

Fig 10.2 Muffins example – one trial

	A	B	Formulae
1	Number of muffins made in first week	99	
2	Number of muffins sold in first week	85	INT((B1+1)*RAND)
3	Selling price (£)	0.65	
4	Variable cost per muffin (£)	0.33	
5	Fixed cost (£)	20.00	
6	Sales revenue (£)	55.25	B2*$B3
7	Fixed cost (£)	20.00	$B5
8	Total variable cost (£)	32.67	$B1*$B4
9			
10	Profit contribution in first week (£)	2.58	B6-B7-B8

Fig 10.3 Muffins example – several trials

A	B	C	D	E	F	G	H	I	J	K
1	Number of muffins made in first week	99									
2	Number of muffins sold in first week	85	69	97	57	18	79	92	78	23	55
3	Selling price (£)	0.65									
4	Variable cost per muffin (£)	0.33									
5	Fixed cost (£)	20.00									
6	Sales revenue (£)	55.25	44.85	63.05	37.05	11.70	51.35	59.80	50.70	14.95	35.75
7	Fixed cost (£)	20.00	20.00	20.00	20.00	20.00	20.00	20.00	20.00	20.00	20.00
8	Total variable cost (£)	32.67	32.67	32.67	32.67	32.67	32.67	32.67	32.67	32.67	32.67
9											
10	Profit contribution in first week (£)	2.58	–7.82	10.38	–15.62	–40.97	–1.32	7.13	–1.97	–37.72	–16.92

DATA AND LOGIC MODELS IN HANDLING UNCERTAINTY

Having described the concept of sampling, we can now set out a more general description of the way in which uncertainty is handled in a spreadsheet model. When dealing with uncertainty, we need to extend the logic model/data model structure introduced in Chapter 5.

It is useful to think in terms of beginning with a model based on conditions of certainty, and then extending it by adding the parts that handle uncertainty. Let us call the logic model under conditions of certainty the *base* logic model, and the corresponding data model the base data model. Their relationship is as shown in Fig 10.4.

In a model assuming conditions of certainty, that is all there is. However, under conditions of *un*certainty, what happens is that part of this data model, the part corresponding to the uncertain input factors, is then replaced with a further logic model. This extension to the logic model comprises the probability distributions that are to be used to produce the sample values for the uncertain input factors. The values in the data model for this extension to the logic model are provided by any parameters of the probability distributions, and by the RAND function (and if necessary the random number seed); it then 'injects' values into the data model for use with the base logic model. This is shown diagrammatically in Fig 10.5.

Fig 10.4 Base logic and data models

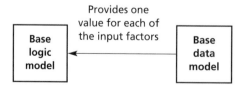

Fig 10.5 The extended logic and data models when dealing with uncertainty

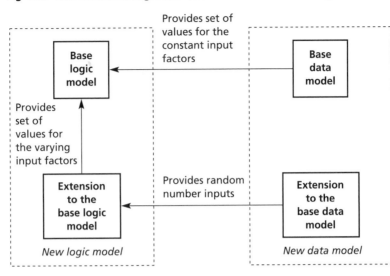

In a model assuming conditions of uncertainty, the part of the data model corresponding to the uncertain input factors is replaced by an extension to the logic model.

Effectively, we deal with uncertainty by using the same base logic model with a large number of different sets of values for part of the data model; the part corresponding to the uncertain input factors. Each set of values is used in one trial. The process of generating these different sets of values includes a random element that helps to represent the uncertainty. The extension to the logic model represents the precise structure of that random element.

Now that we have described the theory, we can explain the steps involved in setting up a risk analysis model in a spreadsheet.

THE STEPS IN BUILDING AND USING A RISK ANALYSIS MODEL

There are six steps in building and using a risk analysis model, as follows.

1 Set up the base logic model, as described in earlier chapters, ignoring the effects of uncertainty on the values in the corresponding data model for the moment.[4] *See* Fig 10.6 for the information flow diagram corresponding to the base logic model in the muffins example. This would then give the spreadsheet shown in Fig 10.2 but with a fixed value in cell B2, not one obtained from a probability distribution.

Fig 10.6 Information flow diagram for the muffins example, not including uncertainty

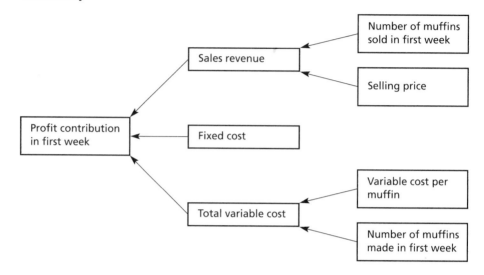

Fig 10.7 Information flow diagram for the muffins example, including uncertainty

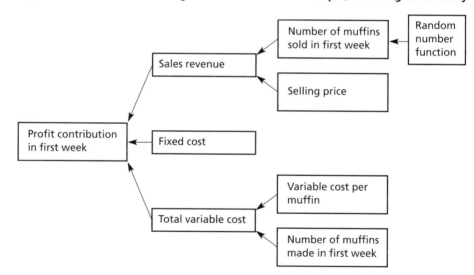

2 Decide which logic model factors have associated values to be regarded as uncertain in the analysis. If an input factor has an uncertain value, then the value of any calculated variable which depends on it will also be uncertain. The muffins example has one uncertain input factor, *number of muffins sold in first week*, in cell B2. The values in cells B6 (*sales revenue*) and B10 (*profit contribution in first week*) are also uncertain, as their values depend on the value of *number of muffins sold in first week*, as may be seen from Fig 10.6. It is unwise to include too many uncertain input factors in a model, or else it may become difficult to understand the pattern of the results obtained. Exactly how

many is 'too many' is a question that has no simple answer. A rough rule of thumb is that there should be no more than the usual '7 ± 2' uncertain input factors, but this number may be increased if several input factors follow the same pattern of uncertainty – for example, the daily production levels achieved by several identical machines. Ideally, it is desirable to start with a large number of uncertain input factors, and then concentrate on those that have the most impact on the calculated variables. However, it can be difficult to establish which factors these are (see the section 'What if I need more?').

3 Choose the appropriate probability distribution to use in the extension to the logic model to represent the uncertainty associated with each input factor. Once this has been done, the uncertainty in the calculated variables will be taken care of by the relationships in the base logic model. For simplicity at this stage, we chose to regard all values from 0 to 99 as equally probable in the muffins example. See Fig 10.7 for the information flow diagram of the muffins example after including uncertainty.

4 Set up the spreadsheet model to produce a sample value for each input factor, using the RAND function and other built-in functions as appropriate. This is the formula INT(100*RAND) in cell B2 for the muffins example. This will be much easier if you have already set up a base set of data model values; in such cases, the fixed value of each uncertain input factor is simply replaced by an appropriate formula to represent the probability distribution identified in stage 3. **N.B.** Don't forget to change the recalculation mode of the spreadsheet from automatic to manual, as mentioned above in the section 'The sampling process in a spreadsheet model'.

5 Copy the logic model produced in step 4, to generate many trials of the same model, each giving a different result. This is Fig 10.3 for the muffins example.

6 Produce summary models from the complete sets of results. However, as we said earlier, the pattern of results in the muffins example seems sufficiently clear that no summary model is needed.

These steps begin in the logical sequence as shown, but in practice backtracking to previous steps is likely to be necessary, as shown in Fig 10.8.

Let's work through another example of risk analysis, to illustrate the use of the six-step approach described above. We shall build up the spreadsheet which is shown (in part) in Fig 10.9. Suppose that a brand manager is concerned about the issue of predicting next year's sales.

Step 1: Set up base logic model

The manager's conceptualisation of the issue is that what happens to sales depends on the total market size and their company's market share. The verbalisation of this is:

sales prediction = {predicted market size} × {predicted market share (%)}/100

Note that the division by 100 is necessary because the manager thinks of market share as a percentage.

Fig 10.8 The steps in setting up a risk-analysis model

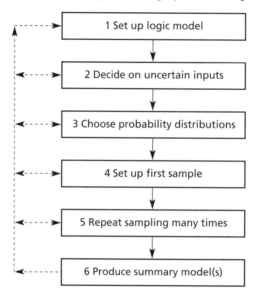

Fig 10.9 Spreadsheet for next year's sales (part)

	A	B	C	D	E	F
1	Sales for next year = market share * total market size					
2	Market share limit (lower) (%)	30				
3	Market share limit (upper) (%)	35				
4	Market size limit (lower) (£000)	1650				
5	Market size limit (upper) (£000)	1815				
6	Predicted market share (%)	32.00	32.08	33.09	34.00	34.42
7	Predicted market size (£000)	1650	1724	1761	1749	1703
8	Sales prediction (£000)	528	553	583	595	586
9						
10	Frequency table: sales values	>= (£000)	510	2		
11			520	6		
12			530	3		
13			540	7		
14			550	15		
15			560	13		
16			570	7		
17			580	7		
18			590	12		
19			600	7		
20			610	12		
21			620	4		
22			630	4		
23			640	1		
24						
25	Average predicted sales	(£000)	568			

The formalisation of this is shown in columns A and B of Fig 10.9, where *sales prediction* (in B8) is defined by formula to be B7*B6/100, cell B7 containing the value of *predicted market* size and B6 that of *predicted market share*. Note that some spreadsheet packages are able to handle percentages in such a way that the division by 100 may be omitted from the formula. For clarity, we have not done this here. The values shown in cells B6 and B7 are the manager's 'static' values; they may, for example, be this year's values.

Step 2: Decide on uncertain inputs

The manager decides that the values of both of the two input factors are to be treated as uncertain. There is no right answer here. Deciding to treat values as uncertain is a matter of judgement, both regarding the nature of the managerial variables concerned and the feasibility of being able to quantify the uncertainty.

In a simple example such as this one, this step will not have a visible effect on the spreadsheet. However, in a more complex example it might, for instance, be necessary to rearrange the spreadsheet so as to group all the uncertain input factors together.

Step 3: Choose probability distributions

To take the simplest case possible, the manager assumes that the uncertainty in each of the input factors values follows a *uniform* distribution, i.e. there is a range of values within which all values are equally probable; see later in this chapter for other distributions. Their decision is that for *predicted market share*, the range is from 30 per cent to 35 per cent, while for *predicted market size* the range is from £1 650 000 to £1 815 000 (the units in the spreadsheet are £000s). These ranges are likely to stem from a combination of studying data and subjective judgement. The limits form part of the extension to the logic model. Following our recommended good practice, the *values* of these limits, which are part of the extension to the data model, are shown in cells B2 to B5 of the spreadsheet.

Step 4: Set up first sample

Further extensions to the manager's logic model now begin in column C. This could have been done in column B, but as mentioned earlier it can be useful to have the 'static' values available for comparison. *Predicted market share* in C6 could now have been defined by the formula 30+5*RAND, but it is better practice to include the lower and upper limits in the logic model, as we have done. The formula in C6 is therefore $B2+($B3–$B2)*RAND, and *predicted market size* in C7 is $B4+($B5–$B4)*RAND. Note the $ signs for anchoring again. Oh yes, and the manager has set recalculation mode to manual, too!

Step 5: Repeat sampling many times

The formulae in cells C6, C7 and C8 are copied into the next 99 columns, as far as column CX, to give 100 trials in total. The number 100 was chosen as a suitably large, 'round number' figure. The only limitation on this is how large a spreadsheet your package and your computer hardware can cope with. Only three more trials (columns D, E and F) are shown in Fig 10.9, to save space.

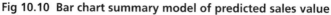

Fig 10.10 Bar chart summary model of predicted sales value

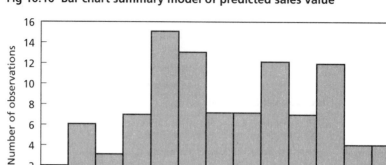

Step 6: Produce summary model(s)

The manager decides to produce two summary models. One takes the form of a frequency table, shown in cells A10–D23 of Fig 10.9; each value in column D represents the number of trials where the value was greater than or equal to the value in column C in that row and less than the value in column C in the row below. For example, the value in D13 is 7; there were seven predicted sales values greater than or equal to £540 000 and less than £550 000. The precise way in which frequency tables are constructed varies between different spreadsheet packages; it is discussed further in Chapter 14.

The second summary model takes the form of the bar chart shown in Fig 10.10. Note that it is not possible to produce such a bar chart without first calculating the corresponding frequency table.

Having described the general process, we now go on to look at the issues involved in generating uncertain values in more detail.

GENERATING UNCERTAIN VALUES

In the case considered above, the RAND function returns a uniformly distributed value that is greater than or equal to 0 and less than 1, as shown in Fig 10.11. Note that in some spreadsheet packages, RAND can never return a value exactly equal to 1. In most scenarios, the difference between a value of 0.99999999 (exactly how many digits there may be after the decimal point varies between different spreadsheet packages) and a value of 1 will not be important, but if it does matter then an alternative way of producing the uncertain values will need to be used.

RAND can therefore be used to produce any values distributed uniformly between two limits. If the lower value is L and the higher value H, then the relationship R=L+(H-L)* RAND will yield the desired result. In our last example,

Fig 10.11 Distribution of values produced by the RAND function

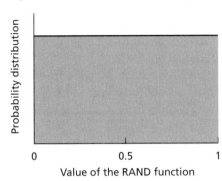

for the input factor *predicted market size*, L is *market size limit (lower)*, i.e. 1650 (£000), and H is *market size limit (upper)*, i.e. 1815 (£000). When RAND=0, R=L; when RAND=1 (or to be pedantic, 0.99999999...), R=H.

Note that by judicious use of INT and ROUND functions, the uniform distribution may be modelled in this manner even if the factor takes discrete rather than continuous values, as in the case of *number of muffins sold in first week*.

Unfortunately for ease of modelling, not all probability distributions can reasonably be modelled as uniform distributions; other shapes of probability distribution will need other functions and formulae. The uniform distribution is also the only distribution where there is really no difference between the discrete and continuous forms. In general, dealing with discrete distributions is more straightforward, and so we shall consider those distributions first.

Dealing with discrete probability distributions

Any probability distribution expressed as a frequency diagram, such as that shown in Fig 10.12 for the number of people absent from work in a manager's department on any one day, or that shown in Fig 10.17 in Appendix A, can be readily transformed into a look-up table.

Fig 10.12 A simple discrete probability distribution

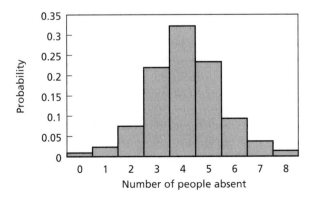

Figure 10.13 shows the corresponding part of a spreadsheet for the distribution of Fig 10.12. The entries in column B are the *cumulative* probabilities that the value is *less than* the corresponding values in column C, for example the probability that the number of people absent is *less than* 4 is 0.32. You may well wonder why the cumulative probabilities are for *less than* the corresponding value rather than *less than or equal to*; this is because of the way that spreadsheet LOOKUP functions work. As mentioned in Chapter 9, if the value being looked up is between two of the values in the table, then it stops its search at the value 'below' the one it is looking for, rather than the one 'above'. Hence the need for the slightly odd layout. All spreadsheet LOOKUP functions seem to work this way. It is fine for the purposes described in Chapter 9, but it is not the way that we would have chosen to design this function for the purposes outlined here!

The function LOOKUP(RAND,B2:B10,C2:C10) used with the table in Fig 10.13, will generate a sample to match the distribution shown in Fig 10.12. The RAND function returns a random value between 0 and 1, which forms the first argument; the value to be searched for in the look-up table. Cells B2..B10 are the function's second argument, the range (in this case a column) where the value is to be found, and cells C2..C10 the third argument, the column containing the value to be returned by LOOKUP.

Thus if RAND returns 0.565873, the search will stop at the value of 0.32 in cell B6 and return the corresponding sample value of 4 from cell C6 for *number of people absent*.

Any discrete distribution, whatever the 'shape' of its frequency diagram, can be handled in this manner.

Dealing with continuous probability distributions

If generating samples from discrete distributions is quite straightforward, generating samples from continuous distributions is much more difficult, except for the uniform one that we have already considered. One way to approach the task is simply to treat the continuous distribution as if it were a discrete one, as follows:

Fig 10.13 A look-up table to be used to generate a sample from a discrete probability distribution

		B	C
1		Cumulative probability	Number of people absent
2		0.00	0
3		0.01	1
4		0.03	2
5		0.10	3
6		0.32	4
7		0.64	5
8		0.87	6
9		0.96	7
10		0.99	8
11			

1 Divide the (continuous) range of values that the variable can take into a series of intervals.
2 Regard the mid-point of each interval as representative of all values in the range, and so as being one of the possible values in a discrete distribution.
3 Associate the same probability with each discrete value as with the corresponding interval of the continuous distribution.

The main problem with this method is that the choice of intervals is arbitrary; we discussed this in Chapter 7 in relation to choosing intervals for displaying continuous variable data as a picture. Too few intervals will not represent the distribution well enough; too many, and the spreadsheet model will become unwieldy. It is also very difficult to predict the likely effects of the rounding-off that is involved in doing this, and so we would only recommend it as a last resort.

The more normal approach to dealing with continuous variable data is to represent the probability distribution by fitting a line of a particular shape. This may also have the advantage of helping to smooth out any fluctuations in the original data.

Unfortunately, although this works well mathematically, it is not so easy to translate into a sampling process, except in the case of the uniform distribution that we have already seen.

For example, suppose the manager decides that a 'flat' distribution like the uniform distribution is not appropriate to represent the uncertainty in a particular input factor, and that a distribution with a peak would be better. Conceptually, the simplest continuous probability distribution that has a peak is the triangular distribution, as shown in Fig 10.14. For simplicity, the peak is shown exactly in the centre of the range at 0.5, but it could lie anywhere. However, this conceptual simplicity is not reflected mathematically; a formula to produce sample values from this distribution needs to be quite complex, because it depends on the geometry of a triangle. It therefore needs to use IF as well as RAND, and for clarity also needs to use two cells, as follows (we suggest that you take the accuracy of this formula on trust – it is intended to illustrate the difficulties of generating samples from distributions). Suppose cell B2 contains the formula RAND. Then the formula:

Fig 10.14 Triangular distribution

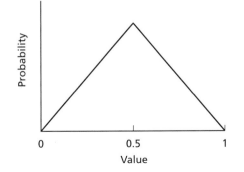

IF(B2<=0.5,SQRT(B2/2),1−SQRT((1−B2)/2))

will generate values from a triangular distribution.

The corresponding formula for a triangular distribution where the peak is not at 0.5 is even more complicated; if the peak value is in cell B3, and cell B2 again contains the formula RAND, it is:

IF(B2<=B3,SQRT(B2*B3),1−SQRT((1−B2)*(1−B3)))

Most continuous probability distributions in real life tend to be made up of curves rather than straight lines. The one most likely to be useful is the normal distribution, which has the characteristic bell-shaped curve shown in Fig 10.15. It tends to crop up when the overall uncertainty results from a large number of small influences, for example the height of a population of individuals depends on small differences in the length of leg bones, gaps between vertebrae and so on. The normal distribution was given its name because it supposedly occurs more often in practice than any other distribution – so such a distribution is 'normal'! Unfortunately, people often interpret it to mean that most variables follow a normal distribution, which is far from being the case.[5] The normal distribution is described in terms of two parameters, its mean, which coincides with the peak, and its standard deviation, which measures how widely the values are spread about the mean.[6]

It is at this point that we reach the limits of the capabilities of current spreadsheet packages. Most spreadsheet packages now have built-in functions that can return a value from a probability distribution, such as NORMAL. These are very useful, as we shall see in Chapter 14. Unfortunately, from the point of view of generating uncertain values, the functions typically operate 'the wrong way round'. Given a particular value, the function NORMAL will return the probability of that value occurring. For example, if a manager knows that the

Fig 10.15 Normal distribution

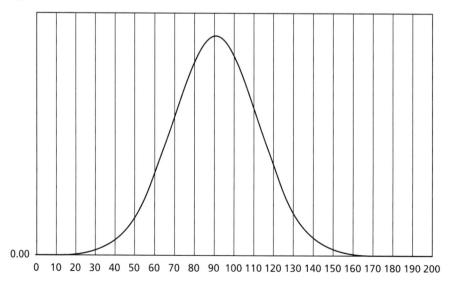

weights of 'one kilogram' packs of a particular product follow a normal distribution with a mean of 1.01kg and a standard deviation of 0.004kg, then NORMAL (1,1.01,0.004) will tell the manager that the probability of a pack weighing less than 1kg is approximately 0.0062. What is needed for generating samples, however, is to start with a probability (which we can produce using the RAND function) and return a corresponding value. Only if your spreadsheet package has *inverse* functions such as NORMALINV can it easily be used to generate sample values. For example, NORMALINV(RAND,1.01,0.004) would generate samples from the distribution just mentioned. Again, good practice would be to include the mean and standard deviation values in cells in the spreadsheet, and refer to them in this formula by their cell references.

Note that if inverse functions for sampling from continuous distributions *are* available, they can very easily be used to return values for discrete variables by means of the INT or ROUND functions, as we did earlier in the muffins example. The rounding in such a case is *not* arbitrary, and so does not raise the problems encountered 'going the other way' (treating a continuous distribution as being discrete) mentioned earlier.

WHAT IF I NEED MORE?

This is one case where the manager might wish to acquire more software sooner rather than later, because there are some extremely good *add-ins* (software packages that can be used directly from within the spreadsheet) specifically designed to perform risk analysis. They include @RISK and Crystal Ball.

These packages offer three advantages over ordinary spreadsheet packages.

1 They contain libraries of additional built-in functions to return sample values from probability distributions, without the need for complex formulae. As we mentioned above with NORMALINV, spreadsheet packages are just beginning to offer these inverse functions, but even where they are included, there is normally only a handful of them. Current versions of the risk analysis add-ins, by contrast, typically contain around 40 different types of probability distribution, including both discrete and continuous variables. This makes steps 3 and 4 of the model building much easier.

2 They make it easier to manage the process of running the model, by avoiding the need to copy formulae at step 5. The add-ins simply run as many trials as the user wishes and record the results of all of them, for use in step 6.

3 They include extensive facilities for building summary models. This includes identifying calculated variables of interest by a simple 'point and click' operation; producing bar charts of the frequencies with which different values of the calculated variables occur, in various different formats; and even identifying which of the uncertain input factors makes the greatest contribution to the variation in the calculated variables. This last point helps the user to cope with the question of 'How many uncertain factors?' by starting with a large number, and then homing in on the ones which really seem to make a difference for investigation in more detail, as mentioned earlier.

SUMMARY

In this chapter we have placed risk analysis within the wider context of risk management, and then looked at the use of spreadsheet models in carrying out risk analysis. The patterns of uncertainty in some of the input factors are represented by generating samples from appropriate probability distributions with the aid of the spreadsheet package's built-in RAND function. A six-step process for building spreadsheet risk-analysis models has been described, and illustrated using samples from uniform distributions. Triangular and normal distributions have also been mentioned.

END NOTES

1 The distinction is that *risk* denotes the general state where the manager does not know exactly what is going to happen; typically, there are several possible outcomes, and the manager cannot estimate how likely each one is. In the 'extreme risk' case, it may not even be possible for the manager to identify all the possible outcomes, so the decision may have completely unforeseen consequences. Modelling is of little help in such situations. By contrast, *uncertainty* refers to the more specific case where the risks can be expressed in a quantitative manner; the manager knows what the possible outcomes are, and can estimate how likely each of them is, in quantitative terms. On these definitions, risk analysis is a contradiction in terms; as it is nevertheless the term in most common use, we shall continue to use risk and uncertainty interchangeably.

2 For simplicity, we shall ignore the possibility that adding chocolate muffins to the range may help increase the sales of the bakery's other products; as we said, very few things in a manager's life are certain.

3 Strictly speaking, computer-generated random numbers are pseudo-random numbers rather than 'proper' random numbers, because there is a process by which one random number is generated from the next. To all intents and purposes there is no difference between pseudo-random numbers and proper random numbers, as long as the random number generator really does generate numbers so that all possible values are equally likely and different values are not correlated with each other (see Chapter 14). It is not easy to achieve this! Thus where genuinely random numbers have to be seen to be provided, physical processes are often used, as in the National Lottery, which is exactly like our numbered pieces of paper, except using numbered balls. Pseudo-random numbers do have the advantage that particular sequences can be reproduced. This enables two possible courses of action to be compared against the same set of uncertain outcomes.

4 It will, however, almost certainly be useful to produce a single set of values for the base data model, to help with validation and testing of this 'static' model and with the construction of the part of the logic model representing uncertainty.

5 In case you are finding this distinction hard to grasp, the following analogy may help. The most common ('normal') make of car on British roads is a Ford, but the majority of cars are not Fords; they only comprise 20–25 per cent of the total. Similarly, the normal distribution occurs more often than any other, but the majority of uncertain variables do not follow a normal distribution.

6 The standard deviation is discussed in more detail, and somewhat more rigorously, in Chapter 14.

FURTHER READING

A good reference to the whole area of managing risk, including the use of models, is C.B. Chapman and S.C. Ward, *Project Risk Management: Processes, Techniques and Insights* John Wiley, Chichester, 1997.

EXERCISES

1 What is the difference between decisions made under conditions of certainty and decisions made under conditions of uncertainty?

2 Explain in your own words how 'top hat' sampling works.

3 What is the difference between a sample and a trial?

4 Think of an uncertain variable, such as the amount of cash you will need next week or your department's expenditure on consumables for the next month. What probability distribution would you choose to represent the pattern of uncertainty of that variable, and why?

5 What formulae would you use to generate sample values for *number of job applicants* if the personnel manager responsible believes that the values are equally likely to be anywhere in the range 200 to 350?

6 Find out what inverse functions your favourite spreadsheet package has, if any.

7 An airline manager is responsible for deciding how many seats of each type of class (Business class and Economy class) are on a particular flight. Data on the past 20 such flights are shown in Table 10.2.

Table 10.2 Numbers of passengers

Economy class passengers	Business class passengers	Turned away
64	26	2
58	21	
64	26	
47	28	
52	26	
51	20	
64	26	5
59	22	
66	24	2
61	29	8
65	21	
62	21	
51	26	
64	26	5
49	27	
50	21	
55	21	
53	27	
57	23	
62	28	

Build a spreadsheet model to produce samples from this distribution.

8 Use the model you developed in Exercise 7 to decide on how large a plane to have and 'where to put the curtain' between the Economy and Business classes.

9 In the muffins example in Figs 10.2 and 10.3, suppose the bakery manager has decided that a uniform distribution for the value of *number of muffins sold in first week* is inappropriate. Build spreadsheet models that represent this as:
a) a triangular distribution with a peak at 85 muffins/week
b) a normal distribution with a mean of 85 muffins/week and a standard deviation of 4 muffins/week.

Compare the financial results of the two assumptions.

APPENDIX 10A: BASIC PROBABILITY AND PROBABILITY DISTRIBUTIONS

Probability is the mathematician's approach to quantifying uncertainty. Probabilities are associated with *events*; any event that can be described can have a probability associated with it. An event may be of any form, for example: 'It will rain tomorrow', 'England will win the next soccer World Cup', 'Sales for the first quarter will be £300 000', 'Consumer reaction to the taste test of our new ice-cream flavour will be favourable'.

The probability of an event is measured on a scale ranging from 0 to 1, 0 meaning that there is no chance of that event occurring, 1 meaning that that event is certain to occur. Where events can be grouped together so that only one of them can occur, and exactly one of them *must* occur, for example the events 'It will rain tomorrow' and 'It will not rain tomorrow', they are said to be *mutually exclusive*. In such cases, the events are often called *outcomes*; it may help to think of them as the different possible results from a given process. In most issues where a decision support system is useful, we will be interested in assigning probabilities to a set of mutually exclusive events/outcomes, rather than to just one event.

There are essentially three ways to estimate the probability of an event occurring:

1 From first principles.
2 By studying data on what has happened in the past.
3 By using subjective judgement (hunch, belief, gut feel).

First principles

If you toss a coin, it will land showing either 'heads' or 'tails' uppermost (we make the simplifying assumption that these are the only possible outcomes; that is, the coin will not land balanced on its edge, or fall through a hole in the floor). For a normal coin, the outcomes 'heads' and 'tails' are equally likely (equally *probable*). The *probability* of each is therefore 0.5, given that the total probability equals 1. If you instead toss two coins (or the same coin twice), there are now three possible outcomes ('heads' twice, 'tails' twice, one 'head' and one 'tail'), but they are no longer equally likely. The outcome one 'head' and one 'tail' is twice as likely as each of the other two, because there are two ways of achieving it (first coin 'heads' and second coin 'tails', or first coin 'tails' and second coin 'heads'), while there is only one way to get two 'heads' or two 'tails'. So the probabilities are now:

Two 'Heads'	0.25
Two 'Tails'	0.25
One 'Head' and one 'Tail'	0.50

Similar calculations from first principles can be done for many situations, especially those involving coin tossing, dice throwing and playing cards. Unfortunately, in most real-life examples in business, such calculations are not possible.

Studying data on what has happened in the past

When first principles cannot be used, but some data about past events are available, then these may be used to estimate the relevant probabilities. Of course, this assumes that the future is going to resemble the past, a point to which we shall return in Chapter 15 on forecasting.

In general, past data are used by simply identifying all the outcomes and then assigning probabilities in proportion to the number of times (the *frequency*) with which each has appeared in the past data. For example, suppose a manager of an electrical spares shop has noted how many replacement remote controls for a particular brand of television were needed each week over the past 50 weeks. The data might appear as in the frequency diagram in Fig 10.16.

These numbers can be converted into probabilities by dividing each of them by the total number of observations, in this case 50. This gives the same diagram, but with a different scale, as in Fig 10.17. In general, any process leading to an outcome which can be expressed quantitatively as the value of a single variable, and where a whole range of values for that variable is possible, can be treated in this way. In such circumstances, the set of probabilities associated with the set of outcomes is called a *probability distribution*. Thus Fig 10.17 shows the probability distribution of the number of replacement remote controls/week. The total area of the bars on the chart is 1, i.e. the total probability.

Fig 10.16 Frequency diagram of number of replacement remote controls/week

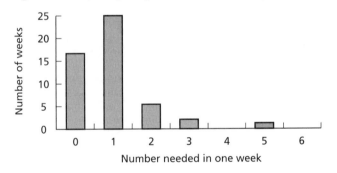

Fig 10.17 Probability distribution of number of replacement remote controls/week

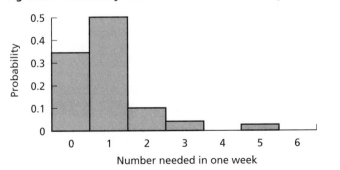

We have changed the format so that the bars now occupy the full width of each category on the axis, to emphasise this point, notwithstanding our comments about histograms and discrete data in Chapter 7.

Probability distributions are perhaps easiest to understand when dealing with discrete variables, i.e. those where the values of the outcomes are whole numbers, such as the number of replacement remote controls/week, as in this example, or the number of people absent from work in a manager's department on any one day. However, the same principles apply to continuous variables, such as the yield of wheat harvested on different farms in kilograms/hectare. That might appear as shown in Fig 10.18.

As with discrete variables, the total area under the curve is equal to 1, i.e. the total probability. However, with a continuous variable, the probability of any specific exact value, say 1171.6000 kg/hectare, is vanishingly small (mathematicians' speak for so near zero as to make no difference). The reason for this is that with continuous variables, there is an infinite number of possible exact values between any two given limits, no matter how close together those limits are. Indeed, the measurement of a continuous variable is, in a sense, only an approximate result. You may measure the yield as 1171.6 kg/hectare, but if you had more accurate measuring apparatus, you would almost certainly get a slightly different result, say 1171.6152 kg/hectare rather than 1171.6000. It

Fig 10.18 Distribution of wheat yields: a continuous probability distribution

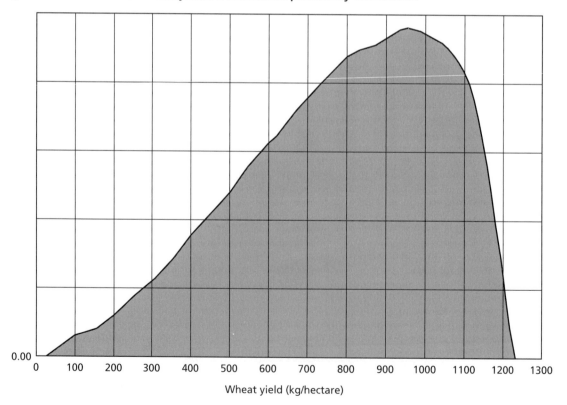

Wheat yield (kg/hectare)

therefore only makes sense to quote the probability of getting a value *between* two given limits. For example, the probability of a value between 1100 and 1200 kg/hectare in the distribution shown in Fig 10.18 is approximately 0.09.

Subjective judgement

When no past data are available, or when past data are inappropriate, the only way to assign probabilities is to use subjective judgement (either your own, or somebody else's). You may consider next year's sales, for example, and judge that there is a probability of 0.6 that sales will increase, 0.3 that they will remain the same and 0.1 that they will decrease.

Note that research has shown that most people are not very good at judging probabilities, especially when considering events that result from two uncertain processes instead of one. For instance, the probability of two events both happening cannot be greater than the probability of one of them happening (irrespective of whether the other one does or not). Suppose we ask a manager in the ice-cream industry their judgement about sales and the weather next summer. For simplicity, assume there are just two sets of outcomes in each case:

- For the weather: 'next summer will be hot' or 'next summer will be cool' (mutually exclusive).
- For sales: 'ice-cream sales will be high' or 'ice-cream sales will be low' (mutually exclusive).

Figure 10.19 shows the four possible joint outcomes from these two events, and how they relate to the individual events. For example, the probability that 'next summer will be hot' (from the first column) must equal the probability that 'next summer will be hot and ice-cream sales will be high' plus the probability that 'next summer will be hot and ice-cream sales will be low'.

Now, because ice-cream sales are very much weather dependent, research has shown that this affects people's subjective judgement of the probabilities. Thus a manager asked to judge these probabilities might well produce the following results:

- probability that 'next summer will be hot' = 0.5
- probability that 'ice-cream sales will be high' = 0.4
- probability that 'next summer will be hot' and 'ice-cream sales will be high' = 0.6

Fig 10.19 The joint outcomes corresponding to two events

	Next summer will be hot	Next summer will be cool
Ice-cream sales will be high	Next summer will be hot and ice-cream sales will be high	Next summer will be cool and ice-cream sales will be high
Ice-cream sales will be low	Next summer will be cool and ice-cream sales will be low	Next summer will be cool and ice-cream sales will be low

The manager's estimate of the joint probability of the event 'next summer will be hot and ice-cream sales will be high' here is greater than either individual probability estimate.

In fact, this is impossible. The probability of the combined event 'next summer will be hot and ice-cream sales will be high' cannot be greater than that of either of the separate events which go to make it up, namely 'next summer will be hot' and 'ice-cream sales will be high'. After all, ice-cream sales might be high even though next summer is cool, or sales low even though next summer is hot. Thus the *maximum* possible probability that both 'next summer will be hot' and 'ice-cream sales will be high' consistent with the two individual estimates is 0.4.

The reason for this inconsistency is that the association between the two parts (the weather and the sales) of the joint event in the manager's mind tends to make both of them seem more likely.

Combining different ways of estimating probabilities

This is very commonly done. For example, when a weather forecaster says that there is a 70 per cent chance of rain tomorrow (i.e. a probability of 0.7), that estimate is usually based on a combination of past data on what the weather has been like in the last few days, subjective judgement as to what the expected weather pattern will therefore be tomorrow, and past data again as to how likely it is to rain when the weather pattern is like the one expected tomorrow.

CHAPTER 11

Simulation

Chapter aims

In a technical sense, this chapter is on exactly the same topic as the previous one, since the models being produced rely for their usefulness on the inclusion of uncertainty. However, the difference in emphasis concerns what is actually being modelled. In the previous chapter we were mainly concerned with the sort of variables that would typically appear in financial reports. Here the aim is to describe simulation, which takes a wider view, to include all aspects of a company's operations.

- Introduction
- Origins in spreadsheet 'What if?' analysis
- Examples
- The use of simulation models
- A simulation built into a spreadsheet
  - More complex models
- Summary of the steps in building and using a simulation model
- What if I need more?
  - Continuous simulation models • Event-driven simulation models

INTRODUCTION

Before going further, we need to tackle a question of terminology. What exactly is meant by the word 'simulation'? There are differences of opinion on this. To an economist, a simulation is any model that is used for 'What if?' analysis. To a human resources specialist, especially one with responsibility for training, a simulation is a training exercise that includes a role-playing element. To a management scientist, a simulation is a model that includes uncertainty in the form of sampling from probability distributions, as was done in the case of risk analysis in the previous chapter. The latter meaning is the one that we shall use for simulation in this book, and is the one most commonly used in spreadsheet circles, although a few spreadsheet models and writers do use the 'economist's definition' instead.[1]

ORIGINS IN SPREADSHEET 'WHAT IF?' ANALYSIS

We discussed in the previous chapter how 'What if?' analysis in spreadsheets led naturally to the idea of incorporating uncertainty into the data model values in a more structured and less haphazard manner. Risk analysis covered the process of examining the effects of uncertainty on calculations which would have been done in a spreadsheet anyway. The addition of uncertainty to the model which was already there, notionally at least, is plainly reflected in the structure of the base logic model and the extension to the logic model.

In simulation, and therefore in this chapter, we look at the same modelling techniques, but we now extend their use to modelling situations where this clear separation into a structure of base logic model and its extension no longer applies. The most likely reason for this would be because it is only the dynamic behaviour of the local scenario that is really of interest. Without the uncertainty, the manager would not bother to use a spreadsheet model to handle the issue. It would, for example, be very easy to plan systems such as supermarket checkouts, bank tellers, taxi ranks and airport terminals if only customers arrived in a pattern that could be predicted with certainty. It is the dynamic nature of the scenario that makes managing it difficult! From the modelling point of view, the spreadsheet must link different time periods, the input factors in the later periods being calculated variables from the earlier ones. This will normally take the form of links between rows, columns or blocks in the spreadsheet corresponding to different time periods. Thus in simulation, unlike risk analysis, it is unlikely that the manager would normally have a base spreadsheet model already available. Indeed, in many cases, it is not even very helpful to *think* in terms of a base model under conditions of certainty when building a spreadsheet simulation, because the uncertainty is so much at the core of the local scenario.

◆ **Key concept**

Simulation covers situations where it is only the dynamic behaviour of the local scenario that is really of interest, and it is the uncertainty that gives rise to the issues. The structure developed for risk analysis, of a base logic model and its extension, no longer applies because of the need to link different time periods. Without the uncertainty, the manager would probably not need to use a spreadsheet model to handle the issue.

EXAMPLES

Spreadsheet simulations have been reported in business management literature in the 1990s for the following applications. There are, no doubt, many more unpublished ones:

- Planning the resources to have available at particular times of the day and week in hotels and restaurants.
- Deployment of equipment in drilling for oil and gas.
- How to organise product development in an engineering company.
- Capacity planning for a chemical-processing plant.
- Demand for machine repair crews.

- Designing an automated product-picking system for a centralised warehouse and distribution centre.
- Deciding how many staff to recruit (and when) for an agency carrying out contract clerical work.

THE USE OF SIMULATION MODELS

Typically, simulation models are used to decide on the structure of the real system, and the policies and procedures to be used in operating it. Simulations are in their element in helping to determine what the structures, policies and procedures should be when the system operates in an uncertain environment. The manager can experiment with the model as a surrogate for the real system, trying different structures, policies and procedures. They can then use the insights gained to decide what to implement in the real world. Note that some books on modelling would phrase this as 'use the solution to the model as the real-world solution'. We do not feel such absolutes are justified, in view of the inevitable assumptions and simplifications in the model, and inaccuracies in the data available. The model can only help; it cannot guarantee a good 'solution' for the real world.

◆ **Key concept**   *Simulation models enable the manager to experiment with the model as a surrogate for the real system, trying different structures, policies and procedures. They can then use the insights gained to decide what to implement in the real world.*

In the terminology used in this book, the experiments may involve not only changing values in the data model, as we have been doing in 'What if' analysis throughout Chapters 9 and 10, but also changing the logic model as well, as we began to do later in Chapter 10.

A SIMULATION BUILT INTO A SPREADSHEET

For this section, we shall work with a simulation model of an inventory or stock-control system, beginning with a simple version, and gradually introducing more complexity as we work our way through the chapter. Essentially, the issue reduces to two related questions: deciding how much to order and when.

To begin with, assume that a manager is dealing with one product. Daily demand is uncertain (that is why the manager needs the simulation spreadsheet) and running out of stock has been a problem. However, cash is short, and thus any excess stock is to be eliminated. The manager wishes to devise a reordering policy of the following form: when the opening stock is less than a certain number of items, known as the *reorder level,* place an order for a fixed amount

– the *reorder quantity*. This policy or procedure, sometimes called a *business rule* by systems analysts, will form part of the logic model for the spreadsheet simulation. The purpose of the experiment(s) will be to help the manager decide when to place an order, and how much to order, i.e. what values to choose for the *reorder level* and the *reorder quantity*.

Initially the manager assumes that the lead time (the time between an order being placed and its arrival) is 0, so that orders arrive the same day that they are placed, and that the uncertain daily demand for the product follows a uniform distribution between a low value of 150 and a high of 250. As was described in Chapter 10, samples from this distribution can be generated from the relationship:

demand = lower demand limit + {upper demand limit – lower demand limit}
× random number

With the values of *lower demand limit* and *upper demand limit* in cells F2 and F3 of a spreadsheet respectively, this can be represented by the formula $F$2+($F$3-$F$2)*RAND, rounded off to a whole number.

Figure 11.1 shows how the information flow diagram for this model is built up. Figure 11.1(a) shows the logic model for a single day, ignoring how decisions about orders are made. This structure is then augmented, to give the more complex model of Fig 11.1b which has to link values for different days together. Note that Fig 11.1a is not the base logic model as in Chapter 10; *demand* is already uncertain.

Figure 11.2 shows one trial of such a simulation model with the current *reorder level* of 100 (shown in cell B2) and *reorder quantity* of 300 (shown in cell B3). The formulae in each row are as follows (taking row 8 as an example):

Cell C8: G7 (today's opening stock = yesterday's closing stock)
Cell D8: IF(C8<=$B$2,$B$3,0)
Cell E8: D8 (no lead time for deliveries)
Cell F8: C8+E8 (stock available)
Cell G8: ROUND($F$2+($F$3–$F$2)*RAND,0) (the uncertain demand)
Cell H8: F8–G8 (closing stock)

As may be seen even from this one trial, this policy does not work very well. On three of the ten days there has been a *stock-out*. This term means that the stock has run out, i.e. the stock available has been insufficient to meet that day's demand. On these days, the closing stock is indicated as negative; the model assumes these orders can be carried over to the next day, and treated as *back orders*, i.e. supplied late. There will certainly be some unhappy customers, however. At least the model appears to have face validity; it is reproducing the stock-out problems! Clearly the manager could do better, although strictly speaking several more trials should be carried out before reaching this conclusion. In this particular example, where the pattern of uncertainty is unchanged from day to day, it would be reasonable simply to

Fig 11.1 Information flow diagrams for stock-control example

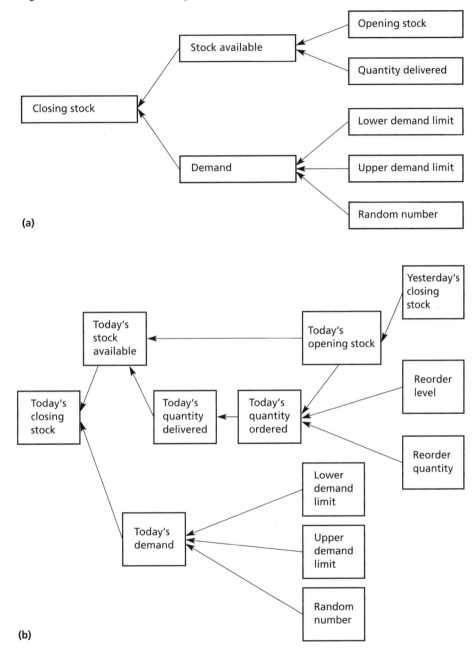

(a)

(b)

increase the number of days using that old faithful, the Copy command. This will make calculating summary measures of performance easier. We shall discuss the use of quantitative summary measures for the performance of the policy later in the chapter.

Fig 11.2 Stock-control simulation – first model

	A	B	C	D	E	F	G	H
1	Stock simulation example							
2	Reorder level	100			Lower demand limit		150	
3	Reorder quantity	300			Upper demand limit		250	
4	Lead time	0						
5			Opening	Quantity	Quantity	Stock		Closing
6		Day	stock	ordered	delivered	available	Demand	stock
7		1	427	0	0	427	249	178
8		2	178	0	0	178	152	26
9		3	26	300	300	326	215	111
10		4	111	0	0	111	175	–64
11		5	–64	300	300	236	222	14
12		6	14	300	300	314	183	131
13		7	131	0	0	131	237	–106
14		8	–106	300	300	194	247	–53
15		9	–53	300	300	247	230	17
16		10	17	300	300	317	215	102

Figure 11.3 shows another trial in which the manager has increased the reorder level to 200, to try to avoid the stock-out problems. Notice also that to give a 'fair' comparison, the same demand pattern has been used as in the previous trial. In this case, this was done using a three-dimensional spreadsheet package by Copying the entire logic model onto a second sheet, and then Copying the demand column from the first sheet into the second one. If your spreadsheet package's RAND function does not allow the use of a random number seed, then the only ways to ensure the same pattern in both simulations

Fig 11.3 Stock-control simulation – second model, first trial

	A	B	C	D	E	F	G	H
1	Stock simulation example							
2	Reorder level	200			Lower demand limit		150	
3	Reorder quantity	300			Upper demand limit		250	
4	Lead time	0						
5			Opening	Quantity	Quantity	Stock		Closing
6		Day	stock	ordered	delivered	available	Demand	stock
7		1	427	0	0	427	249	178
8		2	178	300	300	478	152	326
9		3	326	0	0	326	215	111
10		4	111	300	300	411	175	236
11		5	236	0	0	236	222	14
12		6	14	300	300	314	183	131
13		7	131	300	300	431	237	194
14		8	194	300	300	494	247	247
15		9	247	0	0	247	230	17
16		10	17	300	300	317	215	102

are either to use the Copy command as here, or to enter in the second set of cells the cell references of the first set.

In this trial, the new rule has succeeded in preventing stock-outs. The lowest closing stock level is 14, at the end of day 5. However, this policy does not ensure that there will *never* be any stock-outs, as the trial shown in Fig 11.4 using a different set of *demand* values (produced by using a different set of random numbers to generate them) demonstrates. Only a reorder level at least equal to the maximum daily demand of 250 would guarantee that, because then there would always be at least one day's maximum demand in stock.

A more precise comparison of different policies requires a summary model. As in most examples where simulation is a sensible option, there are several measures that might be used in a summary model, and some of these are conflicting, in that good results cannot be achieved on all of the measures simultaneously. Among the possible measures are:

- Number of days when stock-outs occurred
- Mean closing stock level
- Number of orders placed
- Number of back orders.

◆ **Key concept**   *A precise comparison of the use of different policies in a spreadsheet simulation requires one or more summary models, and running many trials of each of the policies.*

Management science textbooks often attempt to produce a single summary measure by converting everything into cost terms; this entails ascribing costs to holding one item in stock for one day, placing one order and having one

Fig 11.4 Stock-control simulation – second model, second trial

	A	B	C	D	E	F	G	H
1	Stock simulation example							
2	Reorder level	200			Lower demand limit		150	
3	Reorder quantity	300			Upper demand limit		250	
4	Lead time	0						
5				Opening	Quantity	Quantity	Stock		Closing
6			Day	stock	ordered	delivered	available	Demand	stock
7			1	427	0	0	427	195	232
8			2	232	0	0	232	199	33
9			3	33	300	300	333	187	146
10			4	146	300	300	446	207	239
11			5	239	0	0	239	218	21
12			6	21	300	300	321	170	151
13			7	151	300	300	451	248	203
14			8	203	0	0	203	220	−17
15			9	−17	300	300	283	214	69
16			10	69	300	300	369	230	139

back order. This is appealing where the managers involved believe it is appropriate, because a minimum cost solution may then be found, but it is not a universal answer.[2]

The parts of the logic model corresponding to the measures in a summary model are usually quite simple, as shown in Fig 11.5. In most cases there is only a single calculation step; only rarely do summary measures involve intermediate variables that are not already in the logic model of the main part of the spreadsheet.

Figure 11.6 shows the calculations of the four measures mentioned above for the trial shown in Fig 11.4. Note that the value for the *mean closing stock level*, 121.6, is not a whole number. This feature of summary measures such as the mean is discussed further in Chapter 14. The formulae used are as follows.

Mean closing stock level is the most straightforward, being MEAN(H7..H16).

Number of days when stock-outs occurred and *number of orders placed* are also straightforward if the manager's spreadsheet package has a COUNT function including a criterion, such as COUNTIF. They are then COUNTIF(H7..H16,<0) and COUNTIF(D7..D16,>0), respectively.

Fig 11.5 Information flow diagram for summary measures in stock-control model

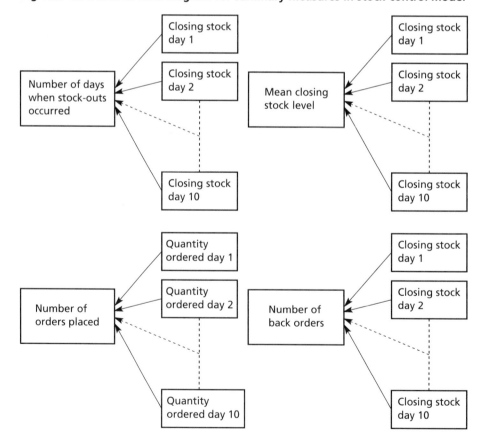

Fig 11.6 Summary measures for trial shown in Fig 11.4

18	Number of days when stock-outs occurred	1
19	Mean closing stock level	121.6
20	Number of orders placed	6
21	Number of back orders	17

Number of back orders is a little more difficult, because here what is needed is a *sum* that includes a criterion; few spreadsheet packages include a SUMIF function. There are two possibilities, each involving adding some cells to the spreadsheet. One possibility with more general applicability for summary measures is to set up another column 'off screen' to the right, for example in column J, in which an IF statement is used to transform all the positive values of *number of back orders* into 0, and the negative values – the back orders – into positive ones. The formula in cell J7 would be IF(H7>0,0,–H7) and so on. The formula SUM(J7..J16) in cell B21 will then give the desired value for *number of back orders*. The other possibility is to use the database DSUM function, which will mean entering a criteria range on the spreadsheet, as we demonstrated for DCOUNT in Chapter 9; the concept of a criteria range is explained in more detail in Chapter 16. Note that with the spreadsheet as shown, where the words 'Closing' and 'stock' appear in different cells, the field name for the DSUM function will have to be just 'stock', as all spreadsheet packages assume a single header row for field names. A minus sign will need to be inserted before DSUM in order to show the total number of back orders as a positive figure rather than a negative one.

It should be clear by now how the manager may try other combinations of reorder level and reorder quantity. Our intention here is not to 'solve' this particular variant of the manager's problem, although you will be invited to attempt this in the exercises. Rather, we intend to add more features to the model, to indicate how more complex simulations may be constructed.

Introducing a non-zero delivery lead time may be done easily by changing part of the logic model, so that E8 is now defined to be D7 (for a one-day lead time); similarly for E9..E16. For a two-day lead time, E9 would be equal to D7, and so on. Figure 11.7 shows one trial of the reorder level 200/reorder quantity 300 policy with a two-day lead time. Here an additional assumption needed to be made that there were no outstanding orders awaiting delivery to the company. Again, you do not need summary measures to see that this policy could be improved.

This approach of incorporating changes in the value of the parameter *lead time* by altering the structure of the logic model works adequately with small models such as this one, but goes against good practice. After all, the logical status of *lead time* is that it should be an input factor; the logic model should therefore treat it as such, enabling it to be set simply by changing the value in cell B4.

Fig 11.7 Stock-control simulation – third model

	A	B	C	D	E	F	G	H
1	Stock simulation example							
2	Reorder level	200			Lower demand limit		150	
3	Reorder quantity	300			Upper demand limit		250	
4	Lead time	2						
5			Opening	Quantity	Quantity	Stock		Closing
6		Day	stock	ordered	delivered	available	Demand	stock
7		1	427	0	0	427	165	262
8		2	262	0	0	262	216	46
9		3	46	300	0	46	233	−187
10		4	−187	300	0	−187	184	−371
11		5	−371	300	300	−71	220	−291
12		6	−291	300	300	9	200	−191
13		7	−191	300	300	109	246	−137
14		8	−137	300	300	163	175	−12
15		9	−12	300	300	288	237	51
16		10	51	300	300	351	167	184

To incorporate lead time in this manner, the manager will need to replace the entries in column E by rather more complex formulae, namely (in cell E7):

=IF(B7–$B$4<=0,0,INDEX($D$7:$D$16,B7–$B$4))

and similarly in cells E8..E16. (No matter how complex the formula is, the Copy command remains just as simple to use!)

Here the condition in the IF function tests whether the lead time is greater than the day number. If it is, the value of *quantity delivered* is set to 0, as it has been assumed that there are no outstanding orders at the start of the simulation. If not, the INDEX function is used to look in the appropriate row of column D, where the values of *quantity ordered* are to be found.

The results from this model are shown in Fig 11.8, this time with a reorder level of 220 and a reorder quantity of 500. These results are notable for two reasons.

The first is that the difference between the logic models of Figs 11.7 and 11.8 in the way that the lead time is treated is not visible from comparing these two sets of outputs. The value of the lead time in cell B4 of the spreadsheet in Fig 11.7 has no effect on the rest of the spreadsheet's logic model; it is effectively a mere label – a note reminding us of the rule linking the values of *quantity ordered* and *quantity delivered*. By contrast, in Fig 11.8's spreadsheet, cell B4 displays the value of an input factor to the logic model. This highlights the importance of putting documentation in the spreadsheet, as we stressed in Chapters 5 and 8.

The second point to observe is that with a two-day lead time, the simple reorder level policy rule seems to be in danger of falling into alternating cycles of understocking and overstocking. Perhaps the policy needs to take into account whether any orders are still outstanding? Or, for example, the quantity

Fig 11.8 Stock-control simulation – fourth model

	A	B	C	D	E	F	G	H
1	Stock simulation example							
2	Reorder level	220			Lower demand limit		150	
3	Reorder quantity	500			Upper demand limit		250	
4	Lead time	2						
5			Opening	Quantity	Quantity	Stock		Closing
6		Day	stock	ordered	delivered	available	Demand	stock
7		1	427	0	0	427	161	266
8		2	266	0	0	266	235	31
9		3	31	500	0	31	184	–153
10		4	–153	500	0	–153	188	–341
11		5	–341	500	500	159	245	–86
12		6	–86	500	500	414	190	224
13		7	224	0	500	724	217	507
14		8	507	0	500	1007	206	801
15		9	801	0	0	801	221	580
16		10	580	0	0	580	151	429

ordered might need to be allowed to vary rather than being a fixed amount each time, perhaps as part of a *reorder cycle* policy where orders are always placed just once a week. Examining the effects of such policies would again need a change to the logic model. The beauty of simulation is that the policies can be tried out (and compared with each other) in the model rather than in the real system. Any policy that can be specified precisely enough to achieve the verbalisation stage of our model-building process could be tried in a spreadsheet simulation model. Any policy that could not be specified sufficiently precisely would almost certainly be unworkable in practice in any case.

More complex models

For clarity, we have concentrated in this chapter on a simple simulation example. It has two features which make it especially suitable for explanation purposes:

- There is only one uncertain input factor, since demand is assumed to follow the same pattern of uncertainty each day; thus only one probability distribution is needed, and only one element of the logic model has to be developed to represent this pattern.
- The uncertain process is repeated many times within the model, thereby achieving the same effect as running several independent trials of the model.[3]

There are three ways in which the spreadsheet model might need to be made more complex:

1 More complex patterns of uncertainty.
2 Multiple, interacting, uncertain input factors.
3 Multiple trials.

More complex patterns of uncertainty

So far, the model has assumed a uniform distribution for the daily demand. As long as the pattern of uncertainty is the same for each day's demand, then changing the logic model to cope with this is straightforward. It would simply be necessary to sample from a different probability distribution, such as the triangular or normal, as was discussed in Chapter 10. This would then be repeated for each day, as before. The only changes to the information flow diagram in Fig 11.1b would be if the new distribution required different parameters to the uniform distribution, in which case the input factors leading into *today's demand* would need to change. For example, with a normal distribution, *lower demand limit* and *upper demand limit* would need to be replaced by *mean demand* and *standard deviation of demand*.

The next step up in complexity in this example might be to have different patterns of demand for different days of the week, as would be typical in many retail businesses. From the modelling point of view this would still be relatively easy to handle; once the first week's logic model had been set up, this could be Copied to the cells for subsequent weeks. Effectively, such a change would be equivalent to having seven uncertain input factors (*demand for Monday*, *demand for Tuesday*, etc.) rather than one. The information flow diagram would then become seven versions of Fig 11.1b linked together, one for each day of the week, with the input factors appropriate to *demand for Monday*, *demand for Tuesday* and so on. We have not included such a diagram in order to save space! The question of multiple uncertain input factors is followed up in the next section. Such a change would also make it more desirable to run multiple trials, as described in the section after that.

A point that we should stress again here is that, however complex the patterns of uncertainty are, the manager using a spreadsheet must always consider how to conduct the experiments with the model. A balance needs to be struck between deliberately using exactly the same set of demand values in different runs of the model to compare different policies, as was done in Figs 11.2 and 11.3, and deliberately using different sets of demand values to obtain a full set of results across the range of possible demand values, as was done in Figs 11.3 and 11.4. In most scenarios, it will be necessary to do both; for example, to compare the results of two different policies over the same 100 sets of different demand values.

Multiple, interacting, uncertain input factors

In general, there may be many uncertain input factors in a simulation model, each with its own pattern of uncertainty; each would need to be handled separately in the same way as has been demonstrated in this chapter for just one such pattern. In the stock control example, one possibility would be differing demand on different days of the week, as mentioned above. Another possibility would be that the manager needed to consider many products at a time rather than just one; we shall now discuss this further.

In the case of stock-control with many products, if stock-control decisions for each product are handled independently, so that the quantity and timing of orders for one product have no effect on the quantity or timing of orders for another, then there is really no issue. The manager might choose to build one big spreadsheet simulation for all the products, but logically this would be no different from having each product on a separate sheet of a three-dimensional spreadsheet, or indeed in different spreadsheets altogether. If we drew the information flow diagram for the logic model in such a case, the parts relating to each product would be separate, i.e. not connected to each other.

The real power of a simulation in such an example comes if the interaction between products affects the way in which a policy operates. Two examples of this (many more are possible) would be:

- Several products are ordered from one supplier, with discounts for orders above a certain value.
- The warehouse space available limits the amount of stock that can be held, so the products are 'competing' for warehouse space.

In the first case, most of the policies that might be tried in the simulation would involve a two-stage process; first determining what the order size would be if there were no interference from other products, then determining what size orders for each product should actually be placed, allowing for that interference. This interference might take the form of order sizes being scaled up to meet the minimum for a discount price, or of some orders being held over until other products are also needed. By contrast, the 'limited warehouse space' example would be most likely to mean order sizes having to be scaled down to avoid exceeding maximum stock levels.

In such a case, rather than a single cell containing a formula to calculate the size of order to be placed, two cells would be necessary for each product. The first would calculate the size of order necessary ignoring the other products, the second the actual size of order to be placed, allowing for the interference of the other products. The parts of the information flow diagram relating to different products *would* now be interconnected.

An aspect of patterns of uncertainty worth bearing in mind is that it may be necessary for the patterns for two or more uncertain input factors to be related, rather than regarded as completely independent. For example, the demand for two (or more) similar products may rise and fall together; the samples generated in the simulation model should reflect this. This may be achieved by using the same value returned by the RAND function to 'drive' all the linked samples by means of references to the same cell.

In addition, unless all the processes are repeated many times, in exactly the same way each time, multiple trials with the model, as in the next section, will be needed for the manager to appreciate the pattern of the uncertainty in the output variables.

Multiple trials

The Copy command will again be the manager's major tool to extend the spreadsheet here. There are two possible ways to set out the spreadsheet model to handle multiple trials.

- If the spreadsheet package permits multiple sheets, put each trial on to a separate sheet.

- Put each trial into a separate block of cells, either side by side or one below the other, one screen at a time.

The difference between these two layouts is simply a matter of personal preference. The use of multiple sheets has the advantage that it can be used whatever the layout of the logic model for each individual trial. Each sheet should be set out in exactly the same way, with one part of the sheet showing the logic model for that trial and another showing the summary model for that trial, as in Figs 11.4 and 11.6. This will mean that built-in functions like MEAN, MAX and MIN can be used on ranges running 'through' the multiple sheets, to produce overall summary models, either on the first sheet or on another separate sheet. For example, a formula such as: MEAN(Sheet1..Sheet10!B27) would return the mean of the values in cell B27 of each of ten sheets, to give a mean value of a summary measure over ten trials.

The 'one screen at a time' approach within a single spreadsheet is used similarly, but the layout of the logic model for each trial dictates whether the different trials can be placed side by side or one below the other. If the summary model is below the rest of the logic model, as in Figs 11.4 and 11.6, then the different trials must be placed side by side. Conversely, if the summary model is beside the rest of the logic model, then the different trials must be placed one below the other. The reason for this is to enable ranges of cells to be used in the creation of the overall summary model; this will only work if there is nothing between the summary model values for each trial.

SUMMARY OF THE STEPS IN BUILDING AND USING A SIMULATION MODEL

If we look back at the process of building the model compared with that described for risk analysis in Chapter 10, it is essentially the same, but the three initial steps have been combined into one: 'build logic model'. Figure 11.9 shows the revised set of steps; compare it with Fig 10.8. Although there are

Fig 11.9 The steps in building a simulation model

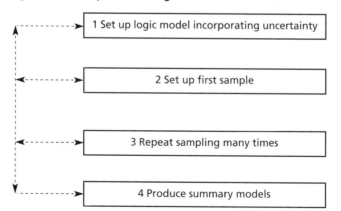

1 Set up logic model incorporating uncertainty

2 Set up first sample

3 Repeat sampling many times

4 Produce summary models

fewer steps, this does not mean that the process is easier. On the contrary, the combined first step may be more difficult for a simulation model, where there is no base logic model to work from, unlike a risk analysis.

The subsequent stages of setting up sample values and generating many trials will be similar for risk analysis and simulation, as will the final stage of producing the summary model(s). However, the latter may again be more difficult for simulation than for risk analysis because of the lack of a base model from which to work.

WHAT IF I NEED MORE?

As discussed in Chapter 10, add-ins such as @RISK and Crystal Ball make it easier to sample from appropriate probability distributions and construct summary models for a spreadsheet simulation. A particular advantage they offer for simulation is when there are multiple uncertain input factors which are partially, but not completely, independent of each other. We mentioned earlier how this may be handled using the RAND function, but these add-ins allow the values of two or more input factors to be associated or *correlated* (see Chapter 14), without being directly linked.

The use of add-ins does not, however, change the basic nature of spreadsheet simulation. We have concentrated here on a stock-control example in which time moves forward in the model in fixed steps or intervals. In this example, each interval was one day, but in different issues the time interval could range from milliseconds to years. In simulation terminology, these are called *time-slicing* models. Time-slicing models are the type of simulation that can most feasibly be carried out using a spreadsheet. There are two other main types of simulation models:

- continuous simulation models
- event-driven simulation models.

Each of these is much better suited to specialised software, as we shall now discuss.

♦ **Key concept** *There are three types of simulation model: time-slicing models, continuous simulation models and event-driven simulation models. Only time-slicing models can reasonably be developed using a spreadsheet package.*

Continuous simulation models

Continuous simulation models, or continuous simulations, are typically used where the time-slice interval is arbitrary, but should ideally be as short as possible for model accuracy. In other words, there is no 'natural' time step such as a daily review of stock levels or a monthly recording of financial performance information. An example might be the water levels and quality in a system of reservoirs. This is the territory of models based on system dynamics, and of related software packages such as Stella/iThink, PowerSim and Vensim. Such models are often conceptualised in terms of stocks and flows, and these packages are designed so that the verbalisation and formalisation steps of the model building can be combined into one. The software does the work of converting inputs in stock/flow terms into equations for the manager.

Note that continuous simulation packages can be used to build time-slicing models; there is an overlap between continuous time and discrete time slices, in much the same way that there is a slight degree of interchangeability between continuous and discrete variables, as we saw in Chapter 10.

Event-driven simulation models

Event-driven simulation models take a different approach from both of the other two types. To explain this, think of a supermarket checkout, the classic starting example of event-driven simulation. This could, of course, be modelled by a time-slicing approach, with a time interval of perhaps one minute or 30 seconds. However, this 'clock-watching' approach is not actually the way that most people looking at a set of supermarket checkouts would think about what they were seeing. Rather, they would be thinking in terms of 'what happens next' – especially if they are standing in one of the queues, when their uppermost thought is likely to be 'When is it my turn?' So, rather than considering the simulation in terms of time ticking forward, it is more natural (and easier) to think in terms of *events*. In this example, the key events are when a customer arrives in one of the queues, and when a customer finishes being served. There is certainly no 'natural' time step to use in a time-slicing model; the time interval of most interest is the *uncertain* length of time that it takes to serve a customer.

The best approach to take, therefore, is to build a model that is event driven, stepping forward not in fixed amounts, but in variable amounts to the next point in time that is of interest. The supermarket manager may then use such a model to help decide how many checkouts to have open at a particular time of day, whether some should be express checkouts, cash only and so on.

It is possible to handle different events in a time-slicing spreadsheet simulation model, normally by producing a column for each event and accessing events as needed. However, this is not event-driven in the true sense, because it will rely on a fixed time step and then testing each event to see if it has happened yet.

True event-driven or continuous simulations using a spreadsheet can only be constructed by doing a large amount of macro programming – almost amounting to writing a small simulation package in the spreadsheet itself.

For event-driven simulation, it is therefore better for the manager to invest in a specialised package. There are many packages available, varying from those that are intended to be accessible to the individual user, such as SIMUL8, to those intended for organisational use, such as WITNESS. There is also a range of facilities and prices, although these two features do not always correspond exactly. One of the great strengths of modern simulation packages is that they offer a broad range of visual display capabilities, going far beyond those of spreadsheets or other modelling packages. These enable the user to 'see' the model working on screen, using detailed, animated (and if necessary highly realistic) graphics. Thus the supermarket manager could 'see' the customer waiting at the checkout and being served and – if they have got it wrong – see the frustrated customers abandoning their shopping trolleys and walking out of the store! This sort of highly sophisticated summary model is well beyond current spreadsheet package capabilities, no matter how much macro programming the manager is prepared to do.

SUMMARY

In this chapter we have looked at the development and use of spreadsheet simulation models, where the key issue is the uncertain dynamic behaviour of the manager's system. We have shown how a simple model can gradually be made more complex in order to be more realistic, and how the manager may experiment with the model in order to gain insights into what policies to adopt in the real system. Finally, we have described three types of simulation model: time-slicing, continuous simulation and event-driven. Spreadsheet simulations are most suitable for relatively small time-slicing models.

END NOTES

1 To make ourselves perfectly clear, what we are discussing in this chapter is, in an economist's terms, Monte Carlo simulation. In the pre-computer era, generating the samples by the 'top hat' method we described in Chapter 10, or by manually calculating pseudo-random numbers, was extremely tedious. One research project therefore used roulette wheels for this task; hence the name 'Monte Carlo' simulation, from the casino in that city.

2 Unfortunately the spreadsheet solver (see Chapter 12) cannot be used to find the minimum in such cases, because it cannot cope with the uncertain values in the model. The best the solver might do, if the logic model happens to be suitable, is to find a minimum-cost solution with the specific values generated by the RAND function in one trial. There would, however, be no guarantee that this was the best solution overall.

3 Strictly speaking, even though each day's demand follows the same pattern of uncertainty, the manager should still run several trials, just in case there is something about the particular starting conditions (in this case, 427 items in stock and no orders) that affects the behaviour of the model. However, in this example the starting conditions have no significant effect.

FURTHER READING One of the best general introductions to simulation is Michael Pidd's *Computer Simulation in Management Science*, John Wiley, Chichester, 1992, now in its third edition. It covers everything from possible application areas to building and validating models, and discussion of the various types of software available. Another book with a good discussion of the problems of applying simulation is Stewart Robinson's *Successful Simulation: A Practical Approach to Simulation Projects*, McGraw-Hill, Maidenhead, 1994. Although it concentrates on event-driven simulation models, the advice on how to use the models is applicable to all types of simulation.

EXERCISES

1 What is the difference between the economist's definition of simulation and the management scientist's?

2 What is the relevance of simulation to establishing organisational policies and procedures?

3 Why are simulation models usually more complex than those for risk analysis?

4 Which type of simulation model are spreadsheet packages most suited for?

5 Build your own spreadsheet for the example considered in Figs 11.2 to 11.6, and use it to find what in your opinion is the 'best' reordering rule.

6 Change the pattern of uncertainty for the daily demand from the uniform distribution to:
   a) a triangular distribution with a peak at 200
   b) a normal distribution with a mean of 200 and a standard deviation of 25
   and examine what difference this makes to the 'best' rule found in Exercise 5.

7 Use the spreadsheet constructed in Exercise 5 to try to find the minimum-cost solution, assuming that holding an item in stock for one day costs 2.3 pence, placing an order costs £35 (irrespective of the order size) and each back-ordered unit costs £2. We recommend that you draw the information flow diagram for these additions to the logic model before amending your spreadsheet; this is one example where what is effectively a summary model will probably contain new intermediate variables.

8 Increase the number of days in the spreadsheet model to, say, 25. Experiment with the model to see if the simple reordering rule does indeed lead to alternating periods of under- and overstocking when the lead time is two days or more.

CHAPTER 12

Goal seeking and solving

INTRODUCTION

So far in Part Two we have covered the use of spreadsheets for automatic recalculation, and the facilities for 'What if?' analysis, enabling the user to explore many of the consequences inherent in a model, even when the values of one or more input factors are uncertain. However, 'What if?' or 'trial-and-error' approaches – even if they are as systematic as we have described in the previous three chapters – are not always what is needed. Sometimes the manager will want to work out 'answers' directly; 'What should be?' rather than 'What if?' It is a waste of time and effort for managers to search for a good solution themselves when it is possible to use the computer to calculate one that has whatever properties they are looking for. That is where the two related, but different, facilities of goal seeking and solving come in. We shall consider the simpler one, goal seeking, first, and then go on to look at solving. Note that for this chapter we return to conditions of certainty rather than uncertainty.

GOAL SEEKING

When would we use it?

We use the term goal seeking for cases when a manager is trying to find a way to achieve a target value for a particular variable. At its simplest – for example 'How many units do I need to sell to achieve a contribution to profit this month of £1200 if the contribution to profit per unit is £3?' – the manager should not need a spreadsheet to work out the answer. However, if several calculations like this need to be done one after another, or the relationship is a more complex one, that is where the spreadsheet comes in.

To explain goal seeking further, let's consider a simple example, as shown in Fig 12.1. Cell B1 shows the value of *number of units sold* for a product. Cell B2 is the value of its *unit price*. Cell B3 is the value of *sales revenue* for this product, which is defined by formula to be B1 multiplied by B2. We have already seen in Chapter 9 how the spreadsheet can be used for 'What if?' analysis on the basis of the values the manager chooses for the input factors: *number of units sold* (cell B1) and *unit price* (cell B2).

Often, however, the manager wants to explore the relationship the other way round, by setting a target value for one of the calculated variables in the model (the only one in this case is *sales revenue*) and seeing what the value of one of the input factors should be in order to achieve it. We mentioned in Chapter 5 that the relationship between types of managerial variable and types of model factor is not a fixed one.

◆ **Key concept**

Goal seeking *is where the manager sets a target value for one of the calculated variables in the model, and the spreadsheet works out what the value of one of the input factors should be in order to achieve it.*

A manager could explore the relationship themselves by manipulating the model at the verbalisation stage so that it could be used for 'What if?' analysis with different input factors, because if:

sales revenue = {number of units sold} × {unit price}

it is equally true that:

number of units sold = {sales revenue}/{unit price}

and:

unit price = {sales revenue}/{number of units sold}

Fig 12.1 Simple relationship before goal seeking

	A	B
1	Number of units sold	35000
2	Unit price (£)	2.78
3	Sales revenue (£)	97300

Thus the values in cells B2 and B3 in Fig 12.1 could be regarded as the input factors, and cell B1, defined as B3 divided by B2, the calculated variable.

Not so long ago, this was how the manager would have had to calculate the value of price or revenue in any spreadsheet package – by reinputting the modified relationships. These days, however, the market-leading packages will find a target value for any cell which is defined by a formula, i.e. for any calculated variable. This is known as goal seeking.[1] What goal seeking does is to enable the manager to reverse the roles of an input factor and a calculated variable, without having to build a new spreadsheet model.

In the example in Fig 12.1, goal seeking means keeping the value in either B1 or B2 fixed, and using the spreadsheet to find the value of the other one that will give a desired value for *sales revenue* (in B3). Figure 12.2 shows the result of keeping the value of *unit price* (one input factor) fixed at £2.78, and seeking the goal of a value of £100 000 for *sales revenue* (the calculated variable) by letting the value of *number of units sold* (the other input factor) vary. We can see that the value of *number of units sold* should be 35 971 in order to meet the target.

Typical uses of goal seeking are for all kinds of breakeven analysis and pricing decisions.

The relationship between the calculated variable and the input factor does not have to be either as direct or as simple as the one shown in Figures 12.1 and 12.2. Suppose that we extend our previous example to include costs (fixed and variable) as well as revenue, and a scrap rate to allow for the fact that some items may be made that cannot be sold because they are unsatisfactory, as for example with the silicon chips for microprocessors in computers. Thus for any given number of units sold, the number of units made will always have to be higher. The information flow diagram from the conceptualisation stage of building the spreadsheet model now looks like that shown in Fig 12.3.

Fig 12.2 Simple relationship after goal seeking

	A	B
1	Number of units sold	35971
2	Unit price (£)	2.78
3	Sales revenue (£)	100000

Fig 12.3 Information flow diagram for more complex example of goal seeking

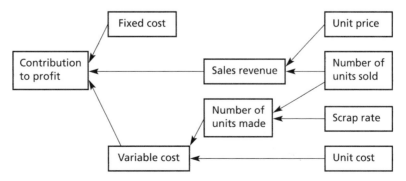

The verbalisation of the model is also much extended. Now, in addition to:

sales revenue = {number of units sold} × {unit price}

our model also includes the equations:

variable cost = {unit cost} × {number of units made}

contribution to profit = sales revenue – fixed cost – variable cost

number of units made = {number of units sold}/{1– scrap rate}

We assume here, for simplicity, that it is a sellers' market, so that we sell all the satisfactory units we can make. As sales should drive production in such circumstances, it is reasonable to treat *number of units sold* as the input factor (especially if we are the sales manager!), but a similar but different model could be built using *number of units made* instead.

This model now contains five input factors (the boxes in Fig 12.3 without input arrows):

- *number of units sold*
- *unit price*
- *unit cost*
- *fixed cost*
- *scrap rate*

Sales revenue has become an intermediate variable, together with two others:

- *number of units made*
- *variable cost.*

The calculated variable is now *contribution to profit*.

In Fig 12.4, we see the result of goal seeking with a target value of £100 000 for the calculated variable *contribution to profit*, by letting one of the input factors vary, in this case *number of units sold*. The result, as seen in cell B2, is a value of 226 978 units.

Fig 12.4 More complex example of goal seeking

	A	B
1		
2	Number of units sold (per month)	226978
3	Fixed cost (£/month)	29756
4	Unit cost (£)	2.12
5	Unit price (£)	2.78
6	Scrap rate (%)	4%
7		
8	Number of units made (per month)	236436
9	Variable cost (£/month)	501244
10	Sales revenue (£/month)	631000
11		
12	Contribution to profit (£/month)	100000

What's going on when the spreadsheet is goal seeking?

Goal seeking may be used whenever a cell in a spreadsheet contains a formula that refers to a value in another cell. It can also apply to several formulae in several cells. The common features are that there is a target value which the manager wishes to achieve for a calculated variable in one cell, that in order to hit that target only one input factor's value is allowed to change (however, the values of intermediate variables may also change), and that there are no other restrictions on the values which cells in the spreadsheet may take. The spreadsheet finds the appropriate value for this one changing input factor.

Referring to Fig 12.4, the target value is for the calculated variable *contribution to profit*, and the one input factor whose value is allowed to vary is *number of units sold*. We can expect, therefore, that as the value of *number of units sold* varies, so also will the values of the intermediate variables on the lines between *contribution to profit* and *number of units sold*, namely *sales revenue*, *variable cost* and *number of units made*.

In this simplest and most common form of goal seeking, with one target calculated variable and one input factor allowed to change, the 'answer' is then the 'What should be?' value for that one input factor. Note that any, or indeed all, of the other intermediate and calculated variables in the model may also change as a result of changing that one input factor.

Linearity and non-linearity in goal seeking

An important feature of the model you build is whether or not it is linear. As we discussed in Chapter 5, linear means that the relationships in the model satisfy the requirements of proportionality and additivity.

The goal-seeking facilities in spreadsheets can be activated, no matter how complex the relationship between the target calculated variable and the input factor – even if they include the use of the spreadsheet's built-in functions. However, it is up to the manager to decide whether the result produced is likely to be usable.

Whether the spreadsheet can find an exact value for the input factor which gives the target value for the calculated variable depends not on how many other input factors are involved in the relationships, or how many intermediate variables, but on whether the relationships between the model factors are linear. If all the relationships are linear, goal seeking is simple, quick and accurate.

◆ **Key concept**   *Goal seeking works best when all the relationships involved are linear.*

Non-linear models are usually harder for the spreadsheet to solve than linear ones, and in most cases this means that the manager will have to put up with an approximate solution rather than an exact one. This does not mean that the answer the spreadsheet gives will be 'wrong', merely that the spreadsheet has to work its way towards the answer over several attempts, getting nearer each time, rather than doing it in a single calculation.

There are, however, some non-linear problems where the goal-seeking facility cannot return an answer at all. This may be either because the target value the manager wants cannot be achieved, or because the operation of the goal-seeking facility is less than perfect. A spreadsheet with a good goal-seeking facility should be able to warn the user that the value it has found for the input factor is incorrect. For example, in Microsoft Excel, a message 'Goal Seeking with Cell . . . may not have found a solution' appears in such a case.

In general, as long as the relationships only involve the basic arithmetic operations +, −, × and /, and built-in functions depending only on arithmetic (such as SUM and MEAN), goal seeking nearly always gives an answer that achieves the target value to within 0.01 per cent.

How do we do it?

Goal seeking is very straightforward, and is usually controlled by a pop-up form or pull-down menu. There are three things the spreadsheet user has to do:

1 Select the cell containing the target calculated variable.
2 Input the target value for that variable.
3 Select the input factor of interest; the cell whose value will be allowed to vary.

The values for the answer, both for the input factor whose value is being allowed to vary and any other calculated variables related to it, will appear in the appropriate cells in the spreadsheet. Where the spreadsheet has to resort to approximate, rather than exact, calculation, another window will appear giving an indication of how close the actual value found for the target variable is to the original target value.

Changing more then one model factor in goal seeking

Some spreadsheet packages allow goal seeking in which several input factors in the same model change simultaneously by the same percentage. Such a facility effectively changes the model by including an extra set of relationships at the verbalisation step, of the form:

new value of input factor = {original value of input factor}
× {1 + {percentage change}/100}

The new input factor values in this type of goal seeking are actually intermediate variables, with *percentage change* as an extra input factor that is really the one changing. It could be argued that a model used in this manner is poorly constructed, unless the manager using it is sure that it is indeed reasonable to assume that the input factors would vary together in this way. At the very least, it goes against good practice since the value of the percentage change and the links between the input factor values are not visible in the spreadsheet itself.

SOLVING

When would we use it?

The crucial point about goal seeking is that the spreadsheet has to be able to work out the desired value for the target variable by changing only a single input factor. However, this approach is only suitable for relatively simple issues. Many issues involving 'What should be?' questions demand something more sophisticated than goal seeking, for one or both of the following reasons:

- Several input factors need to be allowed to change at once, independently from each other, instead of either just one input factor changing, or a range of input factors changing by the same percentage.
- There are constraints on the values that the model factors, or some combination of them, can take. (The principle of constraints was discussed in Chapter 5.)

In such cases, the manager needs the greater flexibility of *solving*. Solving applies to a greater variety of models, and therefore issues, than does goal seeking.[2]

♦ **Key concept** | *Solving involves finding the desired value for a target calculated variable by letting several input factors change at once, independently. There are usually also constraints on the values which the variables in the model can take. The spreadsheet solver calculates what the values of the input factors should be.*

When has solving been used?

The classic situation where the use of solving would help a manager is in any kind of resource-allocation problem. The resource(s) to be allocated might be machine time, people time, money, materials; the list is endless. There needs to be some way of measuring what constitutes the best solution to the problem, preferably so that 'best' means maximising or minimising the value of one variable. The most likely of these is one which maximises contribution to profit or one which minimises costs. Again, however, the list of possibilities is a long one, including minimising waiting time, minimising scrap, maximising investment return, maximising audience size and minimising redundancies.

Examples of applications

The two most basic types of solving applications in resource allocation are *blending* and *product mix* problems.

In blending problems, the issue is treated as being driven by demand. Given what must be produced, and the product specifications, what is the best way to achieve them? Typically here the objective will be to minimise cost.

In product mix problems, the issue is treated as being driven by supply. Given the resources available and the product specifications, what is the best that we can do with them? Typically the objective here will be to maximise contribution to profit.

The first major commercial success of solving techniques was in product mix problems.[3] In the early days – the 1950s – software had to be written specially to do the calculations; there were no solvers – or spreadsheets! The oil industry was in the forefront of this advance; nowadays it would not be reasonable to treat the oil industry as supply driven, but it was then. Models were built covering everything from what to do with the various types of crude oil to its transportation, and led to savings running into millions of dollars.

We list other types of example below, including both general categories of problem and specific examples for which these methods have been used in the 1990s. Note that it is not yet possible to solve all these problems using a spreadsheet solver; some of these problems lead to models which are too large for current spreadsheet solvers to handle, while others require more complicated formulations than we discuss here. They are included here to make you aware of the scope for solving, for the time when the rates of progress of technology and your own understanding bring them within your scope.

- Staffing problems, for example minimum-cost duty schedules.
- Cutting stock problems, where the aim is to minimise waste.
- Situations where cover is required, e.g. doctors or vets.
- Media selection for advertising, to maximise audience exposure.
- Investment portfolio selection, with various financial measures used to judge the best solution.
- Production planning, especially over multiple periods.
- Seat planning for an airline. How many seats of each class should there be on a particular flight?
- Choosing the cheapest way to make animal feed from the available ingredients.
- Blending fertiliser – mathematically much the same as the previous problem!
- Managing reservoir systems to provide water of suitable quality in the right quantities at the lowest cost.
- Deciding where to locate a new brewery.
- Allocating aircraft to flight segments for an airline.
- Determining the purchase and allocation of containers for a liner shipping company.
- Scheduling production for a company making computer chips, including deciding which plant to close when there is a downturn in demand.

Linearity and non-linearity

As with goal seeking, the simpler the formulae connecting the cells in the model containing the values of the variables, especially the one defining the target variable, the easier it is for the spreadsheet to find a solution. A particular point in solving is that it is much easier to find the largest or smallest possible value of a calculated variable, given some constraints, than to find a solution giving a fixed target value for the calculated variable, as in goal seeking. There is a whole area of study concentrating on models where all the formulae, constraints and the target variable are defined by linear relationships, and the manager wants to find the largest or smallest value, often called the *optimum*. This is called linear programming. The reason for the effort put into it is that it is the simplest type of model mathematically, and yet applies to a wide range of issues. We will concentrate on linear programming for the major part of this chapter, although the principles apply more widely.

What's going on when the spreadsheet is solving?

A model suitable for solving consists of three elements. We will call them the input factors, the constraints and the objective function.[4] Unfortunately, just about every spreadsheet solver uses different terms, and professional linear programmers use different terminology again (see Table 12.1 for some of the terms used).

Whatever the three elements are called, they serve the following purposes:

- The input factors make up the 'solution', i.e. they are the managerial variables for which the manager wants to find 'What should be?' values. In a product mix example, these would be how much to make of each product.
- The constraints are the restrictions on the values which the input factors and calculated variables can take. If there were no constraints, the manager might be able to solve the problem by simply goal seeking, or perhaps without needing computer software at all. In a product mix example, these would include the available quantities of each raw material, machine time and labour. Appendix 12A explains the most basic types of constraint using in solving.
- The objective function is the calculated variable for which the best value is to be found. In a product mix example, this might be the maximum contribution to profit. Note that despite the terminology typically used in spreadsheet packages, the objective function is *not* a cell, but a combination of variables, parameters and constants; the cell merely contains a formula by which it is calculated.

The spreadsheet solver's task is to find the set of values for the input factors which gives the best value for the objective function. This is known as the optimal solution. (Optimal is a mathematical term meaning 'best'; it is useful to use it as a reminder that what the spreadsheet solver finds is the best solution to the

Table 12.1 Terminology used in spreadsheet solvers

This book	Input factors	Constraints	Objective function
Wider meaning	The input factors that will be allowed to change	Formulae representing restrictions on the values of combinations of the input factors and calculated variables	The calculated variable for which the maximum or minimum value possible is to be found
Linear programmers	Decision variables	Constraints	Objective function
Microsoft Excel	Changing cells	Constraint cells	Target cell
Lotus 1-2-3	Adjustable cells	Constraint cells	Optimal cell

model.) Best, depending on the model, may mean the largest value (a maximising problem), the smallest value (a minimising problem) or a specific value.[5] Surprisingly enough, in most problems it is actually harder for the spreadsheet to find a solution that reaches a specific target value than for it to find the smallest or largest value possible. This is because achieving a specific value is more difficult mathematically, except in the goal-seeking case when only one input factor is allowed to be changed in order to hit the target. We shall concentrate on the maximising/minimising problems here.

There are likely to be many answers to a typical problem for which the manager needs to use the solver; normally there will in fact be an infinite number, which makes trial and error impossible. A set of values for the input factors that satisfy all the constraints is called *feasible*, or a *feasible solution*. Unfortunately, this terminology is not the same as those used elsewhere in the book, where we reserve 'solution' for the best possible answer; the term ought to be *feasible answer*. However, as *feasible solution* is more or less standard terminology in both solving and linear programming, we shall use feasible solution rather than feasible answer in the rest of the chapter.

◆ **Key concept**

> A **feasible solution** is a set of values for the input factors that satisfy all the constraints. An **optimal solution** is a feasible solution that gives the largest value of the objective function (in a maximising problem) or smallest value of the objective function (in a minimising problem).

An analogy

Solving is like trying to climb a mountain. The constraints of the problem determine the shape of the mountain; not only the parts you can see from where you are, but also what you know about the parts you cannot yet see. Visibility is better when the model is mathematically simpler. The mountain represents all the feasible solutions; every point on (or indeed inside) the mountain is a feasible solution. The objective function (the target calculated variable) tells you how high up the mountain you are. When all the relationships are linear, then you can always see where you are going, and the mountain has only one peak (top) corresponding to the best solution. Both of these make life easier! We shall come back to this analogy later.

Iteration

It is almost certain that the spreadsheet will need to work through several solutions (systematically – remember this is not 'trial and error') in order to find the best one. There are three possibilities for this iterative process.

The first is that the spreadsheet will find an exact solution after a certain number of steps, although we don't know in advance how many steps it might take. This is always the case for problems where all the relationships are linear, and a few other types as well.

The second is that the spreadsheet will produce a series of solutions, gradually getting better, without ever being certain that the best one has been reached. Normally the user can decide either to do a fixed number of tries (say

100), or to carry on until the difference in the value of the target calculated variable between successive solutions is less than a certain amount (say 0.01).

In such approximate solving solutions, you will be given the opportunity by the spreadsheet solver to specify how close an approximation you want it to find (perhaps to the nearest 0.1 or 0.01, say). Note that this is related to how much change there is between successive solutions; it does not guarantee that the final value of the calculated variable found is within 0.1 of the best possible value, or indeed anywhere near it at all. The spreadsheet solver stops when the solution it has found stops changing; that does not always mean that it has found the best solution.

Going back to our mountain analogy, if our mountain has several peaks, we may climb to the top of one of them and stop, because we cannot find an immediate way to go up any further. However, the peak we have reached may not be the highest one; there may be a higher peak that we cannot see. To use a different analogy, it's like going up in a lift/elevator when the display of which floor you are at is not working. You may get in and press the button for the top floor, but that doesn't mean that it will stop first at the top floor. So, when the doors open you have no way of knowing which floor you are on; you can only step out and hope that it *is* the right one.

The third possibility is that the spreadsheet solver cannot find any solutions that satisfy all the constraints at all (there is no mountain there to climb!). This is by no means uncommon. If your spreadsheet is supposed to be modelling an issue in a local scenario which already exists in the real world, then in these circumstances it would be safe to conclude that there is something wrong with the model. Whatever the current real-world answer is, it is certainly a feasible solution, even if it is not a very good one (which is presumably why the manager has built a spreadsheet in the first place). However, if the spreadsheet represents an issue which does not yet exist, it is only too plausible that the constraints cannot all be satisfied; 'you can't please all of the people all of the time'. Some spreadsheet solvers attempt to provide help in these circumstances by listing the inconsistent constraints, but this can be more of an art than a science and we shall not pursue it further here.

How do we do it?

Sensible use of a spreadsheet solver involves building and exploring an appropriate model, relevant to the issue with which the manager is dealing. It is important to remember that the solver only finds the optimal solution to the model in the spreadsheet; this does not mean that it will find the answer to the manager's issue in one go 'at the touch of a button', to use a much-loved phrase of science-fiction films (and even semi-serious advertisements). Even in a simple case, the solver gives us more information about the model than just the optimal solution, as we shall see from the example that follows. This may be extremely important if the manager wishes to change the initial data; remember, the models in this chapter operate under conditions of certainty.

MINICASE   Product mix

A company manufactures three products: umbrellas, anoraks and rucksacks. There are three stages in the manufacturing process, cutting, sewing and assembly, although the anoraks do not go through the assembly stage. Process times for each item (in minutes) are shown in Table 12.2.

Contribution to profit per item is £0.93 for umbrellas, £1.27 for anoraks and £2.16 for rucksacks. The main restriction on production is machine time: the company has two cutting machines, one sewing machine and one assembly machine, and works a standard 40-hour week.

What the manager wants to know is how much of each product to manufacture in order to make the greatest total contribution to profit.

First, the manager needs to formulate this as a problem suitable for the spreadsheet solver. This entails following the conceptualisation, verbalisation and formalisation stages, as set out in Chapter 5. We have already progressed some of the way through the conceptualisation stage by specifying the constraints on machine time and that the objective is to maximise contribution to profit; the corresponding information flow diagram is shown in Fig 12.5.

Verbalisation involves specifying the relationships as follows:

> *total contribution to profit* = sum of {*profit contribution per item* × *number of items made*}

(this is the objective function)

> *total cutting time* = sum of {*cutting time per item* × *number of items made*}

> *total sewing time* = sum of {*sewing time per item* × *number of items made*}

> *total assembly time* = sum of {*assembly time per item* × *number of items made*}

> *maximum cutting time* = *number of cutting machines* × *number of minutes in week*

> *maximum sewing time* = *number of sewing machines* × *number of minutes in week*

> *maximum assembly time* = *number of assembly machines* × *number of minutes in week*

> *total cutting time* ≤ *maximum cutting time*

> *total sewing time* ≤ *maximum sewing time*

> *total assembly time* ≤ *maximum assembly time*

(these form the constraints)

Table 12.2 Process times in minutes for product mix example

Process	Product		
	Umbrella	Anorak	Rucksack
Cutting	0.5	9.0	6.5
Sewing	1.5	6.0	3.8
Assembly	2.5	0.0	3.0

Fig 12.5 Information flow diagram for solving example

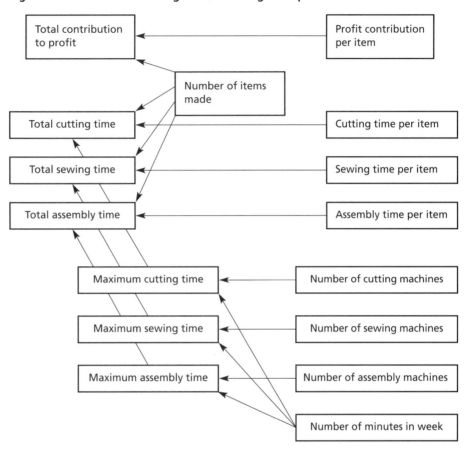

Then the manager enters the data model, and this part of the logic model, into the spreadsheet. Note that the rest of the logic model is built into the solver itself. This is both a strength and a weakness. As always, it is important to lay out the spreadsheet in such a way that it is easy to see and understand both the model and the results. All solvers make assumptions about how the model is set out; these vary between different spreadsheet packages, so we cannot give general advice. However, in most cases it does not make it easy either to separate the logic and data models, as we recommend, or to give the variables exactly the desired names. As we said earlier, there is no one 'right way' for this, but it is important for you to find out any particular requirements of the package you are using. Our version of the spreadsheet now appears as in Fig 12.6. We have managed a partial separation of the data model (shown with thicker borders) and the logic model (shown lightly shaded), but it is far from ideal. Similarly, the total time and maximum time column headings have to be read along with the row labels.

The next step is to tell the spreadsheet solver what to do, by specifying:

1 Which cell contains the objective function/target calculated variable.
2 What to do with it, i.e. maximise or minimise.

Fig 12.6 Product-mix example: spreadsheet before solving

Data model

Data model

	A	B	C	D	E	F	G
1	Process:	Umbrella	Anorak	Rucksack	Total time (minutes/week)	Maximum time (minutes/week)	Machines
2	Cutting time per item (minutes)	0.5	9.0	6.5	0	4800	2
3	Sewing time per item (minutes)	1.5	6.0	3.8	0	2400	1
4	Assembly time per item (minutes)	2.5	0.0	3.0	0	2400	1
5						Total contribution to profit (£/week)	Number of minutes in week
6	Profit contribution per item (£)	0.93	1.27	2.16		0	2400
7							
8	Number of items made	0	0	0			

Logic model

3 Which cells are the input factors allowed to change.

4 Which are the constraints. This is usually by far the most difficult part.

In Fig 12.6, the value of the objective function is shown in cell G6 (formula B6*B8+C6*C8+D6*D8) and it is to be maximised. The formula could also have been written as SUMPRODUCT(B6..D6,B8..D8); the SUMPRODUCT function is very useful in building models for solving. The values of the input factors allowed to change are in cells B8, C8 and D8. Remember that these are part of the logic model, not the data model; the solver will calculate what these values should be. There are three constraints: E2<=F2, E3<=F3 and E4<=F4.

Warning

Many spreadsheet solvers specifically need to be told about the so-called *non-negativity requirement*, i.e. that negative values of the input factors are not possible. Otherwise they may fail to find the best answer, i.e. produce an optimal solution to the model that includes negative values for some input factors.

The main spreadsheet appears as in Fig 12.7.

From this we can see that the best course of action is to make 480 rucksacks and 384 umbrellas this week (and no anoraks at all), giving a value for *total contribution to profit* of £1393.92.

Fig 12.7 Product-mix example: spreadsheet after solving

	A	B	C	D	E	F	G
1	Process:	Umbrella	Anorak	Rucksack	Total time (minutes/week)	Maximum time (minutes/week)	Machines
2	Cutting time per item (minutes)	0.5	9.0	6.5	3312	4800	2
3	Sewing time per item (minutes)	1.5	6.0	3.8	2400	2400	1
4	Assembly time per item (minutes)	2.5	0.0	3.0	2400	2400	1
5						Total contribution to profit (£/week)	Number of minutes in week
6	Profit contribution per item (£)	0.93	1.27	2.16	1393.92		2400
7							
8	Number of items made	384	0	480			

Sensitivity analysis

This result is certainly useful to the manager, but it is by no means the only information which the spreadsheet solver can give. More information is available without any more calculation on the manager's part (or the spreadsheet solver's). Once the solver has finished, three types of information are normally available:

1 The *objective function value* for the optimal solution.
2 The *values* of the input factors for that optimal solution.
3 How much *slack* (if ≤) or *surplus* (if ≥) there is left in each constraint. The slack or surplus is the difference between the left- and right-hand sides of the constraint (for example, between the values of *total cutting time* and *maximum cutting time*). A *binding* constraint is one whose slack or surplus is 0, i.e. the two sides are equal.

Some of this is already displayed in the spreadsheet; some is available in other reports. Exactly what is where depends on the package you are using.

For example, by looking at the spreadsheet in Fig 12.7 we can discover the following:

● The two cutting machines are severely underused in this solution; only 3312 minutes of the available 4800 minutes per week are needed. The constraint on cutting time has a *slack* of 1488 minutes (=4800–3312).
● The sewing and assembly constraints are *binding*, which means that they have reached their limit; the slack is zero in each case. The restrictions imposed by the amount of sewing time and assembly time available are preventing a greater contribution to profit being made.

Fig 12.8 A sensitivity report from a spreadsheet solver

Input factors		Final value	Reduced cost	Objective coefficient	Allowable increase	Allowable decrease
Cell	Name					
$B$8	Number Umbrella	384	0	0.93	0.52	0.08
$C$8	Number Anorak	0	−1.86	1.27	1.86	1E+30
$D$8	Number Rucksack	480	0	2.16	0.20	0.62

Constraints		Final value	Shadow price	Constraint R.H. side	Allowable increase	Allowable decrease
Cell	Name					
$E$2	Cutting Time	3312	0	1488	1E+30	1488
$E$3	Sewing Time	2400	0.52	0	504	960
$E$4	Assembly Time	2400	0.06	0	1600	505

We can also use the *sensitivity analysis* reports, one of which is shown in Fig 12.8. Note that although this was produced from a spreadsheet with exactly the same structure as that in Fig 12.6, the names were changed to make this report easier to read. Once we know what we are doing, we can discover from the sensitivity analysis that, for example:

- The profit contribution from anoraks would have to go up by at least £1.86 before it became worthwhile to make them.
- Any more money for overtime or new machinery would be much better spent on sewing than on assembly.

We shall now explain what the sensitivity analysis reveals in more detail, taking the items in Fig 12.8 in order.

♦ **Key concept**   *The value of using a spreadsheet solver is not just in the 'optimal' solution it finds. It comes as much from the **sensitivity analysis** of what effect changes in the input data values will have on that solution.*

Final value

These have already been seen in the solution as shown in Fig 12.7; no more needs to be said.

Reduced cost

This is the most important information available in the sensitivity analysis report about each managerial variable/input factor. For each managerial variable not included in the optimal solution (not included means that its input factor's value = 0), the reduced cost is the amount lost, compared to the optimal solution, if the manager insists on having one unit of that activity in the solution. Obviously the amount lost is 0 if the activity is already in the optimal solution! So, from Fig 12.8, we see that the reduced cost for anoraks is £1.86; making one anorak would reduce the value of *total contribution to profit* by £1.86. That is where the name comes from: making one anorak would 'cost' us £1.86 in lost contribution to profit.[6]

Equivalently, it is the amount by which the value of that input factor's objective function coefficient (*profit contribution per item* in this example) would have to improve to make the activity worth doing (i.e. to make the input factor's value > 0). The value of *profit contribution per item* for anoraks would have to go up by £1.86, from £1.27 to £3.13, before it was worth making any.

Shadow price or dual price

The most important information available in the sensitivity analysis report about each constraint lies in the *shadow prices* (also known as *dual prices*). For each constraint that has no slack or surplus, the shadow price measures the rate at which the objective function value would improve if the constant term in the constraint (often referred to as the right-hand side), for example *maximum cutting time*, were to increase.

Where the constraint is the amount of a resource available, as in this example, this improvement is, in an economist's terms, the maximum that it would be worth paying for an extra unit of that resource – that is why it is called a price.

From Fig 12.8, we see that the shadow prices are 0.52 for sewing and 0.06 for assembly. We need to think about the units here; they will always be (units the objective function is measured in) per (units the constraint is measured in). In this case, the objective function *total contribution to profit* is measured in £, and all the *maximum time* values in minutes, giving £ per minute as the units for both these constraints. Thus, for example, if the manager can arrange extra *maximum sewing time* (current value 2400 minutes each week, in cell F3) for less than £0.52 per minute, the value of *total contribution to profit* could be increased.

Objective coefficient and allowable increase/decrease

The objective coefficient (or objective function coefficient) of an input factor is the value of the coefficient of that input factor in (the formula for) the objective function, for example £0.93 for *number of umbrellas made*. For each input factor, the allowable increase and decrease indicate the range of values of its objective (function) coefficient within which the current set of input factor values still gives the optimal solution. For example, the value of *profit contribution per item* (the objective function coefficient) for rucksacks could go down by as much as £0.62 from its current £2.16 before it would be better to change from the '384 umbrellas, 480 rucksacks, no anoraks' solution.

Sometimes, no change of a particular kind would make any difference to the optimal solution. For example, we know from Fig 12.7 that anoraks do not contribute enough to profit at present (compared to rucksacks and umbrellas) for it to be worth making any of them. A reduction in their profit contribution will therefore only make them even less worthwhile, so no decrease in the value of *profit contribution per item* for the anorak, however large, will change the optimal solution. Solvers have trouble in expressing this situation elegantly in sensitivity analysis reports. Typically, the allowable increase/decrease value is shown as either 'INFINITY', or the largest number the package can cope with, such as the '1E+30' shown in Fig 12.8 as the 'Allowable decrease' in the value of *profit contribution per item* for the anorak. 1E+30 is mathematical shorthand for the number consisting of 1 followed by thirty 0s; it is used because 1000000000000000000000000000000 would not fit into the space available, as you can see! So don't be worried by such 'odd' values.

Constraint R.H. side and allowable increase/decrease

For the constraints, the ranges are those changes to the 'right-hand side' values (such as *maximum cutting time*) within which the shadow prices apply. For example, the potential worth of extra sewing time of £0.52 per extra minute applies to anything up to an extra 504 minutes per week. Conversely, the loss of any of the current 2400 minutes per week value of *maximum sewing time*, up to 960 minutes per week, would reduce the value of *total contribution to profit* by £0.52 per minute lost. An economist would say that, at the margin, sewing time is worth £0.52 per minute.

Point to note

Note that all the sensitivity analysis information discussed above applies only to a change to one input factor value in the data model. To see the effect of changes to several input factor values, it is necessary to change the data and run the spreadsheet solver again.

Using solving

Our remarks about the sensitivity analysis information and the possibility of changing the data and running the spreadsheet solver again should not be taken lightly. It is very tempting, when using the spreadsheet in this 'What should be?' mode, to think that whatever the spreadsheet tells you must be right, and follow the 'optimal solution' unquestioningly.

However, this is a situation where the old computing adage 'garbage in, garbage out' is even more true than usual. The solution to the spreadsheet model should be regarded as a starting point for what to do in the real world, nothing more. Only when the consequences of changes in the data, potential errors in the model (preferably sought using the techniques mentioned in Chapter 8) and non-quantifiable factors have been carefully considered *might* it then be safe to apply the model's optimal solution in the real world.

♦ **Key concept**   *Only you, the manager, can judge whether the optimal solution the spreadsheet solver has found is the appropriate one for the real-world issue in your local scenario.*

Beyond linear programming

Our analogy again

When all the relationships are linear, climbing to the peak of our mountain (solving) is straightforward. However, in non-linear problems, life is more difficult. The mountain may have several peaks of very strange shapes; it may be very foggy, and the point we are trying to find may not be at one of the peaks anyway, but inside the mountain instead. In such cases, we may need to be a miner as well as a mountaineer!

So, although most spreadsheet solvers will attempt to solve almost any problem matching the input factors–constraints–objective function format, don't be surprised if the spreadsheet solver fails to find the solution to a non-linear problem. In some types of problem, whether the spreadsheet solver will work or not depends on the precise values in the spreadsheet (the data model), not on the general structure of the problem (the logic model) at all. We shall therefore discuss just one of the simpler non-linear solving models here, integer programming. Most spreadsheet solvers cope quite well with this, for small problems.

Integer programming

In many problems, the values produced by goal seeking or solving do not come out exactly as whole numbers. This is not a problem if the input factors involved are infinitely divisible anyway, as in many mixing or blending problems, or if the values may be regarded as averages over a period, so that an item which is part-finished today may be completed tomorrow.

Even where only whole units make sense, if the typical values of the input factors are large enough, this will not matter much. For example, in Fig 12.2, the number of units sold is rounded to the nearest whole number and the sales revenue is rounded to the nearest pound; to achieve exactly £100 000 of revenue, the company would have to sell 35 971.2230... units, while the exact revenue from selling 35 971 units would be £99 999.38. We probably cannot meaningfully make or sell 0.2230... of a unit, but the difference between the exact solution and the rounded one, less than one-thousandth of a per cent, is not likely to be significant.

On the other hand, if the typical values of the input factors are small, rounding effects may be crucial. For example, solving is often used for capacity-planning decisions like the aircraft and container-allocation examples mentioned earlier; a solution which suggested buying 7.28 of one type of container and 3.84 of another would be meaningless. In such a scenario, rounding the solution to the nearest whole numbers often either leaves a solution which fails to satisfy the constraints, or does not give the best solution. In these cases, in which some or all of the input factors are restricted to taking integer (whole number) values only, the solution needs to be found by the technique of *integer programming* instead of linear programming. Many spreadsheet solvers can handle integer programming. However, as solving an integer-programming problem typically includes solving a series of related linear-programming problems, it takes much longer than a linear-programming problem with the same logic model structure.

Integer programming also makes another very useful modelling device available to the manager; the 0–1 variable. This is a variable which can only take the values 0 or 1, and so can be used to represent yes/no factors in a model, as well as many other relationships. For example, in planning a roster, each worker either is, or is not, assigned to a particular shift. Any roster can accordingly be represented by a set of 0s and 1s, the 1s representing the shifts worked.

Carrying out integer programming using a spreadsheet solver is very similar to linear programming. Usually the only difference is that it is necessary to indicate which input factors may only take integer values, in the same stage of model building as specifying the constraints.

WHAT IF I NEED MORE?

The same software, from Frontline Systems, is actually at the heart of the solver in several well-known spreadsheet packages. Although satisfactory for linear and integer programming, all spreadsheet solvers have their limitations, in terms of size of model, speed of solution and handling of non-linear models. There are many specialised packages available for performing linear programming and various other kinds of mathematical programming. The best-known (and one of the cheapest) linear programming packages is LINDO. Non-linear programming is much harder in computational terms, and there are fewer good general-purpose packages available; LINGO and GINO, from the LINDO 'stable', are again among the best known of the cheaper ones.

What the specialist packages offer is the ability to solve very much larger problems. The downside of this is that the input is not quite as flexible as with a spreadsheet, although it is relatively easy to transfer a problem from one format to the other. In the middle ground between these two extremes are spreadsheet add-ins such as What's Best!, again from the LINDO stable.

Many real-life problems are still far beyond the capabilities of even today's PCs to solve, but in such cases the acquisition and use of specialised software are likely to be a major organisational decision, rather than an issue for an individual manager. Devising constraints for more complex issues is also an aspect where expert help is often required.

SUMMARY

In this chapter we have considered goal seeking and solving. Goal seeking and solving are both used to find out what the values of certain input factors in a model should be, in order to give a desired target value for one of the calculated variables. In goal seeking, this target value is a specified figure, whereas in solving it is more commonly the maximum or minimum value possible. Goal seeking applies to the case where only one input factor is allowed to vary. Solving not only allows several input factors to vary, but also allows there to be constraints on the solution produced. We have concentrated here on linear programming, as that is the kind of problem to which spreadsheet solvers are best suited.

END NOTES

1 This facility is variously known as goal seeking, back solving or back substitution. We shall use the term goal seeking.

2 A mathematician's viewpoint would be that goal seeking is just a *special case* of the more general activity of solving.

3 One of the earliest blending problems tackled by solving was diet formulation. In this case there is just one 'product', the diet, and the aim is to choose the ingredients to do this at minimum cost so that nutritional requirements are met. The snag has always been that, while the nutritional requirements are easy to model in an appropriate form, it is virtually impossible to bring taste into the model. Nevertheless, solving has been used to minimise costs in pet food and animal feed manufacture.

4 It is possible to have more than one objective function, but the extra difficulty that this introduces is beyond our scope here.

5 Strictly speaking, finding a target value of the objective function subject to constraints is an entirely different problem mathematically to finding a maximising or minimising value, but as spreadsheet solvers generally offer such facilities, it would be churlish not at least to mention them here.

6 This is an example of an *opportunity cost*, the 'cost' of a lost or missed opportunity; a concept with which you may be familiar from economics. In linear programming, such a cost always appears as a negative amount, because it is a loss rather than a gain

FURTHER READING We are not aware of any books as yet that look specifically at applications of goal seeking or solving spreadsheet models. Chapter 10 of *Decision Support Systems: A Knowledge-based Approach* by Clyde W. Holsapple and Andrew B. Whinston, West, Minneapolis/St Paul, 1996, may be of interest to those who would like spreadsheet solvers put into a wider context.

By contrast, the literature on mathematical programming in general is vast. A good introduction to the techniques is Tony Dacre and Mik Wisniewski's *Mathematical Programming: Optimization for Business and Management Decision-making*, McGraw-Hill, 1990. If you want assistance with building the models, the standard textbook on building mathematical programming models of all kinds, concentrating on going from the conceptualisation to the verbalisation and formalisation stages, is H. Paul Williams's *Model Building in Mathematical Programming*, John Wiley, Chichester, second edition, 1993. Most North American books on management science devote around half their content to mathematical programming. Perhaps the best of them is *Introduction to Management Science* by Anderson, Sweeney and Williams, now in its sixth edition, West, Minneapolis/St Paul, 1995.

EXERCISES

1 From the spreadsheet shown in Fig 12.1, use goal seeking to find what the number of units sold should be at a unit price of £2.78, to give sales revenue of £120 000.

2 From the same spreadsheet, use goal seeking to find what the unit price should be to give sales revenue of £120 000, assuming that 38 000 units are sold.

3 Draw up the information flow diagram for the example in Fig 12.3 for the alternative model that *number of units made* is an input factor, and thus *number of units sold* a calculated variable.

4 In the ABC Company electricity tariff example in Chapter 5, use goal seeking to find out how many units used on the ordinary tariff would give a quarterly cost of £200.

5 Using the sensitivity analysis output shown in Fig 12.8, state how much the total contribution to profit would increase if an extra hour (60 minutes) of assembly time were available per week.

6 In Fig 12.8, what does the shadow price of 0 for cutting time mean?

7 What is the difference between linear programming and integer programming?

8 Explain in your own words when you would use goal seeking and when you would use solving.

9 Use the first example from the goal-seeking section to explain why the relationship between types of managerial variable and types of model factor is not a fixed one.

10 In the ABC Company example, assuming that the number of units used remains at 3000 per quarter and all other costs are unchanged, use goal seeking to find what the cost per unit on the small-user tariff would have to be in order to give the same quarterly cost as for the ordinary tariff.

11 In the example in Fig 12.6, suppose that the company is considering increasing awareness of its brand by putting a new logo on all products. This will increase the sewing times to 2.5 minutes per item for umbrellas, 6.5 minutes per item for anoraks and 4.8 minutes per item for rucksacks. Price changes for these new 'designer products' will mean that the profit contributions are now £1.13, £1.32 and £2.16 per item respectively (designer rucksacks are no big deal!). Use the spreadsheet solver to find the best solution to this modified problem, i.e. the one that maximises the total contribution to profit in £ per week. Would you recommend that the company goes ahead with this plan?

12 A pet food manufacturing company advertises the 1kg 'megamix size' of its premier cat food as meeting the following nutritional requirements:
- energy: at least 2000 kcalories
- at least 25 per cent protein
- not more than 11 per cent fat
- at least 1.7 units of fibre.

Seven ingredients are currently available for the cat food: wheat, poultry meal, meat meal, fish meal, corn, soya and maize. Their properties are shown in Table 12.3.

Table 12.3 Cat food ingredients

	Wheat	Poultry meal	Meat meal	Fish meal	Corn	Soya	Maize
Energy (kcal/kg)	1000	2500	3500	3300	1800	1900	1900
Protein (%)	11	55	81	69	60	43	9
Fat (%)	2	25	11	9	4	2	4
Fibre (units/kg)	2.5	0.5	1.2	0.5	0.8	5.5	2.2
Cost (p/kg)	12.75	17.5	31	28.4	23.15	14.9	16.35

From past experience, the amount of soya should be no more than 0.25kg, since any more than that amount produces a texture which the cats dislike.

How should the company blend the ingredients to meet the requirements at minimum cost? (Hint: You will need to include a continuity constraint (see Appendix 12A).)

APPENDIX 12A: TYPES OF CONSTRAINT IN SOLVING

N.B. There has long been a convention in mathematical books about solving, and in most computer programs for it, that all constraints are written with just the constant term on the right-hand side and all the other terms on the left. Most of the specialist packages require the input data to be in this form. This luckily does not apply in some spreadsheet solvers, however. Some spreadsheet solvers, such as the one in Lotus 1-2-3, represent each constraint as a logical formula, in which case any cell entry acceptable as a logical formula would be acceptable as a constraint. Others, such as the one in Microsoft Excel, enforce the 'right-hand side' style. All constraints here are shown in 'right-hand side' style for general applicability.

The five most common types of constraint are:

1 Using up a resource.
2 Meeting a requirement.
3 Continuity (making sure things add up).
4 Upper and/or lower bounds.
5 Representing ratios.

We shall discuss each in turn.

Using up a resource

Using up a resource means a $\leq$ constraint. The resource might be time, money or a raw material, for example. The information flow chart always looks like Fig 12.9.

The corresponding verbalisation is:

total amount of resource used = sum of {*amount of resource used per item × number of items*}

total amount of resource used ≤ maximum amount of resource available

(Note that the verbalisation usually requires two statements for each constraint.)

Fig 12.9 Information flow diagram for 'using up resource' constraint

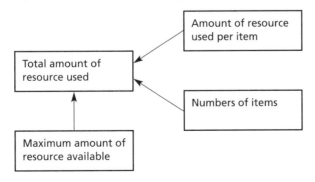

So, for example, if:

- there are 156 units of the resource available
- three products use it up, the values of *number of items* of these products being in cells B2, B3 and B4 respectively
- one item of each product uses 0.38, 0.57 and 0.46 of the resource respectively

then the corresponding constraint will look like this:

$$0.38*B2 + 0.57*B3 + 0.46*B4 \quad \leq \quad 156$$

How much of this resource   *How much of the resource*
the products require   *there is available*

The cutting, sewing and assembly constraints in the example featured in this chapter were all of this form.

Meeting a requirement

Meeting a requirement means a ≥ constraint, for example the minimum number of calories per day needed in a healthy diet. The information flow chart always looks like Fig 12.10.

The corresponding verbalisation is:

total amount provided = sum of {*amount provided per unit of input factor*
× number of units of input factor}

total amount provided ≥ *minimum amount needed*

(Note again that the verbalisation usually requires two statements for each constraint.)

So, for example, if:

- the total amount required is 0.30
- three input factors contribute to it, the values of *number of units of input factor* for these being in cells C1, C2 and C3 respectively
- one unit of each input factor contributes 0.24, 0.95 and 0.71 respectively
  then the corresponding constraint will look like this:

Fig 12.10 Information flow diagram for 'meeting a requirement' constraint

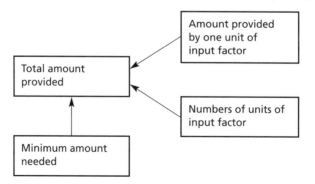

$$0.24*C1 + 0.95*C2 + 0.71*C3 \geq 0.30$$

How much there is as a result   *How much the minimum*
of all the input factors   *requirement is*

Continuity

Computer software has no common sense. We have mentioned in this chapter that it is often necessary to tell the spreadsheet solver that negative values of the input factors are not allowed, even when this would be obvious to a human being. Similarly, we need to tell the spreadsheet solver that, for example, the total weight of the ingredients in 1kg of pet food has to be 1kg! Such a constraint, making sure the whole equals the sum of the parts, is called a continuity constraint: it is always an = constraint. The conceptualisation and verbalisation we leave as an exercise to the reader. Examples of this type of constraint are:

D1 + D2 + D3 = 1   (proportions)
or   D1 + D2 + D3 = 100 (percentages)
or   E1 – E2 – E3   = 0   (component parts)

In the last example, cell E1 might contain the value of *total hours worked*, E2 the value of *hours worked at normal pay rates* and E3 the value of *hours worked at overtime pay rates*.

Upper and lower bounds

Constraints such as maximum anticipated demand or known contracts for a product are typically represented as what are known as simple upper and lower bounds respectively. These constraints consist of a single cell reference, a ≤ sign (upper bound) or a ≥ sign (lower bound), and a number for the right-hand side value. No information flow chart is needed here, as only one input factor is involved.

Upper bound

Suppose that the maximum demand for widgets is expected to be 320 units. There is thus no point in making more than that number.

Verbalisation: *number of widgets produced* ≤ 320. If the value of *number of widgets produced* is in cell F2, the constraint looks like:

F2 ≤ 320

Lower bound

Suppose that we have a contract to supply 250 widgets. Therefore we must make at least that number.

Verbalisation: *number of widgets produced* ≥ 250. If the value of *number of widgets produced* is still in cell F2, the constraint looks like:

F2 ≥ 250

Simple upper and lower bounds involving one of the input factors like this are easier to deal with than other types of constraint, so some spreadsheet solvers have a different way of entering these constraints. It is good practice to put the value of the bound (320 and 250 in our examples) into a separate cell in the model if possible, but some spreadsheet packages do not permit this.

Representing ratios

Many constraints are expressed at the conceptualisation stage in the form of ratios, for example investment portfolio selection with four projects A, B, C and D, where 'investment in A must be at least half of the total investment'. The information flow chart looks like Fig 12.11.

This conceptualisation leads to a verbalisation such as:

Investment in A $\geq$ *0.5 × Total investment*
Total investment $=$ *Investment in A + Investment in B + Investment in C*
+ Investment in D

To represent ratios, a little algebraic manipulation is needed; ignore this part if you don't like algebra! If the value of *Investment in A* is in cell A1, and so on, then we replace *Total investment* with *Investment in A + Investment in B + Investment in C + Investment in D*, leading to the following spreadsheet formalisation:

$$0.5{*}A1 - 0.5{*}B1 - 0.5{*}C1 - 0.5{*}D1 \geq 0$$

Similarly, if we have an advertising media selection problem, including in the conceptualisation 'expenditure on TV ads must be no more than three times as much as on radio ads', than the verbalisation is:

TV expenditure $\leq$ *3 × Radio expenditure*

and the spreadsheet formalisation is:

$$H1 - 3{*}H2 \leq 0$$

where the value of *TV expenditure* is in cell H1 and the value of *Radio expenditure* is in cell H2.

Fig 12.11 Information flow diagram for ratio constraint

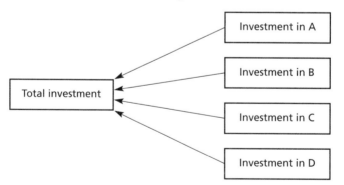

Project management

INTRODUCTION

What is a project?

To begin this chapter, we need to define our terms: what do we mean by a project? A project is a set of activities that together make up a self-contained piece of work with a definite finish, for which a manager is responsible. Managing the project involves organising people and perhaps other resources in order to get the work done. It could be the construction of a new manufacturing plant, or the installation of new anti-virus software on all the department's computers, or even arranging the annual departmental social outing. The crucial point that distinguishes a project from a single activity is that 'what happens when' is important, both in advance planning and in monitoring the project when it is taking place. Thus making a telephone call (to someone whose number you already know) is an activity, not a project. Calling an informal meeting between yourself and the two people working at the desks on either side of you is also merely an activity ('just do it', as the phrase goes), but arranging a meeting of representatives from several companies working together on collaborative research would probably need to be treated as a project, albeit a relatively small one.

◆ **Key concept**

A project is a set of activities that together make up a self-contained piece of work that involves organising other resources in order to get the work done. What distinguishes a project from a single activity is that 'what happens when' is important, both in advance planning and in monitoring the project when it is taking place.

Planning large and complex projects is one of management's biggest problems. The management of a complex project such as building an office block, replacing a generator in a power station, or designing a large computer system, is a difficult task, partly because such projects consist of a large number of separate but interconnected activities; there could easily be as many as 25 000 of them. Even smaller projects, such as producing an advertising leaflet, can present managers with problems. One of the difficulties is that there are three conflicting objectives in project management:

- time
- cost
- quality.

A widely held rule of thumb is that you can only achieve the desired performance on two of these objectives by sacrificing the project's performance on the third!

Modelling techniques to help with project management have been available since the mid-1950s. Strictly speaking, these should be known as project network analysis models, because there are many more aspects that are important to project management than these models alone cover, for example how to motivate the staff working on the project. However, the terms project-management techniques and project-management models are now in common usage with this meaning, especially in the IT industry and the specialised software packages for 'project management', and so we have called the chapter project management.[1]

The best-known project-management techniques are critical path analysis and PERT (project evaluation and review technique). As with many good ideas, several organisations invented them more or less simultaneously:

- critical path analysis was invented by the Dupont Chemical Co
- PERT was invented by the RAND Corporation of California, working for the US Navy
- major sequence planning was invented by the Midland Region of the UK's CEGB (Central Electricity Generating Board)

Unlike the other organisations, the CEGB was not particularly interested in telling others about its technique, and so you will not find major sequence planning mentioned in books or articles about project management. This is a pity in one sense, because we have found that its name gives most people a clearer idea of what the techniques are actually concerned with – planning the major sequences of activities in the project, i.e. the most important ones.

Where are project-management techniques used?

Project-management techniques were originally developed for use on very large projects indeed: building chemical plants for Dupont, developing a submarine-launched nuclear missile defence system for the US Navy, and constructing power stations for the CEGB. All three of these come under the broad heading of 'engineering' projects, and the techniques were rapidly adopted in all types of heavy engineering, including civil, mechanical, electrical and aeronautical. The use of these techniques gradually spread to light engineering and electronics, and to more diverse fields such as planning an audit visit and designing and introducing a new product. With the advent of PCs in the 1980s, the use of these techniques spread even further, for example to information systems development and organising conferences.

A spectrum of recent uses includes (but is by no means limited to):

- all types of engineering:
  - assembling bicycles
  - building houses
  - constructing power stations
- building the Channel Tunnel
- launching a new product
- developing a computer system
- repair and maintenance planning
- audit planning
- planning a university department's student social.

When are project-management techniques useful?

In order for project-management techniques to be useful to the manager, the following requirements must be met:

- The project must comprise several distinct and separable activities; there might be as many as 25 000 of them, in the case of building a power station, but the techniques can be useful for projects with as few as 10 activities.
- The logical links between these activities must be known; for example, the foundations of a building must be laid before work can start on the walls.
- Some of the activities must be able to take place simultaneously; otherwise the technique is not needed, because the manager's decision at any point is trivial.
- The duration of each activity, and the resources required for it, must be able to be estimated.
- The project is finished when (and only when) all of the activities have been carried out. Projects with alternative or optional activities are beyond the scope of the usual range of project-management techniques, and are best modelled using simulation (see Chapter 11).

Techniques such as critical path analysis and PERT[2] concentrate on the first two of the three objectives mentioned earlier, especially time and the interaction between time and cost. They enable the manager to work out the answers to key questions such as:

1 How long will the project take?
2 What is the minimum time in which we can complete the project?
3 Which activities should be done first/next?
4 What effect will a delay in one of the activities have?
5 Which activities must we be extra sure to try to keep going according to the plan?
6 Is the project on schedule?
7 How many people will be needed, and when?
8 How much will the project cost?
9 How much will a deviation from plan or a time overrun cost?

These fall into three categories: timing and scheduling of activities (the first six questions), resource management (number seven), and cost management (numbers eight and nine).

TIMING AND SCHEDULING OF ACTIVITIES

Looking at the six questions listed above that come under this heading, we can see that there are two main issues facing the manager: calculating when the project will be completed, and scheduling the activities that make up the project. These two are related. For example, it may be necessary to schedule the activities in the project in a particular way in order to finish the project in a given time. There is also an iterative aspect to the calculations. They are subject to change, from two main sources:

● management decisions
● outside events.

Suppose that the project is to plan and implement an advertising campaign. The initial calculations may suggest that the campaign will be implemented too late, and so a management decision may be taken to carry out some of the activities more quickly. Later in the project, a photo shoot to provide material for the campaign's posters may be delayed by unsuitable weather – an outside event. In either case, a model of the project may be used to carry out 'What if?' analysis on the consequences of particular happenings.

Before proceeding further, we need to introduce some project-management terminology to identify one of the most important aspects of the models.

A *path* is a sequence of activities, each of which cannot start until the previous one finishes.

The *critical path* is the longest path in the project (in total time) from the project's start to the project's finish. The total time it takes to do all the activities on the critical path is therefore the shortest time in which the project can be completed. By definition, there can be no activities before the start of the critical path, and none after the finish of the critical path. Completion in the shortest possible time is implicitly assumed to be the major goal by all the project-management techniques; the shortest time often also means the least cost, but not always, as we shall discuss later in the chapter.

◆ **Key concept**

A **path** *is a sequence of activities, each of which cannot start until the previous one finishes. The* **critical path** *is the longest path (in total time) in the project. The total time it takes to do all the activities on the critical path is therefore the shortest time in which the project can be completed.*

FINDING THE SHORTEST COMPLETION TIME AND THE CRITICAL PATH

We shall demonstrate how to do this for a very simplified house-building example with 11 activities. The data for this example are shown in Table 13.1. Project-management techniques have standardised data requirements, so they can be laid out in the form of a table. This 'critical path' example is the simplest; the only data required are the activities, estimates of how long each activity will take, and the sequence constraints, expressed in the form of immediate predecessor–successor relationships – B is a predecessor of C means that activity B ('prepare foundations') must precede activity C ('construct walls'), i.e. B must finish before C can start. The relationship is expressed the other way round as 'C is a successor of B'.

Typically, these predecessor–successor relationships are expressed in the form of a picture. These pictures are so standard in project management that they can be used as the basis for the conceptualisation and verbalisation stages of model building. There are two equivalent forms of the *network diagram*, as it is known. Both consist of boxes (called nodes) and lines (called arcs or arrows). In

Table 13.1 Simple critical path example: building a house

Ref. Letter	Activity name	Duration (days)	Immediate predecessor(s)
A	Obtain materials	5	–
B	Prepare foundations	7	–
C	Construct walls	10	A, B
D	Construct roof	4	C
E	Drainage and plumbing	6	C
F	Wiring	3	D
G	Glazing	2	C
H	Flooring	7	E, F
I	Doors and fitting	2	H
J	Landscaping and paths	2	E
K	Painting and clearing	5	G, I, J

the activity-on-arc or activity-on-arrow (AoA) form, the lines represent the activities, whereas in the activity-on-node (AoN) form the activities are represented by the boxes. The AoN form is easier to construct, but the AoA can convey slightly more information. AoN has become more common in recent years, mainly because its ease of construction led to its use in preference to AoA in PC project-management software. We shall therefore use the AoN form in this chapter.

Figure 13.1 shows an AoN network diagram for the house-building example. Conventionally, time flows from left to right across the diagram. Note, however, that it is *not* drawn to scale; the lines represent logical relationships, not the passage of time.

Conceptually, the AoN diagram is in fact a specialised form of our information flow diagram, specifically designed for carrying out critical path analysis, i.e. identifying which activities are critical and calculating the shortest time in which the project may be completed. The only variables involved in the calculation of shortest completion time and the critical path are sets of six variables associated with each activity. The AoN boxes are designed to display the values of these six variables, together with an identifying letter or phrase, as shown in Fig 13.2. Only one set of values, for *duration*, appears in Fig 13.1 – the others will be added later, and their meanings will be explained as we go along. Thus one box on the AoN diagram represents no fewer than six boxes on an information flow diagram. This simplification is only possible because of the special structure of the project network model and the standardised data requirements that we mentioned earlier.

When calculations are being done by hand, the network diagram can be used as the basis for both carrying them out and displaying the results. However, this is impracticable for most real-size projects, and so computer assistance is required. Unfortunately, spreadsheet packages are not yet capable of working

Fig 13.1 Activity-on-node (AoN) network diagram for house-building example, showing only *duration* values and the relationships between activities

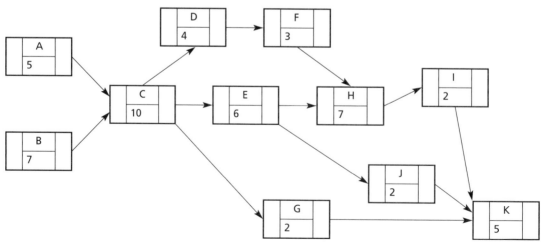

Fig 13.2 The six variables whose values are shown in the AoN network diagram box corresponding to each activity

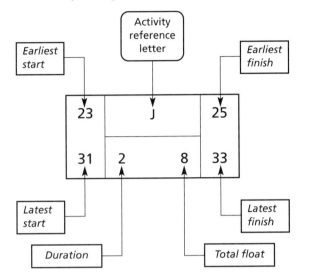

with network diagrams without extensive macro programming, and so the development here will be based on the tabular format of the spreadsheet. In theory, it is possible to get away without drawing any diagram at all. However, the AoN diagram will also be used here by way of illustration, as its simplicity should enable you to understand better the details of project-management techniques.

In order to find the shortest completion time and thus the critical path, it is necessary to calculate the earliest and latest times that each of the activities can start and finish. Logically, these calculations split into two phases, known as the forward pass and the backward pass respectively. However, the use of a spreadsheet enables both sets of calculations to be set out simultaneously.

The forward pass

First, we work through the project from beginning to end, calculating the earliest possible start and finish times for each activity, assuming that no activities are delayed. The earliest an activity can start is immediately after its predecessor activity has finished. For a 'merge' activity, which is one that has more than one predecessor activity, *all* predecessors must finish before it can start. The value of *Earliest start* for an activity is therefore equal to the largest value of *Earliest finish* of any of its predecessors. The *Earliest finish* value for an activity is simply the sum of its *Earliest start* value and its *duration*.

Figure 13.3 shows the forward pass calculations. *Earliest start* values are in column D and *Earliest finish* values in column E; the formulae used to calculate the values in columns D and E are set out in the last two columns of the exhibit. The built-in function MAX is used where an activity has more than one predecessor; these merge activities are C, H and K in this example. Note that the *Earliest start* values for all activities with no predecessors are set to zero; in this

Fig 13.3 Forward pass calculations

	A	B	C	D	E	Formula for D	Formula for E
1	Ref.	Duration	Predecessor(s)	Earliest	Earliest	Earliest	Earliest
2	letter	(days)		start	finish	start	finish
3	A	5	–	0	5	0	D3+B3
4	B	7	–	0	7	0	D4+B4
5	C	10	A, B	7	17	MAX(E3,E4)	D5+B5
6	D	4	C	17	21	E5	D6+B6
7	E	6	C	17	23	E5	D7+B7
8	F	3	D	21	24	E6	D8+B8
9	G	2	C	17	19	E5	D9+B9
10	H	7	E, F	24	31	MAX(E7,E8)	D10+B10
11	I	2	H	31	33	E10	D11+B11
12	J	2	E	23	25	E7	D12+B12
13	K	5	G, I, J	33	38	MAX(E9,E11,E12)	D13+B13

case, activities A and B. Note also that the formulae for *Earliest start* values do not follow a simple pattern; each must be typed in separately. However, those for *Earliest finish* values *do* follow a simple pattern and may be simply Copied from the first one.

The *Earliest finish* value for the last activity, i.e. the largest of the *Earliest finish* values, is the shortest time in which the project can be completed. For this example, it is 38 days, from cell E13. For a larger project, the MAX function could be used on the values in column E, to avoid the risk of human error leading to the largest being overlooked.

Figure 13.4 shows the AoN network diagram with the *Earliest start* and *Earliest finish* values included at the top left and right of each box. You can see how the earliest start time of an activity relates to the earliest finish time of its predecessors.

Fig 13.4 Activity-on-Node (AoN) network diagram for house-building example, with *Earliest start* and *Earliest finish* values included

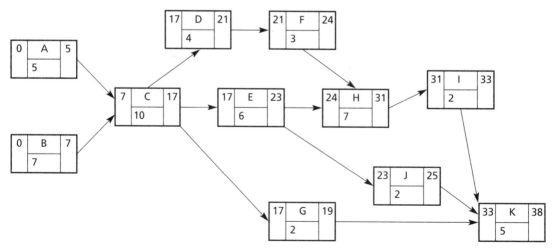

The backward pass

Using the shortest completion time found in the forward pass, we now work back through the project from the end to the beginning. This time we calculate the latest possible finish and start times for each activity, by which is meant the latest times that will not prevent the shortest completion time from being achieved. Everything is the reverse of the forward pass. A 'burst' activity, which is one that has more than one successor activity, must finish before *any* of its successors can start. The value of *Latest finish* for an activity is therefore equal to the smallest value of *Latest start* for any of its successors. The value of *Latest start* for an activity is simply its *Latest finish* value minus its *duration*.

These calculations are shown in Fig 13.5. *Latest start* values are now in column F and *Latest finish* values in column G; the formulae used to calculate the values in columns F and G are set out in the last two columns. Note that the value of *Latest finish* for all activities with no successors, in this case just activity K, is set to the shortest completion time found in the forward pass. This is achieved here by the formula MAX(E3..E13) in cell G13. Activities C and E are the 'burst' activities, for which the MIN function is used, since a burst activity has to finish in time for all of its successors to start without delaying the project. This is analogous to the way the MAX function was used in the forward pass. Again mirroring the forward pass, this time the formulae for *Latest finish* values do not follow a simple pattern; each must be typed in separately. However, those for *Latest start* values *do* follow a simple pattern and may be simply Copied from the first one.

This process is self-checking in three ways:

- Each 'Latest' value cannot be less than the corresponding 'Earliest' value for that activity.
- At least one activity must have a value of *Latest Start* that is 0.
- Negative time values are impossible

Fig 13.5 Forward and backward pass calculations

	A	B	C	D	E	F	G	Formulae for F	Formulae for G
1	Ref.	Duration	Predecessor(s)	Earliest	Earliest	Latest	Latest	Latest	Latest
2	letter	(days)		start	finish	start	finish	start	finish
3	A	5	–	0	5	2	7	G3–B3	F5
4	B	7	–	0	7	0	7	G4–B4	F5
5	C	10	A, B	7	17	7	17	G5–B5	MIN(F6,F7,F9)
6	D	4	C	17	21	17	21	G6–B6	F8
7	E	6	C	17	23	18	24	G7–B7	MIN(F10,F12)
8	F	3	D	21	24	21	24	G8–B8	F10
9	G	2	C	17	19	31	33	G9–B9	F13
10	H	7	E, F	24	31	24	31	G10–B10	F11
11	I	2	H	31	33	31	33	G11-B11	F13
12	J	2	E	23	25	31	33	G12-B12	F13
13	K	5	G, I, J	33	38	33	38	G13-B13	MAX(E3:E13)

If your spreadsheet does not satisfy these conditions, you have made an error in the formulae in either the forward or backward pass. Our spreadsheet does meet these conditions.

Figure 13.6 shows the AoN network diagram with the *Latest start* and *Latest finish* values included at the bottom left and right of each box. The first of the three 'self-checking' aspects means that any of these values cannot be less than the value immediately above it. You can also see how the latest finish time of an activity relates to the latest start time of its successors.

To find the critical path, we now need to calculate the value of the total float for each activity.

Total float

The *total float* of an activity, also known as the *slack* or *slack time*, measures how much the activity can be delayed without affecting the completion of the whole project, assuming all other activities run to time. It may be used up before, during or after an activity.[3]

The total float of an activity is defined by the relationship

Total float = Latest finish − Earliest start − Duration

In the spreadsheet in Fig 13.7, these calculations are shown in column H; for example, cell H3 is given by the formula G3–D3–B3. All the other entries in the column are Copied from the first one. The value of an activity's *total float* is always either positive or zero. Activities with a *total float* value of zero are called *critical activities*. The critical activities form one or more paths from the beginning to the end of the project – the critical path(s).

Fig 13.6 Activity-on-Node (AoN) network diagram for house-building example, with *Latest start* and *Latest finish* values included

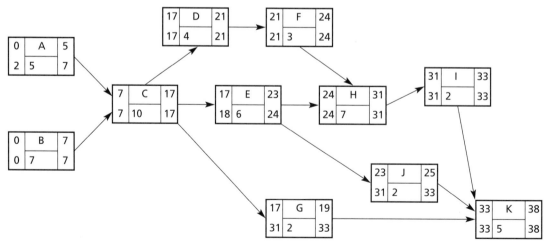

◆ **Key concept**   *The **total float** of an activity measures how much it can be delayed without affecting the completion of the whole project, assuming all other activities run to time. The total float for an activity on the critical path is zero.*

In our example, there is just one critical path, consisting of activities B, C, D, F, H, I and K, as may be seen from Fig 13.7 by finding the zero values in column H. All other paths take less time than the 38 days of this critical path.[4] It would be a simple matter, using the built-in IF function, to display the word 'Critical' rather than the value 0 in the appropriate cells.

Figure 13.8 shows the completed AoN network diagram, including the total float values to the right of the duration values at the bottom of each box. From

Fig 13.7 Completed critical path calculations

	A	B	C	D	E	F	G	H
1	Ref.	Duration	Predecessor(s)	Earliest	Earliest	Latest	Latest	Total
2	Letter	(Days)		Start	Finish	Start	Finish	Float
3	A	5	–	0	5	2	7	2
4	B	7	–	0	7	0	7	0
5	C	10	A, B	7	17	7	17	0
6	D	4	C	17	21	17	21	0
7	E	6	C	17	23	18	24	1
8	F	3	D	21	24	21	24	0
9	G	2	C	17	19	31	33	14
10	H	7	E, F	24	31	24	31	0
11	I	2	H	31	33	31	33	0
12	J	2	E	23	25	31	33	8
13	K	5	G, I, J	33	38	33	38	0

Fig 13.8 Completed activity-on-Node (AoN) network diagram for house-building example

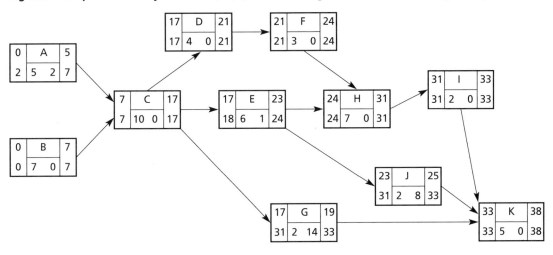

this, you can see how the critical activities B, C, D, F, H, I and K do indeed form a path from the beginning to the end of the project; they all have a 0 in the third element along the bottom of the corresponding node.

RESOURCE MANAGEMENT

Up to this point we have concentrated exclusively on the sequence of activities and the time taken. However, the availability of the resources needed to carry out the activities is another major concern of project management. There are many problems of resource management with which spreadsheet models can offer little help, such as poor-quality materials or low worker morale. However, a major area in which they can help is where the issue is the quantitative one of *resource levelling*, in other words reducing the maximum amount of a particular resource required at any one time by amending the schedule to give a more even usage of that resource over the project as a whole.

We shall demonstrate a very simple example of resource levelling based on the data shown in Fig 13.7. Suppose that each activity requires one person; not very likely, but it will do for our purposes here. We can design a spreadsheet, as shown in part in Fig 13.9, to display the resource usage over time for the project, as follows.

1 Copy the activity reference letters, and the *Earliest start*, *Earliest finish*, *Latest start* and *Latest finish* values, from the original spreadsheet. In this case, that means copying column A of Fig 13.7 into column A of Fig 13.9, and columns D to G of Fig 13.7 into columns C to F of Fig 13.9. Add two columns (G and H here) for the values of *Planned start* and *Planned finish* times for each activity. Copy the *Earliest start* and *Earliest finish* values into them for now; this means that the initial plan will be based on every activity taking place as early as possible.

2 Add a column (column B here) to show the amount of the resource needed for each activity. In this case, one person for each activity, so the value of *number of people* is 1 for each activity.

3 Add a new block to the spreadsheet, which will be used to calculate the amount of resource needed for each activity at a given time. We start in row 15 here. Cell A15 is used for the name of the time unit (day). The cells to the right, beginning with B15, are filled with the times from 1 up to the shortest completion time, identified earlier as 38 days. (The spreadsheet goes on to column AM, but only part is shown in Fig 13.9 to save space.)

4 Copy the activity letters into this new block, starting in the next row. In this case cells A3 to A13 are copied into column A, starting at row 16. We now have a block with one cell for each activity at each time interval in the project. These cells will show the value of the resource needed by that activity at that time. For example, cell B16 will show the amount of resource needed by activity A on day 1. Into each cell we enter a formula to work out whether that activity needs any resource at that particular time; if

Fig 13.9 Resource levelling spreadsheet

	A	B	C	D	E	F	G	H
1	Activity	Number	Earliest	Earliest	Latest	Latest	Planned	Planned
2		of people	start	finish	start	finish	start	finish
3	A	1	0	5	2	7	0	5
4	B	1	0	7	0	7	0	7
5	C	1	7	17	7	17	7	17
6	D	1	17	21	17	21	17	21
7	E	1	17	23	18	24	17	23
8	F	1	21	24	21	24	21	24
9	G	1	17	19	31	33	17	19
10	H	1	24	31	24	31	24	31
11	I	1	31	33	31	33	31	33
12	J	1	23	25	31	33	23	25
13	K	1	33	38	33	38	33	38
14	Block to calculate number of people needed							
15	Day	1	2	3	4	5	6	7
16	A	1	1	1	1	1	0	0
17	B	1	1	1	1	1	1	1
18	C	0	0	0	0	0	0	0
19	D	0	0	0	0	0	0	0
20	E	0	0	0	0	0	0	0
21	F	0	0	0	0	0	0	0
22	G	0	0	0	0	0	0	0
23	H	0	0	0	0	0	0	0
24	I	0	0	0	0	0	0	0
25	J	0	0	0	0	0	0	0
26	K	0	0	0	0	0	0	0
27	Day	0	1	2	3	4	5	6
28	Resource	2	2	2	2	2	1	1

it does, the amount is found in the appropriate cell in the range B3..B13. The verbalisation is that the resource is needed if *day number > planned start* AND *day number <= planned finish*.[5] So, in cell B16 the formula is IF(B$15>$G3 AND B$15<= $H3,$B3,0). The anchoring ensures that this formula may be Copied to all the cells in this block. (Again, this carries on out to column AM.)

5 Add two extra rows at the bottom of the new block; in Fig 13.9, these are rows 27 and 28. Copy the day numbers into the first row (for ease of drawing pictures in step 6) and sum the resources needed at each time in the second row. Thus, for example, the formula in cell B28 is SUM(B16..B26). These values are the amount of resource needed in each time interval.

6 Draw a picture of these values in the form of a bar chart.

7 Perform 'What if?' analysis by changing the values of *Planned start* and *Planned finish* times until a satisfactory result is achieved.

Figure 13.10 shows the bar chart for the case where all activities start as early as possible. You can see that three people are needed on just two days: days 18 and 19. What if all activities start as late as possible? Fig 13.11 shows that again three people are needed on just two days; this time days 32 and 33.

Can the project be done with a maximum of just two people? A look back at Fig 13.7 shows that with the earliest starts, as in Figure 13.10, the activities taking place on days 18 and 19 (when three people are needed) are D, E and G, while with the latest starts, as in Fig 13.11, the activities on days 32 and 33 are G, I and J. These are different, so using only two people may be possible. The only activities we can move without delaying the whole project are those that have some total float. Let us concentrate on activity G, which has a *total float* of 14 days, but a *duration* of only 2 days. (We could equally well choose activity J, but not activity I, as I is critical.) The chart in Fig 13.10 shows that if we could delay the start of one activity taking place on days 18 and 19 to time 25 or later, we could reduce the maximum number of people required from 3 to 2. We *can* do this without delaying the project overall, because the delay of 8 days needed is not greater than G's float of 14 days. Figure 13.12 demonstrates the successful outcome, with never more than two people required.

In this case, a satisfactory outcome was found by a 'What if?' approach that was essentially trial and error. There are in fact many different schedules for the project that never require more than two people. It would be possible to tackle a resource-levelling issue more systematically, by formulating it as an integer-programming problem, so that the spreadsheet solver could be used (see Chapter 12). The detail of how to do this is beyond our scope here. It is also probable that this is unnecessarily complex for the size of project that can reasonably be modelled using a spreadsheet. The 'What if?' approach has the additional advan-

Fig 13.10 Resource usage bar chart, all activities starting as early as possible

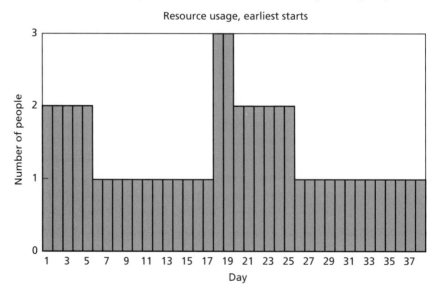

Resource usage, earliest starts

Fig 13.11 Resource usage bar chart, all activities starting as late as possible

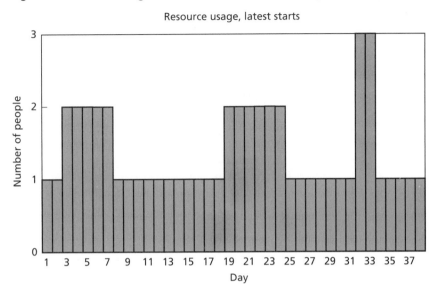

Resource usage, latest starts

Fig 13.12 Resource usage bar chart, all activities starting as early as possible except activity G

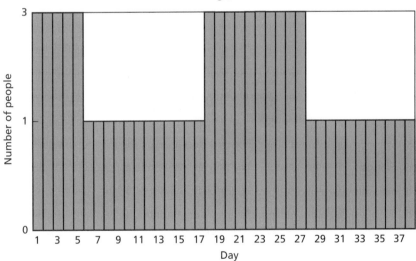

Resource usage, best solution

tage that the manager using the model gains a better understanding of the relationships involved. This may help them to take the non-quantitative aspects of project management into account. Larger projects should be modelled using specialised software (see later in the chapter) rather than a spreadsheet. These project-management packages usually include resource-levelling techniques.

COST MANAGEMENT

Money is a resource, and therefore several issues of cost management for projects could be modelled as issues of resource levelling, as in the previous section, for example reducing the maximum cash outflow in any one day/week.

As with resource levelling, the main use of the spreadsheet in cost management is to support a 'What if?' analysis for relatively small projects. For example, a more specific cost-management issue for projects is that it is often possible to reduce the duration of one of the activities by spending more money on it. For one of the critical activities, this will also reduce the overall duration of the project, and may thus in some circumstances even save money overall. Such a reduction in activity duration goes by the unlikely name of *crashing* the activity.

To illustrate the use of a spreadsheet model in examining whether crashing is worthwhile, we return to the house-building example of Figs 13.1 to 13.7 and Table 13.1. The data from the original problem are now augmented by two further sets of variables:

- the *minimum crashed duration* possible for each activity
- the *crash cost per day* for each activity, i.e. the cost of reducing the activity's duration by one day.

In addition, there will be another variable representing the 'baseline' cost of the project as a whole. This may be a 'lump sum' cost, or a daily cost.

Initially we assume a daily cost. Figure 13.13 shows the layout of the modified spreadsheet model. Columns C and D have been inserted to show the

Fig 13.13 Example of crashing activity durations ('before')

	A	B	C	D	E	F	G	H	I	J
1	Ref.	Duration	Minimum crashed	Crash cost	Predecessor(s)	Earliest	Earliest	Latest	Latest	Float/
2	letter	(days)	duration (days)	per day (£)		start	finish	start	finish	slack
3	A	5	5		–	0	5	2	7	2
4	B	7	5	45	–	0	7	0	7	0
5	C	10	7	60	A, B	7	17	7	17	0
6	D	4	4		C	17	21	17	21	0
7	E	6	4	60	C	17	23	18	24	1
8	F	3	3		D	21	24	21	24	0
9	G	2	2		C	17	19	31	33	14
10	H	7	4	45	E, F	24	31	24	31	0
11	I	2	2		H	31	33	31	33	0
12	J	2	2		E	23	25	31	33	8
13	K	5	4	45	G, I, J	33	38	33	38	0
14										
15			Daily cost (£)	90						
16										
17										
18			Total cost (£)	3420						

values of *minimum crashed duration* and *crash cost per day* for each activity respectively. Only some of the activities may be crashed; the others have a blank entry for *crash cost per day*. Cell D15 contains the value of the *daily cost* of the project, i.e. £90. The value of the *total cost* of the project is given in cell D18, as £3420 (38 days at £90 per day). The reason for the two blank rows 16 and 17 will soon become apparent.

The crashing analysis proceeds as follows. At each step, we choose which activity to crash and by how long, and then insert a row to record the cost.

To choose which activity to crash, we look for an activity which may be crashed and is on the critical path (otherwise there will be no reduction in the overall project duration and nothing will be gained by crashing it). From Fig 13.13 we see that activities B, C, H and K meet these two criteria. When, as here, this leaves us a choice, we choose the activity with the smallest crash cost per day. C has a higher crash cost, so we may choose any of the other three. Arbitrarily we choose K, and reduce its *duration* to the minimum possible (4 days), entering that figure in the appropriate cell (B13) in the spreadsheet. This will change the start and finish times, and may change the critical activities. We enter the cost of crashing this activity (£45) in cell D16. This could be done automatically, but would require Copying the original *duration* values into another column and a complex formula including the use of IF functions. Cell D18 is defined initially by the formula D15*MAX (I3..I13)+SUM (D16..D17), giving the *total cost*. After crashing activity K, this is £3375; this

Fig 13.14 Example of crashing activity durations ('after')

	A	B	C	D	E	F	G	H	I	J
1	Ref.	Duration	Minimum crashed	Crash cost	Predecessor(s)	Earliest	Earliest	Latest	Latest	Float/
2	letter	(days)	duration (days)	per day (£)		start	finish	start	finish	slack
3	A	5	5		–	0	5	0	5	0
4	B	5	5	45	–	0	5	0	5	0
5	C	7	7	60	A, B	5	12	5	12	0
6	D	4	4		C	12	16	12	16	0
7	E	6	4	60	C	12	18	13	19	1
8	F	3	3		D	16	19	16	19	0
9	G	2	2		C	12	14	23	25	11
10	H	4	4	45	E, F	19	23	19	23	0
11	I	2	2		H	23	25	23	25	0
12	J	2	2		E	18	20	23	25	5
13	K	4	4	45	G, I, J	25	29	25	29	0
14										
15			Daily cost (£)	90						
16			Crash K	45						
17			Crash H	135						
18			Crash B	90						
19			Crash C	180						
20			Total cost (£)	3060						

figure would appear in cell D18 at this point. Note that we have not included this 'intermediate' spreadsheet as a figure in order to save space.

We then repeat this process, each time inserting an extra row above row 17 where we enter the cost of the next crashed activity. The formula mentioned above, originally in cell D18, will automatically adjust to the insertion, thus allowing for an unknown number of crashed activities. We need one spare blank row to make this work; that is why there were two to begin with. It may be deleted at the end.

Figure 13.14 shows the final spreadsheet. Activities K, H, B and C have been crashed, reducing the duration of the project to 29 days and the *total cost* (now in cell D20) to £3060. There is no point in crashing activity E, for example; as it is not critical, this would only increase the cost without reducing the overall duration of the project.

In this example, the values of *crash cost per day* were always less than the *daily cost* of the project. In such cases, a cost-minimising approach, as shown here, is possible. If, however, some of the values of *crash cost per day* are greater than the *daily cost* of the project, then the spreadsheet can only address half of the cost-management issue, because crashing may increase the *total cost* value although it reduces the overall completion time. In such cases, the manager will have to judge for themselves how much they are willing to pay to shorten the overall completion time.

Ideally, making this trade-off requires that the completion time and cost figures for all the different levels of crashing be displayed at once. The best way to use a spreadsheet to help with this is to Copy the whole block (cells A1 to J13 initially) elsewhere in the spreadsheet each time there is a new 'solution', to allow one overall summary model to be produced. The effort involved in this makes it questionable whether this is a better option than merely writing down the total cost and shortest completion time at each stage on a piece of paper, given the size of project for which using a spreadsheet for project management is sensible.

This problem also arises if the baseline cost of the project is expressed as a lump sum, rather than a daily cost. In this case, crashing *always* increases the total cost, and so it is again a question of the manager making the trade-off between cost and time.

A MORE GENERAL SPREADSHEET

The approach that we took in the earlier house-building example relies on the user entering the correct formulae in the appropriate cells to represent the predecessor constraints. The predecessor constraints have thus been 'hard-wired' into the logic model. Not only does this go against good practice, but it makes it very difficult to reuse the spreadsheet for a different project.

For these reasons, it may therefore be desirable to build a more general spreadsheet model for project management, incorporating the predecessor constraints partly in the logic model and partly in the data model (the values in the data model being activity reference letters in this case). This can be done, as we shall now briefly outline. However, as will be clear, the amount of extra effort is considerable.

Consider the example of the launch of a new project, from panel testing through to the delivery of the new stock to retailers. The activities and timing calculations will be set out in roughly the same way as for the earlier house-building example, but this more general spreadsheet model, shown in Fig 13.15, involves no fewer than four blocks, one below the other, of which this is only one.

The layout of the spreadsheet model in Fig 13.15 is as follows.

Block 1

The input data (cells A1 to F13) and display of results (cells G1 to K13), as in the earlier spreadsheet. The details of the calculations in columns G to K will be explained later. This spreadsheet allows for an activity to have a maximum of three predecessors, but any number could be catered for, by inserting additional columns after column E. Note that the variable names have been abbreviated in order to keep the width of the spreadsheet down to a single page for illustrative purposes here.

Block 2

A square block with a row and column for each activity (cells A15 to M28). If the column activity is a predecessor of the row activity, then the cell entry is 1, otherwise it is 0. Thus cell A18 shows the value 1 because activity A is a predecessor of activity B, and cell G26 shows the value 1 because activity G is a predecessor of activity J. The formula in each cell is of the same form: IF($C2=$A$2 OR $D2=$A$2 OR $E2=$A$2,1,0) is the formula in A17; they may be Copied down the columns, but each of the formulae in the first row needs to be entered separately – $A$2 becomes $A$3 for the second column, and so on.

Block 3

The same shape as block 2 (cells A30 to M43), this shows the earliest finish time for each predecessor activity identified in block 2. For example, cell A33 has the value 3, the earliest finish time for activity A. The formula in cell A33 is A18*$H$1. Again, the formulae may be Copied down each column, but the first entry in each column needs to be typed in separately. Note that all the values in a column are either 0 or the same earliest finish time.

Block 4

Also the same shape as blocks 2 and 3 (cells A45 to M58), this shows the latest start time for each successor activity identified in block 2, setting it to 999 if there is no predecessor–successor relationship; 999 was chosen arbitrarily and any figure substantially larger than the plausible values for *Latest start* would do. Here, for example, cell A48 shows 8.5, the latest start for activity B. The formula for cell A48 is IF(A18>0,A18*$I3,999). This time the formula can be Copied to all the cells in the block.

Fig 13.15 More general project-management spreadsheet

	A	B	C	D	E	F	G	H	I	J	K	L	M
1	Block 1: Data/Results		Predecessors			Dur	ES	EF	LS	LF	Float		
2	A	Analyse panel test results	–	–	–	3	0	3	0	3	Critical		
3	B	Create concept of ad campaign	A	–	–	6	3	9	8.5	14.5	5.5		
4	C	Select test market area	B	–	–	3	9	12	22	25	13		
5	D	Design advertising artwork	B	–	–	10	9	19	17	27	8		
6	E	Design packaging	B	–	–	3.5	9	12.5	14.5	18	5.5		
7	F	Obtain packaging materials	E	–	–	10	12.5	22.5	18	28	5.5		
8	G	Obtain raw materials	A	–	–	10	3	13	3	13	Critical		
9	H	Book advertising space and airtime	C	D	–	5	19	24	27	32	8		
10	I	Take initial orders	C	–	–	7	12	19	25	32	13		
11	J	Make launch stock	G	–	–	15	13	28	13	28	Critical		
12	K	Package launch stock	F	J	–	4	28	32	28	32	Critical		
13	L	Deliver to retailers	H	I	K	2	32	34	32	34	Critical		
14													
15	Block 2: Predecessors												
16	A	B	C	D	E	F	G	H	I	J	K	L	
17	0	0	0	0	0	0	0	0	0	0	0	0	A
18	1	0	0	0	0	0	0	0	0	0	0	0	B
19	0	1	0	0	0	0	0	0	0	0	0	0	C
20	0	1	0	0	0	0	0	0	0	0	0	0	D
21	0	1	0	0	0	0	0	0	0	0	0	0	E
22	0	0	0	0	1	0	0	0	0	0	0	0	F
23	1	0	0	0	0	0	0	0	0	0	0	0	G
24	0	0	1	1	0	0	0	0	0	0	0	0	H
25	0	0	1	0	0	0	0	0	0	0	0	0	I
26	0	0	0	0	0	0	1	0	0	0	0	0	J
27	0	0	0	0	0	1	0	0	0	1	0	0	K
28	0	0	0	0	0	0	0	1	1	0	1	0	L
29													
30	Block 3: Earliest finish times												
31	A	B	C	D	E	F	G	H	I	J	K	L	
32	0	0	0	0	0	0	0	0	0	0	0	0	A
33	3	0	0	0	0	0	0	0	0	0	0	0	B
34	0	9	0	0	0	0	0	0	0	0	0	0	C
35	0	9	0	0	0	0	0	0	0	0	0	0	D
36	0	9	0	0	0	0	0	0	0	0	0	0	E
37	0	0	0	0	12.5	0	0	0	0	0	0	0	F
38	3	0	0	0	0	0	0	0	0	0	0	0	G
39	0	0	12	19	0	0	0	0	0	0	0	0	H
40	0	0	12	0	0	0	0	0	0	0	0	0	I
41	0	0	0	0	0	0	13	0	0	0	0	0	J
42	0	0	0	0	0	22.5	0	0	0	28	0	0	K
43	0	0	0	0	0	0	0	24	19	0	32	0	L
44													

Fig 13.15 continued

	A	B	C	D	E	F	G	H	I	J	K	L	M
45	Block 4: Latest start times												
46	A	B	C	D	E	F	G	H	I	J	K	L	
47	999	999	999	999	999	999	999	999	999	999	999	999	A
48	8.5	999	999	999	999	999	999	999	999	999	999	999	B
49	999	22	999	999	999	999	999	999	999	999	999	999	C
50	999	17	999	999	999	999	999	999	999	999	999	999	D
51	999	14.5	999	999	999	999	999	999	999	999	999	999	E
52	999	999	999	999	18	999	999	999	999	999	999	999	F
53	3	999	999	999	999	999	999	999	999	999	999	999	G
54	999	999	27	27	999	999	999	999	999	999	999	999	H
55	999	999	25	999	999	999	999	999	999	999	999	999	I
56	999	999	999	999	999	999	13	999	999	999	999	999	J
57	999	999	999	999	999	28	999	999	999	28	999	999	K
58	999	999	999	999	999	999	999	32	32	999	32	999	L

Now, we return to explain the results section (cells G1 to K13). The verbalisation is still the same as in the house-building example.

Column G The values of *Earliest start* are calculated as the maximum of the *Earliest finish* times of the activity's predecessors, i.e. the maximum of the values in the appropriate row in block 3: row 32 for G2, row 33 for G3, and so on.

Column H H2=G2+F2 and so on, as in the house-building example.

Column I I2=J2−F2 and so on, as in the house-building example.

Column J The values of *Latest finish* are calculated as the minimum of the *Latest start* times for the activity's successors, i.e. the minimum of the values in the appropriate column in block 4: column A for J2, column B for J3 and so on.

Column K K2=J2−G2−F2, as before, but this time we have made the formula IF(J2-G2-F2=0,'Critical',J2-G2-F2) to display the word 'Critical' rather than the value 0 for critical activities.

As may be seen from column J, the minimum time needed to complete this project is 34 days.

A problem that may arise with such a spreadsheet is that some of the cell references are circular; they form a chain referring to itself. Some packages will let you enter such a spreadsheet, as long as the recalculation mode is set to manual; others will not. It may well be affected by the order in which you enter the formulae in the cells. In this case, using Lotus 1-2-3 version 4.01, the entries in block 1 in column J had to be entered last, working from J13 upwards. Microsoft Excel version 5.0 worked similarly, but produced an error message when the previously saved spreadsheet was opened again.

DISPLAYING THE RESULTS

Whether you choose to develop a spreadsheet model for a specific project or for more general use, a useful way to display the results as a project plan is in the form of a Gantt chart. A Gantt chart is a special form of horizontal bar chart, in which time is shown on the horizontal scale. Gantt charts are not yet one of the picture formats available in spreadsheet packages, but box plots (see Chapter 7) may be used to achieve the same effect, using the values of the *Earliest start*, *Earliest finish*, *Latest start* and *Latest finish* times as the four sets of data. The ease or difficulty of this depends very much on which spreadsheet package and version you are using!

Figure 13.16 shows the results for the new product launch project. The horizontal bars show the 'window' for each activity, which runs from the *Earliest start* time to the *Latest finish* time. The mark above an activity's horizontal bar shows the *Earliest finish* time, and the mark below it the *Latest start* time. Where these marks are at the ends of the bar, then that activity is critical and there is no scope for it to start or finish earlier or later. Where the marks are not at the ends, there is scope to reschedule that activity within its 'window' (see the section on resource management). The distance between the mark above the bar and the right-hand end of the bar equals the value of the *total float* for that activity, and similarly for the distance between the mark below the bar and the left-hand end of the bar.

A third type of picture in common use in project management is the work breakdown structure, which shows a hierarchical decomposition of the activities in a project, somewhat like an organisation chart. Unfortunately, as with displaying network diagrams, displaying work breakdown structures is beyond the capabilities of current spreadsheet packages.

Fig 13.16 Gantt chart of project

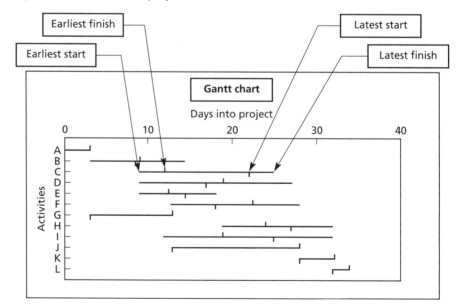

DEALING WITH UNCERTAINTY

PERT (project evaluation and review technique) is intended to handle uncertainty in the activity durations. There are two basic sources of uncertainty in the duration:

- novel activities
- activities with inherent variability; for example, the time it takes concrete to set depends on the weather.

Both of these causes may be present at the same time.

In all such cases, one duration estimate is not a good enough representation of the real scenario. As we have seen in Chapters 10 and 11, it is necessary to use some form of probability distribution in order better to represent the uncertainty. The developers of PERT were actually concerned with novel activities, namely those involved in the construction of the first submarine-launched nuclear missiles, but in fact PERT is probably more often used in practice to handle activities that have inherent variability.

The developers of PERT wanted to use just one type of probability distribution to represent the uncertainty in any activity. As they saw it, this probability distribution needed to have two key properties:

1 It must be able to represent the patterns of uncertainty typical of activity durations. One particularly important pattern is that there is often far more scope for an activity to take longer than expected than for it to be done more quickly than expected; this is probably typical of your journey to work or university, for example.
2 It must be easy to collect the necessary data. This means that data collection should not rely on questions much more complicated than the simple 'How long will this activity take?' and that any mention of mathematical concepts such as variances or standard deviations (see Chapter 14) should be avoided.

Their choice was the beta distribution. It has a variety of possible shapes, as shown in Fig 13.17, thus achieving requirement 1. The shape depends on two parameters, which can be estimated from the mean and variance or standard deviation.

In terms of meeting requirement 2, the choice of the beta distribution enabled data collection to be framed in terms of asking for three estimates of the duration of the activity instead of one, these being the optimistic, most likely and pessimistic estimates respectively. This was found to be acceptable to the supervisors and junior managers who typically supplied the duration estimates. The mean duration of the activity is then given by the following relationship:

mean duration = {optimistic duration + 4 × {most likely duration}
+ pessimistic duration}/6

The mean durations for all the activities in the project are then used to perform exactly the same calculations as for critical path analysis, to identify the shortest mean completion time and the critical activities.

Fig 13.17 Examples of beta distributions

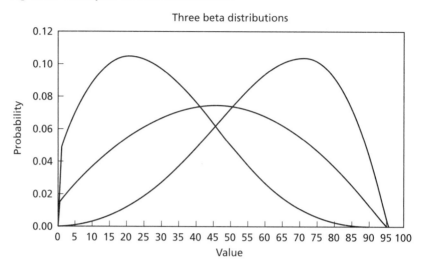

It is then possible to perform further PERT calculations regarding the distribution of the completion time about this mean, but these additional calculations are now rarely done in practice, for three reasons:

1 The accuracy of the estimates of the activity durations does not justify it (see Chapter 5).
2 The additional PERT calculations are based on the assumption that delays to one activity are independent of delays to other activities. This is often not justified, for example if several activities are weather dependent.
3 The PERT results are biased, in that they systematically overestimate the probability of completing the project in a given time.

We shall therefore not discuss this further here.

The greatest bonus of the PERT 'three duration estimates' approach is in determining a more accurate estimate for the mean duration of each activity. When dealing with uncertain durations, people tend to give the 'most likely' value even when asked for the mean/average, and the 'three estimates' approach avoids this tendency.

WHAT IF I NEED MORE?

There is a wide range of packages available for project management, from those aimed at the '25 000 activity' kind of project, to those intended for more modest projects with 'only' between 50 and 100 activities. Project-management packages include Artemis, CA-SuperProject, Microsoft Project and PMW, to name but a few. Their prices range from under a hundred pounds to several thousand pounds, depending (at least in part!) on the capabilities and facilities they offer.

The specialised project-management software provides much more support to the manager than a spreadsheet model can, particularly in four areas:

- diary and calendar facilities
- variety of display options
- resource allocation
- techniques for resource levelling and cost management.

The specialised packages normally operate with proper calendars, rather than starting the project from time 0. This means that weekends, public holidays and overtime can automatically be taken into account. It also avoids any worries about translating from continuous time to discrete time, as we encountered earlier when resource levelling; resource levelling in units of one hour is good enough for anyone! This calendar-based approach is ideal for the manager in charge of a real-life project, although we have found that it is less than ideal for teaching purposes, when starting at 'time 0' still has much to commend it.

The specialised packages also offer a range of display options (for summary models), including Gantt charts, network diagrams and work breakdown structures. Often these displays may also be used for data entry. Allocating resources (including people) to the various activities is also very flexible. The packages typically allow you not only to specify that (say) putting in the doorframes needs to be done by a carpenter, but also name the carpenter who is to do it. Last, but by no means least, the packages include techniques for resource levelling and other resource and cost-management techniques, although often these are based on rules of thumb and it is not always clear exactly how they operate.

A final word about graphs/diagrams

As we have seen, the calculations in project network analysis can be done without drawing any graphs or diagrams at all. However, people find the graphs and diagrams very useful, especially network diagrams for showing the logical relationships between activities and Gantt charts for helping to understand the results.

Indeed, the power of the graphical output is so impressive that in the 1960s, when computers could carry out the numerical calculations but could not produce the graphics, companies often found it worthwhile to have their drawing office staff produce a network diagram by hand from the computer printout – even though, for a large project, this process might take days!

So, although spreadsheet packages are limited in their ability to produce the right types of picture, it is worth your while to use the appropriate chart or diagram format if at all possible.

SUMMARY

In this chapter we have described project-management techniques, and shown how spreadsheets can be used to carry out calculations associated with the timing and scheduling, resource management and cost management of projects. We also indicated how to allow for uncertainty in the activity durations. Spreadsheets are highly suitable for small projects, although they are unable to display data and results in the standard project network diagram form. For larger projects it is essential to use specialised software.

END NOTES

1 Note that this is in contrast to the use of the terms risk analysis and risk management, as in Chapter 10!

2 Strictly speaking, critical path analysis does not allow for any uncertainty in the estimates of how long each activity will take, whereas PERT does (using probabilities). Unfortunately, commercial computer packages for project management tend to use phrases like 'PERT networks' and 'PERT analysis' for what are actually critical path networks and analysis.

3 There are other types of float, but the distinction between them is beyond our scope here.

4 Note that the critical path may be only 'potentially' critical in the happy case where its duration is less than the time allowed overall for the project.

5 The issue arises here of translating from the continuous time scale assumed in project-management calculations to the discrete scale of day numbers needed to display bar charts. We believe it is intuitively reasonable to assume that in a project running from time 0 to time 38 there is no 'day 0', so the project 'happens' on day 1 through to day 38, inclusive. This means that we must treat all start and finish time values as corresponding to the *end* of the day they refer to, i.e. an activity of duration 2 days with a start time of 21 and a finish time of 23 actually takes place on days 22 and 23. Thus the activity needs the resource for the day whose number equals the time period when it ends, but not for the day whose number equals the time period when it starts.

FURTHER READING One of the best books on project-management techniques is Keith Lockyer and James Gordon, *Critical Path Analysis and Other Project Network Techniques*, now in its 5th edition, Pitman, London, 1991. The book by Chapman and Ward recommended in Chapter 10 is also worth reading for those involved in managing really major projects, although we would not recommend that you use a spreadsheet for such projects!

The feasibility of the idea of using a spreadsheet project-management model in practice has been demonstrated in Barrie Baker's paper 'Critical path analysis with a spreadsheet' in *OR Insight*, Volume 9, Issue 2, April–June 1996.

EXERCISES

1 Think of a project that you have been involved in/responsible for in the past. Identify the activities that made up the project.

2 Think of a project that you are likely to be involved in/responsible for in the future. Identify the activities that will make up the project. How will you go about obtaining estimates of the activity durations? Will you need to allow for uncertainty?

3 Explain why the critical path is the longest path in the project, not the shortest.

4 When can the total float of an activity be used?

5 Which of these projects are suitable for the project-management techniques described?
   a) A new advertising campaign.
   b) Cooking your own breakfast.
   c) Auditing a large corporation's accounts.
   d) Painting (i.e. decorating) a house.
   e) Painting a portrait.
   f) Building the main stadium for the Sydney Olympics in 2000.

6 Extend the spreadsheets in Figs 13.3 to 13.7 to calculate mean activity durations based on the three activity duration estimates of PERT.

7 In the resource-levelling example of Fig 13.11, based on the latest starting times, find a schedule for which at most two people are required, by moving activity J.

8 In the example of Fig 13.15, suppose that the numbers of people required are as in Table 13.2.

Table 13.2 People required

A	Analyse panel test results	1
B	Create concept of ad campaign	2
C	Select test market area	1
D	Design advertising artwork	1
E	Design packaging	1
F	Obtain packaging materials	1
G	Obtain raw materials	1
H	Book advertising space and airtime	1
I	Take initial orders	3
J	Make launch stock	3
K	Package launch stock	3
L	Deliver to retailers	2

What is the minimum number of people required for this project?

9 In the example of Fig 13.15, find the minimum cost of the project and the corresponding duration if the cost per day is £180 and the crash costs and minimum durations are as in Table 13.3.

Table 13.3 Crash costs and minimum duration

		Crash cost per day (£)	Minimum crashed duration (days)
A	Analyse panel test results	150	2
B	Create concept of ad campaign		
C	Select test market area	150	2
D	Design advertising artwork		
E	Design packaging		
F	Obtain packaging materials	60	8
G	Obtain raw materials	170	7
H	Book advertising space and airtime		
I	Take initial orders		
J	Make launch stock	150	12
K	Package launch stock	120	3
L	Deliver to retailers		

10 Find the critical path and the minimum completion time for the project in Table 13.4.

Table 13.4 Project details

Activity	Estimated duration (weeks)	Predecessor(s)
A	7	–
B	13	A
C	3	B
D	9	C
E	19	C
F	6	G
G	7	E
H	10	G
I	10.5	E
J	5	D, F, H, I
K	8	L
L	3.5	D, I
M	2	J, K

CHAPTER 14

Statistics

Chapter aims

In this chapter we look at the use of statistics in understanding and exploring the local scenario, and at the facilities that spreadsheets provide for this. As we shall see, the background of spreadsheets in accountancy still shows through, in that some statistical activities are not as easy to carry out with a spreadsheet as they perhaps ought to be.

- Introduction
- Descriptive statistics
  - Measures of central tendency • Measures of spread
- Inferential statistics
  - Confidence intervals • Hypothesis testing • Correlation
- What if I need more?

INTRODUCTION

The relationship between statistical analysis and computers goes back a long way, over a century. One of the key steps on the road which led to the computer as we know it today was the use of mechanical punch-card readers to automate the analysis of the results of the 1890 US census. Nowadays, there is an even greater amount of data available that needs to be analysed. It comes not just from censuses, but from questionnaires, surveys and EPOS (electronic point-of-sale) systems. Almost every central and local government department, and almost every organisation whose customers are the general public, needs access to the results of statistical analyses of large amounts of data. There are also large numbers of researchers in universities with similar needs.

The analyses required can range from, at the simplest, the straightforward counting tasks for which censuses were originally devised ('How many adults are there in our area who will pay the new local taxes?'), through calculations of averages and proportions ('How many packets of our brand of breakfast cereal does each customer buy in a year on average?', 'What proportion of households in this city own a dishwasher?') to the territory of inferential statistics, where inferences are drawn from the data regarding the possible strength of general relationships ('Is our product significantly less reliable than our competitors'?', 'Is there an association between how much people eat of this substance and their chance of developing cancer?').

Statistics may be thought of as the science of summarising and drawing conclusions from data. As its practitioners will tell you, there is a certain amount of 'art' to it as well. There is far more to the subject of statistics and statistical analysis than we can possibly cover in a single chapter. Our concerns here are with statistics as used by managers in general, and with what can be done using a spreadsheet.

We will therefore concentrate on two aspects: descriptive statistics and inferential statistics. *Descriptive statistics* is concerned with characterising the group about which data have been obtained; here we shall cover measures of central tendency and spread. *Inferential statistics*, sometimes called *inductive statistics*, is concerned with trying to infer something that goes beyond the group itself; we shall look at confidence intervals, hypothesis testing and correlation under this heading.

Even this will not take us to the limits of the statistical capabilities of most present-day spreadsheet packages, although one aspect that will emerge during this chapter is that, as the original built-in statistical functions were devised by accountants, they do not always operate in the way that a professional statistician would like.

Before going further, we need some definitions. A *population* is the collection of all the items or entities in which we are interested. Our interest is characterised by a property or properties represented by the values of one or more variables. For example, the heights of all people in the world, or the heights of all adults in the UK, or the heights of all children in a particular school. Note that it does depend on what our specific interest is. A *sample* is a part of a population. For example, the heights of 100 UK adults form a sample from the population of the heights of all adults in the UK. It is therefore possible to take many different samples from the same population. Statistical analyses are normally based on a sample, although sometimes that sample is the whole of the population. The different values in the sample are often referred to as the *observations*.

◆ **Key concept**   *A **population** is the collection of all values of the variable(s) in which we are interested. A **sample** is a part of a population. It is possible to take many different samples from the same population.*

DESCRIPTIVE STATISTICS

The aim of descriptive statistics is to summarise the most important information that can be gleaned from a set of data. The principle is therefore the same as in what we have called summary models. Statistics is mainly concerned with quantitative data, but this does not exclude qualitative data entirely. We saw in Chapter 6 that there are four types of data: nominal, ordinal, interval and ratio levels of measurement. If the data are qualitative data, the only meaningful summary is to count how many there are in each category, or in combinations of categories. This applies whether a nominal scale or an ordinal scale is used (the only possibilities for qualitative data).[1]

Figure 14.1 shows a list of product codes, together with the name of the manager responsible for each. The total number of products for which each manager is responsible can be found using COUNT functions, providing that your spreadsheet (a) counts text values and (b) allows a criterion in the function for what is to be counted. The built-in database functions (see Chapter 16) will do this even if the COUNT ones will not. This produces the result shown in Fig 14.2. The *extra* information – that manager Edwards is responsible for 6 products and manager Finlay for 2 – is shown in the form of a *frequency table* at the foot of the spreadsheet. Note that we have assumed that the list is to be left in order of product code, when it might be more natural (for this purpose) to group together the products for which the same manager is responsible. This issue is addressed again in Chapter 16.

Frequency tables may be used for qualitative or quantitative data, and with either discrete or continuous variables. Continuous variables raise the issue of the choice of category boundaries, as we discussed in Chapter 7. Sometimes this

Fig 14.1 List of products and the managers responsible

	A	B
1	Product code	Manager responsible
2	G1234	J Edwards
3	G1235	J Edwards
4	G1237	P Finlay
5	G1238	P Finlay
6	G1250	J Edwards
7	G1251	J Edwards
8	G1252	J Edwards
9	G1253	J Edwards

Fig 14.2 List of products and managers' responsibilities, together with summary

	A	B	C
1	Product code	Manager responsible	
2	G1234	J Edwards	
3	G1235	J Edwards	
4	G1237	P Finlay	
5	G1238	P Finlay	
6	G1250	J Edwards	
7	G1251	J Edwards	
8	G1252	J Edwards	
9	G1253	J Edwards	
10			
11		Manager	Number of products
12		J Edwards	6
13		P Finlay	2

will also be an issue for discrete variables, if the data contain so many different values that some need to be combined to make the display more understandable. The precise details of constructing frequency tables for quantitative data will be explained shortly. First, we need to introduce some examples.

*A **frequency table** summarises how many values there are in each category, or in combinations of categories; it may be used with qualitative or quantitative data, and with discrete or continuous variables.*

With quantitative data, such as a list of examination marks or the sales revenue for each of a company's salespeople, there is more scope for additional analysis than with qualitative data. We will use three simple example sets of data to illustrate this:

1 The revenue earned by each of a company's salespeople in a particular month, shown in Table 14.1.
2 The salaries of the eight people working in one department, as shown in Table 14.2.
3 Thirty observations of the time taken to carry out a common maintenance operation, shown in Table 14.3.

Frequency tables can be produced as a useful first step in the analysis of quantitative data; this is most informative in the case of the third example, as we show in Fig 14.3. Frequency tables for quantitative data may be constructed in spreadsheets in one of two ways. Some spreadsheet packages contain menu options to perform such an analysis; others include a built-in function, usually called FREQUENCY. In either method, a list of values marking the *upper boundaries* of the categories, often known as bins, needs to be included in the spreadsheet. These are shown in cells B3..B11 in Fig 14.3. The menu commands

Table 14.1 Monthly sales revenue figures for ten salespeople

Name	Monthly sales revenue (£)
Schmidt	10 887
McGrath	11 926
Lewis	2 312
Moody	6 311
Patel	10 354
Simmonds	3 964
Chang	8 949
Robinson	6 499
Dion	8 422
Jones	4 754

Table 14.2 Income figures for one department

Name	Salary(£)
Spriggs	20 000
March	20 000
Elson	20 000
Lee	100 000
Crawford	20 000
Shah	20 000
Kocinski	20 000
Wayne	20 000

Table 14.3 Thirty observations of the time taken for a common maintenance operation (minutes)

10	12	11	16	13
10	10	13	12	11
11	11	26	10	10
9	12	11	8	10
13	10	10	10	11
14	9	11	10	10

or built-in functions are used to give the values for *number of observations* in cells C3..C12; note that there is always one more value than the number of bins, corresponding to those observations that are greater than the highest bin value (in this case a *time* of 20 minutes). The value for each bin is the number of observations that are less than or equal to the upper boundary of the bin, and greater than the upper boundary of the previous bin. For clarity, it might be worth modifying the spreadsheet after such an operation to make the frequency table more readable. In this case, the value 20 in cell B11 could be replaced with the label '16–20' and 'Over 20' inserted in cell B12. An alternative way to display a frequency table is in the form of a picture, in this case a bar chart, as in Fig 14.4; in this case we have modified the labels after constructing the frequency table.

Other forms of picture might also be relevant; we discussed several of these in Chapter 7. However, it can be even more useful to try to summarise a set of observations in the form of one or two numbers which represent important properties of the data. One reason for this is that people can remember numbers more precisely than pictures. The main properties that are usually of interest are the central tendency ('Roughly how big are the numbers?' and/or 'Around which value do the data tend to cluster?') and the spread ('How far between the large values and the small ones?' and/or 'Are the values close together or widely spread out?').

Fig 14.3 Maintenance operation times including a frequency table

	A	B	C
1	10		
2	10	Time(minutes)	Number of observations
3	11	8	1
4	9	9	2
5	13	10	11
6	14	11	7
7	12	12	3
8	10	13	3
9	11	14	1
10	12	15	0
11	10	20	1
12	9		1
13	11		
14	13		
15	26		
16	11		
17	10		
18	11		
19	16		
20	12		
21	10		
22	8		
23	10		
24	10		
25	13		
26	11		
27	10		
28	10		
29	11		
30	10		

Fig 14.4 A bar chart of the frequency table in Fig 14.3

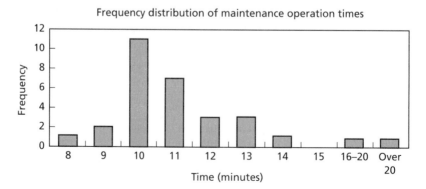

Frequency distribution of maintenance operation times

254

Measures of central tendency

Three measures of central tendency are in common use: the mean, median and mode. The *mean* is the 'average' that most people are used to, when all the figures are added up and the total divided by the number of observations.

The *median* is the 'value in the middle' if all the observations are placed in order. So, if there are 25 observations, it will be the 13th, whether you count from the top or the bottom. What if there is an even number of observations, say 20? In this case the median is defined to be halfway between the values either side of the middle; the 10th and 11th in this case.

The *mode* is the most common value: the one which occurs most often – the typical value, if you like to think of it that way.

Note that the calculated value for the mean is an 'artificial' value. It does not have to be any of the values in the actual data, and indeed it may not even be possible for such a value to occur.[2] The same problem may apply to the median if the number of observations is even.

◆ **Key concept**   *There are three measures of central tendency in common use; the mean (the everyday 'average'), the median (the 'value in the middle') and the mode (the most common value).*

The mode is the most widely applicable, as it can be worked out even for nominal information, as we have seen. The median requires at least an ordinal scale. The mean can only meaningfully[3] be calculated for information that is at least on an interval scale.

All spreadsheet packages have built-in functions to find the mean and median of a set of observations. The names for the mean vary, including MEAN, AVG and AVERAGE, but as far as we know the median is always MEDIAN. Surprisingly, but illustrating the point we mentioned earlier about spreadsheets being designed for accountants (and originally *by* one) and not for statisticians, current spreadsheet packages do not all have a MODE function. If yours does not, you need to carry out the counting as we did for qualitative data earlier, and then use the MAX function on the resulting frequency table.

Tables 14.4 and 14.5 and Fig 14.5 show the mean, median and mode values for the examples of Tables 14.1, 14.2 and 14.3 respectively.

Which measure of central tendency a manager should use in any particular model is a matter of judgement. Each has its pros and cons. We have already mentioned that the mean may give an 'artificial' value, and it also tells you nothing about how many values lie above or below it. On the other hand, it is good for mathematical manipulation; if the values of two variables are added together, such as *labour cost* and *material cost* for each of several products, the mean of the combined values is equal to the sum of the means of the two costs (often abbreviated as 'the mean of the sum is the sum of the means').

The mean also takes every observation into account. This is an advantage in terms of being representative, but is open to distortion by one or two extreme

Table 14.4 Measures of central tendency for sales revenue example in Table 14.1

Name	Monthly sales revenue (£)
Schmidt	10 887
McGrath	11 926
Lewis	2 312
Moody	6 311
Patel	10 354
Simmonds	3 964
Chang	8 949
Robinson	6 499
Dion	8 422
Jones	4 754
Mean	7 438
Median	7 461
Mode	#N/A

Table 14.5 Measures of central tendency for income figures example in Table 14.2

Name	Salary(£)
Spriggs	20 000
March	20 000
Elson	20 000
Lee	100 000
Crawford	20 000
Shah	20 000
Kocinski	20 000
Wayne	20 000
Mean	30 000
Median	20 000
Mode	20 000

values. The median avoids this disadvantage, but is less easy to work with mathematically. The mode, as we have already said, can be applied to any data irrespective of the type of scale used. Unfortunately, it is even more difficult to work with mathematically, partly because in some cases there is more than one mode (when there is a 'tie' for most common value).

Let us look at our three example sets of data. The mean of the ten sales revenue values from Tables 14.1 and 14.4 is £7438. The median is £7461 (rounded to the nearest £1), halfway between the 5th and 6th values. The mode in this example is meaningless, as all ten values are different. The built-in function therefore returns N/A, or 'not applicable'. The mean is probably the most useful

Fig 14.5 Measures of central tendency for maintenance times in Table 14.3

	A	B	C	D
1	10	Mean	11.47	MEAN(A1..A30)
2	10	Median	11.00	MEDIAN(A1..A30)
3	11	Mode	10	MODE(A1..A30)
4	9			
5	13			
6	14			
7	12			
8	10			
9	11			
10	12			
11	10			
12	9			
13	11			
14	13			
15	26			
16	11			
17	10			
18	11			
19	16			
20	12			
21	10			
22	8			
23	10			
24	10			
25	13			
26	11			
27	10			
28	10			
29	11			
30	10			

measure of central tendency to use in this case to judge the performance of the sales team as a whole, because it takes every value into account. However, the median might be used to indicate 'par for the course' for individuals in the sales team, as it is less influenced by the very best and worst performers.

In other circumstances the mode can be important. The mode works best with a frequency table or where there are only a few possible values. If we now look at the example of the salaries of the eight people in one department, as shown in Tables 14.2 and 14.5, how do we judge central tendency? The mean can be calculated, as £30 000, but no one in the department actually earns anything close to that. We think it is clear that if the question is 'What does a person in this department typically earn?', the appropriate measure of central tendency in this case is the mode, i.e. £20 000, because far more than half of the observations are in this category. The median also happens to have this value (£20 000).

Looking now at the times for the common maintenance operation in Table 14.3 and Fig 14.5, the mean is 11.47 minutes, the median is 11.00, but the mode is 10. On the face of it, the mode might again be the most useful, to give the 'typical' time. However, standard operations tend to have standard times for planning purposes, and the manager's concern may be how well the actual performance compares to the plan. In such cases, the mode tells us very little, especially if the standard time for this operation is in fact 10 minutes. On the other hand, the mean may be affected too much by isolated large values, such as the 26 minutes for observation 15. The median may be the best measure of central tendency to use in this case, telling the manager that half the operations take longer than 11 minutes when the standard time is 10.

♦ **Key concept** *The mean is the most commonly used measure of central tendency, but the median may be a better choice to avoid distortion caused by the presence of extreme values, and the mode may be best when a substantial proportion of the observations take the same value.*

Rather than calculating them, it is possible to estimate some measures of central tendency from a picture. The mode may be found from a bar chart or frequency diagram by inspection, i.e. looking for the 'peak'; see some of the figures in Chapter 7. The median may also be found by looking for the 'halfway' point on a *cumulative frequency diagram*. Such a diagram is based on a cumulative frequency table, *cumulative* meaning that the number of observations against a given bin category is not just the number in that category, but the number of observations in that category and all previous categories. A good specialised statistical package will produce such pictures automatically. Unfortunately, this is only helpful to spreadsheet users if the data are already presented (from another source) in pictorial form. Otherwise, since a frequency table will have to be drawn up in order to produce the pictures, it is just as straightforward, and usually more accurate, to find the mode and/or median by formula.

Measures of spread

Spread measures are slightly less obvious than the measures used for describing central tendency. As spread involves the difference between large and small values, it might be thought that the built-in functions RANK and PERCENTILERANK, as mentioned in Chapter 9, could be used to indicate how large the spread is, but these can only reveal where in the set of observations a particular observation comes. To use an analogy, these functions tell us where an athlete finished in the race, but what we want to know (the spread) is whether the race was a close one or not. From the logistics manager's point of view, for example, there is a big difference between a situation in which every order is delivered exactly 4 days later, and one in which the mean delivery time is also 4 days, but half the orders are delivered in one day and the other half take 7 days!

There are four measures of 'how far from the middle' in common use: the range, the interquartile range, the standard deviation and the variance. Some other, more specialised, measures of spread used in forecasting will be discussed in Chapter 15.

Range

The simplest and most intuitive measure of spread is the range: the difference between the largest and smallest values in the set of data. This is very easy to calculate using the MAX and MIN functions, but because it ignores all values except these two, it is rarely used in statistical analysis. The one exception is where the values are successive measurements of the same variable taken over time, such as the temperature in a particular place, or the price of a certain share on the stock exchange. In such cases, the range is a quick and convenient measure, and the hi-lo box plot pictures mentioned in Chapter 7 use the range as a visible measure of spread.

Interquartile range

The interquartile range is most easily thought of as being the range within which the 'middle half' of the observed values lie. It is defined as the difference between the *lower* and *upper quartiles*, i.e. the values which are respectively one-quarter and three-quarters of the way along the ranked set of observations, in the same way that the median is the value in the middle. Its virtues are that, like the median, it avoids any distortion from extremely high or low values, and it can also be estimated 'by eye' from pictures. Its general disadvantage is that it ignores the other half of the values completely! Some specialised statistical packages use the interquartile range in box plots, rather than the range.

The interquartile range is easy to calculate if your spreadsheet package has a built-in function QUARTILE. Such a function normally takes two arguments, the first the cells containing the observations, and the second a number specifying which quartile is required (1 for the lower quartile, 3 for the upper). Thus the interquartile range for the maintenance operation times in Fig 14.3 would be given by the formula QUARTILE(A1..A30,3)–QUARTILE(A1..A30,1). The value of the interquartile range in this case is 2 (minutes).

If your spreadsheet does not contain such a function, it is almost certainly more effort to calculate the interquartile range than it is worth, although it could be done using the built-in LARGE and SMALL functions.

Standard deviation and variance

The standard deviation and the variance are equivalent to each other, because the variance is equal to the standard deviation squared. The reason that both are in use is that each has a useful feature. Mathematicians like to use the variance because it behaves mathematically in exactly the same way as the mean; the variance of the sum of two variables is the same as the sum of their separate variances. For example, if we are measuring the incomes of married couples, the variance of the joint incomes of the couples is the sum of the variance of the women's incomes and the variance of the men's incomes. However, the variance has two drawbacks. The first is that the units of the variance are the units of the observations squared. So, if the observations are the heights of adults in centimetres, the variance will be measured in *square* centimetres. Secondly, the variance tends to be a larger number, because it is a squared term; see Tables 14.6 and 14.7 for examples of this. Both these features can be off-putting to some people. By contrast, the standard deviation is measured in the same units as the observations (like the range and the interquartile range), and yields numbers of a magnitude similar to or smaller than the observations, making it intuitively easy to understand.

The variance of a set of observations is calculated in four steps:

1 Calculate the mean of the observations.
2 Work out the difference between each observation and the mean.
3 Square each of these differences.
4 Add them up and divide by the number of observations.[4]

The standard deviation is calculated by taking the square root of the variance.

All spreadsheets have built-in functions to calculate variances and standard deviations, but there is a complication of which you need to be aware. There are two different definitions for the variance or standard deviation, giving two different values. One is the case where you regard the observations you have as comprising the whole *population* of values, for example ten sales revenue values when your company only has ten salespeople; this is the definition we have just given. The other is the case when your observations are only a *sample* from the whole population, for example, ten sales revenue values when you have a sales force of 789, the whole population, and you wish to estimate the variance of the whole salesforce population from your sample. The spread in the whole population tends to be larger than that observed in any sample taken from it, so in this latter case instead of dividing by n, the number of observations, we divide by $(n-1)$ instead.[5]

Table 14.6 Measures of spread for sales revenue example in Table 14.1

Name	Monthly sales revenue (£)
Schmidt	10 887
McGrath	11 926
Lewis	2 312
Moody	6 311
Patel	10 354
Simmonds	3 964
Chang	8 949
Robinson	6 499
Dion	8 422
Jones	4 754
Variance of sample	9 149 244
Standard deviation of sample	3 025
Estimates for population:	
Variance	10 165 826
Standard deviation	3 188

The crucial thing you must discover is whether the 'ordinary' VAR or STD function in your favourite spreadsheet gives the 'population' or 'sample' estimate. In Lotus 1-2-3 the functions @VAR and @STD give the results assuming that the observations in the data set are for the whole population, whereas @VARS and @STDS give the 'sample' estimates. In Excel it is the other way round, unfortunately; VARP and STDEVP assume the observations are the whole population, VAR and STDEV assume the observations are a sample. If it's any consolation, the difference it makes is small. When $n = 10$, the difference in the two variance calculations is approximately 10 per cent (the 'sample' estimate is larger), and the difference in the standard deviations about 5 per cent; when $n = 100$, the variances differ by around 1 per cent, and the standard deviations by around 0.5 per cent.

Returning to our three examples, the second one (incomes) by definition concerns the whole population of the department; the third (maintenance operation times) is clearly a sample; the first could be either, depending on whether these ten people are some (a sample) or all (the whole population) of the sales staff. Tables 14.6 and 14.7 and Fig 14.6 show the standard deviations and variances for each, including both sets of definitions in Table 14.6; note the size of the difference between the two variances and standard deviations in Table 14.6.

♦ **Key concept**

There are four measures of spread in common use. The range is intuitively reasonable, and very easy to calculate, but ignores all but two of the observations and so is open to distortion by extreme values. The interquartile range is also intuitively reasonable, but ignores half the observations. Mathematicians like to use the variance, but its large numbers and squared units can be off-putting to many people. The standard deviation is often the best compromise between being intuitively reasonable and taking account of all the observations.

Table 14.7 Measures of spread for income figures example in Table 14.2

Name	Salary(£)	
Spriggs	20 000	
March	20 000	
Elson	20 000	
Lee	100 000	
Crawford	20 000	
Shah	20 000	
Kocinski	20 000	
Wayne	20 000	
	Variance	700 000 000
	Standard deviation	26 458

Fig 14.6 Measures of spread for maintenance times in Table 14.3

	A	B	C	D
1	10	Mean	11.47	
2	10	Median	11	
3	11	Mode	10	
4	9			
5	13	Estimates for population:		
6	14	Variance	10.19	
7	12	Standard deviation	3.19	
8	10			
9	11			
10	12			
11	10			
12	9			
13	11			
14	13			
15	26			
16	11			
17	10			
18	11			
19	16			
20	12			
21	10			
22	8			
23	10			
24	10			
25	13			
26	11			
27	10			
28	10			
29	11			
30	10			

INFERENTIAL STATISTICS

Inferential statistics builds on descriptive statistics to try to draw (infer – that's where the name comes from) some *conclusions* from the data rather than simply summarising it. This almost always involves drawing some conclusions about a population on the basis of a sample taken from it. There are many questions which inferential statistics might help a manager to answer. Examples include:

- *Process control.* Is it taking longer to produce a batch of mouldings than it did last month? Is it true that the bolts produced on machine number 12 vary more in length than those from the other machines?

- *Quality assurance*. How does the mean weight of our '1kg' packs actually compare with 1kg?
- *Market research*. Does the public prefer the taste of our lager to the taste of its main competitors?
- *Exam marks*. Is it true that exam results have improved compared with those of the 1980s?
- *Sales*. Have our sales increased/decreased compared with this time last year?
- *Medical*. Does this area have a greater incidence of leukaemia than the rest of the country?
- *Crime*. Does this area have a greater incidence of burglary than the rest of the country?

Previously, in descriptive statistics, the concern was to establish 'what is'; here, the concern is wider – better expressed in the phrase 'What does it mean in general?' There are two difficulties, as may be seen by considering the above examples. One is that in most cases (such as quality assurance and market research) the data can only be a sample from the population; how representative a sample is it? The other is the question of what constitutes a *significant* difference; for example, it would be astonishing if sales were *exactly* the same this year as last to the nearest penny – how large a difference is significant?

Inferential statistics covers far more topics than we can cover in one chapter, so you will not necessarily be able to answer all such questions on the basis of what we include here. Nevertheless, you will become familiar with the principles involved. We consider just three inferential topics:

- confidence intervals
- hypothesis testing
- correlation.

Confidence intervals

Whenever a manager uses values in a sample to estimate the values for a whole population, the results are subject to what is known as *sampling error*; as the sample is smaller than the population, it cannot be completely representative of it. (This is the reason behind the two definitions of variance and standard deviation discussed in the section on descriptive statistics.) Suppose that a manager in an insurance company is interested in knowing the average amount paid out per claim this month, to see if a change in the company's policy for dealing with claims has had any effect. Each 100 claims that come in can be regarded as a sample from the population of the whole month's claims, which would probably number several thousand. One sample of, say, 100 claims might have a mean value of, say, £2342. The next sample of (a different) 100 claims is virtually certain to give a different mean value – say, £1976. The means of the different samples are distributed around the mean of the whole population, just as the individual claims are, but the spread for the distribution of sample means is not as large as the spread for the individual observations. The larger the sample, the smaller the spread of the sample means becomes, and you can see that as the sample size is increased until it equals the entire population, so the sample mean comes closer to, and eventually equals, the population mean. If the values of individual claims follow a normal distribution (see Chapter 10), then in fact the variance of the sample means is smaller than the variance of the individual claims by a factor equal to the sample size. The standard deviation, being the square root of the variance, is smaller by a factor equal to the square root of this. Thus if the samples are size 100, the variance of the sample means is smaller by a factor of 100 than the variance of the individual claims, and the standard deviation is smaller by a factor of 10, as shown in Fig 14.7. Such a distribution of sample means is often called a *sampling distribution of the mean*, and the standard deviation of the sample means is called the *standard error*.

♦ **Key concept**
*The standard deviation measures the spread of individual values around the mean. The **standard error** measures the spread of the means of different samples around the population mean.*

The idea of a *confidence interval* is that, although the mean of a sample is the best estimate of the mean of the population that can be made from that sample, it is also possible to estimate how much confidence should be placed in that estimate of the population mean, using the sampling distribution of the mean. This is done in the form of a percentage, typically 90 or 95 per cent. A 95 per cent confidence interval for the mean of a population, based on a sample, is an interval within which there is a 95 per cent chance that the true (but unknown) population mean lies; there is a 5 per cent chance, i.e. 1 in 20, that the true population mean lies outside this interval. For any given sample, the larger the percentage confidence, the wider the interval has to be.[6]

Fig 14.7 Normal distribution of observations and of sample means (size 100)

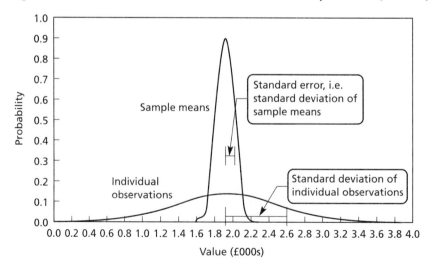

◆ **Key concept**   *A **confidence interval** for the mean of a population, based on a sample, is an interval within which there is a given chance, usually expressed as a percentage such as 95 per cent, that the true population mean actually lies.*

Table 14.8 shows a sample of the first 100 insurance claim values this month. The manager in charge wants to calculate a 95 per cent confidence interval for the mean claim value of the whole population of this month's claims. This is done by calculating the mean of the sample and the estimated standard deviation of the whole population, and using the sampling distribution of the mean – especially the standard error – to find the confidence interval, as shown on the graph in Fig 14.8.

The calculations are then carried out as shown in Fig 14.9, which is a spreadsheet including the data of Table 14.8. This relies on there being a

Table 14.8 Sample of 100 insurance claims (£000s)

2833	1562	1305	1600	2205	2099	1464	2608	1727	1862
2997	2197	2838	2205	1924	2828	1896	1115	1598	3102
2452	2372	1459	2073	945	1533	2131	2453	2399	1857
2377	2124	1923	2211	1998	1869	2194	2097	2152	2589
1833	2523	1490	2017	1960	1834	1919	2010	2885	1592
2287	2592	2411	2218	3279	1649	1925	2561	1404	2094
1868	1430	2483	2710	1858	2842	1504	2236	2956	2332
2362	2480	2245	894	2233	1873	1968	581	2368	2298
1003	1779	2140	2644	1436	2342	2253	1553	1518	2598
1684	2366	2201	1719	2906	2077	846	1189	2273	2585

Fig 14.8 Estimating a 95 per cent confidence interval of the means of a normal distribution

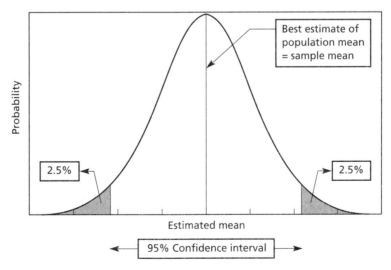

Fig 14.9 Spreadsheet showing 95 per cent confidence interval calculations

	A	B	C	D	E	F	G	H	I	J
1	Sample of 100 claim values									
2	2833	1562	1305	1600	2205	2099	1464	2608	1727	1862
3	2997	2197	2838	2205	1924	2828	1896	1115	1598	3102
4	2452	2372	1459	2073	945	1533	2131	2453	2399	1857
5	2377	2124	1923	2211	1998	1869	2194	2097	2152	2589
6	1833	2523	1490	2017	1960	1834	1919	2010	2885	1592
7	2287	2592	2411	2218	3279	1649	1925	2561	1404	2094
8	1868	1430	2483	2710	1858	2842	1504	2236	2956	2332
9	2362	2480	2245	894	2233	1873	1968	581	2368	2298
10	1003	1779	2140	2644	1436	2342	2253	1553	1518	2598
11	1684	2366	2201	1719	2906	2077	846	1189	2273	2585
12	Sample mean				2063	MEAN(A2..J11)				
13	Estimate of s.d.				529	STD (A2..J11)				
14	Estimated standard error				52.9	E13/SQRT(100)				
15	95% Confidence interval (lower)				1959	NORMALINV(0.025,E12,E14)				
16	95% Confidence interval (upper)				2167	NORMALINV(0.975,E12,E14)				

NORMALINV function in the manager's spreadsheet package; otherwise confidence intervals cannot be calculated in a spreadsheet. Note that the standard deviation is worked out using the built-in function for the 'sample' estimate (@STDS in Lotus 1-2-3, =STD in Microsoft Excel). The values of 0.025 and 0.975 in the first argument of the NORMALINV function are those for a 95 per cent confidence interval that is equally spaced either side of the value of the sample mean. (Note that 2.5 per cent has to be entered as 0.025 and 97.5 per cent as 0.975.) For a different level of confidence, these would need to be changed, for example to 0.05 and 0.95 for a 90 per cent interval. The manager can therefore be 95 per cent confident that the true mean claim value for the whole population lies between £1959 and £2167.

This worked example assumed that it was reasonable to regard the insurance claim values as following a normal distribution. We chose the normal distribution because it is the one with which a spreadsheet package is most likely to be capable of dealing (see also our remarks in Chapter 10). Indeed, at least one spreadsheet package has a built-in function called CONFIDENCE that assumes a normal distribution. The precise details of the calculation of confidence intervals depend on the probability distribution that the variable of interest follows, although the general principles are always the same. The approach shown in Fig 14.9 will always work for the mean as long as the spreadsheet package being used contains the appropriate built-in inverse function for that distribution.[7]

The other crucial assumption is that the samples are reasonably large, in other words a sample size of 30 or more. Below this size, the sampling distribution of the mean ceases to follow the normal distribution, even if the individual observations come from such a distribution. Instead, it follows the *t* distribution, which we shall mention in the next section.

Hypothesis testing

Rather than drawing an inference from a set of data based on no assumption except the type of probability distribution involved, as with confidence interval estimation, a manager may instead wish to test a specific hypothesis. The insurance company manager, for example, might wish to know whether the mean value of claims this month is greater than £2000. In statistical terms, such questions are always stated in terms of a null hypothesis, which is assumed to be true unless the evidence suggests otherwise.[8] In this example, a suitable null hypothesis (usually labelled H_0) would be:

H_0: The mean value of a claim is £2000

As discussed earlier in this chapter, the exact value of £2000 is hardly ever likely to occur, but this is a hypothetical statement (hence the name hypothesis). Hypothesis testing is about looking for differences, and there must be a specific point to serve as a baseline from which differences are judged.

To test such a null hypothesis, the manager needs to know the appropriate distribution to use, and to be able to estimate the mean and the variance/standard deviation of the distribution. This is the same as for calculating confidence intervals; the principles are similar, but the details differ slightly, as we shall see later. The result of the test will also be couched in probabilistic terms, as for confidence intervals.

◆ **Key concept**

*Hypothesis testing looks for differences. It is based on the **null hypothes** is that there is no difference. The data are then used as evidence on which to accept or reject this null hypothesis. If the null hypothesis is rejected, then the data suggests that there is a difference. As with confidence intervals, the result of the test will also be couched in probabilistic terms.*

The manager also needs to decide what the alternative to the null hypothesis is. In this case, it is clearly that the mean value of a claim is *not* £2000. However, it is necessary to be a bit more precise in order to satisfy the assumptions of hypothesis testing. There are *three* possible alternative hypotheses:

- the mean value of a claim is *different from* £2000 (either greater or less)
- the mean value of a claim is *greater than* £2000
- the mean value of a claim is *less than* £2000.

In the first case, where the alternative may lie in either direction, then the manager must carry out what is known as a 'two-tailed' test of the null hypothesis. (The areas corresponding to the parts of a probability distribution furthest from the mean are known as the *tails*. The two 2.5 per cent areas outside the confidence interval in Fig 14.8 are the two tails of the distribution shown.) In the other two cases, then they must carry out a 'one-tailed' test; we shall explain two-tailed tests first, then one-tailed tests.

A two-tailed test Let us first assume that the manager wishes to test the null hypothesis against the alternative hypothesis that the mean value of a claim is *different* from £2000, a two-tailed test. It may help to think of this in confidence interval terms, as in Fig 14.8. The null hypothesis will be rejected if the estimated population mean (i.e. the sample mean) is far enough away from £2000 to be in one of the tails of the distribution. It will be accepted if the estimated population mean is not in one of the tails.

The main difference between this hypothesis test and the confidence interval in Fig 14.8 is that for the hypothesis test the manager sets the test limits when specifying the value of the mean in the null hypothesis (£2000), rather than using the sample mean, as for the confidence interval.[9] The other difference is that probability values used in hypothesis testing are typically quoted in terms of the (small) chance of being wrong, rather than the large chance of being right used in confidence intervals, in other words the area in the tail(s), not the area 'in the middle'. The values chosen are again arbitrary, so the 'round' ones of 10 per cent and 5 per cent are most common, although values of 1 per cent and even 0.1 per cent are occasionally seen. Their meaning will be explained more precisely shortly. Here we shall use 5 per cent.

The formulae for the limits for the test will therefore be (using the Fig 14.9 spreadsheet and with 2000 for the mean rather than 2063):

$$\text{NORMALINV}(0.025,2000,\text{E14}) \text{ and } \text{NORMALINV}(0.975,2000,\text{E14})$$

Note again that 2.5 per cent has to be entered as 0.025 and 97.5 per cent as 0.975. This gives values of £1896 and £2104.

We have also assumed here that the manager has no information about what the spread of the claim values in the whole population is, other than that contained in the sample. If such information were available, for example in the form of a value for the standard deviation, then that value should be included in cell E13 instead of the estimate, to be used in the calculation of the standard error.

The test is therefore:

- Accept the null hypothesis (mean value of a claim is £2000) if the sample mean is between £1896 and £2104.
- Otherwise, reject the null hypothesis and accept the alternative hypothesis that the mean value of a claim is different from £2000.

Using the 0.025 and 0.975 points means that this test has a 5 per cent chance of leading the manager to reject the null hypothesis when it should be accepted. If the null hypothesis is rejected, the difference is said to be *statistically significant at the 5 per cent level*.

Statistical significance is based on distinguishing between random differences resulting from the effects of sampling and other more systematic differences. Thus if the null hypothesis really is true, a test at a level of significance of 5 per cent would give a wrong result (i.e. rejecting the null hypothesis) 5 per cent of the time; 1 time in 20. Note that statistical significance is not the same as practical significance. A statistically significant difference merely tells us that a sample is unlikely to have come from a population consistent with the null hypothesis. Statistical significance does not tell us anything about the magnitude of the difference, or its importance in real terms; although, not surprisingly, large differences are easier to test for than small ones.

◆ **Key concept**

*The **statistical significance** of a hypothesis test is based on the chance of rejecting the null hypothesis when it is really true. It does not tell us anything about the practical significance of the observed difference.*

Carrying out the test in this case, the sample mean is £2063, as was calculated in Fig 14.9. The manager should therefore *accept* the null hypothesis, and conclude that the difference between £2063 and £2000 is not significant at the 5 per cent level. In other words, given the amount of spread in the population, and the sample size, the chance of getting a sample with a mean of £2063 (purely by chance) when the population mean really is £2000 is greater than 5 per cent.

A one-tailed test

Suppose that instead the manager is concerned that the mean value of claims might have *increased*, rather than simply that it has *changed*. Now a one-tailed test is appropriate. The null hypothesis is still:

H$_0$: The mean value of a claim is £2000

However, the alternative hypothesis is now that the mean value of a claim is greater than £2000.

The procedure for a one-tailed test with a significance level of 5 per cent is exactly the same as for the two-tailed test, except that the situation is now as shown in Fig 14.10.

Only if the sample mean falls in the 5 per cent tail (in this case, the one to the right of the distribution) will the manager reject the null hypothesis. This one tail must of course contain twice as much of the distribution as each of the two

Fig 14.10 A one-tailed hypothesis test

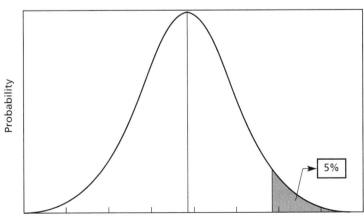

tails for the equivalent two-tailed test, which would look like Fig 14.8. (A test of the alternative hypothesis that the mean value of a claim was less than £2000 would be identical to this except that the one tail would be on the left.)

So, the test now has just a single limit, the formula for which (95 per cent being entered as 0.95) is:

NORMALINV(0.95,2000,E14)

This gives a value of £2087.

The one-tailed test is therefore:

- Accept the null hypothesis (mean value of a claim is £2000) if the sample mean is less than £2087.
- Otherwise, reject the null hypothesis and accept the alternative hypothesis that the mean value of a claim is greater than £2000.

As with the two-tailed test, this test has a 5 per cent chance of leading the manager to reject the null hypothesis when it should be accepted.

The sample mean, as we have seen, is £2063. The manager should therefore accept the null hypothesis. The value of £2063 is not significantly greater than £2000 at the 5 per cent level, given the amount of spread in the population, and the sample size.

The same restrictions regarding sample size apply to this kind of hypothesis testing as we discussed for confidence intervals earlier, namely that the normal distribution is not appropriate for samples of size less than 30, even if the distribution of the population is believed to be normal. In such cases, the t distribution needs to be used instead.

The final type of hypothesis test that we shall discuss in detail here is a test for a difference in spread between two samples. The variance is the measure of spread that is used in such a test, as it is the easiest to manipulate mathematically. It is always a one-tailed test: the null hypothesis, H_0, is that there is no difference in variance between the populations from which the samples are taken; the alternative hypothesis is that the sample with the larger variance comes from a population with a larger variance.

The principle is exactly the same as the one-tailed test described earlier. The test is based on the ratio of the variances of the two samples. Even if these are both from normal distributions, this ratio does not follow a normal distribution, but another distribution called the F distribution. The shape of the F distribution depends only on the size of the two samples, not on the spread of the underlying distributions for the individual observations.

The test is based on the so-called F ratio:

{larger sample variance}/{smaller sample variance}

and is often referred to as the variance ratio test. The null hypothesis, H_0, is that this ratio is equal to one; the alternative hypothesis is that it is greater than one.

The null hypothesis is accepted unless the calculated value of the F ratio is greater than the F distribution value for the desired significance level, for example significance at the 5 per cent level.

To carry out an F test, a spreadsheet package must have a built-in function FINV, to perform the equivalent job to the NORMALINV function used earlier. FINV will have three arguments: the first is the significance level, and the other two are the number of *degrees of freedom* of the two samples, the one giving the larger variance estimate first. The number of degrees of freedom is equal to the sample size minus one.[10] Note also that a 5 per cent significance level is typically input as 0.05, unlike the one-tailed test using NORMALINV earlier, where it was 0.95. This annoying difference is because the F distribution is only used in F tests, whereas the normal distribution has many uses.

Thus, if an insurance manager has the two samples of claim values shown in the spreadsheet in Fig 14.11, and wishes to test for a difference in spread, they should first calculate the ratio of the two variances.

The variances of the two samples are calculated in cells B6 and B7, the formulae being =VAR(A2..J2) and =VAR(A4..J4) respectively (in Microsoft Excel; in Lotus 1-2-3 the manager would need to use @VARS). Cell B8 calculates the variance ratio, as B7/B6. A more general version of this formula, allowing for not knowing which sample had the larger variance, would be IF(B6>B7,B6/B7,B7/B6). Cell B10 shows the limit, or *critical value*, for the F test, in this case FINV(0.05,9,9) for a 5 per cent level of significance and two samples of size 10. (Again, a more general version of the formula would have the significance level as an input factor.)

The calculated F ratio is 4.39, which is larger than the critical value of 3.18 for the desired F test. This means there is less than 1 chance in 20 that this would have happened if the samples were really from populations with the same variance. The manager should therefore reject the null hypothesis, and conclude that the second sample has a significantly larger spread at the 5 per cent level.

The theory of hypothesis testing extends to the testing of many other types of hypothesis, for example testing whether there is a significant difference between the means of the populations from which two samples are taken. This is probably a more common test than those we have mentioned so far. For example, suppose a manager of an electrical company wants to know if light bulbs made

Fig 14.11 Testing for a difference in spread between two samples

	A	B	C	D	E	F	G	H	I	J
1	First sample									
2	1834	1601	2182	2049	2088	2086	2688	2219	2295	1973
3	Second sample									
4	2120	1981	2647	2120	1981	1940	1789	2436	416	2285
5										
6	Variance 1	82677.0								
7	Variance 2	363032.5								
8	F ratio	4.39								
9	Critical									
10	F value	3.18								

in plant A last longer than the same type of light bulbs made in another plant B. Now, there is no fixed value from which to measure a difference; any decision must be based on samples of the light bulbs made in each plant.

Unfortunately, this test is somewhat more complex. It is based on the assumption that the two samples come from populations with equal variances, so that a variance ratio test needs to be carried out first. If the null hypothesis of the variance ratio test is accepted, then the test for a difference between means goes ahead, again based on the t distribution. The full details are beyond our scope here.[11] At least one spreadsheet package has recently appeared that offers such tests as a menu-driven process.

Correlation

The third aspect of inferential statistics that we shall deal with here is that of correlation. The previous two subsections have been dealing with inferences about the values taken by a single variable. Correlation is concerned with inferences about the strength of the association between the values of two variables, where the values are measured in pairs that belong together, such as a person's height and weight, or the age of a machine and the amount spent on maintaining it.

Many different types of association are possible. To explain what is meant here, consider Fig 14.12, which consists of three graphs showing possible relationships between the two variables *Sales of Product A* and *Sales of Product B* in different regions. In graph a, *Sales of Product A* and *Sales of Product B* appear to rise and fall together; the two variables are very closely associated. In graph b, the two variables are also very closely associated, but this time the value of *Sales of Product B* appears to fall when the value of *Sales of Product A* rises, and vice versa. In graph c, there appears to be little or no association between the values of the two variables.

The *correlation coefficient* measures the strength of this type of association. It takes values between +1, indicating that the two variables are completely associated and that the two values rise and fall together, and −1, indicating that the two variables are completely associated but that their values move in opposite directions. A value of 0 indicates that there is no association at all. Positive and negative values of the correlation coefficient are usually termed positive and negative correlations respectively. Most spreadsheet packages have a built-in function CORREL to calculate the correlation coefficient.[12]

Figure 14.13 shows the three data sets that were used to produce the graphs in Fig 14.12. The correlation coefficients, calculated using the CORREL function, are shown in cells B13, D13, and F13. The formula in B13 is CORREL (A3..A12,B3..B12); similarly for D13 and F13. As may be seen, the correlation coefficient for data set A, with a strong association, is 0.985; for data set B, with a strong association but in opposite directions, it is −0.985 (a negative correlation); and for data set C, with virtually no association, it is −0.068.

These values raise the question of 'How strong is strong?' Clearly a correlation coefficient of 0.985 does indicate a strongly positive association – but what

Fig 14.12 Three examples of different strengths of association

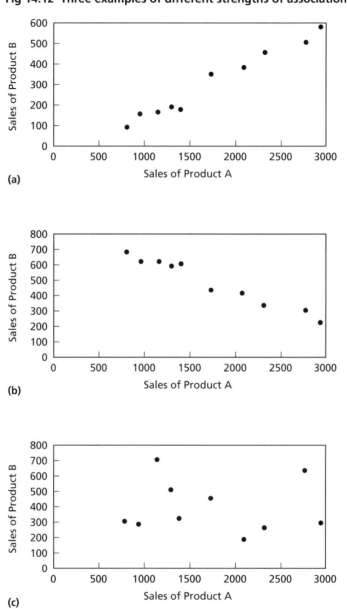

(a)

(b)

(c)

about a value of 0.785? Or 0.485? In general terms, there can be no hard-and-fast answer. What constitutes a high correlation depends on what is being measured and under what conditions. As a rough rule of thumb, a correlation coefficient of 0.7 or more is considered 'high'; one of the reasons for this will be revealed in the next chapter.

There are three important points to note about the correlation coefficient as described here.

Fig 14.13 Correlation coefficients for the three sets of sales data shown in Fig 14.12

	A	B	C	D	E	F
1	Set A		Set B		Set C	
2	Sales of Product A	Sales of Product B	Sales of Product A	Sales of Product B	Sales of Product A	Sales of Product B
3	2323	456	2323	344	2323	269
4	1394	180	1394	620	1394	333
5	2956	578	2956	222	2956	294
6	1159	169	1159	631	1159	717
7	803	97	803	703	803	319
8	2787	500	2787	300	2787	643
9	1301	192	1301	608	1301	521
10	955	161	955	639	955	296
11	2093	378	2093	422	2093	195
12	1738	349	1738	451	1738	460
13		0.985		–0.985		–0.068

1 It is only valid for data measured at the interval or ratio level.

2 It is a measure of *linear* association. Other types of association may not be picked up by it.

3 A high correlation says nothing about *causation*, merely that the numbers representing the values rise or fall together. Two examples of high correlations that have been found in the past where there is generally believed to be no causal relationship are:

- between the number of babies born in Denmark and the number of storks' nests observed on houses there
- between the number of convictions for drunken driving in England and the number of Church of England vicars.

WHAT IF I NEED MORE?

Most spreadsheets nowadays have built-in functions for all the standard statistical measures, but in general do not offer data-entry facilities that are as good as those in the specialised statistical packages. This can be vitally important when there are tens of thousands of observations to be analysed, as is quite usual. The general-purpose specialised statistical packages will perform all the basic functions of elementary statistics as found in any textbook, including descriptive statistics, significance tests, hypothesis testing, correlation, linear regression, analysis of variance and even more advanced techniques. Well-known general-purpose packages include SAS (Statistical Analysis System), MINITAB and SPSS (Statistical Package for the Social Sciences). Some, such as KWIKSTAT and its Windows version WINKS, are specifically targeted at the non-specialist user.

The manuals and on-line help in specialised statistical packages are also usually more careful about stating the assumptions of particular statistical methods and techniques than those in spreadsheet packages.

As well as the general-purpose packages, there are also a considerable number of specialised statistical analysis packages aimed at niche markets. For example, MARQUIS and MARKPACK are specifically aimed at practitioners and students of marketing, to help them analyse market research data. There are also specialised statistical packages for use by the medical profession, in quality control for manufacturing, in oil and mineral exploration and in agriculture, to name but a few. In most cases, the difference between the specialised package and a more general one is not in the functionality so much as in the human interface; the packages use the jargon of the area concerned, so as to make the statistics seem less intimidating. The downside of this ease of use is that the users of specialised packages may not always realise the limitations of the conclusions which they are drawing from their statistical analyses, although this is always a problem whatever software is used.

SUMMARY

In this chapter we have looked at some of the statistical analyses that can be done using a spreadsheet. These included calculating measures of central tendency and spread, under the heading of descriptive statistics, and confidence intervals, hypothesis testing and correlation, under the heading of inferential statistics. Even so, we have covered only part of the statistical analysis that spreadsheet packages can do.

END NOTES

1 As we said in Chapter 6, ordinal scales are frequently treated as if they were interval scales, by using calculated mean values; strictly speaking, the mean of measurements on an ordinal scale is meaningless. Sadly this is widely abused in all kinds of context; for example, UK universities themselves convert potential students' Advanced Level examination results from the ordinal grade scale (A, B, C etc.) to an apparently quantitative ratio scale, by awarding 10 points for a grade A, 8 for a grade B and so on. This implies, for example, that two grade Bs 'equal' one grade A plus one grade C.

2 This question of the interpretation of 'average' accounts for various long-standing jokes, including a UK TV series title, all based on the average family having 2.4 children (see Exercise 2).

3 The emphasis here is on the word 'meaningful', and the old computing adage 'garbage in, garbage out' is worth remembering. If you put 10 numbers which are on a nominal scale, such as telephone or credit card numbers, into cells A1..A10 of a spreadsheet, then MEAN(A1..A10) or MEDIAN(A1..A10) will return a value, but it will not mean anything.

4 If there are n observations, values x_1, x_2, ..., x_n, and the mean is $\bar{x}$, then the expression for the variance is $\dfrac{\sum\limits_{i=1}^{n} (x_i - \bar{x})^2}{n}$ where $\sum\limits_{i=1}^{n}$ means that all of the n different values of $(x_i - \bar{x})^2$ are added together.

5 You will have to take this point on trust. The reason it is $(n-1)$ is rather complicated!

6 We can never be 100 per cent confident unless our sample consists of the whole population, in which case we are *measuring* the population mean, not estimating it!

7 There is a theorem in statistics known as the central limit theorem, which says that as long as the sample size is large enough, the distribution of sample means will closely follow a normal distribution, whatever the distribution of the population values actually is, so the normal distribution is the most general one that we can use here.

8 The popular phrase 'you can prove anything with statistics' could hardly be further from the truth. Actually, statisticians never *prove* anything; the furthest they ever go is to say that the evidence does not *disprove* a hypothesis. The null hypothesis is accepted because there is not enough evidence to reject it, not because it has been proved to be 'true'.

9 Some people think of hypothesis testing solely in terms of confidence intervals, but statisticians would protest that strictly this is incorrect.

10 Confusing, and almost irrelevant though it is in simple examples, the use of the number of degrees of freedom rather than the sample size is essential in more advanced statistical analysis.

11 More mathematically able readers will be able to work them out with the aid of any statistics textbook.

12 If there are n pairs of observations of the variables x and y, the correlation coefficient, also called the Pearson or product moment correlation coefficient, is

calculated as: $\dfrac{n\sum xy - (\sum x)(\sum y)}{\sqrt{[n\sum x^2 - (\sum x)^2][n\sum y^2 - (\sum y)^2]}}$, all summations being from

1 to n.

FURTHER READING There are a huge number of textbooks on statistics, ranging from the introductory to the 'rocket science' level; we won't mention any of the latter type here! A good introductory text on statistical techniques is H. T. Hayslett's *Statistics Made Simple*, Heinemann, 1990, while Darrel Huff's *How to Lie with Statistics*, Penguin, 1973, is a 'light reading' classic. Possibly the best book ever written on statistics and probability for the layperson was M. J. Moroney's *Facts from Figures*, originally published by Penguin in 1951 and last reprinted in about 1976; it would still be well worth reading if you can get hold of a copy.

EXERCISES

1 Why is it necessary to use summary statistics at all?

2 Which one measure of central tendency would you use to summarise the following human characteristics?
   a) Height of male adults in the UK.
   b) Number of children in a family.
   c) Number of cars owned by a family.
   d) Height of all adults in the UK.

3 Which one measure of central tendency would you use to summarise the following information?
   a) Number of lines of program code produced by different computer programmers in a week.

b) Number of ATMs (automatic teller machines – 'cashpoints') in a bank branch.
c) Number of personal computers sold by each of a company's sales staff in a month.
d) Total value of insurance policies sold by each of a company's sales staff in a month.
e) The position in rank order of a company based on market share in each of its different markets.

4 For which levels of measurement/scales is the use of the mean valid?

5 When would you be most likely to use the interquartile range as a measure of spread?

6 What is the meaning of a 90 per cent confidence interval for the mean value of a variable?

7 What is a null hypothesis?

8 What kind of association would a correlation coefficient of –0.95 indicate?

A computer firm has developed a new processor. The data in Table 14.9 below shows the time (in seconds) taken by the new processor to run a standard spreadsheet benchmarking test. There are 28 observations. Exercises 9–13 are based on this data set.

Table 14.9 Time taken for benchmarking test

17	21	20	16	17	23	19
21	19	17	16	18	17	15
19	21	16	18	15	18	19
17	20	20	24	21	20	17

9 Calculate the mean, median and mode.

10 Calculate the range and interquartile range, and estimate the variance of the population from which these observations are taken.

11 Which of the measures in 9 and 10 do you think summarise the data best?

12 Calculate a two-tailed 95 per cent confidence interval for the mean time taken to perform the test.

13 The company's main rival claims that its processor can perform this test in an average of 22 seconds. Carry out an appropriate hypothesis test, and indicate how you would interpret the result for the company's marketing department.

14 Assuming that the maintenance operation times in Table 14.3 may be regarded as following a normal distribution, calculate a 95 per cent confidence interval for the mean time.

15 Again assuming that the maintenance operation times in Table 14.3 may be regarded as following a normal distribution, is it reasonable to claim that the mean time for the operation is now greater than 10 minutes?

16 As a manager in a clothing company that has traditionally used age as its only measure of size for children's clothes, you are interested in the correlation between age and height. Calculate and interpret the correlation coefficient for the data on the ages and heights of a sample of schoolchildren shown in Table 14.10.

Table 14.10 Ages and heights of schoolchildren

Age (months)	Height (cm)
124	136
134	144
128	134
128	138
128	138
129	137
139	143
114	132
131	143
128	145
143	147
127	143
110	136
140	141
125	137
107	123
133	140
124	146
97	128
120	144
98	127
115	122
120	133
132	145
122	132
116	125

CHAPTER 15

Forecasting

Chapter aims The aims of this chapter are to explain two types of quantitative forecasting: time series analysis, where the forecast is based solely on past values of the variable concerned; and causal modelling, where the forecast uses values of other variables as well. We describe some of the techniques that may be used to make such forecasts with the aid of a spreadsheet, and also some of the limitations of these techniques.

- Introduction
- Time series analysis
  - How much data are needed? • Forecasting by identifying patterns in the past data • Measuring the fit of a forecasting model • Forecasting directly from the data values • Dealing with repeating patterns • Forecasting from relationships between variables
- Choosing between different forecasting models
- What if I need more?

INTRODUCTION

Forecasting is something that all organisations have to do if they are to plan for the future. Forecasting what is going to happen, both within your organisation and outside it, is one of the core activities of management. As such, it is likely to crop up in many managerial issues. Most forecasts attempt to use past data in order to identify short-, medium- or long-term trends, and to use these patterns to project the current position into the future.

We have already seen how 'What if?' analysis can help in handling issues connected with what is going to happen. Spreadsheets can help us go further than this, but unfortunately they are not the answer to all a manager's forecasting problems. They will not, for example, be able to tell you what your main competitor's next new product is going to be! The type of forecasts we are going to consider in this chapter are those that meet two requirements:

1 They are concerned with quantitative rather than qualitative matters; how many pairs of shoes we will sell next month, rather than what next year's fashionable styles and colours will be. It is quantitative forecasting, often called time series analysis, which concerns us most here; other types of forecasting are usually too judgemental for computers, never mind spreadsheets, to be of much assistance at present.[1]

2 It is reasonable to assume that the future will resemble the past, whether in a simple or a complex manner. If this is not the case, then the only assistance that spreadsheets can provide is 'What if?' analysis on the basis of figures that stem from managerial hunches or even guesswork; even this must be based on the manager's past – but in this case an inarticulated past!

Taken together, these two requirements also mean that we must have some data available on which to base our forecasts. We shall discuss two types of forecast here:

- Time series analysis, where we forecast future values of a managerial variable based only on what the past values of that variable have been.
- Causal modelling (see Chapter 7), where we forecast future values of a managerial variable based on past relationships that depend on other variables, whose values are easier to obtain. This follows on from the topic of correlation, which we discussed in the previous chapter, and will be considered towards the end of this chapter.

◆ **Key concept**	*Quantitative forecasting models are based on assuming that the future will resemble the past in a manner that can be predicted from past data, either on that variable or other variables. The relationships involved may be relatively simple or highly complex.*

Examples

Any quantitative variable is a candidate for the use of a forecasting model. Among the many possible examples are:

- Sales, of any product or service from paper clips to jumbo jets, and from package holidays to haircuts.
- Raw material prices, again of any kind from wheat to titanium.
- Lead time for delivery of orders you have placed with your supplier.
- Tomorrow's closing value of the FTSE Index for the London stock exchange.
- The number of applications likely to be received for a job vacancy, or a place on a university degree course – and the likely proportion of those offered jobs/places who will accept.
- Demand for gas or electricity. These are somewhat different problems: electricity has the major short-term problem of sudden peaks, such as the end of a major sporting event on TV or commercial breaks during a popular 'soap'; gas has more long-term problems relating to the weather.
- Catering demand at a leisure centre. This would almost certainly require forecasts of the levels of the various activities that take place at the leisure centre.

Even this list only scratches the surface of the possibilities.

TIME SERIES ANALYSIS

A time series is a set of observations of the values of a variable that form a sequence in time. It could be, for example, the sales each month of a particular brand of cola in the USA; or the share price of a company recorded at the close of business each day; or the number of calls made to the West Midlands ambulance service each hour. In each case, the result is simply a set of numbers with the appropriate time period labels. In this section, we shall assume that the period between successive observations is always the same; where this is not the case, the causal modelling approach may be used instead (see later in the chapter).

Time series analysis assumes that the future numbers will resemble the past numbers in a predictable manner. The past numbers are a series of past data values for a single variable measured at different times, for example the sales of a particular product for each of the past 12 quarters, or the £–US$ exchange rate every day for the last month. The number of past values available and the period between observations will depend on the particular variable of interest. Note that the forecast is based solely on the numbers; the model takes no account of what the numbers mean or how they were obtained. The meaning of the numbers must be one of the prime concerns of the manager using the system; as in many other computing contexts, 'garbage in, garbage out' is a phrase worth taking to heart.

The simplest forecast is that the next value will be the same as the last one. In many examples, this is not a bad place to start. Some years back, a study of various methods of forecasting the closing value of the Dow Jones average for the New York stock exchange found that the most accurate forecast was indeed that tomorrow's closing value would be the same as today's. However, forecasting techniques since then have improved, and more recent studies have found that this technique no longer gives the best results in terms of forecasting the Dow Jones.[2]

To go beyond this simple forecasting technique, there are two different families of approach to forecasting from time series data; one is based on forecasting by identifying patterns in the past data, the other on forecasting directly from the data values.

The philosophy of the pattern-based approach is that the way in which the future resembles the past can be thought of as a series of increasingly complex steps:

1 The future will be the same as the past.
2 The rate of change in the future will be the same as the rate of change in the past.
3 The changes in the rate of change in the future will be the same as the changes in the rate of change in the past.

(This can be continued indefinitely.) The aim is to identify a pattern that is sufficiently complex to produce acceptable forecasts, but no more complex than necessary.

The approach based directly on the data values concentrates more on working with the past values as they are than on identifying an underlying pattern in them. The idea here is that the forecast is updated in the light of new data as it becomes available; typically, this will be not only the latest value, but also how accurate (or inaccurate) the last forecast was.

How much data are needed?

There can be no hard-and-fast answers here. Too few observations, and too much of an apparent difference between values may simply be due to chance fluctuations; this is a similar concept to that of sampling error, as discussed in Chapter 14. Too many observations, and not only will the analysis take longer, but there is a danger that the older observations will have been rendered out of date by changing circumstances. It also depends on the frequency with which observations are made; daily or hourly observations do not go 'out of date' as rapidly as yearly ones. As a general rule of thumb, it is pointless trying to forecast the values of a variable unless at least four observations are available, and beyond 500 observations the increasing difficulty of understanding the analysis tends to outweigh any benefits that might result from improved precision. The final decision on this can only be a matter for the manager's judgement, however, in the light of the data available and the purpose for which the forecast is being made.

Forecasting by identifying patterns in the past data

Let us begin with a simple example. Suppose that a manager in an insurance company has collected data on the number of applications for new policies made in each of the past ten weeks, and wishes to forecast the *number of applications* for the coming week. If the manager believes that the market is static at present, then it seems reasonable to take each of the ten observations into account, rather than simply forecasting that the next value will be the same as the last one, as mentioned above. Thus the manager enters MEAN(B2..B11) in cell B12 in Fig 15.1, and uses the calculated value, 108, as their forecast for the coming week. (This pattern is so simple that we will see it again in the section on forecasting directly from the data values.)

Now suppose that the manager looks again at these figures, and wonders if they are really right to think that the market is static. After all, the last two weeks saw the lowest numbers of applications, and the last four weeks are all below the mean figure. This can be seen more clearly from the graph in Fig 15.2. Note that for once the zero has been suppressed, in order to show the variation more clearly.

Fig 15.1 Simple forecasting using the mean

	A	B
1	Week	Number of applications
2	1	117
3	2	104
4	3	110
5	4	115
6	5	110
7	6	110
8	7	104
9	8	105
10	9	102
11	10	102
12	Mean	108

Fig 15.2 Graph of the data in Fig 15.1

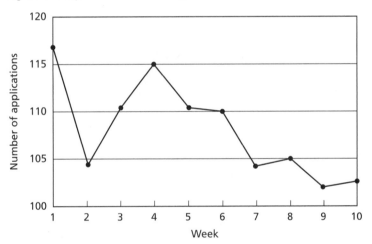

It does appear that there may be a pattern: a trend for the number of applications per week to decrease. The simplest model of such a trend is a straight line, which can then be *extrapolated* (projected) into the future. (It is clear from Fig 15.2 that the existing points do not all lie exactly on a straight line; it is virtually certain that with any real data there will be a spread about any line drawn.) The next step is therefore for the manager to find the straight line which fits the data best. Statisticians have given a lot of thought to what 'fits best' means in these circumstances. The usual choice is the line that minimises the sum of the squares of the distances between the actual data points and the fitted line, the distance being measured in the y-axis direction, as shown in Fig 15.3. This is a compromise between two objectives: being intuitively justifiable and being straightforward to calculate. We shall discuss this further later.[3] Fitting a line in this manner is known as least squares regression.

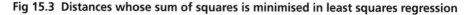

Fig 15.3 Distances whose sum of squares is minimised in least squares regression

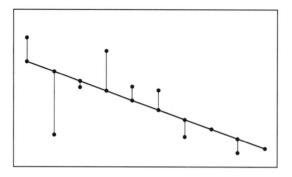

Fig 15.4 Graph of Fig 15.1 data including trend line

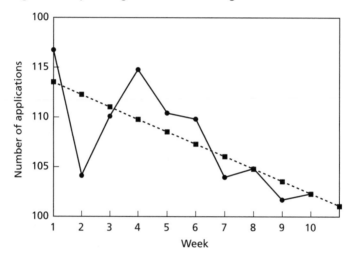

The trend line fitted by regression is shown in Fig 15.4. We can see that it does indeed have a downward slope! From the graph, we can also see that the manager's forecast for next week would now be 101 applications rather than the previous forecast of 108 based on the mean. Somewhat surprisingly, although it helps most people to think about regression in terms of fitting a line, with spreadsheet packages it is often easier to calculate the forecast than to draw the line itself. Most spreadsheets have a built-in function called REGRESSION, TREND or even FORECAST to calculate the forecast (some also have menu commands), but with current spreadsheet facilities for creating pictures, drawing any line requires that there is a series of data values in the spreadsheet to be turned into a picture. This means that at least one extra column of data has to be added to the spreadsheet, containing the calculated y values for the fitted line (again produced with the REGRESSION or FORECAST function) that go with the past x values. We had to modify our spreadsheet as shown in Fig 15.5; we chose to include the x values again in column C as well as the calculated y values in column D, for clarity. Otherwise we would have had to put

Fig 15.5 Modified spreadsheet to draw regression line

	A	B	C	D
1	Week	Actual number of applications	Week	Calculated number of applications
2	1	117	1	114
3	2	104	2	112
4	3	110	3	111
5	4	115	4	110
6	5	110	5	109
7	6	110	6	107
8	7	104	7	106
9	8	105	8	105
10	9	102	9	103
11	10	102	10	102
12	Forecast		11	101
13	(Week 11)	101		

the value of 11 in cell A12, which we felt would be confusing. Some spreadsheet packages do have menu options for including trend lines in pictures. If these are used, it is vital to be aware of the assumptions that the package is making in fitting the line, such as whether it assumes that the x values represent equal intervals, or works on the basis of the actual x values in the cells.

Linear or non-linear?

As in Chapter 12, a crucial aspect in the manager's forecasting model is whether to use a linear model or not; see Chapter 5 for a discussion of the term linear. The linear model (fitting a straight line) assumes that the rate of change in the future will be the same as the rate of change in the past, the second category of pattern in our earlier list; this implies that the rate of change has been constant. Non-linear models assume that the rate of change has itself varied in the past, taking us into our third category of pattern: the changes in the rate of change in the future will be the same as the changes in the rate of change in the past.

Whether the built-in function for fitting straight lines is called REGRESSION or FORECAST, it is still rather a misnomer. Regression can be used to fit curves of all kinds, not just straight lines, as we shall see in an example shortly, and forecasts can be produced by many other means than straight-line regression, as we shall spend the rest of this chapter discussing. Don't be confused by the names!

Non-linear models

Non-linear models aim to find the best-fitting *curve* of a particular type, instead of a straight line. A type of curve which is commonly chosen is the exponential or growth curve, so called because the rate of increase of the values is itself increasing – and at an increasing rate, too! This leads to what is often called *explosive* growth in everyday language, as for example in the 'population explosion'. Microsoft Excel has a built-in function called GROWTH, which makes a forecast based on using least squares regression to fit such a curve. Least squares regression can in fact be used to fit a line of any predefined shape, with the same definition of best fit as was used in the linear case, that is the line (now a curve) that minimises the sum of the squares of the distances between the actual data points and the fitted line (curve), the distance being measured in the y-axis direction.

◆ **Key concept**

*A type of curve which is commonly chosen to model an increasing trend is the exponential or growth curve, so called because the rate of increase of the values is itself increasing – and at an increasing rate, too! This leads to what is often called **explosive** growth in everyday language, as for example in the 'population explosion'.*

Let us consider an example to illustrate the difference between fitting a straight line and fitting a growth curve. A brand manager is interested in forecasting the sales for one product over the next three weeks. This is a relatively new product, so only 12 weeks of past sales data are available, as shown in Fig 15.6.

The manager uses the built-in REGRESSION and GROWTH functions (some packages offer these as menu commands as well/instead) to fit a linear model and an exponential growth curve model to the data. The resulting numbers are shown in table format in Fig 15.7 and pictured in Fig 15.8. Column B of Fig 15.7 contains the actual past data in cells B2 to B13, with cells B14 to B16 containing the forecast sales values for the next three periods from the linear model. Cells C2 to C13 repeat the past data series from cells B2 to B13 for ease of drawing the picture in Fig 15.8; cells C14 to C16 show the forecast sales values for the next three periods using the exponential growth curve model. Cells D2 to D13 show what the values of the past sales would have been if they had followed the straight-line model fitted to the data. These *predictions* (not forecasts, because they are based on data from *after* the relevant time

Fig 15.6 Twelve weeks of past sales data

	A	B
1	Week number	Sales
2	1	1100
3	2	1217
4	3	1301
5	4	1388
6	5	1497
7	6	1613
8	7	1789
9	8	1889
10	9	2001
11	10	2118
12	11	2259
13	12	2525

Fig 15.7 Linear and exponential predictions and forecasts of future sales (table form)

	A	B	C	D	E
	Week number	Sales	Sales	Straight line	Growth curve
1	Week number	Sales	Sales	Straight line	Growth curve
2	1	1100	1100	1048	1122
3	2	1217	1217	1171	1206
4	3	1301	1301	1294	1297
5	4	1388	1388	1417	1395
6	5	1497	1497	1540	1499
7	6	1613	1613	1663	1612
8	7	1789	1789	1786	1734
9	8	1889	1889	1909	1864
10	9	2001	2001	2032	2004
11	10	2118	2118	2155	2155
12	11	2259	2259	2278	2317
13	12	2525	2525	2401	2492
14	13	2525	2679	2525	2679
15	14	2648	2881	2648	2881
16	15	2771	3097	2771	3097

Forecast (linear)

Forecast (growth curve)

Fig 15.8 Linear and exponential predictions and forecasts of future sales

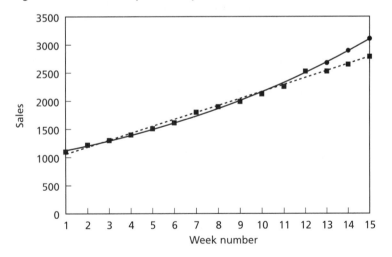

period as well as before) may be compared with the actual values in column B to judge how well the linear model fits the data. This will be considered in more detail in the next section. Similarly, cells E2 to E13 contain the predictions from the growth curve model. The values in cells B14 to C16 were again Copied into cells D14 to E16 for ease of drawing the picture.

As may be seen, by week 15, the two forecasts differ by more than 10 per cent; 3097 units from the exponential growth curve model, as against 2771 units from the straight-line model. Which of these is 'correct'? The manager could only be sure after the event! To an extent, the type of pattern to be fitted is a matter of personal preference, bearing in mind some of the criteria for the validity of a spreadsheet discussed in Chapter 8. Indeed, nothing that the manager can do can actually tell them anything about how well any model fits the (unknown) future data. However, what the manager can and should do is to examine the fit of the forecasting model to the past data, as we consider in the next section.

Measuring the fit of a forecasting model

How do you measure the fit of a forecasting model? This is a little like the old riddle about which is more accurate, a clock that has stopped, or one that loses a minute a day. The answer is supposedly the one that has stopped, as it shows exactly the right time twice a day, while the other one only shows exactly the right time about once every two years! Most people will feel vaguely unhappy about this result (that's why it's a riddle). The point of this analogy is that measuring the fit of a quantitative forecast by whether it is exactly right or not as a yes–no result is not very helpful. We have already discussed two dimensions of exactness in Chapter 6: precision and bias. To judge how well a forecasting model, or indeed any forecast, fits the past observations, it therefore makes sense to consider both precision and bias. We shall now discuss how to measure each of them in turn for a forecasting model.

Measuring the precision of a forecasting model

Whatever the data values in the time series, it is always possible to use least squares regression to find the straight line that fits the data best, by the method used in the first two examples. However, the line that fits the data 'best' may still not be a very good fit; it depends on the data! Consider the data in Table 15.1, for example, relating to maximum daily temperatures during a spell of rather inconsistent weather.

Table 15.1 Data on maximum daily temperatures

Day number	Temperature (°C)	Day number	Temperature (°C)
1	21	15	30
2	21	16	22
3	22	17	19
4	20	18	20
5	16	19	17
6	27	20	24
7	21	21	22
8	26	22	25
9	25	23	25
10	28	24	31
11	21	25	30
12	17	26	26
13	18	27	25
14	19	28	22

Figure 15.9 shows a graph of these data values, together with the 'best fit' linear model. We have again suppressed the zero for comparison with the graph in Fig 15.4. We trust you will agree that 'by eye' the fit of the best straight line to the temperature data in Fig 15.9 appears considerably worse than the fit of the best straight line to the new policy applications data in Fig 15.4. However, as this depends on the scales used in the graphs, it can be very misleading. Let us now see how we can actually *measure* the precision of the fit of these forecasting models.

Fig 15.9 Linear model fitted to daily temperature data

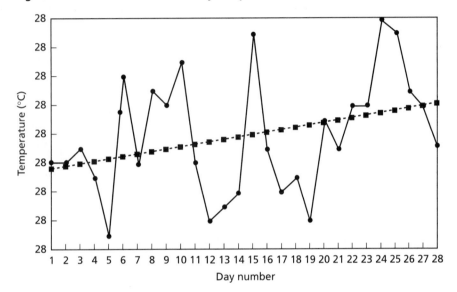

Fig 15.10 Precision of straight line forecasting model – sum of differences

	A	B	C	D
1	Week number	Sales	Straight line	Actual– predicted
2	1	1100	1048	52
3	2	1217	1171	46
4	3	1301	1294	7
5	4	1388	1417	−29
6	5	1497	1540	−43
7	6	1613	1663	−50
8	7	1789	1786	3
9	8	1889	1909	−20
10	9	2001	2032	−31
11	10	2118	2155	−37
12	11	2259	2278	−19
13	12	2525	2401	124
14	Sum of differences			0

Here we will use the concept of the *prediction* or *predicted value* that we introduced in the previous subsection. A prediction or predicted value is a value given by the fitted model for a particular past period; it is not a forecast, because it makes use of data that come after that period as well as before it. The only way to judge the fit of a forecasting model at the time it is built is by looking at these predictions. Fig 15.10 shows the actual and predicted values for weeks 1–12 from the example in Fig 15.7 (sales), using the straight-line model. It might appear that the obvious thing to do to measure precision would be to add up the values of *actual – predicted* for each week. If we do this, Fig 15.10 shows (in cell D14) that the + and – forecasting errors cancel each other out, to give a result of zero. Is this because this model fits very well? Unfortunately, no; if we perform the same calculation for the temperature example of Table 15.1 and Fig 15.9, we would also find that the *actual – predicted* values sum to zero. (We leave this as an exercise for the reader.) Whenever the trend line is fitted by linear regression, the sum of these errors in prediction will always be zero. It is therefore impossible to tell how good the fit of the forecasting model is using this measure.

There are two ways to overcome this problem of the positive and negative errors cancelling each other out. One is to ignore the sign of the error by working with absolute values, the other is to square all the errors; both therefore produce only positive results. We now consider each in turn.

Absolute values When working with absolute values, forecasters typically use the mean absolute deviation (MAD) to measure the precision of the fit. (Make your own jokes about mad forecasters here.) This is the sum of the absolute values of *actual – predicted* for each observation, divided by the number of observations. Most spreadsheets have a built-in function called AVEDEV, but unfortunately what it calculates is not the mean absolute deviation. In order to calculate the MAD, an

Fig 15.11 Precision of straight line forecasting model – mean absolute deviation

	A	B	C	D	E
1	Week number	Sales	Straight line	Actual – predicted	Absolute value
2	1	1100	1048	52	52
3	2	1217	1171	46	46
4	3	1301	1294	7	7
5	4	1388	1417	−29	29
6	5	1497	1540	−43	43
7	6	1613	1663	−50	50
8	7	1789	1786	3	3
9	8	1889	1909	−20	20
10	9	2001	2032	−31	31
11	10	2118	2155	−37	37
12	11	2259	2278	−19	19
13	12	2525	2401	124	124
14	MAD			39	

extra column needs to be added to the spreadsheet, using the ABS function to give the absolute values of *actual – predicted*. The MEAN function can then be used to find the MAD. Figure 15.11 shows this calculation for the sales example. The formula in cell E2 is ABS(D2) and so on; the formula in D14 is MEAN(E2..E13). The MAD for this forecast is 39.

One problem with using the MAD value to measure the precision of a forecasting model is that it varies according to how big the numbers are. It is natural to expect that the errors associated with forecasting large quantities will be greater than when forecasting small quantities. We trust you would agree that a forecasting model for yearly sales of blank video cassettes, which run into millions of units, that had a MAD of, say, 37.5, would be remarkably good, whereas a MAD of 37.5 on sales of a type of aircraft which average 60 a year would not be very impressive.

Sometimes it helps, therefore, to standardise the measurement. A common way to standardise is to use the MAPE (mean absolute percentage error). Again, there is not usually a built-in function for this, so it is necessary to insert a column in which the percentage error is calculated. Figure 15.12 shows these calculations. Cell D2 is defined as ABS((B1–C1)/B1) and displayed as a percentage; remember to divide by the actual value, not the prediction. The MAPE, in cell D14, is MEAN(D2..D13), again as a percentage. The MAPE value of 2.3 per cent generally indicates a good forecasting model.

Squared values   Working with squared values makes it easier to establish the mathematical properties of forecasting models, as we shall see shortly, but compared with the use of MAD or MAPE gives more weight to large errors. Thus an observation that is out of line with the others has more influence on the fitted model when

Fig 15.12 Precision of straight line forecasting model – mean absolute percentage error

	A	B	C	D
1	Week number	Sales	Straight line	Absolute percentage error
2	1	1100	1048	4.7%
3	2	1217	1171	3.8%
4	3	1301	1294	0.5%
5	4	1388	1417	2.1%
6	5	1497	1540	2.9%
7	6	1613	1663	3.1%
8	7	1789	1786	0.2%
9	8	1889	1909	1.1%
10	9	2001	2032	1.6%
11	10	2118	2155	1.8%
12	11	2259	2278	0.9%
13	12	2525	2401	4.9%
14	MAPE			2.3%

Fig 15.13 Precision of forecasting model – sum of squared errors

	A	B	C	D	E	F
1	Week number	Sales	Straight line	Growth curve	Sum of squares (straight line)	Sum of squares (growth curve)
2	1	1100	1048	1122	2700	475
3	2	1217	1171	1206	2109	117
4	3	1301	1294	1297	47	16
5	4	1388	1417	1395	850	43
6	5	1497	1540	1499	1866	6
7	6	1613	1663	1612	2523	0
8	7	1789	1786	1734	7	3067
9	8	1889	1909	1864	412	622
10	9	2001	2032	2004	983	11
11	10	2118	2155	2155	1398	1379
12	11	2259	2278	2317	377	3399
13	12	2525	2401	2492	15262	1112
14	Sum of squared errors		28534	10246		

squared error values are used than when absolute values are used. Figure 15.13 shows these calculations for both of the forecasting models in Fig 15.7. The squared errors for the straight-line and growth curve models are in columns E and F respectively, calculated as the squares of the differences between the respective cells in columns B and C, and columns B and D respectively. The sums are shown in cells C14 and D14. The growth curve model appears to be the more accurate fit to the data, with the sum of squared errors being only 10 246 as opposed to 28 534.

Again, the issue of standardising this measure arises. Not only is this easily done, but it opens up a whole line of thinking about the fit of models that is used in many areas of statistics. We have in fact already seen an example of this type of measure of precision in use, because least squares regression is based on minimising the sum of the squares of the differences between the actual and fitted (predicted) values. Let us look at this in more detail.

As we saw in Chapter 14, the spread of a set of data can be measured by its variance, which depends on the sum of squares of the differences between the values and their mean. If the set of data forms a time series, and we model the trend of the time series (in this case by fitting a straight line), then the spread of the set of data can be conceptualised as the sum of the spread resulting from the trend, and the spread resulting from all other causes. The more of the spread that is accounted for by the fitted model (line in this case), the more precise the fit of the model to the data; a model that went through all the data points would account for all the spread.

Using the variance as the measure of spread (remember, we said in Chapter 14 that mathematicians like the variance because the variance of the sum equals the sum of the variances), then we can verbalise this relationship as:

total variance = variance explained by trend model + unexplained variance

This is shown graphically in Fig 15.14. As the best possible trend model would explain all the variance, and the worst possible model would explain none of it, a standardised measure of precision of fit on a scale running from 0 to 1 can then be obtained by dividing the value of *variance explained by trend model* by the value of *total variance*. As by definition we always have the same number of observations in these two variance calculations, this proportion can be expressed even more straightforwardly as the sum of the squared differences accounted for by the trend model (line) divided by the total sum of the squared differences about the mean, as shown in Fig 15.14. This proportion is known as the *coefficient of determination*, or quite often as just r^2 (upper or lower case *r*). A value of 1 would indicate a perfect fit – the trend line goes through all the

Fig 15.14 Differences between observations and mean, and observations and trend line

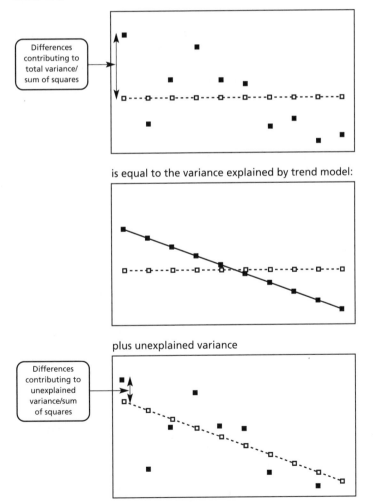

Differences contributing to total variance/ sum of squares

is equal to the variance explained by trend model:

plus unexplained variance

Differences contributing to unexplained variance/sum of squares

points, thus accounting for all the variation in the data. Alternatively, a value of 0 would indicate no fit at all – the points appear to be randomly scattered about the line, which therefore means that the forecasting model tells us nothing about the data.

Why is the coefficient of determination called r^2 rather than just r? There are two reasons. First, it emphasises that we are using squared differences in measuring precision. Second, r^2 as explained here is actually the square of r, the correlation coefficient discussed in Chapter 14.[4] The question 'How good is a particular value of r^2?' arises. There is no hard-and-fast answer, but one rule of thumb often used is that a well-fitting line/model explains at least half of the spread in the variable of interest. Thus a value of r^2 greater than or equal to 0.5 corresponds to a well-fitting model.

The r^2 value is probably the most commonly used measure of precision, since it is used not just by forecasters but in many areas of statistics, and so most spreadsheet packages have a built-in RSQUARED function. The values of r^2 are shown in Fig 15.15 as 0.987 for the straight-line model and 0.995 for the growth curve; both are very good fits indeed, but the fit of the growth curve is marginally better.

By contrast, if we look at the temperature data from Table 15.1 and Fig 15.9, shown in Fig 15.16, we see that the value of r^2 is 0.110; the fit of the straight-line model is very poor. Do not be misled by the fact that the sum of squares in this case (403.5) is much smaller; this is simply because the temperature values are smaller numbers than the sales values. That is the advantage of using a standardised measure such as r^2.

Fig 15.15 Precision of good forecasting model – sum of squared errors and Rsquared

	A	B	C	D	E	F
1	Week number	Sales	Straight line	Growth curve	Sum of squares (straight line)	Sum of squares (growth curve)
2	1	1100	1048	1122	2700	475
3	2	1217	1171	1206	2109	117
4	3	1301	1294	1297	47	16
5	4	1388	1417	1395	850	43
6	5	1497	1540	1499	1866	6
7	6	1613	1663	1612	2523	0
8	7	1789	1786	1734	7	3067
9	8	1889	1909	1864	412	622
10	9	2001	2032	2004	983	11
11	10	2118	2155	2155	1398	1379
12	11	2259	2278	2317	377	3399
13	12	2525	2401	2492	15262	1112
14	Sum of squared errors		28534	10246		
15		Rsquared	0.987	0.995		

Fig 15.16 Precision of poor forecasting model – sum of squared errors and Rsquared

	A	B	C	D
1	Day number	Temperature (°C)	Straight line model	Sum of squares
2	1	21	20.6	0.1
3	2	21	20.8	0.0
4	3	22	21.0	1.1
5	4	20	21.1	1.3
6	5	16	21.3	28.0
7	6	27	21.5	30.8
8	7	21	21.6	0.4
9	8	26	21.8	17.8
10	9	25	21.9	9.3
11	10	28	22.1	34.7
12	11	21	22.3	1.6
13	12	17	22.4	29.6
14	13	18	22.6	21.2
15	14	19	22.8	14.2
16	15	30	22.9	49.8
17	16	22	23.1	1.2
18	17	19	23.3	18.2
19	18	20	23.4	11.8
20	19	17	23.6	43.6
21	20	24	23.8	0.1
22	21	22	23.9	3.7
23	22	25	24.1	0.8
24	23	25	24.3	0.5
25	24	31	24.4	43.2
26	25	30	24.6	29.2
27	26	26	24.8	1.5
28	27	25	24.9	0.0
29	28	22	25.1	9.5
30		Sum of squared errors		403.5
31			Rsquared	0.110

Having looked at the most commonly used measures of the precision of a forecasting model, we now turn our attention to measuring bias.

Measuring the bias of a forecasting model

The bias of a forecasting model is examined on the basis of a similar relationship to that introduced in the previous section. There it was expressed as:

total variance = variance explained by trend model + unexplained variance

because we were working with squared values to avoid the possibility of positive and negative differences cancelling each other out. In considering bias, the sign is crucially important (see Chapter 6). The corresponding 'unexplained' terms – the differences between the actual and predicted values – are often known as the *residuals*, especially in regression. We have already been using these in calculating precision measures. The difference from the previous section is that here the *sign* of the error or residual is important.

Usually the bias of a forecasting model can be investigated qualitatively, by looking at a graph of the actual and forecast values. Figures 15.17 and 15.18 show the same information as Fig 15.8, but on a larger scale, and suppressing the zero for clarity. Figure 15.17 shows the straight-line model. The first three actual values and the last one are all above the fitted trend line (positive residuals); all the others in between are below it (negative residuals), except for the

Fig 15.17 Straight-line forecast (larger scale)

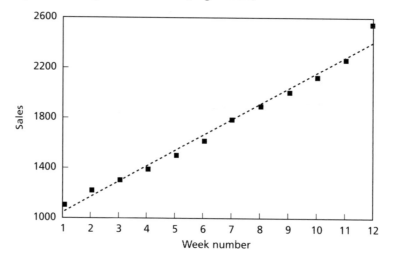

Fig 15.18 Growth curve forecast (large scale)

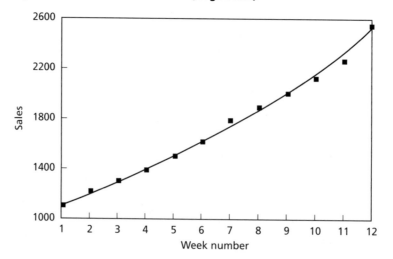

week 7 value which is just above. This 'over–under–over' pattern suggests that a curve increasing at a faster rate than the straight line may give a better fit to the data; one such curve is the exponential (growth curve) shown in Fig 15.18.

Other possible patterns include:

- 'under–over–under', as sketched in Fig 15.19 – this would suggest trying a curve that increases less fast than a straight line
- 'over–under' or 'under–over', as sketched in Fig 15.20 – this might suggest a curve with a point of inflection (mathematical language for an S-bend).[5]

Finally, looking again at Fig 15.18, it is evident that little bias is present in the residuals. The one pattern that does remain is a slight *cycle*; a rise and fall of the actuals relative to the forecast, with peaks in periods 2, 7 and perhaps 12 (the week 13 residual is, of course, unknown as yet). We shall deal with such repeating patterns later in the chapter.

Fig 15.19 Residuals indicating possible logarithmic relationship

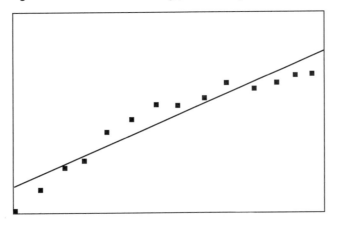

Fig 15.20 Residuals indicating possible S-shaped relationship

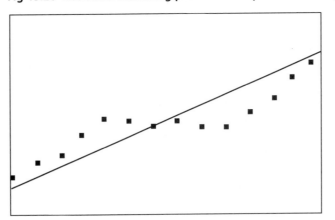

Forecasting directly from the data values

Although there is no effective limit to the number of different kinds of relationship that can be fitted to time series data, all relationship-based methods of forecasting have one feature in common: every observation carries equal weight. This means that the oldest observation has as much influence on the forecast as the most recent one.

In changing circumstances, managers may well wish to use a forecasting method that is capable of giving more weight to more recent observations. These are the methods we shall consider under the heading of 'forecasting directly from the data values'.

We begin from the same point as with forecasting by identifying patterns: the simple method of forecasting that the next value will be the same as the last one. This cannot be faulted in terms of giving weight to the most recent observation, but the downside is that it completely ignores all other previous observations. We shall discuss the two most commonly used methods of forecasting directly from the data values. These are:

- moving average methods
- exponential smoothing.

Moving average methods

Moving average methods differ from the 'identifying a pattern' approach of taking the mean of all available observations (as was done in Fig 15.1) in that only the most recent observations are used. The forecast is the mean of the last n observations. Each of these n still carries equal weight in the forecast as with the pattern-based methods, but after n periods an observation ceases to have any influence on the forecast at all. If the observations are listed down a column of a spreadsheet, with the oldest at the top, we can visualise this as a highlight or a bracket moving down the spreadsheet, showing the observations that are being taken into account in the forecast; hence the term *moving* average.

The choice of the value of n is up to the manager making the forecast: too large, and the forecast is slow to respond to changes; too small, and the forecast will be overinfluenced by chance variations. The only concrete advice that can be given is that if there is a repeating pattern in the data, such as the seasonal pattern of ice-cream sales, then the value of n must be equal to the number of periods between repeats, or an exact multiple of it. Values typically used otherwise are 3, 4, 5 and 6.

Returning to the Fig 15.1 data, forecasts based on a three-point moving average (i.e. using the three most recent past data values) are shown in column C of Fig 15.21. Calculating moving averages could hardly be easier than in a spreadsheet. Simply arrange the past observations in a column or row, enter the built-in MEAN, AVG or AVERAGE function in the cell beside/below the first for which there is enough data available, and use the Copy command to fill in the rest of the forecasts. In Fig 15.21, cell C5 contains the formula MEAN(B2..B4) and the rest of the cells below it in column C are Copied from it.

Fig 15.21 Forecasting model using 3-point moving average

	A	B	C
1	Week	Number of applications	3-point moving average forecasting model
2	1	117	
3	2	104	
4	3	110	
5	4	115	110
6	5	110	110
7	6	110	112
8	7	104	112
9	8	105	108
10	9	102	106
11	10	102	103
12	(11)		103

Precision and bias can be examined for forecasting models based on moving averages in the same way as for pattern-based methods, for example to help the manager choose which value of n to use, although this is perhaps not as commonly done in practice, as moving averages have often been seen as a 'quick and dirty' approach to forecasting. Typically they might have been used where a large number of forecasts needed to be made quite quickly, for example in a stock-control system where next week's demand for every item needs to be forecast.

Exponential smoothing

Moving averages are seen as having two disadvantages:

1 At least n past observations have to be stored for each variable whose value is to be forecast.
2 All the observations that count have equal weight, which drops to no weight at all when they reach an 'age' of n periods. This can lead to sudden fluctuations in the forecast when a particularly large or small past observation 'drops off the end' of the range used for the moving average, as seen with the UK Retail Prices Index when major 'step' changes leave the system.

Exponential smoothing avoids both of these disadvantages. First, it gives weight to *all* past observations, in such a way that the most recent observation has the most influence on the forecast, and an older observation always has less influence than a more recent one. Second, it is only necessary to store two values (the last actual observation and the last forecast – plus the value of the smoothing constant, of course) in order to make the next period's forecast.

Exponential smoothing works on the principle that the forecast is updated in the light of the latest data. Specifically, the forecast is adjusted by a proportion of the difference between the actual value and the forecast. The value of the proportion is called the *smoothing constant*. The verbalisation of the relationship is:

*next period's forecast = last period's forecast +{{smoothing constant} ×
{last period's actual – last period's forecast}}*

As with moving averages, exponential smoothing is extremely easy to do
in spreadsheets.[6] It can be carried out in as small a space as that shown in
Fig 15.22. The formula in cell C3 is C2+C4*(B2–C2). Once the value of *next
period's forecast* has been calculated, it can be Copied from cell C3 into cell C2
using the 'Values' (Microsoft Excel) or 'Formulas as values' (Lotus 1-2-3)
option from the Paste Special command, to be ready for when next period's
actual value is available and inserted in cell B2.

Fig 15.22 Exponential smoothing in a spreadsheet

	A	B	C
1		Actual	Forecast
2	Last period's	107.0	104.0
3	Next period's		104.6
4	Smoothing constant		0.2

The choice of the value of the smoothing constant is another instance where
modelling becomes an art rather than a science. The larger the value, the more
weight is given to the most recent data, and the less smoothing of fluctuations
takes place. The maximum possible value is 1.0, in which case the model is
once again that next period's value will be the same as the last period's.
Correspondingly, the minimum possible value of 0.0 would mean that the forecast never changed. Normally the value of the smoothing constant is chosen to
lie in the range 0.1 to 0.3.

The precision and bias of forecasts produced using exponential smoothing
methods may again be investigated in the same way as for the pattern-based methods, for example to help the manager choose the value of the smoothing constant.

**Stationary and
non-stationary
series**

One feature common to both moving average and exponential smoothing methods is that they work best with a *stationary* series of values; one in which there
is no upward or downward trend. Where such a trend is present, the forecast
will always tend to *lag* behind it, being too low if the trend is an increasing one
and too high if the trend is decreasing. This is a type of bias, and the forecast
needs to be corrected to compensate for it.

This correction is done by first working out the 'age' of the forecast. It is the
reliance on past data that causes the lag effect; even the most recent value has
an 'age' of one period when it is used in producing a forecast. With a three-
point moving average used as a forecast for the next period's value, the three
observations are one, two and three periods old respectively, giving a mean age
of two periods. The values in column C of Fig 15.23 show properly centred
three-point moving average values for the Fig 15.1 data; note how they are two
periods removed from the values shown in column D when this unadjusted
moving average is used as a forecasting model, as it was in Fig 15.21. The
moving average forecasting model has a bias of two periods' worth of trend,
and needs to be adjusted to correct it.

Fig 15.23 Forecasting using three-point moving average, adjusted to remove bias of lag effort

	A	B	C	D	E
1	Week	Number of applications	Centred moving average	Unadjusted three-point moving average forecasting model	Adjusted three-point moving average forecasting model
2	1	117			
3	2	104	110		
4	3	110	110		
5	4	115	112	110	108
6	5	110	112	110	107
7	6	110	108	112	109
8	7	104	106	112	109
9	8	105	103	108	106
10	9	102	103	106	104
11	10	102		103	101
12	(11)			103	100

The trend in the Fig 15.1 data is that the number of applications is decreasing by about 1.3 per period (per week in this case). We actually worked this out in the previous section, but it could easily have been estimated by eye if speed is more important than precision. The forecasts in Fig 15.21 therefore need to be reduced by twice this amount (approximately 2.6) to remove the bias caused by the lag effect. The adjusted forecasts are shown in column E of Fig 15.23.

In general, an n-point moving average forecast needs to be adjusted by $(n+1)/2$ periods' worth of trend, and an exponential smoothing forecast by a number of periods' worth of trend equal to 1/(*smoothing constant*); for example, if the smoothing constant is 0.2, this will be five periods' worth.

Dealing with repeating patterns

In some cases, the manager has good reason to expect that there should be some repeating pattern in the time series, in addition to any other trends that may be present. For example, sales in the UK of ice cream, lager and toys are all highly seasonal. The first two reach a peak in the summer, the latter in the winter (November and December). Similarly, the number of passengers travelling on a particular bus or train route varies according to the day of the week. Any forecast of a time series with such a repeating pattern is likely to be much better if it takes the pattern into account than if it does not.

The values in the time series may be thought of as being made up of four components:

- trend
- seasonal component
- cyclical component(s)
- random variation.

A seasonal component is one that varies with the four seasons of the year; a cyclical component is any other repeating pattern. There may be more than one cyclical component present in the time series data; the larger the number, the more difficult it is to identify them – further discussion of this is beyond our scope here. In practice, there is no difference between a seasonal component and any other cyclical component as far as the structure of a forecasting model is concerned. A seasonal component is simply a cyclical component that repeats once a year. It is simply that, as by far the most common repeating pattern, it was given a special name of its own by professional forecasters. For simplicity, we shall therefore consider an example where a trend and a seasonal component are both present, but no other cyclical component; a random variation – meaning variation not explained by the trend, the seasonal component or any cyclical component – is also almost certain to be present in any data series.

Suppose that a civil servant in the Ruritanian Ministry of Tourism wishes to forecast the number of passengers using Ruritania's main international airport for the third and fourth quarters of 1997, in order to plan the number of people needed to staff the airport. As with most countries, there is a strongly seasonal pattern to the number of tourists visiting Ruritania.[7] The data are shown in Fig 15.24 in the form of a table, and also as a line graph in Fig 15.25. Whenever doing any forecasting, it is always a good idea to display a picture of the data, in order to get a 'feel' for the pattern of the time series.

♦ **Key concept**

Whenever doing any forecasting, it is always a good idea to display a picture of the data, in order to get a 'feel' for its pattern, before deciding on the type of forecasting model to build.

In Fig 15.25, both a seasonal variation and an increasing trend are apparent. The forecasting method to be followed in such a case is known as *decomposition*. The seasonal component is represented by factors by which the trend is modified, in order to synthesise the forecasts; the same would apply to any cyclical component(s).

Decomposition proceeds, in layperson's terms, by breaking down (decomposing) the time series into its component parts (trend and seasonal component in this case), modelling the parts separately, and then putting the parts back together again to make the overall forecasting model. This decomposition may either be done using an *additive* model, in which the seasonal component is added to the trend, or a *multiplicative* model, in which the trend is multiplied by the seasonal component.

Thus for the additive model, the verbalisation is:

forecast of next period's value = forecast of next period's trend
+ forecast of next period's seasonal factor
+ forecast of next period's cyclical factor(s)

The multiplicative model is the same, with the plus signs replaced by multiplication signs.

Fig 15.24 Ruritanian tourist data (table)

	A	B	C
1	Passengers arriving at Ruritania's international airport		
2			
3	Year	Quarter	Number (thousands)
4	1992	3	3719
5	1992	4	1056
6	1993	1	789
7	1993	2	2481
8	1993	3	4090
9	1993	4	1101
10	1994	1	1013
11	1994	2	2320
12	1994	3	4386
13	1994	4	1337
14	1995	1	1095
15	1995	2	2658
16	1995	3	4850
17	1995	4	1367
18	1996	1	1146
19	1996	2	2638
20	1996	3	5380
21	1996	4	1593
22	1997	1	1532
23	1997	2	2999

Fig 15.25 Ruritanian tourist data (graph)

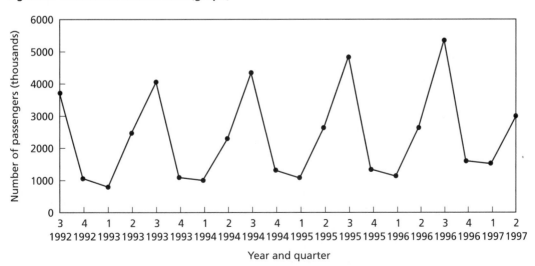

303

An additive model is based on the assumption that the seasonal component is remaining approximately constant over time. The multiplicative model assumes, by contrast, that if the trend is increasing, then the seasonal component also increases, and similarly for a decrease.

◆ *Key concept*

> The **decomposition** method of forecasting breaks down a time series into its component parts, forecasts the parts separately, and then puts the parts back together again to make the overall forecast. This may be done using either an **additive** model, in which the seasonal and cyclical components are added to the trend, or a **multiplicative** model, in which the trend is multiplied by the seasonal and cyclical components.

More formally, the process has five steps, as shown in Fig 15.26.

The first step is to remove the influence of seasonality on the data in the series. An obvious way to remove the influence of seasonality is to use a four-point moving average. As this includes one value for each of the four seasonal components, their influence will be cancelled out. There is, however, one snag. This is because of the issue of centring; as was mentioned above, a moving average always lags behind any trend that is present. Rather than simply replacing each observation by the average of the last four observations, therefore, it is necessary to use a moving average that is correctly centred on the period in question. Now comes the snag; the 'centre' of a four-period moving average is *between* the middle two observations, so that two values come before and two values after. The particular difficulty for a spreadsheet is that if the original data are arranged in a row or column, as good practice suggests, then in order to dis-

Fig 15.26 Steps in forecasting by decomposition method

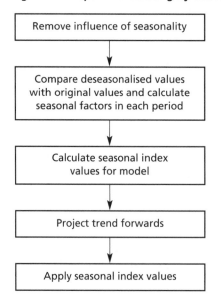

Remove influence of seasonality

↓

Compare deseasonalised values with original values and calculate seasonal factors in each period

↓

Calculate seasonal index values for model

↓

Project trend forwards

↓

Apply seasonal index values

Fig 15.27 Calculations for decomposition model

	A	B	C	D	E	F
1	Passengers arriving at Ruritania's international airport			Four-point moving average (thousands)	Deseasonalised trend values (thousands)	Seasonal factor
2						
3	Year	Quarter	Number (thousands)			
4	1992	3	3719			
5						
6	1992	4	1056			
7				2011		
8	1993	1	789		2058	0.383
9				2104		
10	1993	2	2481		2110	1.176
11				2115		
12	1993	3	4090		2143	1.908
13				2171		
14	1993	4	1101		2151	0.512
15				2131		
16	1994	1	1013		2168	0.467
17				2205		
18	1994	2	2320		2235	1.038
19				2264		
20	1994	3	4386		2274	1.929
21				2285		
22	1994	4	1337		2327	0.575
23				2369		
24	1995	1	1095		2427	0.451
25				2485		
26	1995	2	2658		2489	1.068
27				2493		
28	1995	3	4850		2499	1.941
29				2505		
30	1995	4	1367		2503	0.546
31				2500		
32	1996	1	1146		2567	0.447
33				2633		
34	1996	2	2638		2661	0.991
35				2689		
36	1996	3	5380		2738	1.965
37				2786		
38	1996	4	1593		2831	0.563
39				2876		
40	1997	1	1532			
41						
42	1997	2	2999			

play these moving averages sensibly, an extra row will have to be inserted between each pair of the existing rows – not an operation for which a simple command exists in any spreadsheet package that we know. (Doing this on paper would similarly require working on alternate lines to begin with.)

Figure 15.27 shows the bulk of the calculations. Column D contains the centred moving averages that are 'half a period off' from the original data. The formula in cell D7, for example, is MEAN(C4,C6,C8,C10) and so on. Column E (at last) contains the deseasonalised values corresponding to the original observations, each one being the average of the values above and below it in column D, so that the formula in cell E8, for example, is MEAN(D7,D9).

The second step is to compare the deseasonalised values with the original values. This is done in Column F of Fig 15.27. The manager has chosen a multiplicative model, because it appears from Fig 15.25 that the spread is increasing as time goes on. Thus their forecasting model is:

this period's value = {this period's trend × this period's seasonal index}
+ random variation

The calculated values of *this period's seasonal factor* are thus the best estimates of *this period's seasonal index*. The entries in column F, the estimated values of *this period's seasonal factor* are therefore the original values (*this period's value*) *divided* by the deseasonalised values (*this period's trend value*); the formula in F8 is C8/E8 and so on. (In an additive model, the calculations in columns D and E would be the same, but F8 would be C8–E8 and so on.) The value in F8 is 0.383, because the 1993 Q1 is much less than would be expected from the trend.

The next step is to calculate the seasonal index values to be used in the forecasting model; four of them, one for each season. The seasonal index for the first quarter (Q1) is the mean of all the first quarter values in column F; the formula is MEAN(F8,F16,F24,F32), and the resulting value 0.437, as shown in Fig 15.28. The other seasonal components are 1.068, 1.936 and 0.549. These show that the third quarter is the peak tourist season, as the manager should expect from the picture of the data.

Now the manager can actually make the forecast! First the trend is projected forward, by any of the methods already discussed. Let us assume that the manager has chosen to fit a straight line using least squares regression. This line

Fig 15.28 Seasonal components for decomposition model

		H	I
1		Seasonal index values	
2		Q1	0.437
3		Q2	1.068
4		Q3	1.936
5		Q4	0.549

Fig 15.29 Results of decomposition forecasting model

	A	B	C	D	E	F	G
1	Passengers arriving at Ruritania's international airport						
2							
3	Year	Quarter	Number (thousands)	Four-point moving average	Centred moving average	Seasonal index	Sequence number
36	1996	3	5380		2738	1.965	17
37				2786			
38	1996	4	1593		2831	0.563	18
39				2876			
40	1997	1	1532		2806		19
41							
42	1997	2	2999		2856		20
43							
44	1997	3	5625		2905		21
45							
46	1997	4	1622		2955		22

Forecasting including seasonal factor

Projection of trend

must be fitted to the deseasonalised values in column E rather than the original observations, since they are the best available estimates of the values of the trend. In order to do this, a sequence number for each observation will need to be added, because the regression model cannot cope with 'values' for an independent variable like 'Year 1992 Quarter 3'. The manager needs to project the trend forward as far as the latest period for which a forecast is needed, in this case the fourth quarter of 1997. Finally, the trend value is multiplied by the seasonal index corresponding to that quarter to give the forecast.

Figure 15.29 shows the lower part of the Fig 15.27 spreadsheet, with the results of the forecasting model included. Column G contains the sequence numbers. The trend projections are in cells E40 to E46, done using the REGRESSION function. The formula for E46, for example, is REGRESSION(G46,E8:E38,G8:G38). The final forecasts are in cells C44 and C46, formulae E44*I4 and E46*I5 respectively, the seasonal components being in cells I2 to I5, as shown in Fig 15.28 (this part of the spreadsheet has been omitted from Fig 15.29 so that it fits on the page!). The values the manager needs for the third and fourth quarters of 1997 are thus 5625 and 1622 (remember that the units here are thousands of passengers). Customs, passport control and other planning for the international airport can be carried out accordingly.

Forecasting from relationships between variables

The concept of a causal relationship between variables was mentioned in Chapter 7. It applies in situations where one variable is associated with another, or indeed several others. It is particularly useful to forecasters where one variable is what is called a *leading indicator* for another. This means that the value of the first (leading) variable is associated with the value of the second after a time lag of one or more periods. For example, in the UK, the variable *new housing starts* (the number of new private houses on which work has been started in a given period) is a leading indicator of the variable *white goods sales* (sales of domestic appliances such as refrigerators, cookers and washing machines), because people tend to buy new domestic appliances when they move into a new house. Data on the leading indicator can therefore be used to forecast the variable in which the manager is interested, as long as the values of the leading indicator are available early enough; this may either be through observation, or because the leading indicator is itself easier to forecast. This is fine in the case of new housing starts and white goods sales, since the time lag involved is several months, and greater than the planning horizon for white goods production. However, it is a problem, for example, in the case of the undoubted relationship that exists between UK beer sales and the leading indicator of maximum daily temperature: is good enough data on the temperature (in the form of an accurate weather forecast) going to be available early enough to brew the right quantities of beer?

Similar causal relationships exist even when there is no specific time series aspect involved. For example, consumption of water by a household depends principally on the number of people in the household, and to a lesser extent on whether the household has a washing machine, dishwasher and/or garden sprinkler. Such a relationship could be used, for example, in planning the provision of water supply and drainage facilities for a new housing development; it should be easier to forecast the values of *number of people in the household* than the other variables.

The most common technique used in causal modelling is least squares regression. Technically, this operates in exactly the same way as we have already discussed in time series analysis, when we were using time or even just 'observation number' as the independent variable.

Thus the application of the regression technique with a single independent variable looks just the same in the spreadsheet as it did earlier, in the insurance applications and sales examples. Figure 15.30 shows hypothetical figures for *new housing starts* and *white goods sales* in Ruritania since 1985. It is well known that the value of *new housing starts* is a good leading indicator of *white goods sales* in the Ruritanian economy, with a time lag of one year, so that *white goods sales* in, say, 1994 are strongly influenced by *new housing starts* in 1993. The verbalisation of this is:

white goods sales this period = {constant1 × new housing starts last period}
+ constant2

Fig 15.30 Forecasting a time series using a causal model based on linear regression

	A	B	C
		New housing starts	White goods sales
1			
2	Year	(thousands)	(R$millions)
3	1985	330.6	143.7
4	1986	341.9	180.7
5	1987	387.3	167.0
6	1988	393.7	179.1
7	1989	384.0	198.6
8	1990	444.3	185.3
9	1991	449.2	203.9
10	1992	396.0	228.3
11	1993	481.2	203.7
12	1994	456.3	232.4
13	1995	419.8	209.8
14	1996	510.8	199.2
15	1997	452.5	252.4
16	1998	Forecast:	218.7

Now suppose that a manager of a company manufacturing white goods wishes to forecast the value of *white goods sales* for 1998. To do this, they fit a straight line by linear regression, remembering the one-year time lag, so that the value in C4 depends on B3 and so on. The forecast for the value of *white goods sales* for 1998 is given in cell C16 by the formula REGRESSION (B15,C4..C15,B3..B14). As may be seen, its value is 218.7 million Ruritanian dollars. Note that because of the time lag, the value of *white goods sales* in 1985, in cell C3, is not actually used in the forecasting model, as the value of *new housing starts* in 1984 is not available.

To illustrate the point about a time series relationship being quite unnecessary for a regression-based forecasting model, we must stress that although *you* may know that the independent variable in your model represents time, the regression model does not know that. Any set of numbers works just as well (or badly) as any other. Figure 15.31 shows a spreadsheet with almost exactly the same structure as Fig 15.30. Here the dependent variable is *annual maintenance expenditure* and the independent variable *age of vehicle*. For convenience, the rows are ordered by vehicle number, rather than by the value of the independent variable (*age of vehicle*), as would be the normal practice in a time series case. In fact, the order of the rows makes no difference to the model at all. The manager of the fleet would like to forecast the value of *annual maintenance expenditure* for a two-year-old vehicle. This forecast is again shown in cell C16. The only difference is that as there is no time lag, the formula is now REGRESSION (B16,C3..C15,B3..B15). The resulting forecast is £714.

Fig 15.31 Forecasting a non-time dependent relationship using a causal model based on linear regression

	A	B	C
1	Vehicle	Age of vehicle	Annual maintenance
2	Number	(years)	expenditure (£)
3	1	2	609
4	2	1	552
5	3	2	657
6	4	4	904
7	5	3	845
8	6	3	850
9	7	5	1211
10	8	2	742
11	9	3	901
12	10	1	598
13	11	5	1194
14	12	2	816
15	13	4	1143
16	Forecast	2	714

Where it is possible to identify a meaningful relationship between the values of two different variables, then such a relationship should be used for forecasting in preference to an approach based solely on the values of the dependent variable itself. This is a task that requires the manager's judgement; correlation can be used to examine how strong the association between two managerial variables is, but it cannot indicate whether or not a causal relationship exists, as was pointed out in Chapter 14.

To give a simple example of how important the 'meaningful relationship' concept is, suppose that the values of the sales of a certain type of goods have been as shown in the left-hand part of the graph in Fig 15.32. It would be reasonable to expect that future values of *sales* would continue to follow the downward trend shown in Fig 15.32 rather than the upward trend shown in Fig 15.33, and any of the forecasting models we have so far discussed would yield forecasts of that kind.

However, suppose that we actually know that there is a causal relationship between the values of the variable *sales* and the values of the variable *disposable income*, of the kind shown in Fig 15.34. If we also know that the government's pre-election budget announced the day before will give a gradual but continuing boost to the values of *disposable income* in the future, then the shape of the graph shown in Fig 15.33 becomes a much more plausible forecast than that in Fig 15.32.

Multiple regression

As mentioned above for the case of water consumption, sometimes there may be several independent variables affecting the same dependent variable. In these circumstances, the simplest technique for forecasting is to carry out linear

Fig 15.32 Graph of sales data against time (first possibility)

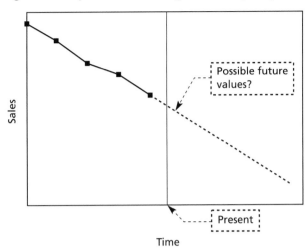

Fig 15.33 Graph of sales data against time (second possibility)

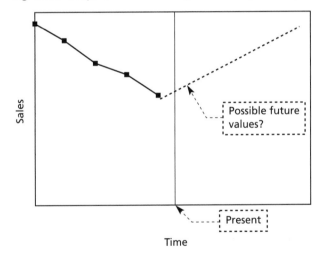

regression with several independent variables. Any regression modelling with several independent variables, whether linear or non-linear, is known as *multiple regression*. Built-in functions to perform multiple regression, at least in linear cases, are beginning to become available in spreadsheet packages, and operate exactly as the FORECAST, TREND or REGRESSION functions already described; they simply have more arguments, because there are more variables in the model. The interpretation of the results of multiple regression requires a more sophisticated understanding of statistics which is beyond the scope of this book.

Fig 15.34 Graph of relationship between sales and disposable income

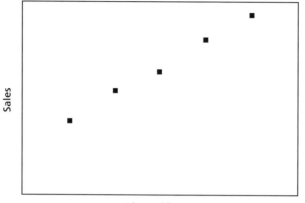

Disposable income

CHOOSING BETWEEN DIFFERENT FORECASTING MODELS

Choice between forecasting models is largely a matter of personal preference, although we have already mentioned certain important points that a manager should take into account, such as how much weight is given to newer data, how much data need to be stored, and whether seasonal or cyclical components are present. We have also advised managers to use the measures of precision and bias that are available, even though strictly speaking these can only ever be used to judge the fit between predictions made using a forecasting model and past data, rather than how good a forecast of a future value will be.

However, it is possible to go halfway towards this, and get an idea of how good the forecasting model *would have been* if it *had been* in use, based on the measures of precision and bias used earlier. (We have chosen our words very carefully here.)

Effectively, we pretend that we are building our model at some time in the past. The steps involved go like this:

1 Divide the past observations into two sets: the 'training' set and the 'testing' set.
2 Build a forecasting model on the basis of the values in the training set.
3 Forecast the values corresponding to the actuals in the testing set, using this model. (Now these really *are* forecasts, not predictions, because all the data used in the model would have been available to make the forecast at that time.)
4 Work out the precision and bias for these forecasts.

For time series data, the testing set should consist of the most recent observations, and cover the same total length of time as that for which a forecast is needed. For example, if monthly sales data for five years are available, and forecasts for the next year are needed, then the testing set should be the data for the last (most recent) year. The model is built using the data for the previous four years, and then its precision and bias are measured relative to the testing set.

For non-time series data, it is usual to divide the observations into two roughly equal sets at random. Each model can then be tested twice, the roles of the training and testing sets being reversed for the second test.

Naturally, this procedure can be used to compare what the performance of several different models would have been if they had been in use, to enable a more informed choice of model to be made. Once the manager has decided which type of forecasting model they prefer, the forecasting model is then worked out again, this time using all the data (from both training and testing sets), before being used to make 'real' forecasts of the future values.

Useful though this procedure is, it still cannot give any definite information about how good the future forecasts will be; as advertisements for certain types of investment in the UK are required to state, past performance is not necessarily a guide to future performance! Nevertheless, to the extent that the future does indeed resemble the past (which is where we came in), a forecasting model that would have worked well in the recent past should produce good forecasts in the future. Certainly, there is no reason to expect that a model which would have been wildly imprecise or biased in the past will suddenly start to produce better forecasts in the future!

WHAT IF I NEED MORE?

Although often (correctly) regarded as a subset of statistical analysis, the extensive use of forecasting techniques such as curve fitting (for medium-term forecasts) and exponential smoothing (for short-term forecasts) has formed the basis of a reasonably substantial software market.

The general statistics packages mentioned in Chapter 14, such as SAS (Statistical Analysis System), MINITAB and SPSS (Statistical Package for the Social Sciences), all offer separate modules which incorporate many of the forecasting techniques currently available. There are also numerous specialised forecasting packages; so numerous that it would be invidious to mention any particular ones! Most are stand-alone packages, although many are designed to work with spreadsheet data formats. There are a few intended to operate as add-ins to spreadsheets, even though spreadsheets are not necessarily the best computational environment for analysing large amounts of past data.

SUMMARY

In this chapter, we have described three approaches to developing forecasting models:

- Forecasting by identifying patterns in the past data on a single variable, specifically fitting straight-line and growth curve models by least squares regression.

- Forecasting directly from the past data values for a single variable, by using moving averages or exponential smoothing.
- Forecasting one variable on the basis of its relationship with one or more other variables, again using regression.

We have also looked at the use of decomposition techniques, to allow for the presence of seasonal and/or cyclical components in the data. In addition, we have looked at ways of measuring the precision and bias of the fit of a forecasting model to past data, and have briefly explained how these can be used to help choose which forecasting model to use.

END NOTES

1 It is worth pointing out that fashion designers, design engineers, architects and even home knitting machine users are making increasing use of computer-aided design (CAD) systems to help visualise possible new designs, but all the creativity needed for such 'forecasting' must at present still be supplied by the user.

2 It is also quite possible that the way investors on the New York stock exchange behave has changed in the time since the original study!

3 The choice of minimising the sum of squares of the 'y-axis' distance, rather than, say, the 'right angles' distance (i.e. the sum of the squares of lines drawn from each data point to the trend line so that they meet the trend line at right angles), is justified because the y-axis values are the ones in which the manager is interested. When the x-axis points are evenly spaced, as they are in this example, the line of best fit most people produce 'by eye' is very close to that found by least squares regression. However, when the x-axis points are not evenly spaced, fitting by eye tends to be influenced too much by outlying points.

4 More able mathematicians will be able to work out that this is the case from the formula given in end note 12 of Chapter 14. We advise other readers to take this on trust!

5 There are many types of curve that might be used in these two cases. The details are beyond our scope here, but among the possibilities are the logarithmic curve in the 'under–over–under' case, and the cubic and the lognormal in the 'over–under' or 'under–over' one.

6 Forecasters have traditionally called the smoothing constant by the Greek letter alpha (α). This was a problem in the days before graphical user interfaces, because the spreadsheets were not very good at coping with Greek letters.

7 The number of tourists follows a strongly seasonal pattern in every country that has a substantial tourist industry, but that pattern is very different for different countries; for example, the seasonal components in Spain are different from those in Switzerland, and those in Japan are different from those in Australia.

FURTHER READING

The top reference work on forecasting for managers is generally regarded as Spyros Makridakis and Steven Wheelwright, *Handbook of Forecasting: A Manager's Guide*, John Wiley, Chichester, 1987. However, there are many better introductory texts, including those by the same two authors. Some books have been specifically aimed at forecasting using spreadsheets, such as Colin Lewis, *Business Forecasting in a Lotus 1-2-3 Environment*, John Wiley, Chichester, 1989.

EXERCISES

1 Explain the difference between forecasting by identifying patterns in the past data, and forecasting directly from past data values.

2 Calculate the sum of the *actual–forecast* values for the temperature data in Table 15.1.

3 What is the advantage of using the mean absolute percentage error (MAPE) as a measure of the precision of the fit of a forecasting model, rather than the mean absolute deviation (MAD)?

4 Why is a value of 0.5 for r^2, the coefficient of determination, often regarded as the minimum necessary for a well-fitting model?

5 Explain the advantages of exponential smoothing, compared to moving average methods.

6 How would you lay out the spreadsheet in Fig 15.22 so as to be most convenient for forecasting the sales of several products?

7 What is the difference between a seasonal component and a cyclical component?

8 Explain why it was necessary to insert a sequence number column (column G) in the spreadsheet in Fig 15.29.

9 The data in Table 15.2 show the number of accesses to a company's new World Wide Web site on each of the first 10 days after it has been set up.

Table 15.2 Site accesses

Day	Number of accesses
1	27
2	225
3	445
4	432
5	494
6	524
7	813
8	903
9	946
10	1081

Forecast the number of accesses on day 11 using:
a) a straight-line model
b) an exponential growth curve model.

(You should assume that there is no cyclical effect due to different days of the week.)

10 Table 15.3 shows the number of patients seen by a hospital's accident and emergency unit in each of the last ten years.

Table 15.3 Visits to A&E

Year	Number of patients
1	59 182
2	58 094
3	56 239
4	60 187
5	59 353
6	61 871
7	58 280
8	60 995
9	60 046
10	59 418

Forecast the number of patients seen by the unit next year using:
a) a three-point moving average
b) an exponential smoothing model with a smoothing constant of 0.2.

11 Work out the precision and bias of the fit of the unadjusted and adjusted moving average forecasting models in Fig 15.23. Do you think that the adjusted model gives a better fit to the data?

12 Forecast the Ruritanian tourist data for the third and fourth quarters of 1997 using an additive decomposition model.

13 A transport company knows that the amount of fuel used by its vans depends principally on the length of the journeys undertaken. On the basis of the data in Table 15.4, forecast the amount of fuel to be used on a journey of:
a) 40 km
b) 80 km.

Table 15.4 Fuel usage

Length of journey (km)	Fuel used (litres)
25	5.4
91	10.9
13	1.0
78	13.1
51	5.0
49	8.7
87	11.4
31	7.3
28	5.1
25	2.5
66	12.0
59	8.0

Spreadsheet data as a base of data

INTRODUCTION

There is no doubt that the spreadsheet package is the leading PC software modelling tool for the individual manager, and (along with the word-processor) the package that any individual business user is most likely to use personally. However, in terms of routine applications, especially on large mainframe computers, the database package is the most important software package for most organisations. Indeed, one of the main responsibilities of an organisation's information systems department is to maintain the integrity of the organisation's main database(s) (see Chapter 17).

Any spreadsheet that is to be used for modelling requires some data. Often, but not always, the data are stored in the spreadsheet itself. In Chapters 5 and 6 we discussed the two crucial parts of any spreadsheet model, namely the logic model, consisting of the factors that are included and the relationships between them, and the data model, consisting of the actual values of the input factors. In this chapter we consider in more detail one form of data model – the database.

Historically, databases and spreadsheets grew up separately. There were already many database packages around when the spreadsheet was just a glimmer in Dan Bricklin's eye, and the first version of the first spreadsheet, his VisiCalc package, had virtually no database facilities to speak of.

However, as with many computing developments, spreadsheets and databases have converged in recent years. This convergence has centred on two aspects:

- extending the capabilities historically possessed by database packages to spreadsheet packages, and vice versa
- making it easier for spreadsheets to retrieve data stored elsewhere.

The first of these was encouraged by the growth of so-called relational database packages during the 1980s. The relational database[1] is now the most common format for database packages, especially on PCs. One of the principles of relational database packages is that the data are stored in two-dimensional *tables* set out in rows and columns; the similarity of this to a spreadsheet is immediately apparent.

The second was originally used mainly for transferring data between different software packages on the same computer. However, as networking of PCs has become more common, and PC–mainframe connectivity has improved, it has also become important for enabling the spreadsheet to access information stored on other storage devices, either within the manager's organisation or further afield.

In the next three sections, we first explain database terminology, then describe how spreadsheet terminology maps on to it, and then examine the uses of basic database activities.

DATABASE TERMINOLOGY

As with most areas of expertise, the topic of databases has its own specialised vocabulary. Most of this terminology applies to all types of database, but we shall concentrate on relational databases here, for two reasons:

- Relational databases are the ones that the manager as hands-on user is most likely to encounter.
- Relational databases are the type of database that is most similar to a spreadsheet.

We will first briefly explain database terminology. There are four levels of information in a database; in ascending order of complexity, these are character, field, record, and table,[2] all within the database itself. So, a database consists of one or more tables, each of which consists of one or more records, each of which consists of one or more fields, each of which contains one or more characters, as sketched in Fig 16.1.

We will now explain these in more detail.

Characters

The character is the lowest form of data in any database system, the 26 letters of the alphabet A to Z and the ten numeric digits 0 to 9 being the most commonly used. All packages allow some specialised characters in addition to these, for

Fig 16.1 Levels of information in a database

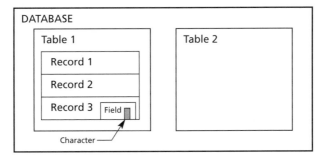

example the dollar sign $ and the underline or underscore _ . However, the characters which are allowed in a database vary between packages. Note also that some database packages do not distinguish between upper- and lower-case letters.

Fields

A collection or group of characters is referred to as a field. In a database package, a field requires:

1 A field name – identifying the attribute (in our terms, the variable) about which data are to be stored.
2 A field type – defining the acceptable contents of the field.
3 A field width – specifying the maximum number of characters that can be contained.
4 The contents, the actual data held within the field.

Common field types include the following:

- Numeric – restricted to the numeric characters 0 to 9, the decimal point (.) and the plus (+) and minus (−) signs.
- Alphanumeric, character or text – restricted to one of the set consisting of the letters A to Z, the numbers 0 to 9 and those special characters which that database package will accept as part of a 'word'.[3]
- Logical or Boolean – restricted to TRUE or FALSE, often as just one character such as T or F, or Y (for yes) or N (for no), or M (for male) or F (for female).
- Date – which may have to be in a specified format such as DD/MM/YY; we discussed spreadsheet date formats in Chapter 9.

Records

A record is a collection of fields. In a database package, the number, type and width of the fields within a record define the record structure.[4] Each record contains information about one instance of a 'thing', where the 'thing' might be a customer, or a spare part, or an employee, or whatever. The fields in the record are the headings under which data are stored for each 'thing'. In an old-fashioned manual filing system, one record corresponds to one filing card.

Database packages automatically include a field called record number (or equivalent). Records in a PC database package are normally held in record number order (referred to as unindexed). By default, records are presented in the chronological order in which they were added to the database.

Tables

A collection of identically structured records is known as a table. Normally the table is conceptualised as having each row corresponding to one record, and each column corresponding to the entries in the same field, although this bears little or no relation to how the data are stored in the computer's memory. Tables may be given names, to help in thinking about the structure of the database, but this isn't essential. Indeed, in a really good relational database, the user should not need to know, or even be aware of, the particular table(s) they are using.

In relational databases, each table must have a *prime key*; a field (or combination of fields) that is unique to each record, so that the records may be distinguished from each other. Often this is specifically included in the record structure for that purpose, for example an ORDER NUMBER field. Figure 16.2 shows parts of two tables. The first table, containing order details, has the ORDER NUMBER field as its prime key, but the second, containing customer details, would need the combination of the CUSTOMER and DELIVERY ADDRESS fields as its prime key. This is called a *composite* key, as it is a combination of fields. CUSTOMER alone would not be suitable as a prime key, as two different customers might have the same name; similarly, two different customers might have the same delivery address. Good practice would be to add a CUSTOMER NUMBER field to that table, to prevent any possibility of confusion.

The contents of the field(s) that make up the prime key to a table must be non-blank for every record in the table, or else it would not be possible to differentiate between all the records. The record number would in theory serve

Fig 16.2 Parts of two tables in a relational database

ORDER NUMBER	ITEM	QUANTITY	CUSTOMER
0354	Chair	12	Smith and Sons
0355	Table	4	Jones and Daughters
0356	Table	6	Smith and Sons

CUSTOMER	DELIVERY ADDRESS	TARIFF	CURRENT CREDIT LIMIT (£)
Smith and Sons	13 Water Street, Randomtown	New Customer	2500
Jones and Daughters	Green Acres Business Park, Anyville	Discount	8000

this purpose, but in many cases cannot be given a reasonable 'business' meaning, unlike the examples of order number and customer number just mentioned, and so could not conveniently be used as the prime key.

◆ *Key concept*	*Each table in a database must have a **prime key**; a field (or combination of fields) that is unique to each record, so that the records may be distinguished from each other. Often a field such as order number, customer number or employee number may be included specifically for this purpose.*

Databases

A database is a collection of one or more tables. Relational database packages allow operations to be carried out using several tables at the same time, relating different tables by the common fields they contain (this is where the name relational comes from). A central principle of relational database theory is that each piece of data in the database should therefore be stored in only one place. For example, for each order placed with a company, the company needs to know the name and delivery address of the customer for that order. Building on the example of Fig 16.2, suppose that one table contains order details and another table contains customer details, including a single prime key field such as CUSTOMER NUMBER. The first table then only needs to include this prime key field to relate it to the customer details table, for use in invoicing and the production of delivery lists. This means that it does not need to include the CUSTOMER and DELIVERY ADDRESS fields in each record as well; a considerable improvement in terms of both readability and storage space used. This is shown in Fig 16.3.

Fig 16.3 Parts of two tables in a relational database, related by the CUSTOMER NUMBER field

ORDER NUMBER	ITEM	QUANTITY	CUSTOMER NUMBER
0354	Chair	12	587
0355	Table	4	211
0356	Table	6	587

CUSTOMER NUMBER	CUSTOMER	DELIVERY ADDRESS	TARIFF	CURRENT CREDIT LIMIT (£)
587	Smith and Sons	13 Water Street, Randomtown	New Customer	2500
211	Jones and Daughters	Green Acres Business Park, Anyville	Discount	8000

DATABASE TERMINOLOGY APPLIED TO SPREADSHEETS

Now that we have described the essential terminology of databases, let us see how it 'translates' into spreadsheet terms:

- A character has the same meaning in both databases and spreadsheets (but see below).
- A database field is equivalent to one cell of a spreadsheet.
- A database record is equivalent to one row of a spreadsheet, or more precisely to one row of the part of the spreadsheet that constitutes the database table.
- A database table is equivalent to all or part of a spreadsheet. Note that it must be all on a single sheet (even in spreadsheet packages that permit three-dimensional or multiple-sheet spreadsheets), and as with all database tables it must be rectangular in shape and have all the records/rows structured identically.
- The concept of a database does not really apply to current spreadsheet package database facilities, since they effectively assume that a database contains only one table.

♦ *Key concept*   *Any part of a spreadsheet that is rectangular in shape and has all its records/rows structured identically may be treated as a **database table**.*

The first four of these are shown for a very simple list of academics interested in business computing in Fig 16.4. The whole spreadsheet is the database table. Each row after row 1 is one record, e.g. the one for Finlay, shown with the darker shading. Each cell is one field, and each cell/field corresponds to the field name shown in the top row of that column, e.g. the entry in the SURNAME field for the 'Finlay' record is actually Finlay, shown with a thicker border. The characters are the letters F, i, n, l, a, y in that cell; one character, in this case the letter F, is shown lighter than the others for illustration.

Fig 16.4 A spreadsheet as a data table

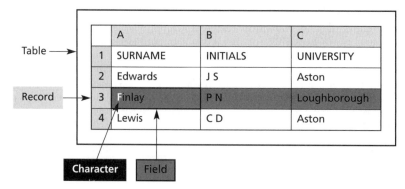

Characters

The meaning in spreadsheet packages is exactly the same as in database packages, but spreadsheet packages typically allow a greater range of specialised characters than database packages. Most modern spreadsheet packages do distinguish between upper- and lower-case letters (but see below, under fields, sorting and selecting).

Fields

Any cell in a spreadsheet can be a database field. Unlike most database packages, spreadsheet databases do not require the field type to be defined in advance, before the data are entered. This is an advantage in terms of flexibility, but can be a disadvantage in terms of data quality if, for example, 'forbidden' characters are included, or what appears to be numeric data is in fact stored as text. The likelihood that the spreadsheet package will accept a greater range of special characters than a database package compounds this first disadvantage. This is because it makes it harder to check for typing mistakes such as hitting the [key instead of the letter p, or releasing the shift key too slowly and thereby inputting the character (instead of the figure 9. It is desirable to check for valid inputs, as we recommended in Chapter 8, but most of these types of input error can only be handled by writing macro programs to do so.

The fact that the contents of the cell/field may include any valid spreadsheet formula is another considerable advantage, since it makes it very easy to have calculated fields, i.e. fields whose values depend on the values in other fields, such as a TOTAL COST field in a database of orders whose value is calculated from the verbalisation:

total cost = unit price × number of items ordered

Another important point to note is that even if a spreadsheet package distinguishes between lower-case and upper-case letters in displaying the contents of a field, it will not do so when it comes to field names. Thus, a field whose name has been defined as FINANCE may be referred to as finance, Finance or any other combination of upper- and lower-case letters.

Records

In a spreadsheet database, the field names are assumed to be shown in the top row of the table. Every other row corresponds to one record. In the example of Fig 16.4 there are just three fields, SURNAME, INITIALS and UNIVERSITY, all of which happen to be text fields.

Although there is a technical limit to the number of fields that can be contained within a record, typically around 256 fields for a spreadsheet database, this is usually so high as not to cause a problem to the average manager. A more significant problem is that records containing more than about 20 fields are difficult to display on the manager's computer screen in any manner that make the data easy to interpret. Indeed, no matter how few fields it contains, any record whose total width is more than that of the computer's screen may well need a special report (see later) to make the output easier to understand.

Tables

Again, most packages have a technical limit on the number of records that may be held in a single table; for example, in some spreadsheet packages this limit is 8191 records. In practice, it may be either the speed of the PC or its storage capacity which provides the effective limit on the number of records; again, this is unlikely to be a problem for the average manager.

Databases

In a spreadsheet package that allows three-dimensional or multiple-sheet spreadsheets, in principle each sheet could represent a separate table within the same database. However, representing this explicitly seems to be beyond the limits of current spreadsheet technology. The concept of a database does not really apply to current spreadsheet package database facilities, since they effectively assume that a database contains only one table. However, it is possible to access several databases (and therefore several tables) from any particular spreadsheet. Normally this will include any other spreadsheet database on the same computer, but may also include spreadsheet databases stored on other computers accessible via a network or modem.

It is, therefore, possible for the manager to decide 'in their own mind' to regard separate sheets of a three-dimensional spreadsheet as different tables in a single database, but care needs to be taken with this, as the package itself will not recognise any database relationship between the different sheets. It is, however, preferable to the alternative of including more than one table in the same spreadsheet. This runs the risk of operations on one table having quite unforeseen (and perhaps unnoticed) effects on another table (see the later section on layout of spreadsheet databases). Again, the spreadsheet database user gains in flexibility at the expense of rigour.

DATABASE ACTIVITIES

There are six fundamental database activities, although only four of them are directly relevant to spreadsheet databases. They are shown diagrammatically in Fig 16.5.

Three of the activities are concerned with operations on the items in the database, and were first mentioned in Chapter 6:

- sorting
- selecting
- merging.

Fig 16.5 Database activities

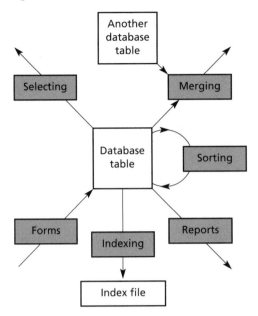

Two are methods of input and output that go beyond the standard spreadsheet display of all the fields in all the records (or at least as many as will fit on the screen):

- input forms
- reports.

The sixth is an important 'internal' operation:

- indexing.

Sorting

Sorting is an operation that can be carried out on any spreadsheet data, although in practice it only works properly if the data are laid out in a form which would make them suitable for use as a database anyway, i.e. a rectangular table with identically structured rows. Figure 16.6 shows sections of two spreadsheets containing roughly the same data about computer equipment. The first, Fig 16.6a, would be suitable for sorting; the second, Fig 16.6b, would not, because similar information is not stored in the same column and is not stored in consistent formats.

All spreadsheet packages have menu commands to Sort numerical or text entries into ascending or descending order. This is a big advantage, but there is an important limitation on spreadsheet database sorting that managers need to remember.

Fig 16.6a Part of a spreadsheet suitable for sorting

	H	I	J	K	L
75	HARDWARE	LOCATION	USER	COST	DATE
76	PC	G72	Smith P	£2199	31/10/97
77	Printer	Reception	Patel N	£495	05/01/98
78	Scanner	AV1	Wong L	£1172	03/12/94

Fig 16.6b Part of a spreadsheet not suitable for sorting

	H	I	J	K	L
75	PC	P Smith	Cost £2199	31/10/97	
76	Printer	N Patel	Reception	£495	05 January
77	Wong L	Scanner	AV1	£1172	03/12/94

As mentioned earlier, database packages automatically include a field for the record number. Spreadsheet databases do not automatically do this, and it is not usually easy to refer to spreadsheet database entries by row and column number, since the requirement for field names to be stored in the first row of a table causes 'off by one' errors even if the table begins in row 1 of the spreadsheet. It is therefore good practice in a spreadsheet database to include a field that numbers the records in order, beginning at 1. This might be called NUMBER or RECORD NUMBER, or a more specific name such as CUSTOMER NUMBER or ORDER NUMBER, if that is appropriate for the data in the particular table. Including this field may be achieved very easily by using the spreadsheet's Fill command. If a record number field is not included, then the manager may find it impossible to recreate the original order of the records after a sorting operation has been carried out. There are at least three reasons why the manager might wish to do this:

- To match the order of data not stored in a computer system, such as correspondence files on paper.
- In case an error is made during the Sorting operation.
- To enable better auditing of the data in the spreadsheet.

This is why Sorting is shown with a circular arrow in Fig 16.5; unlike Selecting, which leaves the original database unaffected, it permanently changes the state of the database.

To illustrate the database activities, we will use the personnel database shown in Fig 16.7. Note that we have inserted a column with field name NUMBER, as suggested above.

Sorting by the field name SALARY(£), a numeric field, in descending order gives the results shown in Fig 16.8. Similarly, sorting by the field name SURNAME, a text field in ascending (i.e. alphabetical) order gives the results shown in Fig 16.9.

Notice that, in Fig 16.8, Smith appears before Jones, although both have the same salary (£12000). This is because that was the order in which they

Fig 16.7 A spreadsheet personnel database

	A	B	C	D	E	F	G	H
1	NUMBER	SURNAME	INITIALS	DEPT	JOBTITLE	AGE	SALARY (£)	DATE OF JOINING
2	1	Smith	P J	Sales	Sales Assistant	28	12000	01/09/86
3	2	Macleod	T C	Finance	Accounts Clerk	35	11000	02/07/84
4	3	Chang	L L Y	IT	Systems Analyst	33	21000	28/07/86
5	4	Dvorak	P D	Sales	Sales Assistant	41	12800	05/07/93
6	5	Roberts	E	R & D	Metallurgist	48	24000	01/04/71
7	6	Shaw	F A	IT	Project Leader	40	25600	29/10/90
8	7	Shah	A J	Finance	Cashier	53	19500	06/06/77
9	8	Hennessey	P W	R & D	Biologist	35	22700	09/05/88
10	9	Jones	H G	Sales	Sales Assistant	21	12000	16/09/96
11	10	Hussain	T M	IT	Programmer	24	19500	07/08/95
12	11	Akindele	E A O	Finance	Accountant	29	24500	05/05/92
13	12	Robb	W H	Security	Security Guard	30	16000	14/11/94
14	13	Shah	R D	Sales	Sales Manager	27	22000	14/06/93
15	14	Gordon	A J	Finance	Accounts Clerk	23	11000	04/06/90

Fig 16.8 Spreadsheet database sorted in descending order of salary

	A	B	C	D	E	F	G	H
1	NUMBER	SURNAME	INITIALS	DEPT	JOBTITLE	AGE	SALARY (£)	DATE OF JOINING
2	6	Shaw	F A	IT	Project Leader	40	25600	29/10/90
3	11	Akindele	E A O	Finance	Accountant	29	24500	05/05/92
4	5	Roberts	E	R & D	Metallurgist	48	24000	01/04/71
5	8	Hennessey	P W	R & D	Biologist	35	22700	09/05/88
6	13	Shah	R D	Sales	Sales Manager	27	22000	14/06/93
7	3	Chang	L L Y	IT	Systems Analyst	33	21000	28/07/86
8	7	Shah	A J	Finance	Cashier	53	19500	06/06/77
9	10	Hussain	T M	IT	Programmer	24	19500	07/08/95
10	12	Robb	W H	Security	Security Guard	30	16000	14/11/94
11	4	Dvorak	P D	Sales	Sales Assistant	41	12800	05/07/93
12	1	Smith	P J	Sales	Sales Assistant	28	12000	01/09/86
13	9	Jones	H G	Sales	Sales Assistant	21	12000	16/09/96
14	2	Macleod	T C	Finance	Accounts Clerk	35	11000	02/07/84
15	14	Gordon	A J	Finance	Accounts Clerk	23	11000	04/06/90

appeared in the original database shown in Fig 16.7. Most packages permit the inclusion of a second sorting field as well; this secondary sorting only takes place for those records with exactly the same value in the first (or *primary*) sorting field. In Fig 16.10, again sorting by the field name SALARY(£) in descending order, SURNAME (in ascending order) was used as a secondary sorting field, so that now Jones appears before Smith among those with a salary

Fig 16.9 Spreadsheet database sorted in ascending order of surname

	A	B	C	D	E	F	G	H
1	NUMBER	SURNAME	INITIALS	DEPT	JOBTITLE	AGE	SALARY (£)	DATE OF JOINING
2	11	Akindele	E A O	Finance	Accountant	29	24500	05/05/92
3	3	Chang	L L Y	IT	Systems Analyst	33	21000	28/07/86
4	4	Dvorak	P D	Sales	Sales Assistant	41	12800	05/07/93
5	14	Gordon	A J	Finance	Accounts Clerk	23	11000	04/06/90
6	8	Hennessey	P W	R & D	Biologist	35	22700	09/05/88
7	10	Hussain	T M	IT	Programmer	24	19500	07/08/95
8	9	Jones	H G	Sales	Sales Assistant	21	12000	16/09/96
9	2	Macleod	T C	Finance	Accounts Clerk	35	11000	02/07/84
10	12	Robb	W H	Security	Security Guard	30	16000	14/11/94
11	5	Roberts	E	R & D	Metallurgist	48	24000	01/04/71
12	7	Shah	A J	Finance	Cashier	53	19500	06/06/77
13	13	Shah	R D	Sales	Sales Manager	27	22000	14/06/93
14	6	Shaw	F A	IT	Project Leader	40	25600	29/10/90
15	1	Smith	P J	Sales	Sales Assistant	28	12000	01/09/86

of £12000. Many people would find this order more intuitively satisfying than the order of Fig 16.8 and, where name and initials need to be used for sorting, two sorting fields are essential. Some spreadsheet packages now even allow a third (or *tertiary*) sorting field.

Fig 16.10 Spreadsheet database sorted in descending order of salary and then ascending order of surname

	A	B	C	D	E	F	G	H
1	NUMBER	SURNAME	INITIALS	DEPT	JOBTITLE	AGE	SALARY (£)	DATE OF JOINING
2	6	Shaw	F A	IT	Project Leader	40	25600	29/10/90
3	11	Akindele	E A O	Finance	Accountant	29	24500	05/05/92
4	5	Roberts	E	R & D	Metallurgist	48	24000	01/04/71
5	8	Hennessey	P W	R & D	Biologist	35	22700	09/05/88
6	13	Shah	R D	Sales	Sales Manager	27	22000	14/06/93
7	3	Chang	L L Y	IT	Systems Analyst	33	21000	28/07/86
8	10	Hussain	T M	IT	Programmer	24	19500	07/08/95
9	7	Shah	A J	Finance	Cashier	53	19500	06/06/77
10	12	Robb	W H	Security	Security Guard	30	16000	14/11/94
11	4	Dvorak	P D	Sales	Sales Assistant	41	12800	05/07/93
12	9	Jones	H G	Sales	Sales Assistant	21	12000	16/09/96
13	1	Smith	P J	Sales	Sales Assistant	28	12000	01/09/86
14	14	Gordon	A J	Finance	Accounts Clerk	23	11000	04/06/90
15	2	Macleod	T C	Finance	Accounts Clerk	35	11000	02/07/84

◆ *Key concept*	*Sorting* rearranges the records in a database table according to the values in one or more sorting fields. These may be numeric or text values, and the order may be ascending or descending. Sorting permanently changes the order of the records in the table.

Case sensitivity in sorting

As we said earlier, most spreadsheet packages distinguish between upper- and lower-case letters in the field contents. This raises an important question: should this be taken into account when sorting into alphabetical order? (If it is taken into account in sorting, then this must also be remembered when inputting the data!) The default is always that it should not; to use the technical term, sorting is not *case sensitive*. Thus, for example, if some of the surnames had been entered as 'smith' or 'SMITH' it would have made no difference to the order of the records in Fig 16.9.

However, it is also possible in some spreadsheet packages to choose a 'case-sensitive sorting' option, in which case the alphabet runs 'AaBbCc...', the upper-case letter being regarded as coming before the corresponding lower-case one. If the case-sensitive sorting option is chosen, then the difference between 'Shah' and 'shah' is recognised. Figure 16.11 shows part of the results of the same sorting operation as in Fig 16.9, with case-sensitive sorting and one entry mistyped as 'shah'. Now R D Shah comes before A J Shah (the one mistyped as shah); even if the INITIALS field is used as a secondary sorting field, the two Shahs will remain in the 'wrong' alphabetical order, since secondary sorting does not affect the sort on the primary sorting field.

Selecting

Selecting (or searching for) records which meet a specified search criterion is one of the most useful facilities offered by a database package. Spreadsheet databases could therefore usefully offer the same facilities as database packages, and nowadays all of the market-leading packages do. They are most commonly accessed in the form of menu commands; as the interface of spreadsheet packages continues to improve, it is becoming very easy indeed to select records. Note that the terminology varies between spreadsheet packages: Microsoft Excel uses the term

Fig 16.11 Example of the effect of case-sensitive sorting

	A	B	C	D	E	F	G	H
1	NUMBER	SURNAME	INITIALS	DEPT	JOBTITLE	AGE	SALARY (£)	DATE OF JOINING
11	5	Roberts	E	R & D	Metallurgist	48	24000	01/04/71
12	13	Shah	R D	Sales	Sales Manager	27	22000	14/06/93
13	7	shah	A J	Finance	Cashier	53	19500	06/06/77
14	6	Shaw	F A	IT	Project Leader	40	25600	29/10/90

filtering rather than selecting, while Lotus 1-2-3 uses both selecting and finding, depending on the form in which the results are returned to the manager.

The selection can be relatively simple, using a single criterion such as all personnel in a certain department; or more complex, using several criteria and the logical operators AND, OR and NOT, such as all personnel in a certain department AND earning above a certain salary AND with at least a certain length of service.

♦ Key concept

Selecting finds and displays the records that meet a specified search criterion. The criterion may be relatively simple, or extremely complex.

Entering selection criteria

There are two different ways in which the criteria to be used in a selection operation may be entered into the spreadsheet:

- by choosing from menus
- by specifying a criteria range.

Menu-driven entry of selection criteria is carried out using the field names in the database table, the field being chosen either from a pull-down menu of all the field names, as in Lotus 1-2-3, or by going to the appropriate cell in the spreadsheet itself, as in Microsoft Excel. A further pull-down menu then shows all the values in that particular field, from which the appropriate one(s) to be selected can be chosen.

All spreadsheet packages have menu-driven commands for this 'exact match' style of selection, including AND combinations of exact matches. However, only one or two packages extend this to include OR and NOT combinations, and criteria such as >20 000 rather than exact matches. Even in these one or two packages, there are limits on the complexity of the search criteria that can be entered by the menu-driven method.

By contrast, the use of a *criteria range*, as it is called in nearly all spreadsheet packages, allows the selection criteria to be as complex as the user wishes. A criteria range has a similar structure to that of a database table: field names to be used for selection appear in the first row, and the values to be used for selection appear in subsequent rows, the value being in the same column as the field to which it applies. It is not necessary to include *all* the field names in the criteria range, only those used in the selection. On the other hand, the use of all the field names has two advantages: it adds to the clarity of presentation, and makes it easier to enter the selection criteria if it is anticipated that the spreadsheet model will be used for many different selections.

♦ Key concept

*A **criteria range** allows the entry of selection criteria that are as complex as the manager wishes. A criteria range has a similar structure to that of a database table: field names to be used for selection appear in the first row, and the values to be used for selection appear in subsequent rows, the value being in the same column as the field to which it applies.*

Where two entries appear in the same row in a criteria range, it indicates an AND condition; where entries appear in different rows, the different rows form the parts of an OR condition. The values included in the conditions may be either exact matches, or relationships such as < or >, and in some packages it is also possible to enter formulae in the value cells. Figure 16.12 shows a criteria range for the personnel database example, here in cells A64..H65 to keep it away from the data. The criteria for selection are all personnel with AGE>40 and SALARY(£)>12000.

The conceptualisation and verbalisation stages of model building can be helpful in specifying selection criteria if these can be prespecified, although it is a little difficult to write down the formalisation stage as it generally involves 'pointing and clicking'. Note that selection is *never* case sensitive, even in spreadsheet packages that allow case sensitive sorting.

- *Conceptualisation* – Select all personnel in the Finance department.
- *Verbalisation* – Select all records with DEPT = Finance

The results of this selection are shown in Fig 16.13.

Table 16.1 shows some of the most common combinations of the logical operators, with examples. Three comments are necessary. The first is that the OR condition in all spreadsheet packages selects all the records that satisfy at least one of the parts of the condition. The second is that in what would be conceptualised as the operation 'AND, but NOT' the 'but NOT' has to be formalised as 'AND NOT'. The third is that it is important to realise the difference between the two different AND/OR combinations. The one we have called AND/OR (1) means select the record if either both the part-conditions 'over 50 years old' and 'joining before 01/01/1980' apply, or if the part-condition 'employed on a fixed-term contract' applies. Our AND/OR (2) means select the

Fig 16.12 Example of a criteria range

	A	B	C	D	E	F	G	H
64	NUMBER	SURNAME	INITIALS	DEPT	JOBTITLE	AGE	SALARY (£)	DATE OF JOINING
65						>40	>12000	

Fig 16.13 Selection of records for all personnel in the finance department

	A	B	C	D	E	F	G	H
1	NUMBER	SURNAME	INITIALS	DEPT	JOBTITLE	AGE	SALARY (£)	DATE OF JOINING
2	2	Macleod	T C	Finance	Accounts Clerk	35	11000	02/07/84
3	7	Shah	A J	Finance	Cashier	53	19500	06/06/77
4	11	Akindele	E A O	Finance	Accountant	29	24500	05/05/92
5	14	Gordon	A J	Finance	Accounts Clerk	23	11000	04/06/90

Table 16.1 Some of the most common combinations of logical operators used in selection

Logical operation	Example: 'All personnel...'
AND	in the finance department AND earning more than £30 000
OR	over 50 years old OR joining before 01/01/1980
NOT	NOT in the company pension plan
Repeated AND	in the finance department AND earning more than £30 000 AND over 50 years old
Repeated OR	over 50 years old OR joining before 01/01/1980 OR employed on a fixed-term contract
AND NOT	under 50 years old AND NOT in the company pension plan
OR NOT	employed on a fixed-term contract OR NOT in the finance department
AND, but NOT	over 50 years old AND joining before 01/01/1980 AND NOT in the finance department
AND/OR (1)	(over 50 years old AND joining before 01/01/1980) OR employed on a fixed-term contract
AND/OR (2)	over 50 years old AND (joining before 01/01/1980 OR employed on a fixed-term contract)

record if the part-condition 'over 50 years old' applies and so do either of the part-conditions 'joining before 01/01/1980' or 'employed on a fixed-term contract' (or both). You need to understand the difference between these two types of condition, and also how to input the two different types in the spreadsheet package that you use.

The results of a more complex selection are shown in Fig 16.14. Here the selection is:

- *Conceptualisation* – Select all personnel earning over £20 000 who are either over 40 or joined the company before 1980.
- *Verbalisation* – Select all records with (SALARY(£) > 20000 AND AGE > 40) OR (SALARY(£) > 20000 AND DATE OF JOINING < 01/01/80)

A criteria range has been used to enter the selection criteria, in cells A18 to H20. Note that the label 'Criteria:' in cell A17 is for clarity only; it is not part of the criteria range. As mentioned above, we have included all the field names for clarity, although only AGE, SALARY(£) and DATE OF JOINING are used in the selection criteria. Row 19 of Fig 16.14 contains the first part of the condition, (SALARY(£) > 20000 AND AGE > 40), the AND being indicated by the appearance of the two criteria in the same row; row 20 contains the second part, (SALARY(£) > 20000 AND DATE OF JOINING < 01/01/80). The OR element of the condition is indicated by the use of the two different rows; note that we had to include the SALARY(£)>20000 part of the condition in both rows. Only one person, the metallurgist E Roberts, meets the selection criteria this time.

A note on conditions involving dates

You may have noticed that in Fig 16.14 we had to enter the specific date 01/01/80 rather than simply 1980 in the criterion cell. The figure 1980 would be interpreted as a day number (see Chapter 9), and thus give incorrect results,

Fig 16.14 Selection of records for personnel with salary greater than £20 000 and either age over 40 or date of joining before 1980

	A	B	C	D	E	F	G	H
1	5	Roberts	E	R & D	Metallurgist	48	24000	01/04/71
2								
17	Criteria:							
18	NUMBER	SURNAME	INITIALS	DEPT	JOBTITLE	AGE	SALARY (£)	DATE OF JOINING
19						>40	>20000	
20							>20000	<01/01/80

since day numbers are calculated from a date early in the twentieth century (the precise date varies between different hardware and software). Note also that when built-in functions such as TODAY are used in conditions relating to dates, for example to calculate which invoices are more than 28 days old and thus overdue for payment, most spreadsheet packages require these conditions to be expressed in terms of day numbers (see again Chapter 9).

Merging

As we said in Chapter 6, merging items from two or more database tables to create another table is a vital operation in large databases. However, as mentioned earlier in this chapter, spreadsheet databases really operate as if each database consists of a single table. Merging is not therefore an operation that is recognised as such in spreadsheet databases, and so will not be discussed further here. However, as a spreadsheet model may refer to any number of database tables in any number of spreadsheets, it is possible to carry out a merging operation as part of the operation of producing a report (see later).

Input forms

Entering data into a database is a process that needs to be done quickly and accurately. However, entering data across a long horizontal row is not very efficient ergonomically, especially if the records extend across several screens and several fields are blank. Specialised database packages therefore tend to offer *input forms*, which are screens designed to make input easier; typically one record takes up the whole screen during input.

There are two main reasons for using input forms:

● reducing the time taken to input data
● decreasing the number of data errors made during input.

Spreadsheet databases tend to be smaller than databases that require specialised packages, and therefore these two issues are not quite so vital for the spreadsheet database user. Nevertheless, improvements in these areas are not to be sneezed at, and so most spreadsheet packages are beginning to offer some assistance of this kind.

Microsoft Excel version 5.0, for example, includes a single type of data form, which lists the fields vertically rather than horizontally; a small but significant improvement, as may be seen from Fig 16.15. (Remember, we said earlier that you don't *have* to think of the fields in a record as running along a row horizontally!) Another advantage of this form is that it is possible to navigate more rapidly between fields by using 'short cut' keys, pressing the Alt key and the underlined letter in the field name to go to that field (e.g. Alt + A to go to the AGE field). This makes it easy to skip fields, and so is especially useful when amending data in existing records.

The buttons on the right-hand side of the form also help the user to navigate between records in the table, and indeed to delete records.

◆ **Key concept**   *Input forms are screen displays designed to make the entry and amendment of data easier and less prone to error.*

Spreadsheet packages at present typically offer only standard input forms. Specialised database packages offer much more flexible facilities, such as being able to design different input forms for different parts of a database, and forms that input data to more than one table. More advanced input forms can be designed for any spreadsheet by writing macro programs, but this is beyond the scope of this book.

Fig 16.15 Microsoft Excel data form for personnel database

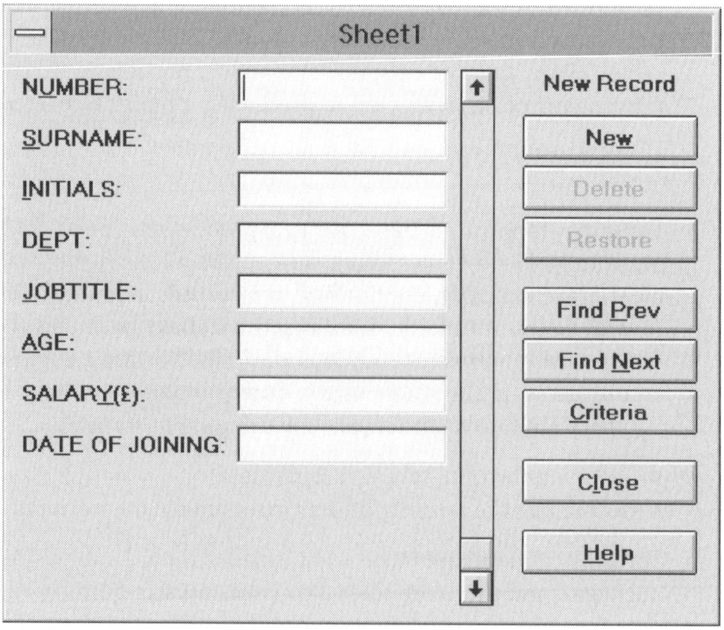

Reports

In most cases, when a manager uses a database already in existence, they will be calling for reports, either displayed on screen or printed. In our formal spreadsheet terminology, a report is a summary model, but we shall use the less formal term report in the rest of this section because it is short and easily understood. We should, however, stress that 'report' means not just hard copy printed on paper to show to other people, but also applies to the on-screen display of a summary model of a database.

♦ **Key concept**   *Reports are summary models, either printed or on screen, that make it easier for the manager to get information from the data in a good database.*

Because reports are so important, specialised database packages include what are termed *report generators*. These are software modules that can be used to create report forms, whose purpose is similar to the input forms discussed in the previous section, except that of course here the concern is with output, not input. The report forms include the details required by the package to produce reports with a prespecified layout. Obviously the *content* (the actual numbers and text) in a report produced by a given report form will vary over time, since the records held within the database will vary from the production of one report to the next. For example, the list of current outstanding invoices this week will be different from last week's list; the employees in post on 31 January 1999 will be different from those in post on 31 January 1998; and so on. The idea of the report generator is to make the interaction with the database easier by separating the layout of the report, which may change only slowly if at all, from the much more rapidly changing content. In our terms, the layout is the logic model for the summary model represented by the report form; the values that make up the data model are in the database table(s) which the report form uses.

The quality of the report generator is one of the features on which different database packages compete with each other, especially regarding the automatic production of totals or subtotals for numeric fields, and the ease with which the actual field contents (as opposed to the totals and subtotals themselves) can be included or omitted when totals or subtotals are produced. Sometimes all the details in every field will matter, as for example with a list of internal candidates for a new job opening. At other times, only the broadest summary information is needed. For example, the finance director of an organisation might wish to know the total salary bill of each department within the organisation without being interested in the salary details of the individual employees. Both the 'job candidate' and 'salary bill' reports would nevertheless be produced from the same personnel database.

Spreadsheet databases are typically stronger in respect of on-screen rather than printed reports, with most spreadsheets offering facilities for producing on-screen reports that are at least as good as those of most specialised database packages. We shall therefore devote most of our space here to on-screen reports. Generally the on-screen reports take the form of new tables; these *report tables* are known as pivot tables in Microsoft Excel and query tables in Lotus 1-2-3.

◆ **Key concept**

*A **report table** is a summary model produced by operations on one or more database tables. It is called a pivot table in Microsoft Excel and a query table in Lotus 1-2-3.*

Report tables in spreadsheets are generally produced by a combination of menu-driven commands and the use of the mouse (or other pointing device). Figure 16.16 shows a report table for the second type of report that we mentioned earlier, one showing salary subtotals by department without individual employees' salary details. (It is again based on the table in Fig 16.7.) It was achieved in Microsoft Excel with just two 'drag and drop' operations. Other spreadsheet packages can do this equally easily for the most basic summary calculations, which are a sum of numeric values and a count of text values. Other summary calculations (see later, in Table 16.2) are also straightforward, but take slightly more operations to achieve. In three-dimensional spreadsheet packages, report tables are always presented on a new sheet, beginning at cell A1; in single-sheet spreadsheets, a separate range for the table to occupy needs to be designated.

Spreadsheets offer a great deal of flexibility in reporting information from databases, because a report table that retrieves data from one spreadsheet model may be used as part of another spreadsheet model. Thus, for example, a human resource planning model concerned with the effect of changing salary scales on the total salary bill could use up-to-date information on salary, length of service and any other relevant variables from the spreadsheet database where that is stored.

This is where the 'database' category of built-in functions comes in. In general, these built-in functions do the same as their 'non-database' counterparts

Fig 16.16 Report table showing total salary by department

	A	B
1	Sum of SALARY(£)	
2	DEPT	Total
3	Finance	66000
4	IT	66100
5	R & D	46700
6	Sales	58800
7	Security	16000
8	Grand total	253600

Table 16.2 Typical built-in database functions and their 'non-database' counterparts

Built-in database function	Corresponding 'non-database' built-in function
DCOUNT	COUNT
DMAX	MAX
DMEAN	MEAN
DMIN	MIN
DSTD	STD
DSUM	SUM
DVAR	VAR

discussed in earlier chapters, especially Chapter 9. For example, SUM and DSUM both add the values indicated in their arguments; MAX and DMAX both find the largest value, and so on. A typical range of database functions is shown in Table 16.2.

The database functions do, however, have the advantage over the non-database functions because they have an extra argument, allowing the user to specify one or more criteria for use in selection operations. This means that the location of values being (e.g.) SUMmed does not have to be specified precisely in the formula. For example, consider the formula DMEAN(A1:H15,"SALARY (£)",A24:A25), where cells A24 and A25 contain the entries DEPT and Finance respectively, thus forming the smallest possible criteria range. Applied to the database table in Fig 16.7, this formula will return the value 16500, which is the mean salary of personnel in the finance department, as shown in cell B26 of Fig 16.17. It is not necessary for the user to know exactly which cells in the table contain values of salaries of employees in the finance department, only to know the location of the whole table (A1:H15).

Report tables are typically capable of including the same calculations as those performed by the built-in database functions shown in Table 16.2, but have only a very limited range of 'table-like' layouts for the outputs. By contrast, the built-in functions can be used to display results in any way of which the spreadsheet package as a whole is capable, thus offering much more flexibility.

Fig 16.17 Use of the DMEAN function (in cell B26)

	A	B	C	D	E	F	G	H
1	NUMBER	SURNAME	INITIALS	DEPT	JOBTITLE	AGE	SALARY (£)	DATE OF JOINING
2	1	Smith	P J	Sales	Sales Assistant	28	12000	01/09/86
3	2	Macleod	T C	Finance	Accounts Clerk	35	11000	02/07/84
23	Criteria:							
24	DEPT							
25	Finance							
26	Mean salary(3)	16500						

Fig 16.18 Use of the DGET function

	A	B	C	D
34	SURNAME	INITIALS		Salary
35	Smith	P J		12000

There is one further important built-in database function in most spreadsheet packages, that has no direct 'non-database' equivalent. This is the DGET function; it returns a single value meeting specified criteria, the criteria being expressed in a criteria range. Thus, operating on the personnel data in Fig 16.7, as usual, the formula DGET(A1:H15,"SALARY(£)",A34:B35) in cell D35 will return the value of P J Smith's salary, £12 000. This is shown in Fig 16.18. The criteria range is in cells A34 to B35. The text 'Salary' in D34 is just a heading for the result in D35, not part of the selection.

The DGET function is very useful for retrieving the contents of a single field, or of several fields in the same record. In theory, the DGET function may also be used to accomplish the equivalent of a merging operation on two tables. However, as the criteria range must be laid out in the format we have already seen, it entails much inserting and deleting of alternate rows to add/remove the field name headers. This is so unwieldy that we shall not discuss it further here. If a merging operation is really necessary, it is probably easiest to sort both tables into the same order based on the field(s) to be used to relate the tables together, and then use Copy and Paste!

We have concentrated on on-screen reports in this section rather than printed ones. Specialised database packages are extensively used for producing printed reports, often on special stationery as in the case of invoices, electricity bills, bank statements and so on; many have sophisticated features to help in the design and layout of such printed reports. Spreadsheet database facilities do not specifically cover these aspects of report design, but their general printing capabilities are extensive enough to be suitable for almost any report-printing task that a personal computer user is likely to need to tackle. As the issues involved in printing depend to a great extent on the printer and operating system that are being used, and are of little significance from the modelling point of view, we shall not discuss them further here.

Indexing

Indexing records is a major issue in database packages, but as yet is not a significant issue in spreadsheet databases. The purpose of indexing is to allow the records to be viewed in a different sequence from the 'usual' one without either having to wait for them to be sorted first, or having the overhead of storing a second database of the same size as the original. Index files store only the data for the field which is the key for that particular index (SURNAME, perhaps) and the corresponding record numbers; this is much more efficient in terms of storage than storing another copy of the whole database, and speeds up both sorting and selection operations. With the very large databases for which specialised database packages are typically used, keeping the time taken for each operation to a minimum is crucial. Much thought therefore goes into deciding which index files to include. However, this issue is not addressed in spreadsheet database packages at present, presumably because the expectation is that spreadsheet databases will be smaller, so that efficiency is less of a problem.

♦ Key concept   *There are six fundamental database activities, but only four of them are directly relevant to spreadsheet databases: sorting, selecting, input forms and reports.*

LAYOUT OF SPREADSHEET DATABASES

In this section, we offer some advice on the layout of spreadsheet databases, to make them easier and more reliable for the manager to work with.

For a single data table, always ensure that there is a clear separation between the table and the rest of the spreadsheet model. Exactly how this is done is really as much a matter of personal preference as anything; the advice about separating the logic and data models given in Chapter 8 should be sufficient, since the data table is by definition part of the spreadsheet's data model.

When it comes to multiple data tables, we consider them under three headings:

- three-dimensional or multiple-sheet spreadsheets
- single-sheet spreadsheets
- external (non-spreadsheet) databases.

Multiple-sheet spreadsheets as databases

The use of three-dimensional or multiple-sheet spreadsheets makes it easy to manage spreadsheet databases, especially producing, and working with, report tables. Each table can be put on a separate sheet, making on-screen display easier and reducing the danger of accidentally deleting or moving a part of the current sheet which is out of sight off the screen somewhere. If you have access to a three-dimensional spreadsheet package, you should always try to ensure that different data tables are on separate sheets.

Figure 16.19 shows the use of a formula that refers to a cell in another sheet. It illustrates an income tax calculation in which the DGET function is used to find the value of P J Smith's salary in the data table shown in Fig 16.7, which is actually on another sheet (named sheet1) in the same three-dimensional spreadsheet. The manager might wish to have one such sheet for each employee, although if it is to be shown to the employee, it would be advisable to omit the formula, which we have shown at the foot of Fig 16.19 for clarification! Note also that the field names shown in cells A4 and B4 are not in the same case as

Fig 16.19 Retrieving data from another sheet

	A	B	C	D
1	Tax allowance (£)	2500		
2	Tax rate	24%		
3				
4	Surname	Initials	Tax Due (£)	
5	Smith	P J	2280	
6				
7	Formula for tax			
8	(DGET(Sheet1!A1:H15,"SALARY(£)",A4:B5)-B1)*B2			

on sheet 1, just to illustrate that there is no distinction between upper- and lower-case letters for selection operations, as we said above.

Three-dimensional spreadsheets also offer another advantage, in that they make it easier to operate with multiple data tables simultaneously. We have said above that current spreadsheet package technology does not fully equal that of relational database packages, and that the spreadsheet database does not actually recognise that the different tables are in fact different sheets in the same three-dimensional spreadsheet. Thus there is no advantage in terms of building the logic and data models. The advantage is that file transfer, back-up and ensuring that you are working with the most up-to-date version of the data are all made much more straightforward. This is a very important point for the manager's actual day-to-day use of a spreadsheet database.

Single-sheet spreadsheets as databases

If you do not have access to a three-dimensional spreadsheet package, or if some other reason such as the requirements of presentation makes it desirable to use a single-sheet spreadsheet to store more than one data table, we offer the following layout guidelines.

The crucial choice is between putting the tables one below the other and side by side. If corresponding columns in all the data tables are of similar widths, then we would recommend the 'one below the other' layout. This is because the most common change to a data table that potentially affects other parts of the spreadsheet is the insertion or deletion of a record, i.e. a row. It is possible that you may wish to insert or delete a new field, i.e. a column, but this is much less likely. If there is nothing beside the data table, then the insertion or deletion of a row cannot cause any unintended effects. Other parts of the spreadsheet should also follow the same 'one below the other' layout.

If, on the other hand, the columns are of greatly varying widths, as may be the case if one of them is a field holding the complete address of a customer,[5] we would then recommend the 'side by side' layout. In this case, the addition or removal of records from a table demands more discipline from you, the user. You must always add new records at the end of the table (this is good practice anyway). More importantly, if a record is to be deleted, you must only delete the cell entries, not the row itself (this, too, is good practice, but unfortunately in most spreadsheet packages the row can be deleted more quickly than the entries in the cells, so it is very tempting to do just that). Fortunately, modern spreadsheet packages can cope with performing operations on tables with blank cells. The rest of the spreadsheet model should also be placed above all the data tables, so that there is no risk of running out of space at the bottom of the data tables.

In either case, there should always be a clear separation between each table and the rest of the model.

Of course, if you are quite certain that you will never, ever need to change anything other than the entries in the cells in the data table, i.e. not the number of records or the field names, then layout problems become less important; but is this likely?

Accessing external databases

Most spreadsheet packages allow a spreadsheet to read data from external database packages in a very general manner. The technical term for this is 'generating a database query'. There are three ways in which this may be done, depending on the spreadsheet package:

- by means of a built-in function, often called DQUERY
- by menu commands
- by means of an 'add-in' package.

Normally these queries are based on the use of SQL (Structured Query Language), which is about as close to being a standard as anything in the world of computing ever gets. The actual operations that can be performed are the same as those we have already been discussing above for data within the spreadsheet: selecting records, or fields within records, that match certain criteria. The user does not need to know any SQL commands; the spreadsheet package translates the query from the usual spreadsheet operations for them.

The reason we are discussing this under layout is nothing to do with the layout of the spreadsheet itself, but because the use of external queries almost always requires the manager to know the correct field names in the external database to use, which can be difficult for some external databases. We shall return to this issue in Chapter 17.

The use of 'add-in' packages is a new development, linked to the growing tendency for a spreadsheet package to be purchased as part of an integrated suite of programs, such as Microsoft Excel as part of Microsoft Office, or Lotus 1-2-3 as part of Lotus SmartSuite. In such cases, the add-in provides an interface designed specifically to query the corresponding database package within the integrated suite, i.e. Microsoft Access or Lotus Approach, and to do so more easily than by using SQL. This can also be used to query other external databases, but without the gain in flexibility over the other methods.

WHAT IF I NEED MORE?

As we have said, spreadsheet databases do have their limitations, principally regarding speed and capacity. The requirements of the database that an organisation might use for its 'engine room' are very considerable; in 1996, for example, the UK financial institution Abbey National had 19 million accounts in its database, and the database was being accessed 1 million times per day. Such a database often has to be developed specifically to meet the needs of that particular application or organisation. Considerations of size and security mean that these databases tend to be standardised and inflexible, often with an interface designed to allow only predetermined operations on the information held in the database, known as *transactions*, to be made.

Because standardised database applications are so common, applying to almost all organisations, the market for specialised database packages is correspondingly large, and it is worthwhile for professional software suppliers to develop them. Even relatively small segments of this market may contain enough businesses to justify a specific development; for example, there is more than one database package available which specifically addresses the needs of dealers in the automobile trade. Such systems are vital to the organisation, but should not be the concern of the manager looking to develop models for decision support, except as a source of data (see Chapter 17).

A more fruitful direction is to consider one of the general database packages available. Most of the leading PC software manufacturers offer one; the leading names include Microsoft Access, Lotus Approach, dBASE, DataEase, FoxBase and Paradox. Database packages for use on larger systems, such as Oracle and Ingres, are alleged to be becoming easy enough for 'ordinary' end-users, but this claim is open to some debate. Both types of package generally offer most of the facilities of relational databases.[6] The PC packages may often be purchased as part of an integrated suite, as we have already mentioned, while the packages for larger systems will often be an organisational purchase, rather than something that a manager would buy for themselves. Prices vary from under £100 to many thousands of pounds; naturally you get what you pay for, at least to a certain extent. A manager looking to go further into databases should make sure they understand exactly what their requirements, and those of their organisation, are likely to be.

SUMMARY

In this chapter we have briefly explained database terminology, including the concepts of characters, fields, records and tables, and looked at how these apply to the database facilities in spreadsheet packages. We have demonstrated the database activities of sorting, selecting, input forms and reports as they are carried out in spreadsheets, and pointed out that the other two database activities of merging and indexing are not yet relevant to current spreadsheet facilities. Finally, we have given a few tips on the layout of database tables in spreadsheets, especially in the more difficult case when more than one table has to be included in a single sheet.

END NOTES

1 There are other types of database, including the older hierarchical database and the newer object-oriented database. The precise distinctions are beyond our scope here. The relational approach enables all data to be shared by all applications. Thus, rather than an invoicing application and a stock-control application each holding its own data on product descriptions, the product codes and descriptions would be held in a separate database and accessed by both applications to retrieve the descriptions as necessary. With this data-oriented approach, as opposed to the older application-oriented one (i.e. databases oriented towards, say, invoicing or stock control), the data tables are organised according to the nature of the information in them, and thus are not affected by new applications. A new application simply involves adding any necessary new data into new or existing data tables, not into the application. This avoids the duplication of data, which is not only wasteful in terms of storage space, but also gives the potential for inconsistency in the data caused by multiple inputs. The main disadvantage of the relational approach is that very large databases can be slow in operation.

2 A table is sometimes called a file. This is really a hangover from older, pre-relational database packages, as discussed in end note 1. Strictly speaking, the term data file applies to the physical location where data are stored (for example, on a computer's hard disk), whereas a table is the correct term for the conceptual level discussed throughout this chapter.

3 A source of considerable annoyance to those with hyphenated names is that many database packages will not accept a hyphen (-) as an alphanumeric character, because of confusion with the minus sign, so that for example the surname Smithers-Jones must be stored as Smithers_Jones, Smithers Jones or, even worse, SmithersJones!

4 Some older database packages still operate with records of a fixed total size, taking up the disk space for the number of characters equivalent to the total width even if all the fields in that record are blank; *not* a very efficient use of storage!

5 One way to avoid this is to split the address into several fields, called ADDRESS1, ADDRESS2, etc. Each field holds one line of the address, such as '64 Larch Avenue', 'Birmingham' etc. This may also make it easier to lay out the address correctly in letters and on printed labels.

6 The issue of exactly what a database package must do in order to qualify to be called relational has caused a great deal of controversy over the past decade or more. We do not wish to get involved in this here.

FURTHER READING A good introduction to database principles for most managers is W. Harris, *Databases for Business Users*, Pitman, 1992. For a more advanced treatment of relational databases by one of the pioneers of the concept, along with E. F. (Ted) Codd, try Chris Date's *Relational Databases: Selected Writings*, Addison-Wesley, 1986. There are many other books on databases, but few even consider spreadsheet database facilities.

EXERCISES

1 What is the difference between a field and a record?

2 In a spreadsheet database, why is it usually necessary to insert a field such as RECORD NUMBER?

3 Which of the six fundamental database activities are not relevant to current spreadsheets, and why?

4 Explain the advantages and disadvantages of using report tables and built-in functions when producing reports from spreadsheet databases.

5   Think of a spreadsheet database that you either have built, or might need to build soon. Which activities need to be carried out most frequently with this database? (for existing databases). How does its layout match our guidelines? (for not yet existing databases). How should you lay it out to comply with our guidelines?

Fig 16.20 Stock at clothing retailer

	A	B	C	D	E	F
1	ITEM NUMBER	ITEM NAME	SUPPLIER CODE	PRICE (£)	NUMBER IN STOCK	VALUE (£)
2	1	Umbrella – gents	T231	9.56	780	7456.80
3	2	Anorak	A104	13.23	19	251.37
4	3	Umbrella – ladies	A003	6.45	294	1896.30
5	4	Raincoat	G110	29.50	914	26963.00
6	5	Umbrella – children	V091	5.02	541	2715.82
7	6	Anorak	H536	15.73	462	7267.26
8	7	Scarf – knitted	K234	4.35	34	147.90
9	8	Gloves – knitted	K234	7.20	531	3823.20
10	9	Hat – knitted	K234	6.84	919	6285.96
11	10	Rain jacket	G110	21.98	357	7846.86
12	11	Anorak – fashion	U001	14.30	997	14257.10
13	12	Waxed jacket – gents	B100	32.65	544	17761.60
14	13	Waxed jacket – ladies	B100	29.79	158	4706.82
15	14	Umbrella – telescopic	T231	8.20	583	4780.60
16	15	Golfing umbrella	T231	21.08	739	15578.12

The remaining exercises are all based on the database table in Fig 16.20, relating to items in stock at a clothing and accessories retailer.

6   If your spreadsheet package has input form facilities, use them to input the data!

7   Sort the database into descending order of VALUE(£).

8   Sort the database into alphabetical (ascending) order of ITEM NAME.

9   Sort the database with a primary sorting field of SUPPLIER CODE (ascending order) and a secondary sorting field of ITEM NAME (ascending order).

10 Select all the items whose price is greater than £20.

11 Select all the items with a supplier code of K234 or T231, which are either priced at over £10 or have a value of over £1000.

12 Design a report listing the total value of stock from each of the different suppliers, in alphabetical order of supplier code, without listing the values of the individual items. (The report should contain only a list of supplier codes and the corresponding total values.)

CHAPTER 17

Internal and external sources of data

| Chapter aims | The aim of this chapter is to consider further the various sources of data that might be useful to managers using spreadsheet models, and explain the key issues entailed in using each of them. The data may be in spreadsheet format, or not; on the manager's own computer, or not; elsewhere in the organisation, or elsewhere in the world. |

- Introduction
- General longer-term data issues
  - Data security and privacy • Data volume • Data formats • Data cost • Data integrity • Data accuracy • Data timeliness • Mapping the characteristics to the issues
- Personal data
- Corporate data
- Commercial databases
- On-line databases
- Databases on CD-ROM
- The Internet and the World Wide Web (WWW)
- Working with sources of data

INTRODUCTION

No matter how good the tools the manager uses are, it is impossible to build a model without data. As data are so important in modelling, there are therefore several aspects of data that a manager needs to think about. Until this point in the book, our concern has been mainly with the creation of data models and what be might be termed their immediate use as part of a spreadsheet, i.e. their use in isolation as if it were a one-off exercise. You might like to think of this as the 'internals' of the spreadsheet. Only in a few places, such as Chapters 8 and 16, have we considered longer-term issues. In this chapter, we reflect specifically on these longer-term problems associated with data, which often tend to be more organisational than technical; the 'externals', if you like. They include four activities:

- maintaining data
- accessing data ('Where do we find the average house prices by region for last month?')

- understanding data ('Is the profit figure from our Ruritanian subsidiary gross or net of tax?' 'What is the definition of a small business in these employment statistics?')
- relying on data ('Who can supply us with accurate data on the demand for specialised forecasting software in Greece?').

Maintaining data ('Are these sales figures up to date?') is only a direct concern of the manager when the data are under the manager's control, although it is worth remembering that *someone* always has to do it, whatever the source of the data! The main problems with this activity are ensuring that the data are updated when necessary, and preserving the data from corruption, whether accidental or deliberate.

Accessing data ('Where do we find the average house prices by region for last month?') covers all the problems associated with knowing where to find the data needed. This might be as simple and 'local' as remembering the right file name, or exactly which cells constitute a particular look-up table, or as complex and wide-ranging as setting up a system to retrieve the previous day's sales data from all the company's retail outlets everywhere in the world. It is therefore the most wide-ranging of the four activities.

Understanding data ('Is the profit figure from our Ruritanian subsidiary gross or net of tax?' 'What is the definition of a small business in these employment statistics?') is, in contrast, a more bounded and technical activity. What *exactly* do the data mean? How are terms defined? We have already given some guidance in Chapters 5 and 8 about how to do this for your own spreadsheets, but this issue can be just as important with data provided (and presumably collected) by others. Professional statisticians are very familiar with the problems this activity raises; they coined the distinction between *primary data* (data you collect yourself, so that you can know exactly what you have measured and how) and *secondary data* (data collected by other people). Statisticians regard primary data as much more reliable than secondary data.

Relying on data ('Who can supply us with accurate data on the demand for specialised forecasting software in Greece?') is the complementary activity to understanding data, concerned mainly with the non-technical matters. Can this source of data be believed? Will it still be available to us in a year's time? Can we afford the cost?

Obviously, these activities overlap. For example, a marketing manager considering whether to rely on data supplied by a market research organisation or to set up their company's own database would certainly need to be thinking about accessing, understanding and relying on data, and possibly about maintaining data as well.

In this chapter, we consider what these activities entail, and how they differ depending on where the data come from. Back in Chapter 6, we identified four sources of data for a spreadsheet model:

1 Data held in databases either inside or outside the organisation.
2 Data obtained from decision aids other than the spreadsheet model itself.
3 Data obtained from look-up tables.

4 The very dynamic data that are changed by the user as they experiment with the spreadsheet model.

This sequence broadly reflects the increasing control that the user has over the sources of data. Our discussion subsequent to Chapter 6 has reversed the emphasis; naturally, since the major concern in this book is with spreadsheets themselves. For example, almost every chapter since Chapter 6 has discussed experimenting with spreadsheet models (the fourth source of data), and Chapters 9, 10 and 16 have all considered aspects of data in look-up tables (the third source).

In considering the activities of maintaining, accessing, understanding and relying on data, control – or more often the lack of it – is a key issue. We will thus look a little further at the second, third and fourth sources of data, but devote most of our discussion to the first source: databases internal and external to the organisation.

Note that in this chapter we have not chosen to highlight any key concepts. This is because all the issues need to be considered together; no one of them is more important than the others. The priorities in each individual case will depend on the particular manager (and model) concerned.

We shall first cover the general issues associated with the activities of maintaining, accessing, understanding and relying on data, and then go on to look at some of the more specific aspects associated with particular data sources.

GENERAL LONGER-TERM DATA ISSUES

Maintaining, accessing, understanding and relying on data are the activities that the manager, or indeed any other user of data, must carry out. In this section we start by looking at longer-term data issues from a different perspective: the characteristics of the data itself. We then map these two views on to each other.

There are seven characteristics of data that are relevant to longer-term, organisational issues. They are (in no particular order):

- data security and privacy
- data volume
- data formats
- data cost
- data integrity
- data accuracy
- data timeliness.

The last three, data integrity, data accuracy and data timeliness, may also be thought of as comprising the three components of a higher-level characteristic, data quality. It may seem that quality is a strange term to apply to data; as we said in Chapter 6, surely data are data are data? We trust that by now we have convinced you that there is rather more to it than that. To give a recent example to show that even the proverbial 'person in the street' has some feel for data quality; consider the proposal for a voluntary national identity card scheme that was made in the UK in 1996. Among the available databases relating to all or most of the UK adult population are those for:

- passports
- income tax
- driving licences
- social security
- health
- electoral rolls.

One of the main criticisms of the proposal was that the identity card scheme would use the driving licence database of the UK's Driver and Vehicle Licensing Authority (DVLA), partly because the DVLA had a remit to try to earn money from its data which the other database 'owners' did not. Unfortunately, the DVLA database is generally perceived to have the lowest quality of data – especially in terms of its accuracy – of those available. During public debate on the proposed scheme, the UK's Data Protection Registrar described the DVLA database as 'probably the least accurate of all databases covering the UK adult population'. Public opinion of the quality of the UK's social security database(s) (there is as yet no single integrated system) is not much better; it was reported, also in 1996, that in 1995 the databases held social security records on over 62 million people when the UK population was only some 58 million.

We now consider each of the seven characteristics in turn.

Data security and privacy

There are three interlinked facets to this characteristic:

- commercial secrecy – preventing competitors from knowing your organisation's 'secrets'
- who is permitted to see which data within an organisation
- confidentiality of personal data.

As may be seen, these cover the organisation as a whole, the people within the organisation, and society as a whole, respectively.

Data security and privacy are issues that have become more prominent in many Western countries recently, as the amount of data held in computerised form has increased. Often this public concern is principally with the third facet listed above, confidentiality of personal data – especially data held by government departments and agencies. It is, however, important for the manager to realise that security and privacy are issues that are (potentially) relevant to all data, no matter who stores it or what it is about.

We distinguish between the two parts of the term here as follows: *data security* denotes the general issue of avoiding unauthorised access to data, while *data privacy* refers to the specific issue of data relating to identifiable individuals. There is a strong overlap between the two, in that consideration of data security for data relating to identifiable individuals should normally include most aspects of data privacy, and in some cases is legally required to do so. The UK's Data Protection Act, for example, requires that where data relating to identifiable individuals are stored on a computer, the use(s) of the data must be registered, so that the *data subjects* (the identifiable individuals) may know what those uses are. There are some exemptions to this requirement, for example for data stored by police forces.

The threefold pressures of legal obligations (where they exist), commercial secrecy and what many people see as a moral duty to maintain the confidentiality of personal data ought to mean that measures should always be taken to prevent unauthorised access to data. However, problems arise in trying to agree how strict those measures should be in any particular case. At the individual level, people do not all agree about which of their personal data need to remain private. Most people in the UK would probably believe that their medical records should be seen only by their health insurance organisation(s) and healthcare professionals, but that their shopping habits should be much more widely known (judging by the success of credit cards and loyalty cards). On the other hand, there are some people who seem to feel that their medical history belongs in the public domain, and others who are unwilling to join a loyalty card scheme.

Within organisations, similar debates occur. Some organisations have an open access policy to all employees; others work on a 'need to know' basis only. Policies and fashions change. For example, in the current business climate, there has been considerable pressure on many organisations for the secrecy traditionally surrounding top executives' remuneration to be removed; not just opening this information to anyone in the organisation, but to the public at large.

Only rarely is the position clear cut, and then normally because of legal requirements, as with the UK's Data Protection Act, or the requirement that any data that might be needed for the grant of a patent *must not* have been made public before the patent application.

We can give no specific guidance on these matters, because in the end they are a matter for the manager and the organisation to decide. However, they must be considered very carefully, especially where data on identifiable individuals are involved.

If a decision is taken to restrict access, the methods include password protection, data encryption (putting it in code) and a very wide range of devices and methods to restrict physical access. A detailed discussion of data security is beyond our scope here.

Data volume

This is a simpler characteristic: the manager must consider the question 'How much data must the model deal with?' In this case, 'how much' covers a combination of the number of data values and the speed of processing, which is why the term data *volume* is typically used, to suggest (not always successfully!) the existence of more than one dimension. Note that 'How much data must the model deal with?' may not be the same question as 'How much data does the model need?' For example, it may be necessary to load an entire database in order to retrieve the values in a particular field, or it may be necessary to search through thousands of records in order to select the few that match the selection criterion. It will therefore be necessary to identify what needs to be done with, or to, the data, in order to work out the data volume correctly.

The data volume has a direct effect on the feasibility of the manager 'doing it themselves'; modern spreadsheet packages and PCs can cope with volumes of data that are orders of magnitude greater than their predecessors, but there are still limits.

Data formats

In what format(s) are the data available? There are four levels to this characteristic:

- Level 1 – the medium (on-line, floppy disk, CD-ROM, magnetic tape, ... , paper(!)).
- Level 2 – the format of the medium (how data are stored on the disk, tape, etc.).
- Level 3 – the format of the file (text, database, word processor, spreadsheet, ...).
- Level 4 – the layout.

We have not had to consider hardware issues much in this book, but this characteristic is one exception. The good news for the manager is that data formats are becoming less of a problem, as networking and on-line access become ever more widespread. It was not that long ago that transferring data electronically from a mainframe database to a PC spreadsheet was such a major operation that it was probably quicker to print out the data and type it in again! This was the result of problems at the first and second levels. They have not entirely gone away, however. For example, data stored on a magnetic tape or a $5\frac{1}{4}$ inch floppy disk is not accessible by a typical modern PC (level 1 problem), and most DOS/Windows PCs cannot read data from floppy disks formatted for an Apple Macintosh, even though they use the same type of floppy disk – the same medium (level 2 problem). Note that the same is not true the other way round; all new Macintoshes can read DOS/Windows format disks.

A big step forward regarding level 3 problems was the emergence in the 1980s of *de facto* standards for file transfer formats on DOS PCs; for spreadsheets, this was the Lotus 1-2-3 version 2.x format, with .WK1 extension, and for databases, dBASE's .DBF format. Even large mainframe databases can usually provide data in these formats. Interestingly, these formats are still the 'lowest common denominator' ones, even in these days of Windows 3.x and Windows 95 operating systems.

Most current PC spreadsheet packages can access data in the following file formats:

- earlier versions of the same spreadsheet package
- other spreadsheet packages (most commonly 1-2-3 or Excel, but could also include, for example, Quattro Pro, Multiplan, Symphony, Supercalc)

- text files, where the cell entries are separated by tabs
- files from database packages (most commonly in .DBF format as mentioned above, but could also include, for example, FoxPro, Paradox, Access, Approach)
- CSV (comma separated values)
- DIF (data interchange format) – dates back to the VisiCalc package!
- SYLK (Symbolic Link – associated with Multiplan)

Up to this point we have considered the question of whether a spreadsheet can open (i.e. read) the file containing a database. Normally, this is how a spreadsheet model would use data stored elsewhere, hence our emphasis on the format of the file. However, there are two exceptions to this, where a spreadsheet model may be able to use data from a file without being able to open the file itself. The first of these is when the data are retrieved from a database by the generation of an SQL query, as discussed in Chapter 16. This widens the range of database packages whose data may be used. The second is where the data may be moved between packages by 'drag and drop' operations within a graphical user interface, the main examples of this being OLE (object linking and embedding) within the Windows operating system and the Publish and Subscribe features of the Apple Macintosh System 7 operating system.

Layout problems (level 4) are really specific to the particular data source, and so we shall leave their discussion until the appropriate section.

If the problem is at level 1, and the only suitable medium for obtaining the data is on paper, the manager has two options for getting it into their spreadsheet model. The first is to scan it in as text. Scanners no longer require text to be printed in special OCR (optical character recognition) fonts, but the performance of a scanner still depends on the font used for printing and the quality of the paper. The final option, of course, is for the manager to type it in themselves, or alternatively pay someone else to do it; definitely *only* to be used as a last resort!

Data cost

How much does it cost to use the data? Little more needs to be said about this characteristic, except that there will often be a need to consider initial costs and recurrent costs separately, and perhaps for some trade-off between them to be made. For example, some data may be available for outright purchase, perhaps in the form of a CD-ROM; other data may only be available by licence, the charging for which may depend either on the period of time for which the licence is valid, or on the number of accesses made, or the volume of data retrieved, or some combination of the three.

Data integrity

What needs to be done to ensure that the data continue to be available when needed? This covers both technical aspects such as the data becoming corrupted, and organisational aspects such as the source of the data disappearing.

Data corruption might occur either accidentally, for example as a result of a disk fault or an error by a user, or deliberately, as a result of a computer virus or unauthorised access, known as *hacking*. Similarly, on the wider scale, the problems might range from an old mainframe system being taken out of use, or a market research company going out of business, to the refusal of the manager of one department to allow continued access by a manager in another department to 'their' data.

This characteristic is therefore the 'internal' counterpart to that of data security. Data integrity is concerned with coping with the (putative or actual) *results* of any virus outbreak or attack of hacking; data security includes preventing them happening in the first place.

Common precautions for internal data include taking of back-up copies of the data and ensuring that they are securely stored, often in a fireproof safe in a separate location from the original. When dealing with external organisations supplying data, some kind of check on their financial health may be in order, as with any other kind of supplier.

Data accuracy

How accurate are the data available? Basically, can the manager believe the data? Note that the accuracy necessary depends on the purpose for which the data are to be used; we have already made some comments about measurement in Chapter 6, and the accuracy with which values are presented in a spreadsheet in Chapter 7. If data values only need to be presented to (say) the nearest million, as in area population figures, then the data source does not need to be any more accurate than that.

Data timeliness

This characteristic has two facets:

- How up to date are the data?
- How frequently do the data values typically change?

The first facet is related to the initial suitability of the data source, and the second to its subsequent suitability. What the manager really needs to know for the latter is how much the data values will change during the lifetime of the model; this means knowing what the expected life of the model is. There is a certain similarity between the structure of the thinking here, and that for data cost; this should not be surprising, because data timeliness is one of the major determinants of data cost. Up-to-date, fast-changing data are always likely to cost more.

For a one-off issue, the frequency of change is not a problem; the data only need to be obtained once. However, for recurrent issues, the frequency with which data need to be updated may be a more important aspect than how up to date the data are.

Mapping the characteristics to the issues

As we said above, the seven characteristics are in no particular order. In general, all of them will have to be considered whatever the source of the data, although naturally the significance of each characteristic will depend on the particular spreadsheet model and data source involved.

In Table 17.1, we display our ideas of the relative importance of each of the characteristics to each of the four issues of maintaining, accessing, understanding and relying on data. Accessing data involves all seven of the characteristics, as might be expected from what is probably the most central issue. Maintaining data is most associated with data security and privacy and the three components of data quality. Relying on data is also closely connected with data quality, while data accuracy is paramount for understanding data.

Table 17.1 is intended to show the general level of importance of the characteristics. In the subsequent sections, we look at how likely each of these characteristics is to pose a particular problem when using each of the following specific data sources:

- personal data
- corporate data
- commercial databases
- on-line databases
- databases on CD-ROM
- the Internet and the World Wide Web (WWW).

Note that there is a certain overlap between these categories, especially the four that are external to the manager's own organisation. Note also that how problematic something is is not necessarily linked with its importance. To use an analogy, whether you can get a seat is a particular problem when travelling by train, compared to travelling by car or plane, but its importance depends on the particular journey; most people would be happy to stand up for a 5-minute local train journey, but few would be willing to stand throughout the 100-minute trip from London to Birmingham.

Table 17.1 Data characteristics mapped onto the manager's activities (the greater the number of stars, the more important is that characteristic to that activity)

Characteristic	Maintaining data	Accessing data	Understanding data	Relying on data
Data security and privacy	***	**	*	
Data volume	*	**		*
Data formats		***	**	
Data cost		**		*
Data integrity	***	***		***
Data accuracy	**	**	***	***
Data timeliness	***	***	*	***

PERSONAL DATA

For the manager, one of the great strengths of building their own decision support system is that it can make use of personal data, without any problems of data security or privacy arising. By personal data, we mean data 'belonging' to the manager, not to be confused with data on identifiable individuals, as already mentioned; our point is that problems of data being confidential, and thus unavailable to the manager, are avoided with this source. Where legislation exists regarding the storage of data on identifiable individuals, as in the UK, that still applies to data held on the manager's own PC. However, the manager should find it easy to comply with legislation when the data are under their own direct control, unlike the other sources. Data security and privacy should therefore not be problems.

The personal data may take many forms, of which the following are only a few:

- data specifically stored for this issue, whether in spreadsheets or other packages
- data stored on the manager's PC for other purposes, which again may be in spreadsheets, or the output from other decision aids
- data discovered during the exploration of the local scenario
- subjective judgements.

In most cases, especially if working in a Windows, Macintosh or OS/2 operating system environment, any data stored on the PC should be accessible to the spreadsheet, thus reducing data format problems to those of layout only.

Data cost is also negligible; there are no direct costs at all, only the opportunity cost (see Chapter 12) of the manager's time. The downside is that this is the only data source where the manager must take responsibility for maintaining the data. Referring back to Table 17.1, this potentially increases the importance of data security and privacy, data volume, and the three components of data quality, but as we have said, data security and privacy do not cause a problem.

Data volume *is* a problem; if the manager's spreadsheet or database package and PC cannot cope, then the only alternative to using another data source is to acquire a better package and/or a faster and more powerful PC. This is, however, a relatively straightforward decision to make.

Data quality is the main concern. The manager should worry particularly about the integrity and timeliness of the data. They must be responsible for ensuring that back-ups of important data are taken, and if necessary stored elsewhere (we have to admit from personal experience that this is something that many managers – and academics and students – find hard to take on board). They should work out a plan for keeping the data up to date if this has to be done. Data accuracy also becomes more important, but this is mitigated by the degree of control that the manager has over their personal data. If our earlier guidelines on documenting the spreadsheet model are followed properly, then the manager should not be able to 'forget' what the data mean, and the only problem is whether or not the measuring system used to obtain the data actually measures what it is supposed to. This is by no means a trivial point, but is one that goes far beyond the realms of spreadsheet modelling.[1]

To sum up, we show what we believe to be the likelihood of problems for each of the seven characteristics when using personal data as a data source in Table 17.2.

Table 17.2 Likelihood of problems for the seven characteristics when the source is personal data

Data source: Personal data	
Characteristic	*Likelihood of problems*
Data security and privacy	Low
Data volume	Moderate
Data formats	Low
Data cost	Negligible
Data integrity	High
Data accuracy	Low
Data timeliness	High

CORPORATE DATA

All organisations nowadays have accumulated vast amounts of data; increasingly this tends to be stored in computer form. One of the reasons why 'do-it-yourself' modelling has become much more feasible in the past few years is that the advent of PC networking in organisations has made it much easier for the manager to access corporate data at their own desktop, and to transfer it to their own computer.

Not all data are freely available, however. There are still technological limitations, both in terms of connectivity, and in terms of the PC's ability to cope with the vast amount of data that can be residing on a corporate database. The problems of this kind come under the characteristics of data format(s) and data volume. There are also data security problems; exactly who in an organisation should have access to particular information is an issue that occupies a great deal of the time of database administrators, and it would be unwise to believe that just because the technological links exist, it automatically means free access to data for all. Try to access the managing director's personnel (or indeed personal) file, for example! As we said earlier, in some organisations this might be acceptable; in others it would come close to being an offence warranting instant dismissal.

In virtually all industrial and business organisations it can be assumed that the following databases will exist:

- *Personnel* – employees' personal details.
- *Payroll* – employees' salary/wage calculation details and method of payment
- *Stock* – item details and movement information such as issues and receipts.
- *Customers* – name, address and other delivery details, and financial information such as items sent and payments received (often called the sales ledger).
- *Suppliers* – name, address and other details, and financial information such as invoices received and payments made (often called the purchase ledger).

Often some of these are combined; typically personnel and payroll, sales ledger and purchase ledger, or stock and suppliers.

Almost all organisations that have a proper budgeting system will have it in computer database form, but it is surprising how many organisations still do not have such a system at all.

With these 'core' databases, it should be reasonable for the manager to expect that problems of data integrity, accuracy and timeliness have already been addressed. For most organisations, this will certainly be true of data integrity and timeliness. However, in the case of data accuracy, it is worth recalling that different parts of an organisation often define the same thing in different ways. For example, a part-time employee or student may count as 1.0 or a whole person for one purpose (personnel or student records) but only 0.5 or half a person for another purpose (departmental overhead or student 'load' calculation).

Legacy systems

At the time of writing, and in the foreseeable future, corporate data will continue to be stored on *legacy systems*, i.e. systems built using technology which is now out of date. Since in the PC field anything over two years old is likely to be obsolescent, it may come as a sobering thought to realise that some existing mainframe systems have been in constant use, with very few changes, since the 1970s.[2] Not only does this raise the prospect of difficulty in retrieving the data because of data format problems, it should also raise concerns with the wise manager about data accuracy: does anyone now remember the definition of the data items stored in those databases? Even personal computers can raise legacy systems issues; a 1996 UK survey found that the average life of companies' personal computers was approximately four years, and in a quarter of companies the majority of PCs were over three years old. Again, problems of data format and data accuracy may arise – especially as new hardware capabilities tend to lead to software advances with correspondingly different formats. There may perhaps also be problems of data integrity resulting from hardware failure in older systems.

Gatekeepers

Political problems (political with a small 'p') in organisations should not be underestimated, even when it comes to obtaining data. The term *gatekeeper* is often used to refer to a person, or perhaps a department, who controls the use of certain data. Information is power, as the phrase goes, and many people seek to maintain their power by restricting access to information or data for which they are responsible. Improved connectivity in organisations has reduced the influence of gatekeepers somewhat, but only somewhat; almost by definition, those people who have happily made 'their' data more widely available were not the ones who guarded it most jealously in the first place! These problems come not only under the heading of data security, but also under data accuracy and integrity, since (for example) data may be made available but with little or no explanation of what they mean, or without warning data may suddenly cease to be available.

In studying any issue that goes outside the manager's immediate sphere of responsibility, it may be necessary to cultivate the appropriate gatekeeper(s) of the data needed to explore the local scenario adequately. Even if the gate-keeper's willingness to supply the necessary data is not a problem, their ability to do so may be. The days when different computer systems used completely incompatible hardware are behind us but, as we said earlier, transferring data electronically from a large mainframe, or even a specialised workstation used for computer-aided design (CAD) or artificial intelligence (AI) work, to a per-sonal computer is still not a trivial problem. The consolation is that any organisation that has large mainframes, or specialised CAD or AI workstations, should also have some technical experts who are more competent than the man-ager to tackle these data format problems!

To sum up, we show what we believe to be the likelihood of problems for each of the seven characteristics when using corporate data as a data source in Table 17.3.

Table 17.3 Likelihood of problems for the seven characteristics when the source is corporate data

Data source: Corporate data	
Characteristic	*Likelihood of problems*
Data security and privacy	High
Data volume	High
Data formats	High
Data cost	Negligible
Data integrity	Moderate
Data accuracy	High
Data timeliness	Low

COMMERCIAL DATABASES

Commercial data services go back a very long way. News agencies have been supplying data to organisations since the nineteenth century, and market research companies joined them in the early years of the twentieth century. These services moved into computer format in the 1960s, when delivery at best took the form of punched cards or magnetic tape, and at worst the proverbial reams of computer printout.

Some commercial databases offer highly aggregated data, such as the pur-chasing habits of a particular market segment or the financial health of an industry sector; others offer very specific data, perhaps tailored to the client's requirements, such as monitoring of wage rates in similar companies. Organisations such as Reuters or A C Nielsen cover the whole range from the general to the specific, while others concentrate on specific niches, such as IDS (Income Data Services) on data about pay and remuneration.

One example of a commercial database for a specific purpose is that offered by CACI to investigate the operation of an organisation's network of branches. Their database is called Branch *Base. Many organisations have agreed to pool their data for mutual benefit. Typically this would consist of data on location, facilities and so on for the branches, to be combined with statistics on population numbers and market research on buying habits. The hardest part in this particular example is finding out data on what a branch's typical catchment area is. Specific data on local markets include the Mortgage Market Database and the Current Account Market Database.

With any commercial database, data cost becomes a problem. (We feel it reasonable to assume that any additional direct cost to the manager is a problem *per se*.) Unlike the previous two sources internal to the manager's organisation, obtaining the data now involves a direct cost that can be very considerable. By contrast, the manager's worries about the other characteristics should be much reduced. Data security is now the database provider's problem, and any reputable provider should also do its best to minimise problems of data formats, integrity and accuracy. Data volume may be a problem, especially as it often has a direct impact on data cost, and data timeliness may also be a problem; there is an inevitable time lag with regard to the compilation of industry-wide data compared to internal data. Nevertheless, it mainly comes down to the question of whether the manager (or their organisation) is willing to pay the cost of the desired data (assuming it is available, that is).

To sum up, we show what we believe to be the likelihood of problems for each of the seven characteristics when using commercial databases as a data source in Table 17.4.

Table 17.4 Likelihood of problems for the seven characteristics when the source is commercial databases

Data source: Commercial databases	
Characteristic	*Likelihood of problems*
Data security and privacy	Negligible
Data volume	Moderate
Data formats	Low
Data cost	High
Data integrity	Low
Data accuracy	Low
Data timeliness	Moderate

ON-LINE DATABASES

As we said earlier, we do not wish to get hung up on definitions here; there is some overlap between the middle three categories. The main difference in our minds between on-line and commercial databases is that these on-line databases are ones where the manager carries out operations to select the relevant data interactively. This is often called *on-line search*, although that term is slightly inconsistent with the terms we defined in Chapter 16. Some commercial databases may be on-line, but are still accessed in a prespecified manner, one example being market research reports in a predetermined format. On-line databases include:

- library catalogues
- *LEXIS* (legal data)
- *FAME* (Financial Analysis Made Easy – company financial data)
- directories of patents
- directories of business organisations.

The use of on-line databases tends to split into two stages:

- Stage 1 – Setting up criteria and selecting the data that match them.
- Stage 2 – Downloading the results.

It is wise for the manager to finish stage 1 to their satisfaction before carrying out stage 2. On-line databases are often very large; this comprehensiveness is one of the main reasons for using them. When working with such large databases, it is sensible to count the number of records that meet the selection criteria before attempting to list or download the record contents. This is standard practice, for example, when doing literature searches on a library's bibliographic database. If the count reveals that too many records meet the selection criteria, then further criteria may be added. This prevents unnecessary downloading expense, but increases selection time. Thus data volume is likely to be a problem, more so than for the commercial databases, because the manager must cope with it themselves. Data cost is also likely to be a key problem, because of the time and the data volumes involved; the manager should check whether they are being charged by subscription, by connect time, by number of records downloaded, or some combination of the three.

For similar reasons, i.e. that the manager is doing more of the work, data formats and data accuracy may be more of a problem than for the commercial databases.

You might think that the one characteristic in which on-line databases would clearly be superior to commercial databases would be data timeliness, but this is not necessarily so. Although on-line databases do allow up-to-the-second access to the data that are stored in the database, the sheer size of many on-line databases means that there is often a substantial delay before the data are actually entered into the database.

To sum up, we show what we believe to be the likelihood of problems for each of the seven characteristics when using on-line databases as a data source in Table 17.5. Comparison with Table 17.4 shows that, overall, problems are more likely when using on-line databases than when using commercial databases. The compensations are those of being in control of the selection, and of not being restricted to preformatted reports. However, only on rare occasions will the same data be available from both commercial and on-line sources so that the manager has to make this trade-off decision directly.

Table 17.5 Likelihood of problems for the seven characteristics when the source is on-line databases

Data source: On-line databases	
Characteristic	*Likelihood of problems*
Data security and privacy	Negligible
Data volume	High
Data formats	Moderate
Data cost	High
Data integrity	Low
Data accuracy	Moderate
Data timeliness	Moderate

DATABASES ON CD-ROM

The CD-ROM is revolutionising the computer storage industry in much the same way that the CD has almost completely replaced the vinyl record in the music industry. It has not had quite the same far-reaching effects yet, because as the name CD-ROM (compact disc read-only memory) implies, it is read only. That means that the data on the CD-ROM cannot be altered or added to after it has been produced (without specialist equipment). A really successful CD format offering the capabilities to write as well as read data appears to be just around the corner at the time of writing. Nevertheless, CD-ROMs are an excellent way to distribute data that are to be used for reference, and much data that would formerly have been available only from commercial or on-line databases is now available on CD-ROM. Typically this is from the same providers, too.

There are other products more specific to CD-ROM. The CD-ROM has transformed the newspaper and magazine archive industry, so that it is now possible to acquire the full text of articles in publications such as the *Financial Times* or *The Economist* on CD-ROM. Although a CD-ROM encyclopaedia such as Microsoft *Encarta* or the *Hutchinson Multimedia Encyclopaedia* is more likely to be of interest to the manager at home rather than at work, the existence of such data sources should not be forgotten, especially where highly aggregated data on general topics such as populations are what is required.

The benefits of data on CD-ROM are that they are under the manager's control, unlike the commercial databases, and that the cost is not affected by how long it takes to select and download the data, unlike on-line databases. Data cost may still be an issue – CD-ROM databases are far from cheap – but data volume and data formats are not likely to be problematic. Data integrity is also helped by the fact that the data on the CD-ROM cannot be changed, thus avoiding virus and overwriting problems, although it is still possible to damage a CD-ROM, or indeed lose one!

Faster CD-ROM drives and larger hard disks mean that data volume is no longer a major problem for most users.[3]

The main drawback is, of course, in data timeliness: the data can only be updated by replacing the CD-ROM with another one. Often such a service is available from the data provider, but only at an increased cost. This is in addition to any delays in the compilation of this external data, as with commercial and on-line databases.

To sum up, we show what we believe to be the likelihood of problems for each of the seven characteristics when using CD-ROM databases as a data source in Table 17.6. Whatever the problems, as the inclusion of a CD-ROM drive in new personal computers has now become more or less standard, the market for CD-ROM databases must surely increase. This ought to lead to a consequent drop in price and a broader range of databases becoming available from this source.

Table 17.6 Likelihood of problems for the seven characteristics when the source is databases on CD-ROM

Data source: Databases on CD-ROM	
Characteristic	*Likelihood of problems*
Data security and privacy	Negligible
Data volume	Low
Data formats	Low
Data cost	High
Data integrity	Low
Data accuracy	Moderate
Data timeliness	High

THE INTERNET AND THE WORLD WIDE WEB (WWW)

It seems no exaggeration to claim that the growth of the Internet and the World Wide Web has been one of the major historical events of the 1990s. Many of the previous categories of data may nowadays be accessed via the Internet and/or the World Wide Web. This includes many of the commercial and on-line databases, and even some of the corporate data may be accessed using the same technology, usually referred to as an 'intranet' rather than the Internet. This means using a Web *browser*, a package such as Microsoft Internet Explorer or Netscape Navigator that enables the user to find particular Web *pages* or *sites*. The *page* is the Web equivalent of a data table, although it is much less restricted in layout, including pictures and sound as well as text. A *site* is a collection of pages stored on the same file server (or group of servers). The *home page* of a site is the one that explains what other pages there are on that site. Each page has its own URL (universal resource locator), the Web equivalent of a telephone number. URLs look like these:

> http://www.abs.aston.ac.uk
> http://www.lboro.ac.uk/departments/bs/

These are the home pages for Aston Business School and Loughborough University Business School respectively.

Progress in this area is so fast that almost anything we write now will be out of date tomorrow, never mind by the time you read it. Nevertheless, we feel that we must offer some advice, which we trust will prove useful.

The first piece of advice stems from the pace of change itself. Just because a manager may have found a useful source of data on the Web, they should not assume that it will be available in the same place the next time they look for it! Some sources are by their very nature ephemeral, for example pages by students at university or college. Even a reliable source such as a newspaper or 'household name' company may change the URL of its home page, or the way in which its Web site is organised, so that the manager can no longer find the information that they want. There is a trade-off here on which the manager must make up their own mind. If the manager *bookmarks* (saves the URL for) the site as a whole, then they will have to do more work to find the specific data they want, but the URL for the site is unlikely to change, especially if it is already a standard format. For example, the home page for most UK universities has a URL like

http://www.*name*.ac.uk

where *name* is an abbreviation of the university's name.

Similarly, for many companies the URL is:

http://www.*name*.com
or http://www.*name*.org
or http://www.*name*.co.uk   (for some UK companies)

Examples include http://www.ft.com for the *Financial Times* and http://www.telegraph.co.uk for the *Daily Telegraph*.

On the other hand, if the manager bookmarks the specific page, that may change whenever the site itself is reorganised. With the current state of sophistication of the Web, sites may well need to be reorganised fairly frequently, as the patterns of use become apparent. At the moment, for example, it seems that no one really understands exactly what people want from a Web site, except that it is clear different people want different things.

As if these problems of data integrity were not bad enough, there are also major potential problems of both data accuracy and data timeliness. The Web contains data on almost any conceivable topic, but its source could be anyone from a reputable market research agency to a pathological liar or someone deliberately aiming to cause confusion! Internet *search engines* (software that selects according to criteria) for data selection treat all sources equally; our advice is that the manager must try to judge the credibility of the source provider in order to judge the accuracy of the data. As for timeliness, the experimental nature of much Web activity at present means that data may not be up-dated rapidly, or indeed at all. We know of one software company, which shall remain nameless, that was still displaying its pricing information from June 1995 in October 1996, even though some of the packages listed were no longer even available, never mind the prices being out of date!

Data volume, in sorting the wheat from the chaff, may well also be a problem with the World Wide Web. Data security and privacy raise just one specific issue, related to that of data accuracy; as the manager cannot always tell who is responsible for the data on a particular page, they cannot tell if the provider was entitled to put it there, or indeed if they themselves are entitled to read it!

The attractions of the World Wide Web are that data cost is low compared to the other sources, and that data formats are becoming more standard. We would expect the World Wide Web HTML (HyperText Mark-up Language) standard file format to be added to the list we gave earlier under 'data formats' in new releases of spreadsheet packages.

Literally during the course of us writing this chapter, it has been revealed that the next versions of the market-leading spreadsheets to appear will be able to include formulae in cells that refer to particular URLs on the World Wide Web. Given what we have already said about the transient nature of URLs at present, our guess is that this is most likely to be useful for retrieving data via 'intranets' – systems within an organisation that use the same technology as the Internet. In such a case, the facility to include a URL in a formula is more like an addition to the file or medium formats available under the 'corporate data' heading.

The Web's other major advantage – the inclusion of sound, video, animation and links to other Web pages – is not yet of great benefit in terms of providing data for spreadsheet models.

To sum up, we show what we believe to be the likelihood of problems for each of the seven characteristics when using the Internet/World Wide Web as a data source in Table 17.7.

Table 17.8 summarises the likelihood of problems arising with each of the seven data characteristics in a single table, i.e. the information in Tables 17.2–17.7. Remember that, as we said before, this can only be a general list, to indicate what needs to be thought about carefully with each data source. It is not the same as a list of the importance of particular characteristics in a particular case. There may, for example, be models where the timeliness of the data is of paramount importance, or where the importance of the data justifies a 'money no object' approach to data cost.

Table 17.7 Likelihood of problems for the seven characteristics when the source is Internet/World Wide Web

Data source: Internet/World Wide Web	
Characteristic	*Likelihood of problems*
Data security and privacy	Moderate
Data volume	High
Data formats	Moderate
Data cost	Low
Data integrity	High
Data accuracy	High
Data timeliness	High

Table 17.8 Summary of Exhibits 17.2–17.7

Characteristic	Personal data	Corporate data	Commercial databases	On-line databases	Databases on CD-ROM	Internet/World Wide Web
	Likelihood of problems	*Likelihood of problems*	*Likelihood of problems*	*Likelihood of problems*	*Likelihood of problems*	*Likelihood of problems*
Data security and privacy	Low	High	Negligible	Negligible	Negligible	Moderate
Data volume	Moderate	High	Moderate	High	Low	High
Data formats	Low	High	Low	Moderate	Low	Moderate
Data cost	Negligible	Negligible	High	High	High	Low
Data integrity	High	Moderate	Low	Low	Low	High
Data accuracy	Low	High	Low	Moderate	Moderate	High
Data timeliness	High	Low	Moderate	Moderate	High	High

WORKING WITH SOURCES OF DATA

In the previous sections, we have highlighted what we believe to be the main problems associated with data from different sources. Each type of source has its advantages and disadvantages; there is no overall best choice. What the manager must do is to make the appropriate trade-offs about the data for the particular spreadsheet model that they would like to build. This will depend on the manager's circumstances, the organisation's circumstances, and even the manager's personal preferences. For example, if a spreadsheet model is developed while a manager is away from the office, it may not be possible to use some or all external sources of data.

It is also worth bearing in mind that any data that is not personal data may need to be downloaded to the manager's own PC before it can be accessed by the spreadsheet model. This will then raise minor issues of maintaining the data, although not to the same extent as for 'real' personal data, since it can always be recreated from the original source. This is most likely in the case of commercial, on-line and Internet/World Wide Web sources, and may also apply to some corporate data from legacy systems.

In general, the trade-offs the manager can make between different sources for a given set of data are limited. For example, most of the personal data and corporate data are simply not available from any other source. The guidance we now offer relating to the four activities of maintaining data, accessing data, understanding data and relying on data, described earlier, is therefore so that the manager may be aware of the likely difficulties with each activity. It will also help on the rare occasions when a direct trade-off decision between different data sources is possible.

Maintaining data is very much the key activity for personal data. If this is done well enough, then most of the problems associated with accessing and relying on personal data should also be avoided. Since there should be few problems of understanding personal data, the importance of maintaining personal data becomes apparent. The manager needs to worry especially about data security and privacy, data integrity and data timeliness when maintaining personal data. With the other data sources, maintaining the data is not the manager's problem.

Accessing data from the other five sources raises two more general and two more specific issues. The first general issue is that the less structured, more flexible sources of data (corporate, on-line and Internet/World Wide Web) may give the manager problems in dealing with the data volumes involved. The second is that the use of any commercial, on-line or CD-ROM data sources is likely to require a data cost/timeliness trade-off by the manager, especially if similar data are available from more than one of these sources. More specifically, gatekeepers may hinder access to corporate data, either deliberately or accidentally, causing the manager problems with data security, accuracy or integrity; and the World Wide Web's dubious data quality may simply make it impossible for the manager to find data that 'ought to be there somewhere'.

Understanding data, as we have said, should not be a problem with personal data; nor should it be a problem for any commercial data source worthy of the name. In principle, the same should be true of on-line and CD-ROM data sources, although in practice the more flexible retrieval these sources offer puts more onus on the manager to ensure that they have understood the definitions of the data correctly. Corporate data sources, strange as it may seem, may raise greater problems for the manager here, especially those of data formats with some legacy systems, and data accuracy problems simply because one part of an organisation does not define a term in quite the same way that another part does. A commercial database provider has to sort out such anomalies before making the data available, but corporate data may often be left for many years in such a state. We know of one case where a manager, on taking up a new post, requested a particular report about their department from a legacy system, and was surprised to find that the data in it bore no resemblance at all to the real situation. Further enquiries revealed that this was the first time that report had been asked for since the system was installed five years earlier!

The World Wide Web is at present in a class of its own when it comes to understanding data – at the bottom, that is. All the problems already mentioned for corporate data may arise, especially if the manager's spreadsheet package deals with .htm or HTML format files as if they were text files; this is likely to 'mangle' the layout of any tables and omit any graphs completely. The issue of deliberately incorrect data also arises with this source.

Finally, relying on data raises perhaps the greatest range of issues according to the different sources, many similar to those mentioned for the other three activities. Commercial, on-line and CD-ROM databases all raise the cost/timeliness trade-off again, with the timeliness of CD-ROM data a particular point. There is also the added question of the manager's willingness to make a long-term (financial) commitment to a particular source of data. In the current state of the market, it would be prudent to consider the financial health of the supplier, if the data are really important to the manager's organisation. With corporate data, data accuracy may decrease over time because definitions used in other parts of the organisation change, and it is also possible that data volume may become a problem even if it is not one initially, especially if computers are relatively new to the organisation. Finally, the World Wide Web's constantly changing URLs also pose a potential data-quality problem.

SUMMARY

In this chapter, we have looked at the main activities associated with the longer-term use of data in spreadsheet models, identifying them as maintaining data, accessing data, understanding data and relying on data. We then described seven characteristics of data that may give rise to problems in carrying out these activities: data security and privacy, data volume, data formats, data cost, data integrity, data accuracy and data timeliness. These characteristics were then examined for the six different data sources of personal data, corporate data, commercial databases, on-line databases, databases on CD-ROM and the Internet/World Wide Web. Finally, we attempted to make the connection back to the four activities.

END NOTES

1 It may, for example, depend on what might be called organisational perspective. One insurance company had traditionally measured the time it took to process new policy applications as the time its staff spent working on them; a matter of a few hours, or perhaps a day or two for complex cases. Then someone asked how long it took from the customer's perspective. The answer turned out to be measured in weeks; the applications spent most of their time waiting in in-trays! The insight gained from this change of perspective led to a radical redesign of the way in which applications were processed – and a tremendous improvement in the time taken (from the customer's perspective, of course).

2 For those who prefer to take the more optimistic view, the early 1970s computer technology on board the Voyager spacecraft, that is now on its way out of the solar system into the wider universe, was reprogrammed many times during the mission and the hardware made to do things of which its designers could hardly have dreamt.

3 In the early days of CD-ROM databases it was a problem, because the typical CD-ROM capacity of 660 megabytes was far greater than the personal computer with, say, a 100 megabyte hard disk normally had to deal with. Now that hard disks with sizes measured in gigabytes are the norm, this is no longer the case.

FURTHER READING

There is little that we can recommend by way of reading specific to the topics covered in this chapter, although if you are not familiar with the Internet and World Wide Web it might be worth getting hold of one of the many introductory books about them. A more useful activity, once you have particular data in mind, would be to go and discuss potential sources for that data with your information specialist or librarian (for external data) or your information systems department (for corporate data).

1 Maintaining data is only likely to be a major issue for the manager with one data source; which one is it?

2 At the present stage of its development, what is the biggest problem with the Internet/World Wide Web as a data source?

3 If the same or similar data are available from a commercial database, an on-line database and a database on CD-ROM, what is the main trade-off that a manager would have to make in deciding which of these sources of data to use?

Think of three spreadsheet models that you have built, or would like to build. Then answer the following questions.

4 Identify the sources of the data for these models.

5 What are the major problems likely to be with these data sources in your particular case?

6 How would you go about making the trade-offs between data sources?

CHAPTER 18

Beyond the spreadsheet

Chapter aims The aim of this chapter is to look beyond the spreadsheet as we have discussed it so far, in two senses. The first is to consider other software that a manager might wish to use for building decision support systems, especially spreadsheet add-ins; this will summarise and extend what has been said in the individual chapters of Part Two. The second is to speculate on what extra facilities are likely to become available in spreadsheet packages in the near future. Naturally, these two overlap to some extent.

- Introduction
- Beyond the spreadsheet
  - Add-ins for financial modelling • Add-ins for database work • Add-ins to help with building and using the spreadsheet model • Other add-ins
- Beyond current spreadsheet packages
- What if I need more?

INTRODUCTION

The main intention in this book has been to look at ways in which the spreadsheet can be used to help managers to handle the issues they face in their organisations, by building and exploring appropriate models of parts of the local scenario. However, it is clearly impossible to cover the whole of this topic in one book. The main part of this chapter is divided into two sections, in each of which we look at one of two areas in which you, the reader, may wish to pursue the topic further.

The first, and longer section, 'Beyond the spreadsheet', looks at other software that a manager might wish to use for building decision support systems, especially spreadsheet add-ins.

We trust it has become clear by this stage in the book that the spreadsheet is not the only tool that can be used for modelling the local scenario, although it is certainly the most commonly available and most familiar, perhaps the cheapest and for many people the easiest to use. However, we have already seen in Part Two that there will be times when the manager needs to go beyond the spreadsheet; to use other software in order to build an adequate model for decision support. This will be because the issue in question has some or all of the following characteristics:

- It is too complex for a spreadsheet model.
- It is too specialised for a spreadsheet model.

- It is too novel for a spreadsheet model.
- It needs to be shared with other people who are more familiar with other software than with spreadsheets.

In the first section of this chapter we review some of the likely directions in which the manager might need to go, summarising what we have said in earlier chapters and also mentioning some other packages not covered so far. We concentrate on packages available as add-ins to current spreadsheet packages, since these do not require the manager to learn to use a new interface.

Finally, in a more speculative mood, in the second section, 'Beyond current spreadsheet packages', we try to guess what improvements are likely to appear in new versions of spreadsheet packages in the near future, and how they will affect model building for decision support.

BEYOND THE SPREADSHEET

In previous Part Two chapters, the 'What if I need more?' sections have mentioned various specialised software packages. Here we are concentrating specifically on add-ins that can be used directly with a spreadsheet package; the advantage being that the manager does not need to learn a new human interface. One point that we should make is that, although there are at least 20 different spreadsheet packages on the market for various different hardware and operating systems, the great majority of add-ins are available only for a PC running DOS/Windows, and to work with one or more of the 'big three' PC spreadsheets (Microsoft Excel, Lotus 1-2-3 and Quattro Pro). Managers who use other spreadsheet packages and platforms will find a much narrower range of offerings. Note also that the add-ins available range from commercial software costing over £1000 to 'shareware' – software that is distributed freely and relies on the honesty of the purchaser to make a donation to its developer. A wise manager should not discount the use of shareware, especially for a one-off and highly specific issue, but many information systems departments may have quite justifiable reservations about the use of such software on company computers.

The add-ins that we have already mentioned are @Risk and Crystal Ball for risk analysis and simulation and What's Best! for solving. The latest versions of Crystal Ball are now being marketed as suitable for forecasting as well, using the curve-fitting facilities that were originally included to find the best probability distribution to represent the pattern of uncertainty for a particular variable. @Risk also includes facilities of that kind.

Add-ins for financial modelling

Looking at other add-ins, the most highly developed area is that of financial modelling, as is only to be expected given the spreadsheet's original development to meet the needs of accountants and financial managers. Generally these add-ins simplify 'What if?' analysis by including extra built-in functions specific to particular tasks; in our terms, these are ready-made sections of logic model.

They may also include improved facilities for constructing summary models. We give a little more detail on four of them: FinancialCAD, Options @nalyst, Bond @nalyst and BPS. These are chosen simply to indicate the range available; there are many others.

FinancialCAD offers detailed financial modelling functions covering all kinds of investments from bonds through to commodities, and specifics such as options, futures and so on. It also has risk analysis functions built in, to handle uncertainty, and includes a wide range of picture-display facilities.

Options @nalyst offers much the same range of extra built-in functions as Financial CAD and has the wonderfully named Exotic Basket, Exotic Barrier and Exotic Asian/Lookback advanced versions for use with specific financial markets and types of investment.

Bond @nalyst is more specific and so less generally appealing, working with another specific type of investment – fixed income instruments. Unlike many add-ins, it is also available for the Apple Macintosh.

BPS takes the 'ready-made sections of the logic model' approach even further. Rather than simply offering extra built-in functions, it aims to be a complete financial modelling package; i.e. a prespecified logic model that enables financial modelling and 'What if?' analysis to be done by merely specifying what the variables of interest are (excuse the pun) and where the values of the data model are to be found. Obviously this is less flexible than some of the other add-ins, but it would save a great deal of time for a manager whose issue fits BPS's structure.

Add-ins for database work

The other large area of the add-in market is that for database retrieval. The add-ins here take many forms, but by and large perform the same tasks as we have already discussed in Chapter 16. Their common aim is to simplify and speed up tasks when dealing with large volumes of data. For example, SQLPro Agent is designed to retrieve data from very large databases for use in a spreadsheet; FlexFilter is a tool to simplify and speed up highly complex selection and sorting activities; and Informer extends the capabilities of report tables to allow the inclusion of formulae (we discussed the trade-off between report tables and the use of built-in functions in Chapter 16). IDD Plus combines this category and the previous one, by allowing on-line retrieval of data on financial securities through the use of built-in functions.

As in the previous category, there are many other add-ins available.

Add-ins to help with building and using the spreadsheet model

A few add-ins are specific to the problems faced by model builders and users. We mention three here: Spreadsheet Professional, Top Rank, and Baler.

Spreadsheet Professional includes facilities for helping to verify and validate spreadsheet models that go far beyond those provided by the spreadsheet package itself. These include tests for errors and the production of audit trails. It also contains facilities for producing input forms (see Chapter 16), and has a novel tool to help understand other people's spreadsheets, which attempts to produce a verbalisation of the model from the formulation! This is advertised as 'Translates calculations into English'.

Top Rank carries out the more specific, but equally useful, task of displaying pictures of *sensitivity analysis* for any spreadsheet model, to show which input factors have the greatest impact on a given calculated variable. Remember that we identified this as one of the key features of the risk analysis/simulation add-ins in Chapters 10 and 11, as well as discussing sensitivity analysis in solving in Chapter 12.

Baler, now Visual Baler in its Windows version, enables a spreadsheet model to be *compiled*, i.e. turned into a self-contained piece of executable software that does not need to be connected to the spreadsheet package at all. This means that the spreadsheet model can:

- run faster
- not be altered unintentionally
- be distributed free of charge if desired
- be used without a copy of the originating spreadsheet package.

This is of great use to anyone who needs to develop a spreadsheet model that has to be used, but not modified, by others. However, we suspect that relatively few managers will have such a need.

Other add-ins

Again, we can only scratch the surface here. For the mathematically trained manager, there is MathLink to exchange data between Excel and Mathematica, the leading computer algebra package. There is the fascinating MapLand software add-in, that enables spreadsheet summary models to be displayed in the form of geographically accurate maps. There is Schedule Master for scheduling, SQC for statistical quality control, Sapling for decision tree analysis, and there are many others. To form a link between this section and the next, our final example is an add-in for a very new modelling technique.

Evolver is a an add-in that performs similar tasks to the spreadsheet's solver (see Chapter 12), but by using genetic algorithms; these are a product of artificial intelligence research rather than the mathematical methods used in the solver.[1] The advantage of a genetic algorithm is that it makes fewer assumptions about the nature of the relationship between the variables. As with the solver, there must be input factors whose values are allowed to change, a calculated variable that is used to measure how good the solution is, and some constraints that make finding a good solution difficult! Unlike the solver, a genetic algorithm is not restricted to relationships expressed as arithmetical functions, but can include results returned by relationships of any kind that can be entered as a formula in a spreadsheet cell, even look-up tables or external database queries. Remember that in Chapters 5, 12 and 15 we discussed the issue of linearity and non-linearity; not only can genetic algorithms cope with non-linearity, they can also handle much worse problems, such as some of the values in the data model being missing. The only necessity is that the manager has plenty of patience, because it can take a long time for good solutions to evolve, even on a very fast and powerful PC, because this approach is very close to 'trial and error'. The manager also has to accept that it may be very difficult to see why the genetic algorithm's solution is a good one, so that any changes in the data set may make it necessary to rerun the entire modelling process from scratch. Examples of the use of genetic algorithms in warehouse location, production scheduling and portfolio optimisation have been reported.

BEYOND CURRENT SPREADSHEET PACKAGES

Finally, we gaze into our crystal ball (not the package mentioned in the previous section!) and try to speculate on the future of spreadsheet packages. Two trends in the history of spreadsheet functionality have been quite consistent. The first is a continuing increase in the number of built-in functions. The second is a tendency for spreadsheets to absorb the capabilities of specialised packages. What has tended to happen on the latter front is the following:

1 First, a modelling capability of some kind is only available in a specialised package.
2 Then it becomes available as an add-in for the major spreadsheet packages.
3 Finally, it becomes part of the functionality of spreadsheet packages.

The most visible example of this happening has been with the solver. In the early 1980s, the facilities offered by the solver were only available in specialised packages such as LINDO and GINO. Then the add-in What's Best! appeared in the late 1980s, using the LINDO calculating 'engine' but able to work with Lotus 1-2-3 and Microsoft Excel. Now in the 1990s, solver facilities have become standard in all the leading spreadsheet packages.

Similar processes have occurred with database facilities and with regression, although in both these cases the add-ins had less time to succeed before being overtaken by the facilities incorporated in the spreadsheet packages.

Our guess is that in the next couple of years this process may be most apparent with the risk-analysis add-ins. As we mentioned in Chapter 10, built-in functions that allow sampling from named probability distributions such as NORMALINV are beginning to appear in the latest versions of spreadsheet packages. This is a significant step on the road to including easy-to-use risk-analysis capabilities, but easier facilities for producing summary models and carrying out sensitivity analysis are also needed.

The second-best candidate as an area for progress may be improved verification and validation capabilities, of the kind offered by Spreadsheet Professional.

Better facilities for on-line database access are also likely to appear; we have already said in Chapter 17 that direct access to a World Wide Web URL from a spreadsheet cell is to be available in the new versions currently being tested.

Forecasting *ought* to be a strong candidate for improved facilities in spreadsheets, but here the specialised packages are more strongly developed and so add-ins have always had a harder task in trying to establish a market. As we mentioned in Chapter 15, some of the leading spreadsheet packages are now in fact capable of generating forecasts with little intervention by the manager, but the assumptions made in building the forecasting model are usually left unstated.

The final possibility is a rather different direction to the usual trends. This one comes from outside the spreadsheet world altogether. One of the reasons that spreadsheet modelling has been so successful in business organisations is that specialised database packages were designed for data handling rather than modelling. Most of them do have extensive model-building facilities, but these are not easy for a manager who is not a computing expert to use. Database vendors have realised this threat to their market, and commissioned relational database guru Ted Codd to do for decision support what he had done for databases. Codd's contribution was OLAP, which stands for On-Line Analytical Processing. The intention is to extend the data-modelling techniques of specialised database packages to handle logic models better.[2] One of the key concepts in OLAP is that of the user-analyst, regularly doing new things with existing data. To us, this sounds very much like the manager as model builder, whom we identified as the target readership for this book. OLAP packages for use with the specialised database packages used in the 'engine room' systems of organisations are now available. It will be interesting to see if this begins to work its way into the spreadsheet field in the way that the use of SQL for queries from large databases has done.

To conclude this section, we believe that the evolution that we have described here means that the spreadsheet, as part of an integrated suite of software, will more and more become the manager's point of entry to the IT infrastructure – of their own and of other organisations. This can only mean that spreadsheet model-building skills will become even more important to the manager of the future.

WHAT IF I NEED MORE?

In a way, this whole chapter addresses this question. However, in such a fast-moving field there are one or two specific pieces of extra advice that we can give. One is to talk to other people – at work, at university or college, at any professional societies to which you belong. Find out whether they have any ideas that you could use; you may also find that you have ideas they can use! Many academic and professional societies also organise meetings on topics relating to spreadsheet models, for example the Operational Research Society (telephone +44 (0)121-233 9300; URL http://www.orsoc.org.uk), the British Computer Society (telephone +44 (0)1793 480269; URL http://www.bcs.org.uk) and the various professional accounting bodies.

Another avenue that you would be well advised to follow in order to keep up with what modelling software is available as spreadsheet add-ins is to obtain the catalogues provided by organisations such as Eastern Software Publishing Ltd (telephone +44 (0)1206 44456; URL http://www.ip7.co.uk/eastern).

SUMMARY

In this chapter we have tried to look beyond the earlier material in two senses. First, we looked at spreadsheet add-ins, especially those for financial modelling and for working with databases; and second, we speculated on what improvements future versions of spreadsheet packages may offer.

Whatever the future may hold, the best way to learn about spreadsheet models is to build them and use them. We hope you find it enjoyable and rewarding to do just that!

END NOTES

1 The name *genetic algorithm* comes from the idea of 'survival of the fittest' in biological evolution. What happens is that a population of different solutions compete with each other to survive into the next generation; at each step, the next generation's population is produced by applying various changes to the members of the existing population, to mimic the effects of breeding and mutation. Fortunately, no more knowledge of genetics is needed than this to use a genetic algorithm package.

2 Codd described this as 'a new category of database processing not allowed for in the relational model'.

APPENDIX A

The Readyread Printing and Publishing Company

Case Part A: A simple trading account

The Readyread Printing and Publishing Company produces one type of book for the children's market. It manufactures and sells this book (and no others) in the UK.

It is the end of 1996. You are the chief executive of Readyread and you have already built a spreadsheet to produce a simple trading account for the next three years. (Inflation has not been included.) The data used is as in Table A.1.

The model calculates the *Sales revenue*, *Total variable costs*, *Profit*, *Profit per month* and *Percentage change in profit from year to year*.

(Note: this is exactly the same spreadsheet as asked for in the Exercises in Chapter 5. If you haven't already built this spreadsheet, this is your **first assignment**.)

Case Part B: Modelling material costs

You now become concerned about the raw materials costs and plan to extend the simple trading account to include a module to calculate these costs. This is your **second assignment**.

The situation is as follows. Each book is made up from one large sheet of paper. After cutting and folding it is bound, using glue and staples, into a thick board cover. Inks of several colours are used in the printing of both the sheet and the cover.

Waste has been around 5 per cent for paper and around 2 per cent for board. In 1996 the costs and usages of paper and board were as given in Table A.2.

Table A.1

	1997	1998	1999
Sales estimates (million)	2.7	3.0	3.0
Sales price (£)	5	5	5
Raw materials costs (pence/book)	40	40	40
Royalty (pence/book)	75	80	80
Labour costs (pence/book)	170	180	180
Fixed costs (thousand £)	5000	5200	5600

Table A.2 Materials costs

	Material cost (£/unit)	Usage per 1000 books (excluding waste)
Paper	£150/ream	2.0 reams
Board	£550/tonne	200 square metres
Sundries	£1 per 1000 books	

Note: 100 square metres of board weigh 1 tonne.

Case Part C: Modelling labour costs

You realise that you are unable to predict the labour costs associated with the production of the books. You want the spreadsheet to calculate the labour costs for a variety of situations, particularly for the 2.7 million books that the sales director expects to sell during the year. In his more expansive moments, the sales director has also mentioned the possibility of selling 3.3 million books. Extending the spreadsheet to incorporate labour-cost modules for the printing and binding sections is your **third assignment**.

In the past, sales estimates have been at considerable variance with actual sales. Over the last four years, sales of books have remained fairly constant at around 2.5 million p.a.

The sales forecasts for these years are given in Table A.3.

It can be considered that there are two activities involved in the production of a book: printing and binding. The operation is so organised that the printing section prints all the pages of one book in the form of a large, single sheet. Thus the number of sheets printed would form the 'insides' of the same number of books. The business is of such a form that both the quantity of work in progress and the amount of finished goods stock held are insignificant.

The staffing requirements and the labour costs associated with the printing and binding sections are set out below.

Staffing requirements in the printing section

The printing section has four printing machines, each capable of producing 1 million sheets per year. Thus the maximum number of sheets that can be printed in normal working is 4 million.

Each printing machine needs a crew to run it. There are eight skilled craftsmen per crew, each of whose cost to Readyread in 1997 is expected to be £30 000 p.a. These craftsmen have been difficult to replace when lay-offs have been followed by a pick-up of trade, and management is keen to keep enough

Table A.3 Sales forecasts

Year	Sales (millions)
1993	2.8
1994	2.4
1995	2.6
1996	2.2

craftsmen to run all four machines. In practice, because of sickness and holidays, this means keeping five crews in all. Crews have never worked overtime.

Also employed in the printing section are 20 'print assistants'. These assistants are responsible for loading machines with paper, collecting sheets etc. The production manager has stressed that the number of assistants does not vary with the level of output, but they work overtime when production is over 3 million sheets per year. Each assistant is expected to cost the company £20 000 p.a. in 1997 (excluding overtime). Overtime is paid at time and a half.

It would be possible, without much effort, to purchase new printing machinery. A new printing machine capable of printing 1 million sheets p.a. would cost around £500 000.

Staffing requirements in the binding section

When producing 2.7 million books p.a., the production manager believes that roughly 100 people would be needed. (There is not the split between craftsmen and assistants as there is in the printing section.) Each of these employees is expected to cost the company £17 000 p.a. in 1997. Traditionally, overtime has never been worked.

The normal maximum binding capacity is 3 million books p.a., using three machines, each with a capacity of 1 million p.a. With a lot of effort, although at no extra cost, this can be increased to 3.5 million books p.a.

When pressed, the production manager has indicated that the number of people he would require for production volumes at and around 2.7 million p.a. would be as given in Table A.4.

Table A.4 Binding staff requirements

Production volume (million p.a.)	People required
2.0	75
2.5	90
2.7	100
3.0	110
3.5	130

He says that it is very important to have these numbers of people available to produce these volumes. This can be difficult, as absenteeism is running at around 20 per cent.

The assignment

You are required to produce a spreadsheet model of the situation described, in order to be in a position to answer 'What if?' questions about the situation.

It is suggested that you:

1 Read and understand the case.
2 Develop an understanding of the spreadsheet package you intend to use.
3 Follow the modelling methodology of Chapter 5 to construct first an information flow diagram and then a verbalisation.

4 Enter the model into the spreadsheet incorporating the 'good practice' suggested in Chapter 7.

5 Use the resulting spreadsheet decision support system to answer such questions as the following:

- What are the total costs for labour if the output required is 3.2 million books?
- What is the average labour cost per book if the skilled printing-crew workers are paid at a rate of £35 000 p.a.?

Strongarm Arcade Games Inc (A)

Strongarm Arcade Games Inc is a UK company engaged in renting electronic games of the 'space invader' type to pubs and clubs. Strongarm are developing a new pub game called Mutant Mania which they are planning to release in January. You are a member of a small management team which has been set up by the chief executive to assess the strategy that Strongarm should use when selling Mutant Mania into the pubs and clubs game market.

The team consists of the sales, marketing, production and personnel managers, and the chief management accountant.

Because the chief executive is known to be very prone to asking 'What if?' questions, the group has decided to develop a computer model that will allow sensitivity analysis to be performed.

The sales and marketing position

The sales and marketing manager believes that the new game is such an advance on current games that it offers the opportunity of expanding the market and Strongarm's market share. She also believes that Strongarm will have a year's grace after the launch of Mutant Mania before competition reacts in force and then the rental that can be charged will fall to the industry average (expected to be £15 per week in January).

Strongarm is planning to recruit new salespeople for December when the new salesforce will attend an intensive training course. Thus the new salesforce will be ready to begin selling at the beginning of January. It is reckoned that each salesperson will be able to make an average of 150 visits to pubs and clubs per month (taking into account illness and leave entitlement).

The number of potential outlets for Mutant Mania is extremely large, and the sales and marketing manager reckons that three out of every ten visits will result in a sale. The after sales service for Mutant Mania includes a revisit to the outlet three months after the sale.

The production position

The maximum production level in any given month is reckoned to be 3000, with unit costs of £300 per machine.

The financial position

The financial implications of the move to produce and market Mutant Mania are not trivial for Strongarm.

Each salesperson has an associated company cost of £10 000 p.a. This is also paid in full during training. Additionally, each salesperson costs a further £1000 while being trained.

The rental from each of the Mutant Mania machines is estimated to be around £25 per week for the first year.

The problem

You have drawn the short straw. Your brief is to develop a spreadsheet model to work out the costs and show the consequences associated with producing and selling the Mutant Mania machines into the new outlets.

The chief executive is known to be sceptical about the whole project and is only willing to look as far as the end of the second year after the launch for results. One thing he has said is that he wants to see the sensitivity of the costs to the assumptions made, e.g. how sensitive is the cash flow to changes in staff level, uptake rate of Mutant Mania, rental charge etc.

The assignment

Develop a spreadsheet model that can be used to investigate various selling strategies. Your answer should contain conceptualisation and verbalisation sections. To obtain a good mark you must specify the assumptions you have made and you must list all the relationships that enter your model. You should indicate the scope of sensitivity analysis possible with your model by including some examples of such analysis and discussing them, but you are not expected to anticipate every single analysis that the chief executive might want. You must use a spreadsheet and your answer must include a diskette copy of your model.

Note that in the Strongarm problem, certain features appear imprecise. This is intentional to encourage scenario building. You are free to add elements to the problem statement.

Credit will be given for the layout of the model, e.g. use of separate pages for the various parts of the model, names used for variables rather than (meaningless) cell references, graphical displays of important information, good use of colour etc.

In summary, the requirement is:

- Detail the conceptualisation and verbalisation stages of model development.
- Provide examples of sensitivity analysis carried out (i.e. printouts of model instances).
- Provide a diskette copy of model.

APPENDIX C

Strongarm Arcade Games Inc (B)

Strongarm Arcade Games Inc is a UK company engaged in renting electronic games of the 'space invader' type to pubs and clubs. Already Strongarm has its games installed in 20 per cent of the 300 000 pubs and clubs in the UK.

It is the beginning of July and Strongarm is planning to launch a new pub game called Mutant Mania in January. You are a member of a small management team which has been set up by the chief executive to assess the feasibility of further penetrating the pubs and clubs game market.

The team consists of the sales, marketing, production and personnel managers, and the chief management accountant.

Because the chief executive is known to be very prone to asking 'What if?' questions, the group has decided to develop a computer model that will allow sensitivity analysis to be performed.

The sales and marketing position

The sales and marketing manager believes that the new game is such an advance on current games that it offers the opportunity of expanding the market and Strongarm's market share. She also believes that Strongarm will have a year's grace after the launch of Mutant Mania before competition reacts in force and then the rental that can be charged will fall to the industry average.

The Sales and Marketing manager believes that she can sell into 20 per cent of the pubs and clubs where as yet Strongarm does not have a presence. Unfortunately, she does not know which of the 240 000 outlets to which she is not currently selling will take the new game. However, she does believe that she can categorise them as in Table C.1.

Table C.1 Categorisation of outlets

Class	Probability of renting MM	Number of outlets
A	0.4	80 000
B	0.2	55 000
C	0.1	105 000

Naturally, the sales and marketing manager intends her new salesforce to visit the class A outlets first, then the class B outlets and finally the class C outlets. Once an outlet decides to take the Mutant Mania machine, it must then be visited by the salesperson in all subsequent quarters; thus the number of new outlets that can be called on in later periods will reduce. If an outlet is visited and the visit is unsuccessful, no further visits are made to it.

The sell-in to new outlets cannot be achieved overnight, as the sales and marketing manager will need to recruit additional salespersons. She estimates that each salesperson will take one month to be trained, during which period they will not be selling. Thereafter they will be able to operate in the same way as a member of the established salesforce.

The production position

Production costs will vary with the number of machines purchased and with the output from the machines. Because of the novel nature of the assembly machines, the production manager feels that he can only hazard a guess at the unit production costs. Because of congestion, lack of skilled people etc., it is estimated that the least-cost and maximum levels of working shown in Table C.2 will apply.

With either one or two extra machines the production manager reckons that the unit costs will follow the curve shown in Fig C.1.

Table C.2 Levels of working

Extra machines	Least-cost output level (units/week)	Least cost unit production cost (£)	Maximum output (units/week)
1	400	200	800
2	600	220	1200

Fig C.1 Variation of unit production costs with production level

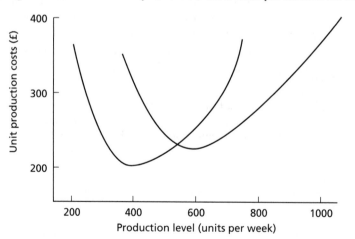

The financial position

The financial implications of the move to produce and market Mutant Mania are not trivial for Strongarm. Each assembly machine costs £500 000. Each salesperson has an associated company cost of £10 000 p.a. This is also paid in full during training. Additionally, each salesperson costs a further £1000 while being trained. The rental from each of the Mutant Mania machines is estimated to be around £25 per week, as compared to the industry standard of £15 for this type of game.

The issue

You have drawn the short straw – the team has asked you to build an appropriate spreadsheet to work out the costs and show the consequences associated with producing and selling the Mutant Mania machines into the new outlets. The chief executive is known to be sceptical about the whole project and is only willing to look as far as the end of the next year for results. One thing he has said is that he wants to see the sensitivity of the costs to the assumptions made.

The assignment

Your answer should contain conceptualisation and verbalisation sections. To obtain a good mark you must specify the assumptions you have made and you must list all the relationships that enter your model. You should indicate the scope of sensitivity analysis possible with your model by including some examples of such analysis and discussing them, but you are not expected to anticipate every single analysis that the chief executive might want. You must use a spreadsheet and your answer must include a computer printout of both the logic and data models. You should include a diskette copy of your model and a series of runs of selected scenarios. The package (including version number and computer, i.e. PC or Mac) you used for this assignment should also be clearly stated.

Note that in the Strongarm case, certain features appear imprecise. This is intentional to encourage scenario building.

APPENDIX D

Your own issue

If you choose to tackle an issue in your organisation certain provisos exist. These are:

- You must describe the issue clearly in an introductory section.
- The model must contain a minimum of 15 variables.
- At least two relationships between the variables must be 'judgemental', i.e. where you have modelled a relationship which is not known precisely. (Note: not imprecision in the value of a variable, but imprecision in the connection between variables.)
- The model must contain a minimum of ten relationships.

GLOSSARY OF TERMS

Absolving: deciding that a potential issue does not become an issue to be tackled.

Application system: a computer-based system to deliver processing power directly to an employee.

Argument: a value or a symbol used in a function. Sometimes an argument can be a range of values or a set of symbols.

Arithmetical operation: the process of working with or on one or more numbers. Examples are addition, multiplication and the calculation of a square root.

Base data model: data model under conditions of certainty used in the first stage of building risk-analysis spreadsheet models.

Base logic model: logic model under conditions of certainty used in the first stage of building risk-analysis spreadsheet models.

Bias: a measure of the systematic error in a piece of information.

Calculated variable: a variable whose value is calculated within the logic model.

Causal modelling: the modelling of the cause-and-effect relationships that govern the behaviour of a system.

Certainty: the situation in which an action always leads to a single known outcome.

Chart: the generic term used in the Microsoft Excel spreadsheet package to encompass all forms of non-numeric representations of information (pictures, graphs, diagrams).

Coefficient: the ratio of two or more factors.

Conceptualisation: the first stage in logic modelling in which the relationships between the model factors sketched out.

Confidence interval: are the two values between which a value applicable to a population can be expected to lie with a specified confidence when the value has been estimated from a sample.

Constant: a factor whose value is fixed.

Constraint: a limitation on the value that a variable can take.

Continuous variable: a variable that can take any values within a specified range.

Correlation: the degree of the relationship between the corresponding values of pairs of variables.

Correlation coefficient: a measure of how well a relationship fits the set of data values of two or more variables.

Cumulative frequency: the total frequency of all values in a data set or distribution less than or equal to a specified value. For a discrete variable, this is the total *number* of all values less than or equal to a specified value.

Data: those stimuli from outside the system that pass the rules embedded in the interface between the system and its surroundings.

Database: a formal collection of data.

Database management system: a set of computer programs used to create, maintain, access, update and protect one or more databases.

Data management: the efficient and effective disposition of data.

Data model: one of the major elements of a spreadsheet. It is made up of the values for all the input factors in the logic model.

Data privacy: concerned with the holding and access of personal data.

Data security: concerned with the general issue of unauthorised access to data.

Decision support system: a system that enhances decision making in conditions of high or ill-defined uncertainty, by evolving, structuring and evaluating relationships and/or options. Such systems take information as input, reconcile and mesh together these inputs to form intelligence.

Decision variable: a variable in the manager's system whose value they can alter.

Definitional relationship: a relationship that is as it is because it has been defined to be so.

Dependent variable: a variable whose value depends on the value of one or more other variables (the independent variables).

Descriptive statistics: measures that describe the features of a set of data.

Deterministic: a situation where the value of outcomes is known exactly.

Discrete variable: a variable that is restricted to taking only a set number of values.

Dissolving: occurs when conditions change or are changed so as to eliminate or fundamentally change an issue.

Empirical: an attribute that can be measured.

Empirical measure: one that will provide data. It is in contrast to a theoretical measure which will not. For example, height and weight are empirical measures since a tape measure and a weighing machine will produce data. Goodness and evil are theoretical rather than empirical measures since data cannot be obtained about them – certainly not directly.

Enhancement: a change to a spreadsheet that provides an additional feature: for example, adding the calculation of monthly totals where previously only weekly totals were available.

Environment: a manager's environment encompasses those things that are of relevance to them doing their job, excluding those things over which they have control (which comprise their system).

Environmental variable: important variables in the manager's environment

Exactness: a general term encompassing bias and precision.

Extrapolation: the extension of the application of a relationship outside the range over which the relationship has been validated. In general, the greater the extent of the extrapolation, the less valid the application of the relationship becomes.

Feasible solution: a solution that satisfies all the constraints that are imposed.

Forecast: a prediction about the future.

Formalisation: the third stage of logic modelling in which it is translated into the set of verbal relationships that were developed in the verbalisation stage into the final spreadsheet form in terms of formulae.

Formula: the form of a relationship that appears in an individual cell of a spreadsheet.

Function: a combination of variables, constants and coefficients. Suppose it was known that there was a relationship between *contribution, unit price* and *units sold,* but the form of the relationship was not known. What is known about the relationship can be expressed as:

revenue = f{*unit price, units sold,*}

and read as

revenue is a function of *unit price* and *units sold*

Note that a letter other than f can be used to denote a function. A *different* function to that given above might be written:

contribution = g{*revenue, variable costs*}

Graph: the generic term used in the Lotus 1-2-3 spreadsheet package to cover all forms of non-numeric information (pictures, charts, diagrams).

Hard information: information that is well defined. Often quantitative and objective.

Hard system: a system for which objectives can be clearly defined and in which causal relationships between factors are well understood.

Human–computer interface: the boundary between the human using a computer and the computer input and output devices.

Hypothesis: a preliminary and untested statement about a situation of interest.

Hypothesis testing: a formal method of testing the strength of a hypothesis to fit a set of data.

Identity: a definitional relationship that is an equation.

Independent variable: a variable whose value does not depend on the value of any other variable.

Inferential statistics: the method and techniques whereby population measures are inferred from sample measures; also the inferred measures themselves.

Information: data that is perceived by an employee to be of use or potential use to them in their job.

Input factor: a factor whose value would be input to the logic model. These values make up the data model.

Intelligence: the outcome of the meshing and reconciliation of a set of information.

Interface: the boundary between the human using a computer and the computer input and output devices.

Interpolation: the use of a relationship in a region between the points at which the relationship has been tested. The greater the distance between the tested points and the point where the application is to be used, the less confidence one can have that the relationship applies.

Interquartile-range: a measure of the spread of a set of data. It is the interval between the value below which 25 per cent of the data points lie and the value above which 25 per cent of the data points lie.

Issue: a situation potentially calling for decision/action: any facet of a manager's daily grind that they have to attend to. This would include opportunities, problems, decision situations and threats.

Issue definition: the process of determining the fundamental attributes and broad scope of an issue.

Issue detection: the initial awareness that an issue exists.

Judgemental relationship: a relationship for which data cannot be obtained that would unequivocally allow one relationship to be generally accepted as an adequate representation of the real world.

Knowledge: a generic term to include data, information and intelligence.

Legacy system: a computer system built using technology which is now out of date.

Linear: a relationship in which the effects are in constant proportion to the causes and where the effects of more than one factor acting at the same time must be additive.

Local environment: that part of the environment where a manager can exert a significant influence or exercise indirect control, and where their performance has a significant effect.

Local scenario: the portion of the scenario brought into focus under pressure from an alerting stimulus. A local scenario is likely to be wider than an initial consideration of the single in-focus issue might suggest, but narrower than the whole scenario.

Logic management: is about good practice in developing the logic model – knowing how relationships were developed, over what range they are applicable and whether the relationships are appropriate or not.

Logic model: one of the major elements of a spreadsheet. It is the combination of relationships between variables, constants, coefficients and parameters that encapsulate the managerial issue of concern.

Macro: a program written in a programming language offered with the spreadsheet package to automate commonly used sets of keystrokes. Microsoft Excel offers Visual Basic. Lotus 1-2-3 offers its own macro language.

Maintenance (of a spreadsheet): the process of keeping the spreadsheet in a state where it remains valid. It involves keeping both the logic and data models current.

Management information system: an organisational subsystem for providing information to support the operation, management and decision-making functions in the organisation.

Managerial variable: the term used for all the variables in a manager's scenario: this includes the decision, environmental and output variables.

Maximum: the largest value a variable can take in a particular circumstance.

Mean: usually taken to be the same as the commonly termed 'average' value. It is calculated by summing the individual values in a data set and dividing the sum by the number of data values in the set.

Median: the value such that 50 per cent of the values in a data set are greater than or equal to it and 50 per cent are less than or equal to it.

Minimum: the smallest value a variable can take in a particular circumstance.

Mode: the most frequently occurring value in a set of values.

Model: a representation of reality – either that which already exists or a view of what might exist in the future.

Modelling factor: a general term encompassing the input factors and the calculated and intermediate variables.

Moving average: the mean value obtained by averaging the values associated with a set of time periods. As each new time period provides a data value, this value is used to calculate the mean with the value from the oldest time period being discarded.

Normal distribution: a 'bell-shaped' curve describing the probability of occurrence of specific values of a variable. This distribution is also sometimes known as the Gaussian distribution after the German mathematician Gauss.

Objective: the value of an output variable set for a manager by their bosses.

Objective function: a combination of variables (*cf* function) such that the value of this combination is the objective of interest.

One-tailed test: a form of statistical testing to judge whether one value is either larger than a second value or, alternatively, smaller than a second value, but not both at the same time.

Operation: *see* Arithmetic operation.

Optimum/optimal: either the maximum or the minimum value of a variable in a specific case.

Output variable: the dimensions along which a manager would measure themselves and be measured by others.

Parameter: a factor whose value is held constant over a given period of time or during the exploration of given relationships.

Population: in statistics, the entire collection of things of interest: e.g. the number of people living in the UK, the number of defects in a factory's annual production.

Precision: a measure of the random error in a piece of information.

Predictive validity: is shown when data produced by the spreadsheet is matched to those subsequently produced by the system.

Prescription: a judgemental relationship where the amount of judgement is small and the form of the relationship is seldom seriously a contentious issue.

Any controversy over the form of the relationship would be handled according to the rules of scientific method.

Principal model: the totality of the model in the spreadsheet.

Probability distribution: a relationship describing the linkage between the chance of a specific values or a range of values of a variable occurring and that value or range of values.

Project: a set of integrated activities that need to be completed by a specified date.

Random number: a number chosen so that all values are equally likely.

Random number generator: a facility that, given a random number seed, will generate a series of random numbers. To be strictly accurate the random number generators in spreadsheets generate pseudo-random numbers: pseudo since there is a relationship between the numbers in the series.

Random number seed: the initial value used to start the generation of a series of random numbers from a random number generator.

Range of application of the model: a statement of the scope of the model.

Regression: the relationship obtained between the values of one variable and those of another using least squares fitting procedures.

Relationship: a meaningful link between variables, parameters, coefficients and constants.

Relative frequency: of a class is the frequency of the class divided by the total frequency of all classes, generally expressed as a percentage.

Remote environment: that part of the environment over which the manager has no influence.

Replicative validity: is shown if the data produced matches data already produced by the real-world system.

Resolving: obtaining an answer to an issue that is good enough.

Risk: a) a management definition of risk is the same as that for uncertainty, where a particular action will lead to one of several possible outcomes; b) a specialist risk analyst's definition of risk is the general state where there are several possible outcomes and the probability of their occurrence is unknown. In 'extremely risky' situations, it may not even be possible to identify all the possible outcomes.

Risk analysis: paradoxically, given the definition of risk, risk analysis is the investigation and understanding of the effects of uncertainty on a system. It involves the development and use of quantitative models. It is part of risk management.

Risk management: the overall activity of considering the sources of risk and uncertainty, determining the likely consequences and identifying possible responses.

Sample: in statistics, a part of the (total) population in which you are interested.

Scenario: an outline view of the world in which the manager is currently operating and thinks they will operate in the future. It provides the context within which an issue will be tackled.

Scenario manager: a facility within a spreadsheet that allows the storage of a set of values for some of the input factors that correspond to a particular set of managerial assumptions about their scenario.

Soft information: information that comes informally, usually verbal (gossip and rumour).

Soft system: a system whose objectives are difficult to define and impossible to state with any precision, and where cause and effect are only hazily understood.

Solution: an optimum answer.

Solving: obtaining an answer to an issue that is optimum or best.

Standard deviation: the square root of the variance.

Structural modelling: a systematic way of capturing the manager's perceptions of their world. It attempts to identify all the important factors in an organisation and its environment, to specify the broad relationships between these factors and to recognise the broad ranges of values associated with them.

Summary model: an extract from the principal model that constitutes the 'results' of using a spreadsheet.

Synoptic validation: concerned with checking 'around the spreadsheet', by being satisfied that acceptable outputs are obtained from a set of inputs applied to the spreadsheet.

System: a set of interdependent things connected so as to form a complex unity. One crucial feature of a system is that the whole is greater than the sum of its constituent parts – the system has properties that the elements do not. These properties are called emergent properties. A manager's system may be defined as encompassing those things over which they have control.

Systems software: computer systems which work 'behind the scenes' and are not themselves used directly by management. Operating systems and compilers are examples of systems software.

Tackling: a generic term for an approach to an issue: it encompasses absolving, dissolving, resolving and solving.

Test pack: a set of data used to test the logic model in a spreadsheet.

Time series analysis: the analysis of a set of data points corresponding to a continuous time periods (e.g. weeks, months or years) into a set of components (e.g. a trend and a seasonal component).

Trial: the results of a spreadsheet (or other) model with one particular set of values for the uncertain variables in the model.

Triangular distribution: a probability distribution with one peak value and with the probability falling off linearly on either side of this peak.

Two-tailed test: a form of statistical testing to judge whether one value is different from a second value – either larger or smaller than the second.

Uncertainty: describes the situation in which all the possible values of a variable are known together with the probability of each of these values occurring.

Uniform distribution: a probability distribution in which all values have an equal probability of occurring.

Validation: the process of testing the fit between a spreadsheet or parts of it and the real world system being modelled.

Validity: an expression of the confidence we have in the appropriateness of a spreadsheet to help understand a real-world problem. A valid spreadsheet would be one that has passed the validation process.

Variable: any factor whose value is not fixed.

Variance: the variance of a sample data values is the average of the squared values of the deviations of a set of data points from their mean. The best estimate of the variance of the population from which a sample of n data points was taken is $n/(n-1)$ times the sample variance.

Verbalisation: the second stage in logical modelling in which the relationships between the model factors is specified verbally (in 'organisational' English in the UK and North America for example).

Verification: is the process of testing spreadsheets to see that they perform as expected – for example, that totals are calculated correctly, and that exceptions are reported appropriately. It is the testing and debugging of the spreadsheet.

Version manager: *see* Scenario manager.

INDEX